1991

THE AMERICAN JOURNALS OF Lt JOHN ENYS

AN ADIRONDACK MUSEUM BOOK

THE AMERICAN JOURNALS OF Lt JOHN ENYS

ELIZABETH COMETTI, Editor

Preface by Harold K. Hochschild
Foreword by Julian P. Boyd

THE ADIRONDACK MUSEUM · SYRACUSE UNIVERSITY PRESS   1976

First Edition

Elizabeth Cometti is Professor Emeritus of West Virginia University.
She is the editor and translator of *Seeing America and Its Great Men—
The Journal and Letters of Count Francesco dal Verme, 1783–1784* (1969)
and the author of dozens of journal articles on the American Revolution.

Library of Congress Cataloging in Publication Data

Enys, John, 1757–1818.
  The American journals of Lt. John Enys.

  Includes bibliographical references and index.
  1. United States—History—Revolution, 1775–1783—
Personal narratives, British. 2. United States—
Description and travel—1783–1848. 3. Enys, John,
1757–1818. I. Cometti, Elizabeth. II. Title.
E267.E58   1976   973.3'41'0924   76-13884
ISBN 0-8156-0121-2

Manufactured in the United States of America

PREFACE

IN OCTOBER 1776, JOHN ENYS, a nineteen-year-old ensign in the British army, participated in the battle of Valcour Island on Lake Champlain and the defeat of the American fleet under the command of Benedict Arnold. Eight and a half years later, the Revolution over, Enys, now a captain stationed in Canada, returned to Lake Champlain on a fishing trip. It took him up the Saranac River, which rises in the Adirondack Mountains. During this trip he encountered some of the earliest settlers of what was to become the city of Plattsburgh and amazed them with both the salmon he caught and the artificial flies with which he caught them. At the end of his tour of duty in North America in the autumn of 1787, Enys took a furlough and traveled from Montreal south through the United States as far as Virginia in order to know the people against whom he had fought.

It is with the consent of Miss Elizabeth Enys and her brother, the Reverend C. R. S. Enys, of Enys, Cornwall, England, that the Adirondack Museum, in association with the Syracuse University Press, now publishes John Enys' engaging journals of his American travels.

To Dr. Julian Parks Boyd, editor of *The Papers of Thomas Jefferson*, we are indebted not only for the discovery of the Enys manuscripts and our introduction to Miss Enys but also for the guidance and encouragement that enabled us to overcome unexpected difficulties to bring the book to completion.

Blue Mountain Lake, New York   Harold K. Hochschild, *President*

January 1976   THE ADIRONDACK MUSEUM

CONTENTS

Preface, Harold K. Hochschild   v

Foreword, Julian P. Boyd   xiii

Introduction, Elizabeth Cometti   xvii

    John Enys   xviii

    John Enys in America   xxxv

    The American Journals   xxxix

    Editorial Method   xli

    Acknowledgments   xliii

The American Journals of Lt. John Enys   1

    The American Rebellion, 1776–1782   3

    Return to Canada—Garrison Duty, 1784–1787   69

    Niagara Falls and a Royal Visit, 1787   115

    Visit to the United States, 1787–1788   171

    On to Virginia and Home, 1788   227

Notes   271

Index   361

LIST OF FIGURES

Capt. John Enys, age 26   *Frontispiece*
1.   Enys House, Cornwall, England   xix
2.   Boston and British ships of war   xxi
3.   Sword presented to Lt. Col. John Enys   xxxiv
4.   Lt. Col. John Enys when retired   xxxvi
5.   Page from the Enys journal   xlii
6.   The Bason of Quebec   9
7.   Quebec: British army arrived from sea   11
8.   His Majesty's armed vessels on Lake Champlain   19
9.   New England armed vessels on Lake Champlain   22
10.   Ticonderoga   41
11.   Sawmill and block house on Fort Ann Creek   43
12.   Falls of Montmorenci and Gen. Haldimand's country house   55
13.   Montmorenci River   57
14.   Cathedral, Jesuits' College, and Récollet Friars Church   83
15.   Orphan's or Ursuline Nunnery   85
16.   The City of Montreal   88

ix

17. Encampment of the Loyalists at Johnston   97
18. Cataraqui on the entrance of Lake Ontario   107
19. Capt. John Montresor's tramway and cradles on the lower
     Niagara River   123
20. Plan of Niagara Falls   127
21. Niagara Falls   133
22. Western branch of Niagara Falls   135
23. French Castle at Old Fort Niagara   145
24. Fall of the Grande Chaudière   161
25. State Street, Albany   182
26. Van Rensselaer manor house   184
27. Bryans Place, formerly the Schuyler mansion   186
28. Peter Waldron Yates mansion, Albany   187
29. Monument to Gen. Richard Montgomery   195
30. Bridge over the Charles River   201
31. Bay of New York from Paulus Hook   210
32. Nassau Hall, Princeton   213
33. Philadelphia   216
34. Lt. Gen. Thomas Musgrave   220
35. Landsdown, Pennsylvania   223
36. Old Light Street M.E. Church, Baltimore   236
37. Belvidere, Howard family home in Baltimore   237
38. Mount Vernon, Virginia   247
39. Dove with olive branch, Mount Vernon   248
40. Advertisement offering stud services   250
41. Richmond, Virginia   254
42. William and Mary College   257
43. The Right Honorable Norborne Berkeley   259
44. Bruton Parish Church and William and Mary College   260

LIST OF MAPS

I.   Inhabited part of Canada from the French surveys   2

II.   Richelieu River   17

III.   Northern end of Lake Champlain   21

IV.   Southern end of Lake Champlain   25

V.   Lake George, Ticonderoga, and Crown Point   38–39

VI.   Map of North America   70–71

VII.   Possibly the outlet of the Onondaga River into Lake Ontario   111

VIII.   Plan of Carleton Island   114

IX.   Route of the Canadian Couriers from Montreal to Skenesborough   170

X.   The northeastern states   181

XI.   Claverack, New York   189

XII.   City and suburbs of Philadelphia   225

XIII.   Middle Atlantic states   228

XIV.   Plan of Baltimore   233

XV.   Plan of the investment of York and Gloucester   262–63

FOREWORD

IN *Life on the Mississippi* Mark Twain described in unforgettable terms the torments of mind and body he experienced as an apprentice river pilot. He soon learned that a master pilot, most envied and respected of all river men, achieved his awesome authority only by fixing in memory a myriad of facts about the location of bars, points, reefs, bends, islands, plantations, and towns through twelve hundred miles of river. What is more, these things had to be learned with such precision that the pilot could discern them in their infinitely varied aspect in winter and summer, in high water and low, in sunshine and fog, and in moonlight, starlight, and pitch dark. Worst of all, they had to be learned and relearned endlessly because the landmarks and other characteristics were constantly shifting as the river itself changed its course, altered its hidden traits, and multiplied its various dangers by capriciously obliterating some and silently substituting others.

The river, Mark Twain soon discovered, had to be read like a book—a wonderful book, to be sure, but not one to be read once and thrown aside, for it had a new story to tell every day and "never a page that was void of interest, never one that you could read without loss." A passenger might not notice the faint dimple on the surface or might only find it charming. But to the pilot it was an italicized passage, shouting that beneath it lay buried a rock or a wreck that could tear the life out of the stoutest vessel afloat. "In truth," Mark Twain declared after he learned to tell the difference between a harmless wind reef on the surface and a deadly bluff reef below, "the passenger who could not read this book saw nothing but all manner of pretty pictures in it, painted by the sun and shaded by the clouds, whereas to the trained eye these were not pictures at all, but the grimmest and most dead-earnest of reading matter."

So, too, must the editor of texts learn to read the evidence that lies invisible beneath the surface. Human lives and valuable cargoes might not be placed in jeopardy by the editor's errors and oversights, but something even more precious—the truth—could be distorted by them. The misreading of a single digit in a cypher or a single letter in a word—*1* for *7* or *now* for *not*, for example—could puncture truth just as a hidden snag could rip open the hull of a boat. But accurate reading of the surface is the easiest and most elementary obligation of the editor. In discharging it the editor has a considerable advantage over the pilot of Mark Twain's day, for written texts do not change their features through whim or caprice. *Litera scripta manet* is axiomatic, though a manuscript might be mutilated by mice or men so as to eliminate an all-important negative or otherwise entrap the unwary. Once a text is established, it remains fixed and does not go wandering off into new channels, creating new hazards.

But in editing as in piloting what truly distinguishes the master from the apprentice is the ability to discern the evidence not visible, to perceive the silences in the documents, to understand those unuttered assumptions which are so obvious to writer and recipient as not to require expression. This is the supreme test. It is not surprising that this trial of editorial skill presents itself in its most exacting form in diaries and letters, the most personal of all varieties of the human record. D'Israeli's observation that we converse with the absent by letters and with ourselves by diaries is apt but not wholly correct. Both diaries and letters are composed in varied form and for diverse purposes, sometimes interchangeably, but they share in common the fact that they are more immediate, personal, and individual in nature than other forms of record. For this reason no editor can truly read the meaning of the diary or letter presented without understanding as best as one can the character of the person who wrote it. The task of probing the unseen text through the character of the author is made all the more difficult by the context of the varying times, places, and circumstances in which the author wrote. What is more, as has been pointed out by the distinguished student of British and American diaries, William Mathews, "No diarist tells all, not even Pepys." The same applies to writers of letters, even the greatest of them, such as a Walpole or a Jefferson. To explore what is not seen in the record and not told by the author is at once the most rewarding experience and the most creative act of an editor.

That Elizabeth Cometti has mastered the craft of editor is demonstrated in this and other works from her hand. Here she presents to us in his own words and in the fuller amplitude of her skillful commentary an engaging, observant, and admirable young British officer whose curiosity led him to wish to know more of a people who conceived of themselves as inaugurating a new order in human affairs. Lieutenant Enys' diary is a fresh contribution to the literature of the young Republic, made all the more acceptable because of what Elizabeth Cometti has added to it.

Princeton, New Jersey   Julian P. Boyd
January 1976

INTRODUCTION

JOHN ENYS (1757–1818), Lieutenant Colonel and historian of the Twenty-ninth (or Worcestershire) Regiment of Foot, made two visits to America in the service of Britain during the final quarter of the eighteenth century. As a young ensign in the Twenty-ninth, he arrived in Quebec in the spring of 1776 with the contingent that helped to preserve British sovereignty over Canada. Other than the engagement off Valcour Island in October 1776, Enys saw no major action during the Revolutionary War. But he did take part in raids against the Vermont frontier in 1778 and against the New York frontier in 1780. His vivid description of the ravages inflicted by the invading Regulars, Loyalists, and Indians illumines one of the minor chapters of American history.

Two years later, Enys, now a captain, reluctantly returned to Canada, where he did garrison duty at various posts in what is today eastern Ontario. Despite the isolated location of these posts, Enys managed to find some diversion while discharging his limited responsibilities. Before leaving this early West, he visited Niagara Falls, the wonder of wonders for him. On his return to Quebec in 1787, he participated in the festivities occasioned by the visit of Prince William Henry, later William IV.

Instead of returning to England with his regiment, Enys journeyed to the United States, passing through such places as Albany, New York City, Princeton, Philadelphia, and Baltimore. Traveling in the dead of winter, generally by public conveyance, he had no easy time on the road, especially while en route from Philadelphia to Alexandria. The highlight of his visits in the homes of prominent citizens was the day spent at Mount Vernon in company with General Washington and his family. Shortly thereafter, he continued on to Norfolk, from which port he sailed back to England in the spring of 1788.

JOHN ENYS

John Enys came of a Cornish family that can trace its origin to the reign of Edward I, at the latest. In an ancient Cornish play entitled *Creation of the Universe*, the Enys and some neighboring lands are given as a reward to the builders of the universe. In another play, the Enys estate is given as a present to King Solomon. These legendary compliments to the Enys properties were not without basis in reality, for the superb park and fine gardens that are seen to this day were already celebrated by Stuart times.[1]

Marriages with heiresses extended the family holdings and enhanced its prestige in the southwestern corner of England. In May 1678, John Enys, the great-grandfather of the Colonel, married Anne, the heiress of Henry Gregor of Truro. His son, Samuel, married Dorothy, daughter of Thomas Willys, sister and co-heiress of Sir William Willys. Samuel and his son, John Enys, each held the honorable post of High Sheriff of Cornwall. The latter married Lucy, the second daughter of Francis Basset of Tehidy, a member of another prominent Cornish family. Six children, three sons and three daughters, were born of this union. John, the youngest of the sons, was born at Enys on December 19, 1757. Francis, the "Frank" of John's letters and his traveling companion on the tour of Scotland, was four years older.[2]

Both Francis and John attended Eton College and were there together some of the time. "I left my two boys at Eaton well recovered from the measles," wrote their father in July 1766. "I wish I could say that Jack was as well got over the small pox (but must trust to providence for that)." Between June 1773 and March

1. A view of the Enys house, Parish of Gluvias, Cornwall, England. Engraving by William Borlase in Borlase, *Natural History of Cornwall* (Oxford, 1768), plate VII. *Courtesy of the Curators of the Bodleian Library*

1775, the father paid £202/11/2 for young John's education at Eton. He also spent £600 for the purchase of an ensign's commission, which was granted April 22, 1775. This sum was £200 more than the official cost of such a document.[3] Ensign Enys was assigned to the Twenty-ninth Regiment of Foot.

The Twenty-ninth had recently become notorious in the seething thirteen American Colonies as being responsible for the "Boston Massacre." Far from restoring calm in turbulent Boston, the stationing of troops there in 1768 had resulted in numerous confrontations between radical townspeople and the sorely-tried Regulars. The explosion long feared by the latter and welcomed by the former occurred on the chilly night of March 5, 1770, when a tumultuous mob, aroused by shouts of "fire" and the ringing of bells, began insulting and snowballing the frightened guards on King Street. The Captain of the day, Thomas Preston, tried to disperse the crowd, which responded by taunting the soldiers to fire. At length, one of them opened fire, and other shots followed. Blood stained the snow, and soon people learned that four men had been killed and another mortally wounded. To the dismay of the radicals, a Massachusetts jury acquitted Captain Preston and six of the eight soldiers charged with murder; the other two, found guilty of manslaughter, claimed benefit of clergy and escaped with no more punishment than having their right thumbs branded.[4] But the patriots of Massachusetts, realizing the "massacre's" high propaganda value, never let the public forget the event. "From hence then we may date the Commencement of the American War," Enys wrote some years later in his History of the Twenty-ninth Regiment. "And that the Americans esteemed it to be so cannot be doubted since they always called the 29th the Vein Openers."[5]

At the time John Enys received his commission, the Twenty-ninth had returned to England and was stationed at Chatham Barracks. Enys' entry into the Regiment coincided with the opening of hostilities in America. In May 1775, a body of Green Mountain boys under Ethan Allen, accompanied by Benedict Arnold, obtained the surrender of the small garrison at Ticonderoga together with valuable military stores so needed by the Americans. On June 17, 1775, occurred the bloody engagement on Breed's Hill, which the Americans had fortified. After three attacks the British took the hill, but not before incurring heavy losses. Of the approximately 2,500 British troops who participated in the engagement, 19 officers and 207 men were killed and 70 officers and 758 men were wounded.[6]

On December 16, 1775, the Twenty-ninth was ordered to be in readiness to

2. A view of Boston and of British ships of war landing their troops, 1768. Engraving by Paul Revere (1735–1818), Boston. *Courtesy of the American Antiquarian Society; photograph by Marvin Richmond*

embark for service in America. The first contingent, Captain James Basset's company (he had been stationed in Boston in 1770), departed from Sheerness in mid-February on a small transport for conveyance to Plymouth; from there the troops set sail on March 21 for Quebec on the frigate *Surprize* and the sloop *Martin.* Joining these vessels was the *Isis,* with the grenadiers on board.[7]

Encouraged by the proddings of Allen and Arnold and by their recent successes, the Americans decided to try to conquer Canada. General Richard Montgomery advanced from New York toward Montreal. After taking that place he was to proceed against Quebec. There he was to meet Benedict Arnold, who moved northward through Maine. Fort Chambly fell to Montgomery's army in October, St. Johns capitulated on November 2, and Montreal surrendered November 13, 1775. In the meantime, Arnold's force reached Quebec, after an incredibly difficult march through the Maine wilderness during which men were lost through desertion, illness, and starvation.[8] When Hector Cramahé refused to accept Arnold's demand to surrender, the American commander had no alternative but to await Montgomery's arrival, which occurred on December 2. Three times the garrison inside the walls of Quebec was summoned, and three times the Americans were refused.[9] On the last day of the year the Americans launched their expected attack against the fortress of Quebec, despite their deficiency in artillery support. Montgomery was among the first to be killed. Arnold was wounded, and their troops were driven back with heavy losses, perhaps as many as 750 killed, wounded, or taken prisoner.

The British military situation in Canada improved in May 1776 with the arrival of the vessels that had finally departed in March from Plymouth. Since his repulse in December, Arnold had received enough reinforcements to maintain a blockade of Quebec, but his position was precarious, his force having been reduced by smallpox and desertion. Taking advantage of his favorable position, General Guy Carleton forced the Americans to retreat from Quebec up the St. Lawrence valley. At Sorel the Americans were joined by reinforcements under General William Thompson, who, hoping to stem the adverse tide, attacked General Simon Fraser's division at Trois Rivières on June 8, 1776. The Americans were repulsed with heavy losses, and Thompson himself was captured along with more than 200 of his men. Carleton continued the pursuit to Sorel, but there he halted and permitted the Americans to fall back to Lake Champlain.[10]

During the remainder of the summer of 1776, Carleton was unable to penetrate into New York. The Americans, among whom Arnold was very active, constructed and equipped a flotilla of fifteen vessels and some gondolas on the lake. Carleton, too, unable to move forward without command of the lake, assembled a fleet, which included a large radeau, the *Thunderer,* with fourteen guns, and a square-rigged three-master, the *Inflexible,* which carried eighteen twelve-pounders. "The exertions used to form this fleet are hardly to be credited," Enys commented in later years. These vessels went into action in the important naval battle off Valcour Island, October 11–13, in which the Americans were defeated. Arnold, whose remarkable skill, courage, and resourcefulness undoubtedly make him the hero of this short campaign, fell back to Crown Point, and, after burning the fort, retired to Ticonderoga.[11]

The necessity of dealing with the American fleet had forced Carleton's army to remain quiet. It was now too late in the season to make an attack on Ticonderoga, Enys recounted. On November 1 and 2, Carleton's forces moved northward to Canada and dispersed to winter quarters. Enys' regiment was stationed at Montreal.

Only a portion of the Twenty-ninth participated in the ill-starred campaign of General John Burgoyne in 1777. The remainder, which included Enys, did garrison duty at St. Johns and passed the winter at Montreal—a winter so severe, Enys reported, that a sergeant and fourteen rank and file, overtaken by a snowstorm on Lake St. Peter, froze to death. On February 16, 1778, Enys, then only twenty years old, was promoted to the rank of lieutenant.

In the autumn of that year, Enys, with detachments of the Twenty-ninth, Thirty-first, and Fifty-third, as well as a contingent of royalists and "savages," participated in a destructive expedition against the Vermont and New York frontiers. Despite the systematic ravaging they carried out, the officers had so little to do from time to time that for want of better amusement they played tetotum on the drumhead, thus labeling the raid the "Tetotum Expedition."[12]

In 1780, Enys took part in another raid of devastation into the New York frontier. On their return to the ships that waited for them on Lake Champlain, the raiders encountered unspeakably bad roads; "surely," commented Enys, "never was such a road marched by Troops either before or since." To add to their difficulties, they were encumbered with as many captives as there were captors. To prevent the escape of the prisoners, the raiders cut the waistband strings of the Americans' breeches, thereby forcing them to keep one hand employed in holding them up. This strategem, coupled with the captives' fear of Indian attack, kept them under control.[13]

Enys saw no further combat while he was stationed in Canada during and after the Revolution. Although the definitive treaty of peace was not signed until September 3, 1783, hostilities practically ceased after Cornwallis' surrender in October 1781. Enys passed the following winter at Saint-Henri-de-Mascouche in command of light infantry and two battalion companies.

On obtaining leave to return to England, Enys set sail from Quebec on July 18, 1782, and debarked on Hoy Island the following month. From Scotland he went by cutter, chaise, horse, and foot to London in company with General Frederick Haldimand's courier, Lieutenant Atkin. From London he proceeded to Richmond Green where he celebrated the first of several homecomings with members of his family, with whom he appears to have had very cordial relations.

About the time that Enys arrived in England, General William Evelyn, who commanded the Twenty-ninth, learned that the Government had adopted a plan to attach each regiment to some particular county in England, doubtless, Enys concluded, to facilitate recruiting. It fell to the lot of the Twenty-ninth to be connected with the County of Worcester.[14]

Enys was promoted to captain of an additional company of the Twenty-ninth on January 25, 1783, but when the company was reduced later that year, he was placed on half-pay. A profile view of Enys at this time in the Worcestershire Regimental Museum shows a young man in uniform wearing his cocked hat, laced with silver, over hair that is clubbed, all according to regulations.[15]

Enys had acquired a zest for traveling while he was serving in America, and this feeling had been enhanced on his return journey through Scotland in 1782. It is not surprising, then, that he and his brother Francis, former schoolmates and, in 1783, both on half-pay, should have decided to go touring together. Perhaps it was insularity and the desire to see old friends that led the two young men to go to Scotland rather than to take the "Grand Tour" across the English Channel. The two set out from Cornwall on July 8. Their first and principal stop was Harrogate, where they remained until September. At times, especially on good days, they

traveled by horse; at other times they took gig or chaise. Their intellectual background, especially in British history, stimulated their interest in what they saw. At
Kendal they visited the castle where Catherine Parr was born; farther north they
noted the remains of a Druid temple, a church built by William Rufus, Eleanor
crosses, the wall of Antoninus, and other sites learned about in the colorful pages
of English history. Both of the young travelers kept memoranda, on which John later
relied in the preparation of the "Tour of Scotland," now among his papers.[16]

By October 29 the brothers were back in Richmond. Here they parted company, Francis going to Bath, John remaining behind in order to procure an exchange
into the Twenty-ninth. Although it gave him "great pleasure" to be once more on
active duty, he was anything but happy when he received orders to join his regiment
in America, of which continent he had had enough. In August, he obtained passage
on a packet commanded by Captain Philip d'Auvergne, a genial young man, re-
putedly a good sailor. His vessel, properly named the *Speedy,* carried only three
passengers: Lieutenants William Haughton and Thomas Hughes and Enys. The
captain kept a table "fit for an alderman" and provided "all sorts of wines and every
convenience." Two large cabins were used as drawing room and parlor and the
smaller ones, of which there were twelve, for sleeping.[17]

Enys spent the winter of 1784–85 very comfortably and enjoyably at Montreal.
In the spring, the Twenty-ninth received orders to proceed to the upper forts as
soon as communications opened. The command of these posts—Oswegatchie, Carleton Island, Cataraqui, and Oswego—was entrusted to Major Archibald Campbell,
a capable and highly respected officer, who was charged with the very difficult task
of introducing and administering an entirely new economic policy designed to
eliminate a great many perquisites without offending those who had been enjoying
them.[18] Enys was stationed at Cataraqui, now Kingston, Ontario, which he reached
on June 9, 1785, after an exciting journey up the spectacular rapids of the upper
St. Lawrence. Fishing was the chief diversion at this remote place which was
beginning to take on the appearance of a permanent settlement.

In October, Enys went to Montreal to obtain stores for the winter. While
there he witnessed the phenomenon known as "Dark Sunday," which many people
erroneously supposed was an earthquake. On his return to Cataraqui, Enys settled
down to make the most of another winter in only "tollerable Society."

Even so, Cataraqui society was better than what he found at Carleton Island the following April; here he remained until he was ordered to Fort Ontario, an assignment he had been anticipating with little pleasure. His expectations regarding this "most loansome place" were justified, but, as usual, he made the best of it. At least the winter of 1786–87 was mild. At the end of June 1787, Captain Enys was relieved of the command at Fort Ontario and ordered to conduct a party of replacements to the garrison at Niagara. Nothing could have pleased the English romantic more, and he availed himself of this opportunity to see that grandest of sights, Niagara Falls.

In early August, the still-young veteran returned to Quebec. Here he found the town agog over the arrival of Admiral Herbert Sawyer's fleet, one of whose ships, the *Pegasus,* was commanded by Prince William Henry, afterwards King William IV. With relish Enys described the varied highlights of the memorable visit, among which was an elaborate military exercise planned by him.

Having obtained leave to visit the United States, Enys did not join his regiment when it set sail for England in October 1787. Instead, he again turned his steps westward to Montreal, the first stopping place on his journey to New York via Lake Champlain and the Hudson. His American tour was much like that taken by other foreign visitors of the day: he inspected scenic spots and battlefields; he met the best people, for some of whom he had letters of introduction; he inquired about the population and industry of the burgeoning towns; he noted educational institutions and churches; and he listened to tales about the recent war. If there was anything unique about his tour, it was the extraordinary inconveniences he encountered while traveling in winter. On March 17, 1788, Enys embarked at Norfolk on the brig *Abby* bound for Liverpool, where he arrived exactly a month later.

On his return to his native land, Enys probably enjoyed a long visit with his family before joining his regiment at Cheltenham. For the next five years Enys must have moved with the Twenty-ninth from one English cantonment to another, discussed with fellow officers the change in the regiment's high command from Lord Charles Harrington to Lord William Cathcart, and laughed at the meticulous regulations concerning uniforms and hairdress. For instance: "the Hair to be dressed with one curl on each side; the toupee turned up, and not too long; the club to be tyed high, and to be more spread at the top than at the bottom. The rosette to be of ribband, and not more than three inches in diameter; the ribband and rosette to be perfectly black, and put on after powdering." And so it went to hats, stocks, coats, epaulettes, waistcoat, breeches, gaiters, boots, gorgets, sashes, great coat, shoes, and swords.[19] Above all, they must have watched the progress of the French Revolution and wondered how long Great Britain could stay out of war with France.

Since Enys rarely identified himself with the events described in his history, it is difficult to follow his own career during the last decade of the century. For example, although the Twenty-ninth participated in Lord Howe's important victory over the Brest fleet on June 1, 1794, Enys does not reveal whether he, personally, took part in this engagement.

The difficulty of obtaining recruits at this time (1793–94) led the government to award to such regiments as could raise a certain number of men in a given time an additional lieutenant-colonel and a major, the promotions to remain within the respective regiments. By successful recruiting in Birmingham, Manchester, and Nottingham, Major Hugh Dixon (Dickson?) was promoted to the former rank and Captain John Enys to the latter, on March 1, 1794.[20]

At the end of this year, Colonel Archibald Campbell embarked at Plymouth with all effectives for a secret destination, but owing to contrary winds the troops were detained until the following February (1795). In the meantime, a number of men having been attacked by a virulent fever resulted in Major Enys' being left ashore in charge of the sick. This was a fortunate turn of fate for the Major, for Campbell's troops were bound for the West Indies, where the climate, as Enys put it, "was more destructive than the enemy." After their departure, Enys wrote to Lord Cathcart explaining his own uncertain situation and complaining that he was almost "destitute" of help, with only himself and two "sickly sergeants" to do anything. Indeed, the Major confessed that he felt "unequal" to cope with his responsibilities since for the past three months he had been confined by the gout and was hardly able to walk.[21]

A few weeks later, Enys again wrote to Cathcart urging him to send orders regarding a new battalion of the Twenty-ninth, for without them he lacked authority to introduce necessary changes. Enys was further disturbed by an order from the War Office to the effect that he and his men were to be transferred to Jersey, "one of the worst places in the world to form a Regiment, provisions being extremely dear, and liquor of all kinds very plentiful and cheap," which extremes in prices, with the large sums of prize money the troops had to spend, would "be enough to ruin the whole Regiment." Their stay in Jersey, after their departure from Plymouth in June, justified Enys' fears. "I was rather surprised," wrote the Major, "one day to hear that a soldier of my company . . . had invited the whole company to sup with him on roast duck and green peas. On enquiry I found it was not only true, but that the same man, on a former payment of prize money, not being able to go ashore at the moment he wished to spend it, had eaten a £20 note!"[22]

In August Enys again wrote to Cathcart (whose continued silence must have been exasperating) that since his arrival in Jersey he had been busy arranging the companies and putting their confused accounts and regimental books and returns into some kind of order. He had managed also to provide clothing for his men. "We may not be said to be a parade Regiment, [but] I think no one can deny we are as noble a Detachment as ever were seen," he commented. The sick report contained only 62 names, "the same set of fellows, . . . with sore legs, sore backs, and Venerial." To be sure, there had been some irregularities in the ranks of the Twenty-ninth, but on the whole no regiment had been better liked by the inhabitants. "Would to God I could send you so good an account of the first battalion but their melancholy horrors [in the West Indies] meet us at every line of their letters." Some of the men who died there had been fellow officers of Enys in Canada.[23]

Enys was next ordered to Southampton to hold his troops in readiness for service in the West Indies under General Sir Ralph Abercromby. While awaiting embarkation, Abercromby became "outrageous" over the excessively high number of desertions from the ranks of the Twenty-ninth. To punish the troops, he ordered the regiment to embark immediately and not to permit any man to land without close check. Dutifully the regiment obeyed orders. Only later was it learned that while Enys was in Southampton on regimental business, an officer had reported that there were 42 deserters and 4 sick on the weekly list, whereas there were 42 sick and 4 deserters.[24]

In mid-November 1795, the troops set sail but were forced to return to port by a gale of such violence that the vessels were dispersed. In December, the fleet once again left port, but after a few days of good weather, a near gale buffeted them for about a month, disabling some vessels and leaving others without water, so that a signal was given for the ships to put in at St. Helens. Once more, fate had prevented Enys from going to the West Indies.[25]

Still in England, Major Enys' battalion was ordered in February 1796 to disembark and place itself under the command of Lord Cathcart at Southampton. Instead of toward a deadly climate and a fierce enemy, Enys directed his attention to the improvement of the "ornamental parts" of the Regiment, particularly the band. Also, he cooperated with the mayor of Southampton in suppressing a disturbance among the men who were working on a canal nearby. The grateful town authorities conveyed their thanks to Major Enys "for the readiness with which he complied with the request of the magistrates" by sending a detachment of the Twenty-ninth to lend assistance in case of trouble.[26]

The "poor remains" of the unfortunate contingent of the Twenty-ninth that had gone to the West Indies rejoined those who had remained in England in October 1796. A few weeks later, Enys was sent to Worcester to stimulate recruiting and "to re-instate the 29th in the favor it had formerly enjoyed in Worcestershire." His efforts were initially quite successful. He attended many public meetings and assured all the men raised that they would doubtless be assigned to their county's regiment, the Twenty-ninth. Enys was justifiably dismayed, then, when he received orders from the Adjutant-General to return to camp and transfer the recruits to the Forth-sixth Foot. Enys expressed his indignation to Lord Cathcart with customary frankness: "I am very sorry to find that this is the case as we should probably have gotten many very good men as I am told several respectable Magistrates have exerted themselves very much under the Idea they were serving their County Regiment who now as well as myself feel themselves hurt at being duped in such a manner." Considering the perennial difficulty in filling the ranks, the Adjutant-General's order was indeed self-defeating.[27]

John Enys was promoted to the rank of Lieutenant-Colonel on September 6, 1796. It had taken him twenty years to advance from ensign to colonel in a regiment that had acquired a reputation of being one of the best in the armed forces. "The 29th was always one of the most exact Corps in the Service, even to trifles," wrote a young officer in 1797, "every officer [sitting] down to dinner with his sword on." Colonel Enys had charge of the mess accounts, and every Friday afternoon each officer was called upon to pay his week's bill. "We wore powder in those days, and the hair was formed in a club behind, with a black rosette; shoes, and black cloth gaiters to the cap of the knee, with Regimental buttons. The Coat was cut off at the sides. . . . The other parts of our dress were, a white kerseymere waistcoat, cut off in front, with flaps to the pockets, with 4 buttons to each: the Breeches of white kerseymere, with Regt. buttons at the knee; a cocked hat worn square to the front, the least more over the right eye than the left. We had a corps of Black Drummers [blacks from the West Indies]: the one beating the Big Drum in the centre was a handsome man, 6 feet, 4 inches."[28]

The twin fears of a French invasion and an Irish insurrection were intensified in the summer of 1797 when it was reported that French troops had embarked at Brest with the intention of making a descent on the Cornish coast. Enys must have felt keen anxiety as his regiment marched to Truro, Falmouth, and back again to Truro. One detachment was stationed at Penryn, adjacent to the Enys estate. The regiment did not remain in Cornwall for long, however, but shifted to several points in the southwestern part of England, always poised to meet either danger. In mid-June 1798, the Twenty-ninth Foot embarked for Ireland. Disciplined troops were certainly needed there to put an end to the looting, burning, and murdering on the part of the disaffected Irish. On their arrival in Ireland, the Twenty-ninth entered the town of Wexford, where the rebels had indulged their fanatical hatred against the Protestants by murdering their prisoners.[29] The "English Brigade," consisting of the "Queens," the Twenty-ninth, and the One hundredth regiments, was placed under the command of Major-General Peter Hunter, who, in turn, was under the able command of Lord Charles Cornwallis, who had just arrived in Dublin in the capacity of Lord-Lieutenant and Commander-in-Chief.[30] In August information was received that three French frigates with a thousand men under General Jean Humbert had reached Killala Bay. The news produced an order for the Twenty-ninth to move to Kilkenny. This was the start of a series of marches that took the regiment as far north as Carrick-on-Shannon in pursuit of the French. At Mohill some prisoners provided the welcome information that the French were nearby. Engaged by a strong force under General Gerard Lake and cut off from retreat by that under Cornwallis, Humbert and eight hundred French surrendered.[31]

In late December, Enys escorted a number of prisoners from Kilkenny to Waterford. As they proceeded through the mountains after a halt at Thomastown, the cold, accompanied by sleet which cut their faces, became the "most inclement" Enys had ever experienced in Europe. By the time the column reached Millinavat many of the men were so numb that it was difficult to get them to move. Recalling the effects of the Canadian cold, Enys ordered that no one should fall back unless he could be accommodated in a house, an unlikely prospect in this desolate region. He therefore ordered that a dram of rum be given to each man, but before the men in the rear had got their portion, those in front were worse off than before and had to keep moving. By the time they reached Waterford, one man of the Twenty-ninth and two prisoners had died, and many did not recover from the effects of the cold for some days. "The Dragoons were as much affected as the Infantry," Enys reported, "for they acknowledged that had they been called on to act, they were all so benumbed that they could not have drawn their Swords."[32]

Rumors of another French invasion kept Enys in Ireland until July 1799. On the 24th, his regiment embarked at Cork and landed at Deal six days later. Immediately after their arrival they marched to Barnham Downs to join other regiments then being assembled under the command of Major General Eyre Coote for the expedition to the Helder. As proclaimed by General Ralph Abercromby, the commander of the English forces, the object of this ill-conceived and ill-starred operation was to help deliver the Dutch from French "tyranny and domination" and reestablish their former government under the Stadholder.[33]

The Twenty-ninth, commanded by Colonel Enys, embarked at Margate August 13, but because of bad weather did not land at the Helder until August 27! Here the troops were obliged to move on top of sand-hills, where high winds blew fine sand all over them and their food, so that those who ate most meat, commented Enys, were sure to eat most sand. After eating the prepared rations they had brought, they resorted to stacks of broken muskets for fuel to cook more food.[34]

On August 28, the Helder was evacuated by the enemy and occupied by a part of Abercromby's army. Two days later, Admiral Andrew Mitchell summoned the Dutch Admiral, Story, to hoist the flag of the House of Orange and transfer his ships and stores to the British. Alleging that his troops refused to fight, Story surrendered. So far the campaign had gone much better than expected. But in this area of sand dunes, ditches, and canals, these early successes did not insure final victory.[35]

In mid-September, the Duke of York, not the best of generals, assumed the chief command with reinforcements consisting of three brigades of British infantry, a few squadrons of British cavalry, and two divisions of Russians, allies of the British—a total of 33,000 men. Important and costly engagements were fought on September 19 and October 2. On the former date, Coote's brigade, as Enys put it, was "merely Spectators," there being a wide dike of considerable depth between them and the enemy. Not until a temporary bridge was constructed from materials from a neighboring house could the Twenty-ninth cross the canal and join in the pursuit of the Dutch. Early the following day Coote's brigade returned to its old quarters near Schagen.[36]

Bad weather impeded further significant operations until October 2, when a vigorous attack was launched on the enemy's left at Bergen. Colonel Enys was ordered to form the Twenty-ninth on the edge of the sand hills and to advance always slightly ahead of the Russian line moving toward Schorl. Casualties were light, since the enemy gave way before them. As they neared Bergen, Enys received orders to dislodge a party of the enemy posted on a hill near that village. This was accomplished, and by nightfall the French had retired to Bergen, which they evacuated during the night.[37]

In the ensuing days, operations continued, chiefly around Alkmaar and Egmond-aan-Zee. Although the British could in this brief campaign claim a victory, it was, at best a Pyrrhic one, partly because the expected support from the Dutch never materialized. Negotiations between the Duke's staff and the French opened on October 14. Four days later a capitulation was agreed to. Its terms provided that hostilities should cease and that the British should evacuate the country by November 30 and surrender eight thousand Dutch and French prisoners; the Dutch fleet, however, was to remain in British hands.

Enys' regiment embarked on the *Trusty* October 28 and landed at North Yarmouth on November 4.[38] In contrast to the other troops who disembarked at that time, the men of the Twenty-ninth wore cocked hats and white breeches with black gaiters. For their smartly uniform appearance the men were hissed by the crowd, who supposed that they had not seen combat, whereas those of the Eighty-fifth, who had also been on the *Trusty,* were cheered as heroes because they wore nondescript trousers and round hats tied up with pack thread and fastened with pieces of tobacco pipes. Later, Enys and his men were to have another disappointment when Guild-hall would deny them permission to march through London with their drums beating and colors flying, a privilege to which they had supposed they were entitled.[39]

Shortly after his return to England Enys resigned from the army. His reasons for taking this step at the age of forty-two were given in the regimental orders of March 20, 1800, issued at Dover: ". . . Lieut. Colonel Enys cannot take leave of a Regiment, in which he has passed almost the whole of his life, and from which he now retires only because he finds himself unequal to the fatigues of so active a profession, without returning his most sincere thanks to all and every part of the Corps. . . . To leave such a Corps, after having served in it for nearly twenty-five years, must naturally be a very painful task. . . . " As a farewell present, the officers of the Regiment gave Enys a fine sword made in London. On its blade in embossed letters were these words: "As a Tribute of Sincere Regard and as a Testimony of their Perfect Approbation of his Conduct during Twenty Five Years' Service. This Sword is presented to John Enys, late Lieut.-Colonel of the 29th Regt. by his Brother Officers."

In his valedictory, Enys told his regiment that it would always be "one of the greatest pleasures of his retirement" to show "his gratitude . . . by using every means of serving those, who [had] served with him."[40] With what interest, then, he must have followed the movements of his former comrades in the Peninsular campaign under Arthur Wellesley, Duke of Wellington, in the American War of 1812, and in the occupation of Paris following Napoleon's defeat at Waterloo. Ever concerned about his country's military problems, during these critical years he pre-pared a "plan for establishing a system of communication throughout each county by the appointment of lieutenants, inspectors, superintendents, and agents to super-intend and to carry out the measures to be directed in case of invasion" and entitled it "Defence during Napoleonic Wars." This undated manuscript is in the archives of the Cornwall County Council, Truro.

Little is known about Enys after his retirement. Very likely he spent some of the remaining eighteen years of his life in the preparation of the notebooks which contain his journals and the history of the Twenty-ninth Regiment. For this highly detailed work he doubtless relied on copious memoranda which are no longer extant.

3. Sword presented to Lt. Col. John Enys by his fellow officers upon his retirement from the 29th Regiment of Foot. *Courtesy of the present members of the Enys family*

Enys never married—not, however, because he was indifferent to the ladies. That he enjoyed feminine company is often evident in the pages of his journals. These also reveal a man of great affability, one who lived on the best of terms with colleagues, friends, and family, including in-laws.

At some time before 1809 Enys moved to Bath and occupied a house at 11 St. James Square. Whether he went there for reasons of health or because he liked the social life at the spa is not known. Probably both factors led him away from his native Cornwall. As early as 1795, when he was still in his prime, he was complaining of such a bad case of gout that walking was difficult. His condition must have become increasingly worse as the years passed, for his obituary notice reported that he died "after a lingering illness," July 30, 1818.[41] He was buried in Bath Abbey next to his sisters Mary (d. 1775) and Dorothy (d. 1784).

JOHN ENYS IN AMERICA

In the two extant likenesses of Enys—one a profile portrait of him as captain, the other a miniature of him in colonel's uniform—he appears serious, kindly, somewhat melancholy. His arduous military experiences during the years between his captaincy and colonelcy left their mark on him; for one thing, his nose, probably frozen while Enys was serving in Canada, became prominently bulbous, but, according to family tradition, he was never sensitive about it. That he must have been tall for that day is evidenced by the "honor" of appointment in 1781 to a grenadier company, an elite corps composed of the tallest and strongest men in the regiment.

If little is known about John Enys aside from the bare facts of his military career, his journals reveal much about him as a man—this in spite of the tone of detachment that characterizes his writing. While he chronicles events of the American Revolution with terse objectivity and displays no rancor toward the Americans, his patriotism is still evident. "It gave us pleasure to See even the most distant part of the Island we were Born in, and from which we had been so long absent," he exclaimed when he sighted the coast of Scotland after six years in America. "It was with the greatest satisfaction" that he left the battlefield at

4. Lt. Col. John
Enys when retired.
Miniature. *Courtesy
of the present
members of the
Enys family*

Saratoga, for the scene of General Burgoyne's surrender engulfed him in gloom. He felt equally depressed on seeing the site of the Battle of Bunker Hill (Breed's Hill). The British victory had been a costly one. "For the honor of our Nation," he later expressed the hope that it was not true that the British had despoiled the college library at Princeton. And he was "agreeably" surprised to learn that the people of Norfolk did not hold the British entirely responsible for the burning of that seaport.

As a soldier, he never missed an opportunity to visit battle sites, noting the extent of the remaining fortifications and sometimes recalling the tactics employed. In these respects his journal may be likened to a field-book of the American Revolution. In Canada, upper New York, on Manhattan Island, in the environs of Boston, and in Connecticut, New Jersey, Pennsylvania, and Virginia he covered the scenes of military action with a professional eye.

But his curiosity was not restricted to such places. Far from it. Like an eighteenth-century romantic or natural scientist, he noted the awesome icebergs off the coast of Newfoundland, walked on the ice which held the ship firm in these northern waters, and experimented with distilling fresh water from salt water. He went to some effort to observe Indians directly. He delighted in contemplating waterfalls, especially the grandest of them all, Niagara, where he marveled at the evidences of nature's altering the position of the falls through the long course of time. And he never failed to find pleasure in a good "prospect."

Little escaped his attention, neither the old nor the new, neither the works of nature nor those of man. Near Fort Niagara, for instance, he wanted to open some Indian mounds he saw there, but the Indian chief, Joseph Brant, discouraged the investigation. Enys sketched an Eskimo kayak, Niagara Falls, General Haldimand's summer home, and the Chew house in which some British defended themselves in the battle of Germantown. He became something of an authority on fishing. He observed the operation of gang saws, visited a beaver house and dam, took note of the inspection and marketing of tobacco, described garrison sports and an Indian regatta, and witnessed not one, but two veilings of young nuns in Quebec.

Only rarely was his lively curiosity held in check. At Niagara Falls he would not venture beyond a third of the way down the side of the cataract. And in Albany he refused to enter a coffee house because it was permeated with "intollerable" tobacco smoke. Unlike other foreign travelers in America, Enys did not denounce slavery, and indeed made no mention of the unfortunate blacks except to give their population figure in Virginia. This seeming indifference probably stemmed from the fact that he visited only two states where slaves were numerous—Maryland and Virginia. Also, he stopped at public houses rather than large plantations teeming with blacks.

Enys was a very young man, only eighteen years old, when he first came to America early in 1776, and only thirty when he left it for the second time, in 1788. During these years he saw combat, performed arduous garrison duty, traveled under conditions that would dishearten all but the most inveterate tourist, and still had energy to spare for diversion, especially dancing. Enys never missed an opportunity to attend an assembly, a kind of dancing club composed of the most fashionable people in the town. Traveling at the height of the social season, he had an opportunity to attend a number of such balls, on which he commented with taste and discernment. Any day of the week, including Sunday, found him ready to dance. He danced in the Governor's Palace at Quebec, in the homes of social leaders, in assembly rooms, even in isolated western posts where there was a dearth of feminine partners. He postponed for a week his departure from Philadelphia in order to attend a ball at the mansion of William Bingham. When he reached Baltimore after a day that would have sent the average person straight to bed, he attended a dance at the home of Luther Martin that lasted until nearly two o'clock in the morning. Always he enjoyed the company of young ladies, the customary "elegant" suppers, and above all, the minuets, country dances, cotillions, jigs, and reels that were performed. So sociable was Baltimore society that while Enys was in that town he attended four dances in eight days. Always he was an enormously appreciative participant, never patronizing or making invidious comparisons. So impressed was he by a party given at the Chew mansion in Philadelphia that he expressed the hope that Truro society would have similar entertainments.

Enys' varied interests and youthful vigor rendered him immune to boredom regardless of where he was. Stationed at the lonely post on Carleton Island, he used his spare time in planting a garden which included a field of Indian corn. He kept a record of the shipping that passed from the Great Lakes to the St. Lawrence River. On a fishing trip to the Saranac River, Enys' party used flies for bait to catch all the salmon they could consume, with enough left over for supplying the local people and for pickling. It was his avid curiosity that impelled Enys to see something of the young republic before returning to his own country, despite the generally bad condition of the roads, the scarcity of good accommodations, and the rigors of the weather. On reaching Norfolk, he intended to proceed to Charleston, South Carolina, by boat, but on finding that a sloop had just departed for that port, he decided to entrust his next move to fate and so cut short his tour.

Whether Enys read the travel literature mentioned in his journal before or after his two sojourns in America remains open to question. In the case of Chastellux, *Travels,* it was probably at the latter time, since the English version of that notable work was not published until 1787.[42]

THE AMERICAN JOURNALS

There is abundant evidence that Enys compiled his journals from on-site memoranda or from letters written to his older brother, Francis. "Nothing happened that day to put down in my Memorandum that I had like to have forgot the day altogether," he once wrote. In his account of the journey from Cap Rouge to Montreal in 1784, he cites the rates of the post for 1786. After describing a large turnip so formed as to resemble the male genitalia on one side, and on the other, the female, he adds: "The one was more perfect than the other but having lost a Remark I made I cannot remember which was more so." In his prefatory statement to the description of "Dark Sunday," he writes: "The Account here given is what I saw myself in Montreal and took notes of it on the following day." Recounting his visit to Mount Vernon, he remarks: "I am sure my dear Frank you will expect me to give you some account of this family [Washington] of whom we have so often spoken and for whom from the General public character I know you have so high an esteem." These memoranda and letters have not been located; very probably they are no longer extant.

The Enys documents were deposited at the County Record Office, Truro, Cornwall, in 1967, and a catalog of them was compiled by Miss Sheila Pratt. Prior to that time they were kept in the Enys home in Enys, Penryn. Mrs. Sarah L. Enys, the mother of the present owners of the Enys journals, Miss Elizabeth Enys and the Reverend C. R. Saltren Enys, wrote that the journals looked like "eighteenth century exercise books." These vary in shape, size, and color. One of them is dark blue; three are bound in parchment; five are covered in marbled red and blue paper; and the remainder have brown paper covers. The writing is fairly clear and legible.

Copies of the Enys journals are in three depositories:

1. The Public Archives of Canada, Ottawa, has a microfilm reel containing the history of the Twenty-ninth Regiment and the journals covering the years 1784–87. These were copied in 1957 from originals loaned for filming through the courtesy of the National Register of Archives, London. The Public Archives of Canada also has a nineteenth-century edited transcript of the journal covering Enys' trip to Niagara Falls in 1787. In publishing this account of the Niagara Falls visit in the *Canadian Archives 1886* (Ottawa, 1887), Douglas Brymner, the Archivist, wrote that this "original" manuscript was once in the possession of a son of Captain Enys who emigrated to New Zealand. At the 1876 Centennial Exposition in Philadelphia, Dr. Alfred Selwyn, then Director of the Canadian Geological Survey, met Mr. Enys, who, in the course of conversation about the changes that had taken place at Niagara Falls, mentioned that at his home in New Zealand he had his father's manuscript of the visit to the Falls in 1787. On Enys' return to New Zealand, he sent the transcript, which included the marginal sketch of the Falls in the original manuscript, to Dr. Selwyn. This explanation of the provenance of the transcript was repeated by Frank H. Severance in *Studies of the Niagara Frontier* (Buffalo, 1911). An account of the same visit, but without the Brymner-Severance introductory statement, has been printed in Charles M. Dow, *Anthology and Bibliography of Niagara Falls,* 2 volumes (Albany, 1921). As has been stated, Colonel John Enys never married and he had no children. The donor of the transcript to Dr. Selwyn was probably Enys' great-great-nephew, John Davies Enys, who, with his two brothers, Francis Gilbert and Charles, went to New Zealand and bought a sheep farm.

2. The Princeton University Library has microfilm copies of the journals of Enys. This material was made available to the Library by the National Register of Archives through the Public Archives of Canada in London.

3. The Adirondack Museum, Blue Mountain Lake, New York, has typescripts of the Enys manuscripts now in the County Record Office, Truro, with the excep-

tion of the one entitled "Defence during Napoleonic Wars." In addition, the Museum has microfilm copies of the "History of the 29th Regiment" and of the journals covering the years 1784–87, and photostatic copies of the journals covering the years 1776–82 and 1787–88.

In spite of his indifference to orthography and punctuation, Enys was both a credible and a creditable journalist. This is evident in Major Everard's reliance on the Enys journals in the preparation of *The 29th (Worcestershire) Foot* and in the inclusion of Enys' memorable account of his visit to Niagara Falls in the Selwyn-Severance-Dow publications. Fresh, contemporary accounts of the Revolutionary period are becoming increasingly scarce; the Enys journals will come as a welcome addition to this category of historical literature.

EDITORIAL METHOD

The text that follows is as literal a presentation of the Enys journals as seems practical. Qualification is necessary only because the journals display some peculiarities that would impede their readability were they not corrected. Sentences often begin without capitalization of the first letter and end with a comma or dash or both. Paragraphing is generally ignored except for an occasional indentation or a series of dashes or multispacing. Misspelling is prevalent; common nouns, prepositions, conjunctions, and verbs are frequently capitalized; and place names consisting of two or more words, such as "three Rivers" and "point au Lac," lack proper capitalization. Names of ships and titles of books are sometimes misspelled and never italicized. First names of persons mentioned in the journals are usually omitted.

Not all of these peculiarities have been eliminated. The original orthography has been retained, but when necessary for the sake of clarity, the correct spelling has been enclosed in brackets. Whenever a person's name is mentioned for the first time, the correct spelling of the surname and the given name is likewise enclosed in brackets, with an added question mark in case of doubt. Every effort has been made to identify persons, places, inns, and ships and to provide the reader identifications either within brackets in the text or in footnotes. Where such identifications do not appear, the Editor has been unable to trace the names. No biographical or geograph-

parts infinitely more Beautiful we at length however struck
again into the wood and passing down its skirts Mr H brought us
out a few Yards below the fall. Here I for one sett down for some
time in silent Admiration and Astonishment at a Sight which
I am fully persuaded no pen or Pencil can ever convey across the Sea
In our present situation we were too near to the highest part of the fall which in
a kind of a Shelf or Plan Shore onward is Marked to to enjoy its full beauty but
we had a tolerable good view of the great or as it is in general called the Horse shoe
fall which is here Marked 4.5.6 To give any adequate Idea of the astonishing
Variety which here crowds upon your mind is impossible and it may
be well said to be the real sublime and beautifull conveyed in the Language of
Nature infinitely more strong than the united Eloquence of Pitt Fox or Burke
even if we give them the Assistance of Luther himself to help them, As the water
during its fall from different parts meeting the Rays of the Sun in different
directions takes an infinite number of different Colours and Shades. to this
we must add the numberless beautifull breaks in the water the delightfull
verdure which covers the Islands and neighbouring Shores. the beauty of the
most Noble Rapid which can be conceived before it ever Reaches the Brink
of the Precipice, the Astonishing Column of Spray which Rises from the
great fall the Thundering noise which the Whole makes by its fall on
the heap of Stones below from whence it Runs no longer like Water but
Absolutely in such a State of foam as to appear like a perfect River of
Milk for about 100 or 150 Yards after which it resumes its Natural State

ical information has been provided for names that are easily identifiable in biographical dictionaries and contemporary atlases. The ampersand has been retained as well as abbreviations. Raised letters have been lowered and periods have been added to designations of rank. Symbols for units of money, weights, and measurements, as well as abbreviations and contractions, have been retained as written. Superfluous dashes, such as those occurring after commas and periods, have been eliminated. Where letters are not clearly distinguishable, modern practice has been followed. Sentences and paragraphs that are inordinately long have been silently shortened. Commas have been supplied where absolutely necessary for the convenience of the reader, while commas at what appears to be the end of sentences have been eliminated in favor of periods. Where additions and alterations represent an educated guess, a question mark has been added in brackets. The marginal dating employed by Enys has been retained. For ease in distinguishing dates, they have been italicized.

Enys' interpolations, many of them of considerable length and value, appear to be mostly random observations or hearsay. Occasionally, though, he includes material that might properly belong in the text, as his account of the "depredations" of the sand flies on the upper St. Lawrence or his visit to a beaver dam. It should be noted that the journal covering the war years contains no interpolations. These asides, as the interpolations might be called, are here treated as notes and appear with extra indentation in the notes section. All other notes are by the Editor.

ACKNOWLEDGMENTS

Many individuals have greatly assisted me in the preparation of this work.

I am particularly grateful to Elizabeth Enys for making available family papers and pictures; to Anita Hutcherson for editorial assistance; to Julian P. Boyd for his many kindnesses, not the least of which was the loan of his unpublished manu-

5. Part of a page from the Enys journal describing the plan of Niagara Falls. Dated July 18, 1787. *Courtesy of the Cornwall County Record Office, DD. EN 1811; photograph by Charles Woolf*

script, "Royal Gift"; to John R. Alden for valuable comments on the Quebec campaign; and to William K. Verner for his meticulous reading of the manuscript.

I am also very grateful to the following specialists in various fields: Giselle D. Beauvais, Public Archives of Canada; Clark L. Beck, Rutgers University; Stefan Bielinski, State Education Department, New York; James B. Bell, New England Historic Genealogical Society; Gordon Bowen-Hassell, Naval Historical Center; Vivian Bryan, Vermont Department of Libraries; Harriet R. Cabot, the Bostonian Society; John A. Castellani, Mount Vernon Ladies' Association; Carl A. Christie, Public Archives of Canada; Nancy F. Chudacoff, Rhode Island Historical Society; Earle E. Coleman, Princeton University; Rebecca B. Colesar, New Jersey State Library; Richard J. Cox, Maryland Historical Society; Michael Gibson Fitch, Connecticut Historical Society; Stephanie Glover, Ministry of Defence Library, London; Armand Gogue, Les Archives de l'Archidiocese de Quebec; Cliff Hamrick, West Virginia University; Mary M. Jenkins, West Virginia Department of Archives and History; Robert H. Land, Library of Congress; Gilles Langelier, Public Archives of Canada; Donald E. Loker, Niagara Falls Public Library; E. Richard McKinstry, New Jersey Historical Society; James E. Mooney, the Historical Society of Pennsylvania; Patrick J. Mullin, Marietta College; Christine North, County Record Office, Truro; Dennis O'Brien, West Virginia University; Francis J. Petrie, Official City of Niagara Falls (Ontario) Historian; William M. E. Rachal, *Virginia Magazine of History and Biography;* Tony Roth, the Historical Society of Pennsylvania; David L. Salay, New York State Historical Association; Elizabeth Silvester, McGill University; Dortha H. Skelton, the College of William and Mary in Virginia; Frances L. Stone, West Virginia Library Commission; John A. Williams, Editor of State Papers, Vermont; Mathilde D. Williams, Peabody Library Association of Georgetown, D.C.

I am also greatly indebted to Gloria Fisher for providing competent typists for this project.

Charleston, West Virginia   Elizabeth Cometti
January 1976

THE AMERICAN JOURNALS OF Lͭ JOHN ENYS

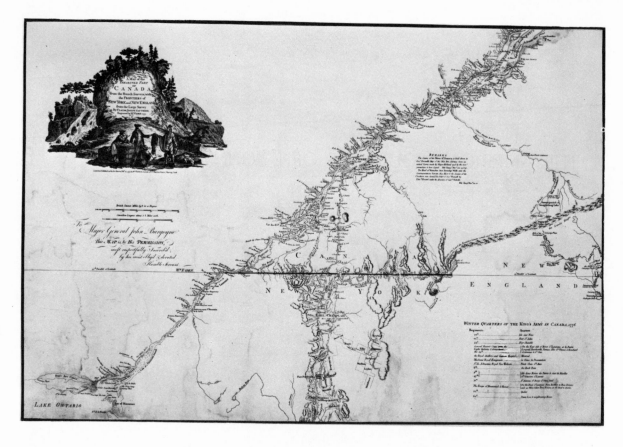

Map I. A Map of the Inhabited Part of Canada from the French Surveys, with the Frontiers of New York and New England from the Large Survey by Claude Joseph Sauthier. Engraved and published by William Faden, London, February 25, 1777. From a copy among the Enys papers. *Courtesy of the Cornwall County Record Office, DD. EN 2073; photograph by Charles Woolf*

THE AMERICAN REBELLION

O<small>N THE</small> *15th of Feby 1776* the Company to which I belonged Marched from Chatham Barracks, and embarking on board a tender proceeded to the Nore,[1] where we found the Transport destined to take us to Plymouth. Having previously obtained leave from General [William] Evelyn[2] to go by land to Plymouth in order to Settle some business, I left Capt. [Thomas?] Basset and Lt. [Thomas] Hill with the Company and returned that Evening to Chatham, from whence I set out Next Morning towards the place of our final embarkation (Plymouth) at which place the Surprize an[d] Morten [*Martin*] Men of war were waiting to receive us.[3] At this place I waited untill the *17th of March* before the Company Arrived after which no time was lost. The Company embarked on board of the Men of War the Next day altho we were prevented from Sailing by Contrary winds untill the *21st,* when the Wind being fair Capt. Basset and I embarked on board the Surprize (Lt. Hill) having embarked the evening before on board the Morten. About four in the evening *22d* we got under way. Next day about 12 OClock we took our departure from

3

the Lizard and that Night were Supposed to pass Scilly of which we Saw Nothing. It was Impossible to have had better weather that we had all this Month but on the *first of Aprill* it began to blow very hard & continued so to do for two days the greatest part of which time we were obliged to lie too.

On the *Eighth* we struck Soundings on the outer bank of Newfoundland, and on the Same day saw some Islands of Ice, one of which we Supposed to be Near a Quarter of a Mile Square and about Sixty feet perpendicular hight. This Must have been an Imence body of Ice, As According to some experiments Made on board of our Ship we found that Ice floated only one eighth out of the Water, and I am told Capt. Douglass [Charles Douglas] of the Isis⁴ made some experiments of the same kind whilst we lay in the Gulph who says only one twelfth appears above Water. On the *Ninth* we had a very thick fog which Froze to our Ropes as it fell, by which means the Ship Appeared as if Rigged with Ropes of Cristal Near four times their usual diameter, which formed a Sight both new and Strange. However Agreable this might be to the Eye yet the Situation was far from a pleasant one, as not a Rope in the waul [*sic*] run until by dint of beating them we had got them Clear of the encrustation of Ice which had formed Round them, which was not until near 12 OClock in the day, when we again got in Sailing trim Meeting every Now and then with Small Islands of Ice.

On the *twelfh* about Noon we made the land which proved to [be] the Island of St. Peters [St. Pierre], a Smal French Island about 3 Leagues South of Newfoundland. Having assertained what land it was we bore away for Cape Ray one of the Capes that form the Gulph of St. Laurence [St. Lawrence], but the Wind blowing hard and the drift Ice setting out of the Gulf we were obliged to lie too all that Night. On the *13th* in the Morning we made Sail again, & as our pilot imagined could we once get thro the Strait we Should find no more Ice, we were hopes of making a remarkable good passage, but think how we must have been disappointed when Instead of getting rid of the Ice we came to a peice so long that we could not see the end of it. At first we attempted to find a passage th[r]o it as it was but a very Narow Slip but finding that impracticable and being Anxious to proceed it was determined to atempt to force a passage thro it, which was done with very little difficulty it being extreemly rotten. After having passed this we again began to imagin our dificulty's over as we could see no more Ice, but in the evening were convinced of our Mistake by finding a peice of Ice ahead of us to which we could See no End. At first we attempted to force our way thro this as we did the former one. As we were now better fitted for attacking it, having been employed all the day in Making fenders out of old Cables and peices of Wood, and Nailing a three Inch plank round the bow of the Ship to prevent the Ice from cutting of her, for some time we had a prospect of Success as the Ice imperceptably opened & admited us, but in the course of the Night it closed upon us so firm that we could get Nither backwards or forwards. On Morning of the *14th* the fog which had been very thick the day before Cleared off and we found ourselves within Sight of cape Ray distance about four Leagues. This afternoon the Ice being perfectly firm all round us, I and some others took a walk about a Quarter of a Mile round the Ship which you may Suppose was very Agreeable after our being on board Ship so long. Here we also made a trial of the Ice Water by Melting down large blocks of it which we found produced excellent fresh water tho the Ice was certainly formed from Sea Water. The greatest difficulty is the getting pices free from Cracks or perforated parts in which the Salt is apt to lodge in which case it disolves with the Ice and Spoils your water, but when made with care we preferred it to the water we had on board. He[re] we also tried the Machine for distilling Salt Water fresh (from the Steam) which is said to produce good fresh Water from the pots which they boil the Ships provisions in. It was first tried with plain Salt Water and produced a Water not unlike barley Water.[5] It was afterwards tried on the pot where they were cooking the provision and produced a fresh water but not quite so good as the first, nor yet so bad as I should have supposed it would have been.

From this untill the *twentieth* we were sometimes making Saill and pressing thro the Ice and sometimes laying quite steady in it to all appearance, tho it is plain we altered our Sittuation every day tho sometimes it was without any attempt on our part and even without our knowledge. On the *20th* in the Morning we Saw an immence Number of Seals and as the Ship was Still fast i[n] the Ice, we amused ourselves by killing them, one of which was brought on board, and I was Surprized to See the quantity of blood there was in it, tho I could make no Guess at it as it had bled partly on the Ice, partly in the pinnace, and the rest on the deck. I had the curiosity of tasting part of this Animal, so we had the heart broiled and I do not think it eat badly but some of our men were Made Sick by eating of its flesh which is of a very oily Nature and produces great quantity of Train oil to the fisheries on that Coast. On the *21st,* the Ice began to be Rotten and lesser than usual, and on the *22d* a breze getting up broke up the Ice so much as to let the ship Make way through it, and about one OClock to our great joy we got quite Clear, and after having Sailed a few leagues toward evening we saw the Island of Anticosti which is Situated in the Mouth of the River St. Laurence. It is a prity large Island but not Inhabited excpt by wild beasts and some Goats that were Sent there by Sir Guy Carleton (whilst he was Governor) for Subsistance of any one who Should be so unfortunate as to be wrecked on its inhospitable shores, as a Ships Crew who were cast away there some years ago were very near perishing for want of food.[6]

On the *23d* we had another very hard Gale of Wind which prevented us passing the Island untill Night when the Wind Sinking with the Sun we proceeded up the River, very Seldom Seeing land until we came to Cape Chat which we made on the *26th*. Near this place are a Number of Mountains called the [Our] Lady Mountains[7] the tops of which being covered with Snow and all the rest of the Mountain Green with the pines and other evergreens which grow at the foot of it made an apearance agreeable an picturesque enough. On the *29th* we got Sight of the Island of Bic at which place Capt. [Robert] Linzee[8] had orders to Land on Shore for Inteligence, for which purpose he intended runing between the Island and the Main, but a very thick fog came on which prevented his intentions, and obliged him to lie too until the fog cleared up, which was not until the *1st of May* early in the Morning. Just as the horison began to be a little Clear we Saw a Ship which to all appearance was a very large one coming directly down upon us. As we did not know what she might prove our Ship was Imediately Cleared for Action. It is Surprizing to see how Active and Cleaver the Sailors are at this Work. It was quite finished before I thought they had time to begin it and looked pretty enough all bulk-heads and births being knocked down so that She appeared fore and aft a compleat double Battery without the Smalest obstruction from one end to the other. By the time every thing was ready it was discovered to be the Mortin Sloop, which Saild from plymouth the same day we did and had on board party of our Regt. As soon as we knew each other we join'd and came to an Anchor between the Island of Bic and the Main.

As soon as every thing in the Ship was set to rights a Boat was maned to go on shore for Inteligenc. The boat was commanded by Lt. [Thomas] Bennet[9] the first Lieut of the Ship Accompanied by Myself and the Pilot. I confess what led me on Shore was my curiosity to see a Savage which I expected to See leaping from Hill to Hill in the Manner Goats do in England, for which Curiosity I payed dearly, as the wind blew very fresh aganst us & the Spray of the Sea beat all over us which freezing as it fell made us compleatly uncomfortable. I realy believe the portugal Cloak I had on would If tried have stood upright so much was it froze.

After having hunted a long while for an Inhabitant we at lenth saw a fire at a distance and rowed towards it. When we Arrived we found and old Canadian sitting by it, who as a picture of poverty beggar'd all discription, indeed such was his figure and Dress, that it would be Impossible for Words to discribe him to one who had never Seen any of the lowest order of Canadians, every part of his dress being the work of his own family, and of a sort peculiar to this country. So very cold was I when I got on Shore that altho before that time I had never tasted a drop of raw Rum in my Life, I then drank it without perceiving its heat or its taking the least effect on me until I got on boad Ship again. After having warmed ourselfs by his fire Lt. Bennet began to examine the Canadian who gave us the following Inteligence which he said he got from an Indian from Quebec who had passed by some days before, Viz. that at the time he left Quebec it was still in the hands of Genl. Carleton, but that the Rebels had 22000 Men[10] before the town Adding that they were employed in fitting up fireships, floating Batteries fire Rafts &c. &c. to destroy any Shiping who attempeted to relieve the town, that they had also very strong Batteries on point Levi and point Orleans which commanded the entrance into the Bason of Quebec. He also told us that a very large Man of War had passed on the Night before which from his desscription we soon found out to be the Isis, which had Sailed from the Nore about the Middle of february with some of our Regt on board. With this Inteligance we went on board, and very early Next Morning we got under way and that evening reached the Island of Caudre [Coudres] where we found the Isis. This Night 13 pilots came on board to offer their Service who were all retained and taken up to Quebec. Here we were detained for want [of] wind untill the *fourth* at Night, at which time the Isis having some of her boats on shore in pursuit of a Scooner we saw in Shore could not proceed that tide, but suffered the Surprize to proceed at the request of Major Carleton (now Lt. Col. Carleton) who came on board togeater with Capt. [Archibald] Campbell of our Regt before daylight on the *5th* bringing orders from Capt. Douglas[11] for us to proceed with all haste to Quebec. As soon as ever day light appeared we got under Way and that day passed the traverse [Traverse] at the end of the Isle of Orleans, a place very difficult to pass as the Channel in that part is very Crooked and extreemly Narrow. Having passed that we Saild along the Banks of the Isle of Orleans, a most beautyfull well Cultivated Island. This afternoon being Sunday we Saw a great Number of Inhabitants coming out of Church, who upon Seeing us Crowded to the beach, on Which Capt. Lindzee ordered a Gun to be fired to Leeward and the Colours to be hoisted which done instead of any of them coming on board as we expected they all dispersed so much that after that we could hardly see a Creature on shore. At dusk in the evening the Wind began to fail us we being then off a place Called St. Patrick hole [Hole] distance

6. A view of the Bason of Quebec, with the Island of Orleans, Point Levi, and Fall of Montmorenci. Drawing by James Peachey. *Courtesy of the Public Archives of Canada*

about five or Six miles below Quebec but not within Sight of it. I beleive we could have got something Nearer the town that Night had we pushed, but as we had no certain intelligence withir the town was taken or no and Imanagining there were very Strong Batteries on the points Levi and Orleans according to the Intelligence we had received at Bic, I believe was the reasons which determined Capt. Lindzee to come to an Anchor here in preference to proceeding further, as there was a very great probability of our getting off those Batteries without wind to carry us, by them, as it was every Moment growing Calmer as Night came on. As soon as we had Anchored every thing was prepared for towing off any fire rafts which the[y] Might attempt to send down with the tide which at this place runs very Strong. Every thing being ready for the worst we all lay down to Sleep the Ship remaining Cleared for Action and all the Men ready at a Call during the Night. At day light on the *6th* we got under way once more. And just as we were turning Point Levi we saw a Canoe with two Men in her put of and make toward the Ship. When they had got Near enough to know who we were they would have wilingly have returned but it was then too late as they were within Shot of us, which obliged them to come on board, tho much aginst their wills. As soon as they were on board they were seperated and examined one after the other, When they gave Nearly the following intelligence (Viz.). That the Garrison of Quebec was Still in the possession of General Carleton consisting of about 1500 Men for the most part the Militia and Merchants of the town who had taken Armes on the Occasion, as did also the Judges and the rest of the Civil Magestrates.[12] The remainder were partly regulars and Sailors with McLeans new Regt (then very Weak).[13] On the part of the Rebels they had between 2 and 3000 Men before the town great part of which were Ill of the Small pox which at that time raged in their Army. Secondly, that they expected a very large reinforcement that day or next from above. On the Arrival of which they had determined to assault the town once more for which purpose they had withdrawn all their force from Point Levi and the Isle of Orleans on the preceeding Night. (The last boat from the Isle of Orleans was seen by us about the time of the examination of the two men which appeared to go towards the falls of Montmorency). On these men being Asked why they wanted to return Said they were afraid to come on board, but it seems since that the Rebels had perswaded them they would have a large french fleet to their assistance early in the Spring and as we had the St. Georges Ensign hoisted they took it for the french Colours, there not being wind Sufficient at that time to Blow out the flag they could not see the Red cross in it, and that it was on the Discovery of that they wanted to turn.

During the greatest part of this examination we had been in Sight of the City and were Surprized that they made no Signal although ours had been hoisted the whole time. At lenth the Signal being made we proceeded into the Bason, When Capt. McKenzy [Thomas Mackenzie] of the Lizard frigate[14] came on board of us and took Capt. Lindzee, Coll. Carleton and Capt. Campbell on Shore with him. Very soon after they had been on shore Orders were sent on board for us and the Marines on board to disembark Immediately which was very soon done as we had every thing ready before we rec'd the

7. Quebec: British army arrived from sea, May, 1776. Engraving in a scrapbook at the Public Archives of Canada; engraver and date of publication unknown. *Courtesy of the Public Archives of Canada*

Order. Just as we were landing the Isis and Mortin came into the Bason who as us landed all the Soldiers they had on board as soon as possible, among which was our Grenadier Company.[15]

We were no sooner on Shore than we received Orders to March out of the Garrison as soon as our Men had refreshed themselves a little. Accordingly About twelve OClock every thing being ready we left the town with about as I have since been told 850 Men for the Most part English When to our great Surprize the Rebels abandoned the place and that with so great precipitation that they even left a feild peice Loaded in the field with only a Nail put into the Vent which was easyly drawn from thence. At first they seem'd as if they would form in a Smal wood at the end of the hights [Heights] of Abram [Abraham], but it was very soon known they had decamped for good. During this time I am told some few Shots were fired tho I do not remember to have heard above one or two which were fired by some Canadian Voluntiers at a body of men three Shots distance from them. A party of Coll. McLeans Corps was detached from the hights to examine the houses w[h]ere the rebels had been Quarter'd and to bring in all the Sick and Wounded, togeather with all the Armes they could find in them.

Among other things that were found was the Commanding officers Dinner which he had left at the fire, and served as a refreshment to the Soldiers. After having remaind on the hights untill between four and five OClock we returned and that day all our Officers dined with the General. I Never heard the Quantity of stores that were taken which were however very considerable.

I had not been here above four or five days (during which time all the rest of our Regt were Arrived) before I was Ordered on detachment to Cape Rouge a place about 9 or 10 Miles above Quebec, where I was Stationed at a ferry at the foot of the Hill. The time I spent here was I think the Most disagreeable I ever yet saw as I was obliged to live in a very Small house with nothing but thin deal partitions in it togeather My party of 20 Men, and two family's of Canadians who were for the most part Ill of the Small Pox. I remaind here nearly a Week in this Situation And on my return found the 47th Regt was Arrived from Hallifax [Halifax], and about 100 Recruits for the 8th Regt from England. Among the Officers of the former was Capt. [Thomas] Aubrey who I had very often Seen at Mr. Carters and who I believe you [i.e., Francis Enys] also know. About two or three days after My return to Quebec the 47th Regt and the Grenadiers and Light Infantry of our Regt proceeded 20 Miles Up the River to a place called point au Tremble [Pointe aux Trembles], All the rest remaining in the Garrison of Quebec until the *21st* in the Evening when we were ordered on board Small transports to go up the River in, the Indiamen which brought out greatest part of our Regt being too Large to pass the falls of Richelieu. Early on the *22d* we Saild and coming up with the Shiping above the town Near the above mentioned falls we all proceeded as far as three Rivers [Trois Riviéres] Nothing material happening untill our Arival at that place. Our Small fleet under the Command of L. Coll. [William] Nesbit of the 47th Regt came to an Anchor about 1 Mile or 1½ above the town. Soon after our Arrival here (as we had been for some time detaind by contrary Winds) the remainder of the Army from England and Ireland came up to three Rivers w[h]ere they lay.

On the *7th of June* Genl. [Guy] Carleton arrived at that place, and on the *8th,* a boat belonging to our fleet which had been up the River was fired upon by the Rebels About 2 OClock in the Morning, and about day light Capt. [Henry] Harvey of the Morten ordered our Ship to drop a stern Clear of the reach of his Guns as he was going to fire on Shore.[16] On looking on Shore we could See a Large body of Men near the Edge of the wood. A good deal of firing took place from the Mortin Sloop and an Armed transport Named the British Queen[17] but beleive it had no effect except making the Rebels just enter the Skirts of the Wood that they might not be Seen. The Signal for our party to land was very Soon made which we accordingly did togeather with two Six pounders which came from England on board one of our transports under the command of Lieuts. Smith and York of the Artilery. As soon as we were all on Shore we Marched and took post in there rear in order to cut of their retreat. A very Short time after we taken up our Grownd, a Scatering fire began with the pickeks of the Army Near the town which was soon Succeeded by a very Smart one from the 62d and some other Regts which lasted about ten or twelve Minutes when the Rebels retreated into the Wood. About this time we were joined by 4 Companies of the 24th Regt and a field piece from three Rivers, so that when the Rebels had retreated as far as our post, finding us too strong they never attempeted to fire upon us but tried to go round us by Striking deeper into the Wood in order to gain their Boats which they had left at a place caled Machiech [Yamachiche] about 15 Miles further. This occasioned us another March in order to get possesion of the Boats before them, and as we had taken a good Many Prisoners very good Intelligence was got of the place where they were. But unfortunately on our Way we Saw 5 other Boats full of Men just as we came to the Banks of Lake St. Peter at a place Named point au [Pointe du] Lac at whom we fired a few Shot from our Cannon which Alarmed those we were in pursuit of and gave them time to get off which they did before we reached Macheich. Balked in our hopes and being now 18 Miles from our Ships and the day prety far advanced we were orderd to take post, which was accordingly done, on the Banks of the River Machieche we found convenient for the purpose. Here we lay all Night very quiet. In the Morng some of the Rebels Shewed themselves at the Shore of the Wood but on Seeing us Retired.

About 7 or 8 in the Morning great Numbers began to come in to us and give themselves up as prisoners, among whom was General Thomson [William Thompson] who commanded, Coll. Irwin [William Irvine] Second in Command, one Aid de Camp and many other inferior Officers and about 80 privates.[18]

Soon after these had come in who informed us many others were preparing to do the Same an order was rece'd from General Carleton for us to return to our Ships which was Imediately complied with. When we Arrived at Point au Lac we found Generals Carleton & Burgoine [John Burgoyne] with the 31st and 62d Regts at that place who joind our Line of March as we passed, and

About 4 OClock in the Evening we all Arrived Safe at our Shiping and imediately embarked whilst the rest pursued their Rout to three [Three] Rivers. Our loss in this great Action was I am informed only one Sergeant and three or four Privates Killed and 7 or 8 Wounded, as for the Rebels tho I never could hear of more than 22 or 3 that were found dead, nor were there more in all than between 4 and 500 Prisoners Yet I am told they Accknoledged to have lost 700 Men by the Expedition, which consisted of about 1500 or 2000 Men under the Command of General Thomson.[19] Their March seemed pretty well and Secretly conducted and had not they been mislead by one of their Guides we Should in all probability have lost more men as they Meant to have made their Attack before day light on the town of three Rivers where they expected to find only a few men instead of the Whole Army, which shews what bad inteligence they had.

We were after this detained by Contrary Winds until the *13th* when the Wind being fair we proceeded towards Sorel a Strong post of the Rebels at which it was said they Meant to Make a Stand. Our fleet being now all to-geather on Lake St. Peter made a Most beautyfull appearance where we had an opportunity of seeing it all att once which consisted of more than 90 Sail altogeather. At the End of this Lake is a very great Number of Small Islands thro which the fleet were obliged to pass. I think it was one of the most Agreable prospects I ever saw, the Islands and Shiping being so interspersed one with another, and the Shiping being eager to get on were very often almost near enough to Leap from one to another.

On the *14th* about four in the afternoon we Arrived at Sorel which we found abandoned as usual. Sorel is Situated at the mouth of River Richelieu tho it is more commonly called the River Sorel which formes a Comunication between the River St. Lawrence and Lake Champlain Navigable for Small Scooners as far as Chambly which is no more than 19 Miles from St. Johns where the Lake commences in which there is plenty of Water. This evening the Grenadiers & Light Infantry of the Army Landed And Next Morning *15th* great part of the Army did the Same in order to pursue the Rebels by

Route of that River and our Regt and some others continued our Route towards Montreal. Before we had got within 30 Miles of the town an express Arrived to let the Generl know that the Rebels had abandoned the town, on which our Regt was ordered to Land and March thither. The Wind being foul it was the *16th* in the After Noon when we landed about 30 Miles from Montreal and that Night reached point au Tremble [Pointe-aux-Trembles] a

17th   place about Nine miles from town and Next Morning about Nine OClock we Marched into it to the great joy of some of the Inhabitants. A few hours after our Arrival Sir John Johnson Arrived with about 200 Men which had been Most of them tenants of his on his Estate on the Mohak [Mohawk] River and near as many Indians who brought with them a Six pounder which the lat[t]er had taken at the Cedars a short time before.[20] I confess I was a little alarmed being at Breakfast when they Arived and knowing our Regt to be Scatered all over the town. When the Indians began firing their Salute according to custom I thought the Rebels had returned but was soon convinced of the Contrary.

The remainder of the Army having as before Mentioned pursued the Rebels by the way of the River Sorel who at their approach abanoned and burnt the forts of Chambly and St. Johns after which having boats Ready at the latter place they embarked and got over the Lake without our Army being able to overtake them tho I am told some of their Rear boats were Still within Sight of St. Johns when our people Arrived at that place.[21]

The Rebels being now entirely drove out the Province the Army encamped at, Isle aux Noix, St. Johns, Chambly, and on the Roads leading to Sorel and Montreal at which place our Regt remaind. No time was lost in preparing a Naval force Sufficient to cope with the Rebel fleet on Lake Champlain. Accordingly Scooners were Bought and being taken to peices at Chambly were tranported over the Carring place [carrying place or portage] between that and St. Johns where they were rebuilt for the lake Service. A great many Gun Boats the frames of which came from England were rebuilt as was also a Ship Large enough to carry 20 Guns the frame of which was built at Quebec.

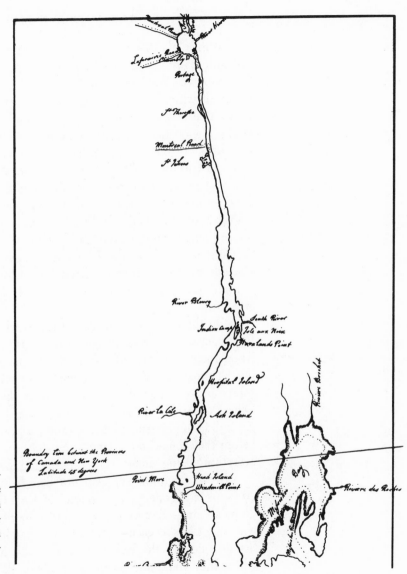

Map II. The Sorel, or Richelieu, River and the outlet of Lake Champlain. Copy by Michele Wynn of the northern portion of a manuscript map probably originally drawn by John Enys. *Courtesy of the present members of the Enys family*

Whilst all this was preparing Nothing of any Consequence happened until the *25 of July* when Brigadier Genl. [Benjamin] Gordon returning from St. Johns was fired upon and wounded from a Wood within 3 Miles of the Camp of which Wound he died on the *1st of August*. The person who Shot him was afterwards known to be one Lieut. Whitcombe [Benjamin Whitcomb] of the Connecticut Rangers, who notwithsanding he was Imediately pursued by party's of Soldiers and Indians found means to escape them all.²² Montreal was now full [of] Indians of all Manner of Nations you can Suppose who came down to receive their presents and offer their Service to the General. In the latter part of Augt I being then at the Isle aux Noix our most advanced post on a Visit to our Grenadier and Light Company, the Rebel fleet were Seen a little above point [Point] au Fer, and on the *3d of September* in the evening an Account was rec'd at the Island that they were then within 5 Miles of that place, from whence they retreated Next Morning after having fired a few Shot at some Savages (who were sent to watch their Motions) without doing them any harm.

On the *6th* being on my return to Montreal I met a detachment of our Regt consisting of one Officer, two Sergts., two Corporals and Eighty Privates who brought me an order from the Commanding Officer of the Regt to take the Command of the above detachment with which I was to proceed to St. Johns and put myself and them under the Command of the Commanding Officer of Artilery at that place. Our Regt left Montreal at the same time this party did, and encamped at Laprarie [Laprairie] where they lay until the *12th* before they joined the Camp at St. Johns which was now Augmenting dayly everything being almost ready for crossing the lake.

In the *beginning of Octr* our fleet being ready consisting of one Ship of 20 Guns, a Scooner of 14, another of 10, a Gondola with 7, a Radeau with 10 Guns all Brass Battering peices and four Howitzers and about 20 Gun Boats with one Gun in each.²³ After having rendevous'd at point au Fer we all Set Sail in quest of the Rebels. On the *10th* in the evening we got inteligence where they were, and on the *11th* about 12 OClock we saw and some of our

8. A view of His Majesty's armed vessels on Lake Champlain, October 11, 1776. Watercolor by C. Randle, 1776, showing from left to right in the foreground the ships *Carleton* (1), *Inflexible* (2), "A Long Boat" (6), *Maria* (3), *Convert* (4), and *Thunderer* (5), and, in the background, "Gun boats" (7) and "Valcure Island" (8). *Courtesy of the Public Archives of Canada*

headmost Ships fired at them. They were lieng at an Anchor behind the Island of Valcore [Valcour], so that our fleet had passed them before they knew it and were obliged to tack in order to get into the Bay. This rendered the Vessel I was on board totaly useless she being flat bottomed and consequently could not work to Windward. We fired some few Shot at the time we first Saw their *Oct. 11* fleet but believe it might have been just well lett alone. The Gun Boats bore the blunt of their whole fire the Greatest part of that day untill at lenth the Carleton Schooner got in tho She was of very little Service to them ebing very Soon in Such a Shattered Condition as to be towed out of the Bay by the boats of the fleet for fear of her being taken. The Inflexible and Maria fired also some Shot in the course of the day but I believe with as little effect as Radeau, being bothe to far off. The firing continued until evening when the boats withdrew leaving the Rebel fleet formed in a line in the Bay whilst our fleet formed in a Semicircle round the Mouth of it, in Such Manner that it might well be thought they could not have escaped, which however they did in the course of the Night by passing between us and the shore unpersieved by any one.

The Rebels lost this day one of there largest Vessels called the Royal Savage which Ran on shore when the firing first began in the Morning and was Burnt by our people that Night.[24] I never heard the Number of men we lost on that day. One Midshipman was wounded, our Regt had 5 or 6 Men and a Drummer Killed and one wounded on board the Carleton and one man wounded on board of a Gun Boat. The rest of the loss fell Mostly on the

12th Artillery.[25] Early Next Morn it was found the Rebels were escaped and at day light some of their fleet were Seen at a distance. Our fleet attempted to pursue them but the wind was so hard against us we were obliged put back again, the Inflexible and Radeau having both been in Some danger, the Reason of the former I don't know but the latter was occasioned by her lee boards giving way which made heel so much as to let some water into her lower parts.

In the evening one of our tenders discovered their fleet a second time and on the *13* early in the Morning a Breeze Springing up in our favour we all made Sail once more in pursuit of them, when the two Schooners and the Ship overtook and came to Action with them the rest of our fleet not being able to get up. This force however proved Sufficient as in a very short time, one of their Gallies Named the Washinton [*Washington*] Commanded by one Brigadier Genl. Waterbury [David Waterbury] Struck her Colours and Seven others of their fleet under Command of General [Benedict] Arnold ran on Shore in a bay Named Ferries's Bay [Buttonmould Bay] where having burnt their Shiping they took to the Woods and returned to Ticonderoga. The Same day a party of Canadians found a Gondola Named the Jersey on the opposite

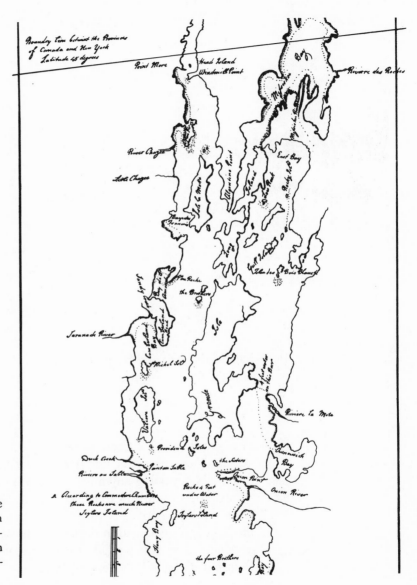

Map III. Northern end of Lake Champlain. Copy by Michele Wynn of the central portion of a manuscript map probably originally drawn by John Enys. *Courtesy of the present members of the Enys family*

9. A view of the New England armed vessels in Valcour Bay on Lake Champlain, October 11, 1776. Watercolor by C. Randle, 1776. The ships from left to right are *Revenge* (2), *Washington* (6), *Philadelphia* (8), *Congress* (7), *Jersey* (10), *Lee* (4), *Royal Savage* (1), *Spitfire* (14), *New Haven* (13), *Providence* (12), *Connecticut* (11), *New York* (9), *Enterprise* (3), and *Trumbull* (5). *Courtesy of the Public Archives of Canada*

Side of the lake and Soon after a Small Sloop Named the Lee was found and brought up to Crown point where we Arrived on the *17th* in the Morning so that out of all the 14 Sail of Vessels they had on the lake only four got off Clear and one of them was Not with their fleet being at Teconderoga Changing her Guns as I am informed. On our Arrival at Crown point General Waterburry and his Crew were Suffered to return on their Parole.[26]

2nd

A day or two after our Arrival here the Army came up, where they all Stood without doing anything Material untill the *1st of November* when we reimbarked to return to Canada as did all the rest of the Army The day after. On the *third* I Arrived at St. Johns and on the *ninth* reced my Orders to join the Regt again who had in the mean time passed and got into Winter Quarters at Montreal at which place we were soon joind by the Artilery where we Remaind all the Winter very Quietly.

1777   General Burgoine Arrives at Quebec on the *5 of May*. Arrives at Montreal on the *17th of May*. The 29th Regt March to Chambly Portage and St. Therese on the *19th of June*. The last part of General Burgoines Army Quit St. Johns on the *20th* or *21st* of June. The 29th Regt March to St. Johns on the *21st of Septr* to releive the 31st Regt who proceed to Ticonderoga on the *22d* which was at that time invested by the Rebels commanded by one Coll. [John] Brown.[27] Return to Montreal on the —— of *November* at which place we remain'd all the Winter and a great part of the Summer following without anything happening worthy of Mention.

On the *Eleventh of Sept 1778* we Marched from Montreal to releive the Emigrants at Isle aux Noix, and that Night Slept at St. Theresee [Thérèse]. Early Next Morning we Marched into St. Johns and embarking imediately we Arrived at Isle aux Noix by dinner time on the *12th*.

About the Middle of October there were orders given for a party to Cross the lake under Major [Christopher] Carleton of our Regt, and on the *24th* the following party embarked at Isle aux Noix.

	Majr	C	Lt	En	P	
29th Regt	1	2	5	1	120)	with Noncomissiond
31st Regt		2	3	1	96)	Officers in
53d Regt		1	0	2	50)	Proportion
Sr. J. Johnsons			1	0	30)	
Savages					80)	
	1	5	9	4	376	

The Savages were under the Command of Captain [Alexander] Fraser of the 34th Regt deputy Superintendent of Indian Affairs, and Lieut. Houghton [Haughton] of the 53d Regt who has the Charge of the Village of Caughnawaga.[28]

I have to prevent Confusion Said that all these party's embarked at Isle aux Noix which they did not exactly do, the 31st Regt having Slept the preceeding Night a Short distance above and the Savages a Short distance below the Isle Aux Noix. Each embarking from the place they Slept Joind us **24th** in the Course of the day when we all incamped at the upper end of Isle la [La] Motte. On our way to this place we halted at Point au Fer, from whence Capt. St. Clare [David St. Clair] of our Regt was prevaild on to return his health not permiting him to proceed. Early on the *25th* we proceeded on our Voyage untill About 1 O'Clock in the Afternoon at which time we were off Point au Sable [Ausable]. Here Major Carleton put into a River of the above Name it being now dangerous to proceed during the day, for fear of our party being discovered by some of the Rebel Scouts from the East Side of the Lake then well Inhabited.

During our Stay here a Mr. [Colin?] Campbell came to us who had been into the Country for Inteligence. What News he brought I know not but I am apt to think his Accounts of the frontiers was not altogeather Suitable to our purpose.

We lay on this River (which is a very good place for Shelter when once you are in it although very difficult of access on Account of Some Sand banks which lay off it on which some of our boats got aground) until 2 O'Clock in the Morning of the *26th* when we all got under way again and to my great Surprize got over the Bar at the Mouth of the River without difficulty, although the Night was quite dark. This Morning a fog rising with the Sun enabled us to proceed as far as Flat Rock point [Point], a tolerable Bay against Southerly Winds, but quite open to the Northerly, & but very Indifferent Shellter for to hide our boats and fires Notwithstanding which we lay here 5 days without being Seen that I could ever hear of. The day after our Arrival **Sept.** here the Major Sent off a Mr. Johns into the Country. During our Stay here our party went into the Woods a little way to practice treeng as they Call it, that is to Say the Manner of hiding ourselves behind Trees S[t]umps &c. &c. &c. and at our return the Major was pleased to say the Men had exceeded his

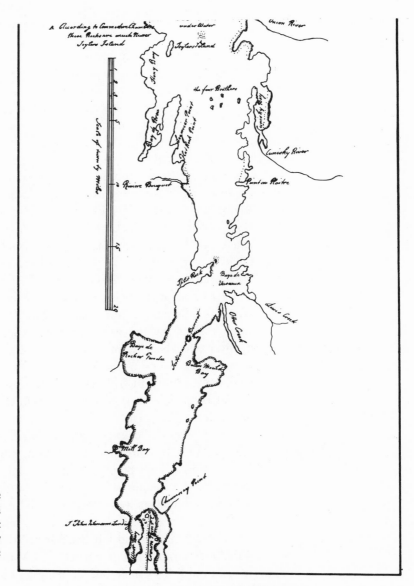

Map IV. Southern end of Lake Champlain. Copy by Michele Wynn of the lower third of a manuscript map probably originally drawn by John Enys. *Courtesy of the present members of the Enys family*

expectations tho I could See very plainly our Aukwardness diverted the Indians and Roialists [Loyalists] who are by far better hands at this Work being bred in the Woods from their Infancy, and Accustomed to this Manner of hiding themselves in order to Shoot Deer, and other Wild Beasts.

On the *30th* in the Morn a very unlucky Accident happened by one of our Men Cutting down a Tree carlessly which fell on a Wigwam where there were several Sitting, by which three men were hurt. One died of his wound the Same Morning another was obliged to return to Canada, the third was hardly worth mentioning as he was able to do his duty again in a day or two.

31st About Sun Set we Moved from this place with a fair Wind and passing Split Rock about 12 O'Clock at Night we Arrived in the Baye de Roche Fendu where we lay the remainder of that Night, and all Next day. About two OClock in the Afternoon we had all the reason possible to Suppose we were discovered, as we saw a boat enter the Bay with her Sail Set and just after She had got Clear of the point Struck her Sail and rowed a little Distance into the Bay. After Staying a short time we Saw her row out again in Company with another Boat. Scouts were Imediately Sent by Major Carleton to try and discover what boat it was. At lenth an Indian came in and Said he Saw her go on board of one of the Vessels. It afterwards proved to be the Boat of the Carleton, Sent by Lt. [Hercules?] Harrison (who was Ignorant of our being in that Bay) to fecth [fetch] of a Batteau which he had left at that place some time before.

Novr. 1st At twelve OClock at Night we left this Bay and before daylight Arrived safe in West Bay at the back of Crown point. There was still one house Standing on Crown point Inhabited by an old Man and his Wife commonly known by the Names of Lord and Lady North, in whose house some of our Soldiers and roialists were when an Inhabitant of the Lake Named Ferrero put in there to get some refreshment on his return from hunting who was immediately secured. He had left his Son in his Canoe at the Water Side which it was also Necessary to take for which a Man was sent. The Boy on seeing him at first put off his Canoe but on being told his father wanted him in the house came on Shore and was by that Means taken also. We found in his Canoe a Very fine Buck which was very Acceptable to us, as our fresh Meat was out.

2d   On the Next day one of our Indian Scouts took a prisoner, who was known to some Men in our Camp who told us if he was not bound he would escape in a quarter of an hour. This proved but two true for during the time a rope was fetching he made his escape Not only from the Guard but also from a great many bye Standers, among whom was Myself and two or three More Officers, one of which had just Cautioned the Centry to take care of him. During this time he was walking with his Armes Across upon his breast Apparently very thoughtfull, when on a Sudden he Sprung into the Wood, and Notwithstanding he was *Imediatly* pursued by Some of the Spectators, and some Indians (as Soon as they could get their Armes) He was Active enough to get Clear of them all.

3d   Next day some of our Indians Saw two Batteaux full of Rebels and were pursued by them which obliged them to land and hide their Canoe in the Wood which they did and came into Camp to inform Major Carleton of it. On the *4th* a party Crossed the Lake to Chimny point [Chimney Point] where they learnt from an Inhabitant that a party of Rebels had been there the Night before Commanded by one Lt. [Joseph?] Crook who Meant to Sleep that Night at a house called the red house about 6 or 7 Miles down the Lake.[29] He also showed them where the Rebels had left their boats which were found and taken.

It was very late at Night when this News came into Camp so that it was 5th   1 OClock in the Morning before a party was ready to pursue them when Capt. Dickson [Hugh Dixon] of our Regt with 40 Soldiers and as many Savages set off and landed on the east Side of the Lake, with Orders to endeavour to take the above mentioned party and to bring of all the Men betwen the Red house and Chimny Point. Unfortunately the party of Rebels apprized as I imagin of our being so Near, had left that place and taken to the Woods at Sun Set the evening before. Capt. Dickson returned about Noon after having execcuted the latter part of his Orders. The prisoners where Sent on board the Maria

Schooner, where there were also four More who where taken by Lt. [William] Alder of the Navy, and who proved afterwards to be Inhabitants of Otter Creek. On the *6th* about 11 OClock in the day we Crossed the Lake and landed a little way above Chimny point, from Whence two deta[c]hments were ordered one Commanded by Capt. [Andrew] Ross of the 31st Regt consisting of 100 Soldiers and all the Savages but 6 or 8 who remaind with Major Carleton and the other under the Command of Lt. Forquhar [William Farquhar] of our Regt. The latter was to destroy a Mill and Some houses Near Ticonderoga, and the former of which I was one were to March thro the woods to Otter Creek in Order to burn and destroy that Settlement. About one OClock both party's Marched. We continued untill it was very Near dark Marching Nearly due East, when we arrived at a deep Valley surrounded on every Side by very high hills so that our fires could not well be discoverd. Here

7th the Savages Agreed to pass the Night. Next Morn we Marched at day light and after having Marched about 5 Miles we came to a prettey large Creek the Name of which I have never been able to learn.[30] We passed this by means of a large tree fallen across it as it was by no means fordable at this place. A very Short distance from the place we Crossed this Creek we found a large trunk broke open and some empty flour Barrells. From this we continued our rout about 4 Miles further when we came to two Small Houses one of which was a Blacksmiths Shop but found no body in either of them, altho there was a very good stock of Corn, and one Horse left. After we had destroy'd these houses we proceded two Miles further, when we came to another house which from the furniture must have been a Weavers. Here were also two very large barns well stocked with all Sorts of Grain. This place did not Stop us at all as an Advanced Guard appointed to burn all they could See had totaly destroyed this place before our rear came up. So continuing our March about twelve OClock we came in upon Otter Creek at a place called Bladgets [Blodget] House, in the upper part of the township of Middlebury. At this place we found only a very Small house and barn with a very little Corn no Inhabitants.[31]

From hence two detachments were sent out one under Lt. Houghton of the 53d Regt composed of Savages and Royalists, to burn a farm house about two Miles up the Creek at which they found a large quantity of Grain but Neither Cattle or Inhabitants. The Other was commanded by a french Interpreter one La Motte and consisted of only 6 or 7 of the uper Country Indians, who Swam across the Creek and burnt a farm or two on the other Side but found niether Inhabitants or Cattle. The Main body waited here for the return of the above party's who were no sooner come in than we proceeded and Burnt a great Many Houses, Barns &c. and a very great quantity Hay, Corn &c. &c. but found Niether Cattle or Inhabitants in the course of this day. After we had quit the Village if it may be called so as the houses are ½ a Mile or a Mile Sunder, our Guide I know not for what reason thought proper to quit the direct road and Struck into the Woods. After having Marched near 5 Miles we found our selves at the house we had burnt in the Morning which I before mentioned to have been a blacksmiths shop. After this we were a long while before we gaind the proper path again and when we did the day was so far advanced that we got but a very little way forward in the course of our afternoons Marching although we had gone over a great deal of grownd.

8th   This Evening we encamped a short distance from the ford at which we were to pass the Creek. Next Morning we Moved Early and about 7 or 8 OClock arrived at the ford which the Indians immediately passed and began so warm a fire upon the Cattle and poultry that most of us who were in the rear Imagined they had been Attacked in the passage. We all Crossed the ford a[s] fast as we came up. Here for the first time we found Inhabitants, who appeard very glad to See the Soldiers cross the ford as the Savages had frightened them almost to death before our Arrival. The family we found here consisted of one Man, two Women and Eight or nine Small Children.

You can hardly suppose how quietly all these Yankees take any distresses, so much so that they appear to have lost all sort of feeling. They expressed no Sort of Surprize or Greif at our Coming and only Said very cooly they did not Suppose we Should have come so far into their Country. One of them appeared

THE AMERICAN JOURNALS OF LT. JOHN ENYS   30

a little destressed however when She was told that her Husband was to be carried into Canada and that She herself must return to them [their?] friends higher up the Creek or indeed where She chose, so She did not attempt following her Husband which would not be permitted. She said it was very hard to be treated so when they had never done any thing against the Kings troops which by the bye I beleive to be a d——d lie as from all appearance the house was fitted up as a place of defence to command the passage of the ford. At this place was found great plenty of Cattle of all kinds, hay, Corn, Indian Corn, Flax and many other things. The Inhabitants were Suffered to take a certain quantity of every thing Necessary for their Journey to the first Settlement, after which the Savages where admited to plunder the House, a thing they allways look upon as their undoubted right. As this was the uper most House we found any thing in there was [only?] a very small outhouse left standing to Shelter the Inhabitants who might pass that way on thire road home as the Nights were getting very cold at present. There were also left here a small proportion of provisions of different kinds and one Cow to give Milk to the Children on there passage for which Indulgence the woman promised to wait some time for the rest of the Inhabitants coming up and to give them all a share of the things which were left.

After we had destroyed all that was here except what I mentioned to be left, and were about to proceed an account came to us that there were Some Rebels in a house a little way down on the opposite Side of the Creek on which Lt. Arburthnot [Robert Arbuthnot] of the 31st Regt with 30 Men and some Savages repased the ford but on their Arrival at the house mentioned found none but the family. Meanwhile after having collected all the Cattle we could find and sent them off before us we proceeded down the Creek to opposite where Lt. Arburthnots party were, at which place we burnt another house and Waited untill his party had destroyed all on the other Side of the water and Crossed which was effected by means of a canoe found at that place. Our whole party being joind again we proceeded down the Creek burning and destroying all we found untill Near dark when we encamped at a Mile or two's distant from the lower falls [Vergennes]. It would be endless to Mention every house that was destroy'd this day, nor could I do it if I was inclined as I do not know the Number. During this days March our Guide Mislead us again, tho not so Materialy as before.

I Confess I was a good deal diverted at an old woman who had shewn more than common philosophy whilst She had been a Spectator to the destruction of every thing She had in the world. When every thing was over She began to Make a most dreadfull outcry that She was totaly ruined and undone that She could never live two days. It was very Natural to Suppose it was for her house and Cattle She was lamenting so deeply but it appeared when She was question'd about it that what She was so much distressed about was her having quit the house in such a fright as to leave her tobacco pipe, behind her. As to the rest She said was only the fortune of war and that the Rebels treated the Friends to Government much worse.

I must here also mention a circumstance of Generosity in one of the upper Country Indians who have very little intercourse with white people and are supposed to be more barbarous and Cruel than the Canadian Indians. I observed this young Man among the other Indians more active than common in striping one of the houses, in which he was very succesfull, having got a great quantity of different things. I supposed at first he meant them for himself as all the rest did but to my great Surprize saw when he found he could get no more that he colleted all he had got togeather and gave them to the poor Woman to whom they belonged nor would he suffer any of the other Indians to take them from her tho they would have been very glad to have done it. Early Next

9th Morning we rece'd accounts that Major Carleton was at the Mouth of the Creek and intended coming up to the falls. As soon as this Account was received we all Marched again and soon arrived at the falls and were Surprized to find the Blockhouse burnt which we found afterwards was done by La Motte and his Indians who had left the camp during the Night without our knowledge and I beleive without Capt. Rose's knowledge and finding no one in it had burnt it. Near this place was a very fine farm belonging to a Scotchman one MacIntoch [Donald McIntoch?] who was one of the Men taken at Crown point by Lt. Alder as before mentiond. This was by far the best farm we Saw in the Country as it was a very good house agreeably Situated with a View of the falls and an imence quantity of Grain, Cattle, poultry, and every thing which could render his Sittuation Agreeable. This Man had formerly been reconed a roialist, but his name being fownd to [found on?] Some paper or other was I believe the reason all his things were destroy'd as well as the rest, however he was Suffered to bring his Wife and another Woman who lived with her into Canada an Indulgence granted to no one else.

During our Stay here one Mr. Jones of the Royalists was Sent to destroy a Small Village Called Monkton a short distance from hence and to endeavour to bring off a Man Called Hayet [Winthrop Hoyt?] who Spoke the Indian Language very well and Who had been very often sent as an emissary to the Canadian Indians.

About the Middle of the day Major Carleton Arrived with all the boats (Gun boats excepted). From them we learnt that the party under Lt. Forquhar had miscarried having prior to there reaching the Mill come to a house in which a party of Rebels before Mention'd under the command of Lt. Crook had taken part. The Centry at the door Chalendged our party on their Approach, and on receiving no Answer fired and retreated into the house. The party being thus Alarmed it was impossbl to attack the house without very evident disadvantage and a Chance of losing a great many Men, particularly as the Rebels had thrown a party of men into small Log house which flanked the door. Some few Shot were fired on both Sides by which one man of our Regt was Wounded of which he died after his return to Canada. Thus circomstanced he quit the house and Joined Major Carleton again. We also learnt that Capt. Dickson had Crossed the Lake and burnt a large Mill and Some other houses on the opposite Side, and that the remainder with the Major had destroyed all the Settlements on the East Side of the Lake. I cannot here omit giving you some little Idea of the falls [Sutherland Falls?] of this place which I think are the pretiest I ever Saw. The Creek just above the fall is about 40 or 50 yards wide, and just before it comes to the fall is divided by a Small Island which has a Small rivulet falling down its center. The Whole is about 20 feet high and had on one Side of it the Block house and on the other a Saw Mill. A little before dusk Mr. Jones returned from Monkton having Executed his orders fully. No Sooner was he returned than the Whole embarked and went down to the Bottom of the Creek where we encamped that Night after having Sent all the prisoners on board of the Ships which were lieing off the Mouth of the Creek.

10th   Early Next morning we began to pass the Cattle across the lake which were very Numerous so that it was not finished untill 4 O'Clock in the afternoon when the whole embarked again to return to Canada. Capt. Ross and his party of the 31st Regt Crossed the lake to burn two or three houses in and Near the River Bouquet, at which place he was also to wait untill the Cattle had passed him.

The Carleton Schooner burnt 3 or 4 houses on the East Side of the lake which had been evacuated for Some time all the Rest of the party keeping Strait down the Lake. Just after Dusk it began to blow very fresh which encreased as it became Dark into Gale of wind by which our little fleet was totaly Seperated, each making the Safest part they Could, so that when we put in there was but our own boat an two others togeather. We were very Singularly fortunate in finding a bay that Night as tho it was so dark we could not tell where we were but very lukyly found at our first attempt to put on shore a Small Sandy bay, so as to secure our boats to which no damage was done, tho we had some of our Amunition Spoiled by the Surf bracking over their Sterns

11th   at our landing. It was not before Next Morning we found out where we were which we found to be on a Small Island [at the] uper end of Grand Isle. We lay in this place until past twelve O'Clock that day supposing the Lake to be too rough for a boat about which time we Saw a boat of Savages under Sail in the Middle of the Lake. On this the Major Resolved to proceed and when we had got out in the lake we could See Some more boats behind us. The Wind continued to blow very hard all day, so that some of our boats got into Point au Fer in very good time that evening, but that was not the case With me for before I reached the point it was dark and raind as if heaven and earth were coming togeather. We were all perfectly ducked and it was so very dark we should have passed the point without knowing it had not the people on shore who heard our oars made a Signal to us. On our landing here we found, a good many of our boats Already Arrived and Many others joind us in the Course of the Night. In the Morning we were all togeather except Capt. Ross's party left at River Bouquet on a boat loaded with things for the Savages, so without waiting for them, we proceeded to Isle aux Noix where we Arrived safe about the Middle of the day, and in a day or two after we were joind by all the boats we had left behind and all the party returned to there respective Winter Quarters our being at Isle aux Noix.

12th

The Whole of our Regt remain at this place untill *Novr 1779* when four Companys moved to St. Johns to releive the 31st Regt who went to Quebec. The head quarters of our Regt still remaind at the Island untill the *Summer 1780* when the regt were all brought down to St. Johns except one Company, who remain at that place as a Garrison for it.

In this Sittuation was the regt when we rece'd Orders for a Second Expedition under Major Carleton. This party was very considerable stronger than the first, tho not quite so Strong as was at first expected as we had only 108 Savages instead of all that cold be got, the rest having gone on another Expedition.

On the *27th of Septr.* the whole of the undermention'd party Arrived at St. Johns and on the *28th* they all Embarked and proceeded as far as Isle aux Noix.

		Ma.	Capt.	Leiut.	Ensn.	Sert.	Corpl.	Drum.	Private
Major Carleton	29th Regt	1	2	3	2	5	5	1	182
	34th Do	–	1	2	1	4	4	1	100
	53d Do	–	1	2	1	4	4	1	100
	84th Do	–	1	2	0	2	2	0	50
	Chassures			1	0	1	1	1	30
	Royalists	2	4	8	2	9	0	0	125
	Savages			1					108
Capt Monro [John Munro]	Royal Yorkers		1	2	2	2	2	1	120
	Rangers				1				30
	Mohawk Indians								30
	Total	3	10	21	9	27	18	5	875

In this I have mentiond the Savages as Embarking with the Rest (in order to have the total Strenth of the detachment in one place,) wheras they did not join untill we had been on the lake a day or two as you will find hereafter. Brigadier [Henry Watson] Powell accompanied our party as far as the Isle aux

29th Noix and Next Morning Saw the whole detachment under Armes. This parade being over we all embarked on board our boats and that Night encamped on the Isle La Motte, except Major Carleton who remain behind us at Isle aux Noix and passed us in the Night in company with Comodore [William] Chambers on their Way to his Vessell which lay a little way above us, on board of which the Major Slept this Night.[32]

On the *30th* we proceeded and found the Major on board the Maria Schooner, who embarked with us. We had hardly put off from the Maria when the wind began to blow very hard against us which obliged us to put into the Bay de Francois not being able to Make any way against it. In the Evening the wind being Somewhat abated we again Moved and got into the Bay de St. Ammand [Amand], when Night came on and the Wind rose very high so that

Oct. 1st it was not without some difficulty we reached the shore.

The wind Continued so strong all next day that we could not proceed. This day was employed in Aranging our boats.

On the *2d* we Moved and making but a short Stritch got in early to the Isle of Valcore where we lay that Night. During our residence here the Mohawk Indians join'd us togeather with Claws's Rangers Mentioned as part of Capt. Monro's party.[33]

Early on the *third* we got under way and having a little wind we reached River Bouquet in good time where we Stay'd that Night and next day.

In the Evening of the *fourth* about 6 O'Clock we came out of the River and proceeded that Night to Split Rock Bay where we again encamped. Next

5th Morning some of our Scouts Saw and Spoke with two Indians, and asked them if they were going to Major Carleton on which they answered in the Affirmative, & the Scout took no further Notice of them. When they returned to Camp they told this Storey adding they appeared to be very much fateagued and heavy loaded. This led to a Suspision they were not Friends on which a party of Mohawks pursued them but without success. In the Affernoon Lt. [William] Johnson of the 47th Regt, who has the Charge of the St. Regis Indians join'd us with 108 Indians principaly from the above Nation, telling us at the same time that the rest of the Canadian Indians were gone on another rout under the Command of Lt. Houghton of the 53d Regt towards the Head of the Connecticut River.[34]

7th
In the Evening of the *6th* we left this bay and got into West bay behind Crown point, about 2 O'Clock in the Morning. Soon after day light Capt. Monro's detachmen left us and crossing the Bay hid his boats in the same place Sr. John Johnson had done the preceeding Spring, and which for distingtion Sake I shall call Sr. Johns Landing—after which he sett off on foot for the place of his destination then totaly unknown to us.[35]

Capt. Monro having left us, the remainder of the day was employed in Making up our packs and preparing everything for our March, taking twelve day provisions with us, and in the Evening every thing being ready we proceeded towards Teconderoga, Our Boats all in a line each boat following his leader. In this Situation my boat got upon one of the Piers of the Bridge at teconderoga which had been burnt down to the Water Edge when our people left that place, and whilst I was fast upon it, the boats which were before me got out of Sight.[36] I endeavoured to overtake them as much as lay in my power, Supposing they had been before me, but after having Rowed for a Considerable time to no purpose, and not knowing where the Major meant to Sleep, who was with the headmost boats, I stoped and told the Officer Commanding my Sittuation that I was totaly lost as I had never been above Crown point before.

The Commanding Officer then present Capt. [Hugh?] Fraser of the 84 having enquired of a man formerly an inhabitant here, where was the best place to lay by conceald next day, was told there was but one place where it could be done, which was in the Creek leading into Lake George, to which place we all returned.[37] On endeavouring to enter the Creek some of our head-

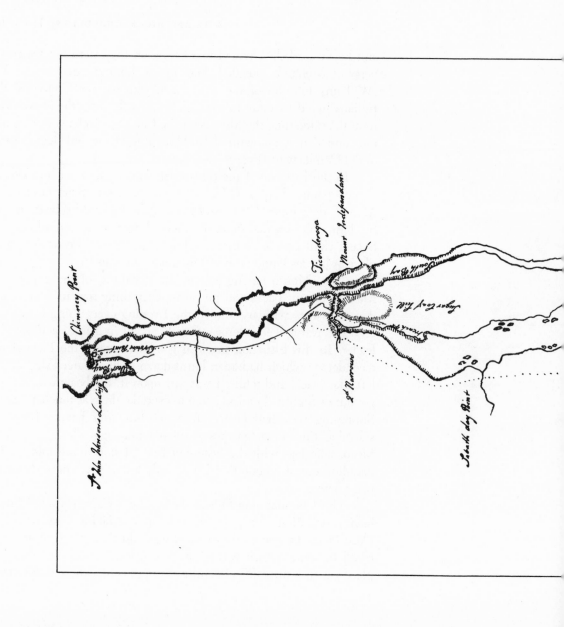

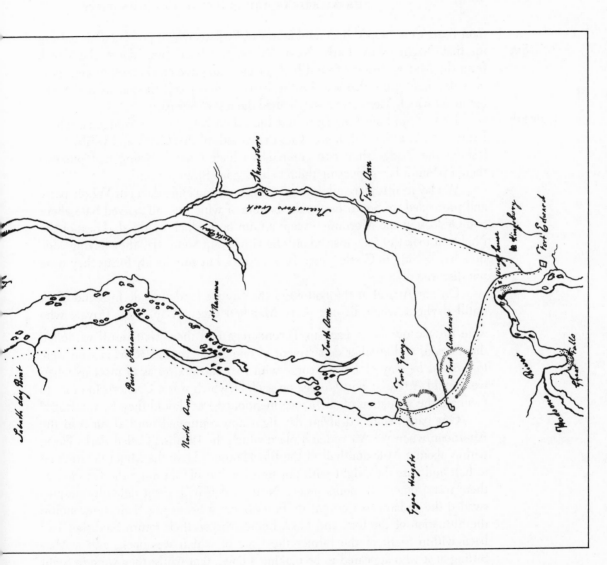

Map V. Lake George, Ticonderoga, and Crown Point. Copy by Michele Wynn from a manuscript map probably originally drawn by John Enys. *Courtesy of the present members of the Enys family*

8th

most boats were Stoped by a double row of Picketts which prevented us getting up that Night. Very Early Next Morning a boat came down the Creek from the Major, who we found had got into the same creek, and it being now near day light we could see the the Picketts that [had] Stoped us the Night before by which Means we easly joined the rest of our party.

Octr 8th

I now found out how I was lost the Night before as the Bridge on which I run was but a Short distance from the Mouth of this Creek and whilst I was fast on the Bridge they had entered it which I not knowing had pursued them up South bay supposing them to have gone Strait forward.

We lay in this place all day and in the evening embarked our Whole party and proceeded up South bay at the bottom of which we all arrived Safe about two OClock in the Morning, except a Gun boat which by the darkness of the Night mistook the way, instead of following us up South Bay they having gone up a bay leading to Castle Town [Castleton?], but very luckly for us they were not discovered.

On our Arrival at the bottom of the bay we landed made fires and Slept untill daylight when all our party Marched except Cap. Sub. Private who were to take our boats back to Teconderoga and there wait untill we join'd them again, and another detachment of one Subatern and 30 Men who were to proceed by way of Lake George with two bateaux, so as to meet us when we Should Arrive at Fort George on each of which was a Coehorn in order to facilliate the reduction of the above mentioned fort should they be wanting.[38]

Our party Marched about day light and continued until about 3 in the Afternoon when we Arrived at a place which the Roialists Called Parks Farm, within about a Mile and half of the Blockhouse.[39] Here the Major determined to halt and pass the Night with out fires for fear of Alarming the Country as there were some Setlements preety Near, which with great difficulty he pursswaded the Indians to Consent to. From hence a Scout was Sent to reconoitre the Sittuation of the fort, and block house who on their return Said they had been within Sight of the former the Gate of which was open, and a Man Sitting at it who appeared to be making a bowl, that whilst they were in Sight

10. A view of Ticonderoga from a point on the north shore of Lake Champlain, 1777. Watercolor by J. Hunter. The boats are bateaux. *Courtesy of the Public Archives of Canada*

of the fort they heard someone call for the Sergt. of the Guard on which they returned and passing by the block house found no one in it. About two Next Morning Lt. Forquhor of our Regt Marched with 30 Soldiers and as many Roialsts to way lay the road leading to Fort Edward, and between four and five our whole party got in Motion.

Octor 10

It is impossible to conceive what a disagreable March we had from this until day light, our way laying through Swamps and broken grownd with an emmence Number of fallen Trees, over which [we] were continualy falling as it was so very dark it was with the utmost difficulty we could see the Man before us. This kind of Marching is as uncertain as it is Slow and disagreeable. For Instance our Front came up with the Rear of Lt. Forquhors party who had Marched two hours before us owing to their having Mistaken the Road by the darkness of the Night. The Same reason may be Aledged for our party being divided in three for a short time this Morn. The Indians had Marched before our line and thought we were diretly after them though in fact we were at some distance behind them and at a halt we made a little before daylight one half of our party got up and Marched without the knowledge of the Rear, thus was our Small party divided into three Sepperate body's. Just after daylight we came up with the Indians just after we had been joind by our rear party (before mentioned to have been left behind,) thus being one more united. After a very Short March we reached the Block house which we found abandoned. It was a large well built block house well sittuated in a Strong Situation, appeared to be Intended for the protection of a large Saw Mill at which there was a very great Quantity of Timber ready for Sawing. We passed

11. A view of a sawmill and block house on Fort Ann Creek, the property of Gen. Skeene, "which on Gen. Burgoyne's Army advancing, was set fire to by the Americans." From Thomas Anburey, *Travels through the Interior Parts of America,* 2 vols. (London, 1789), I, facing p. 350. *Courtesy of the Public Archives of Canada*

this place without halting leaving a Sergts. party to destroy it and after we had proceeded about a Mile our front came in Sight of fort Ann.[40]

Imediately on our Arrival a Flag of Truce was sent to Summons the place, & after some Conversation, the Commanding Officer agreed to Surrender provided the British Troops should take possession of it before any Savages were permited to approach it. This proposal being agreed too we took possession of it when we found it to be no more than a Wooden house surrownded with large Pickets, through which were cut loop holes to fire through, but so Ill was this done, those on the out Side had an Equal Chance with the Garrison as the holes were low enough to be fired into from the outside. This place was altogeather as Ill provided as contrived, not having more than 3 or 4 day provision in the place, nor more than four Rounds of Amunition Pr Man upon an Average. Add to this that their Gate had Niether lock nor hindges, and so loosly was it fastened with a Bar I am told that some of the Indians trying to get into the fort pushed it down. The Garrison consisted of one Capt. two Lieuts. and 72 Privates all Millitia except the Captn. who I beleive was one of their Regulars as they call them.[41] From him we learnt our party was discovered just before we landed in South bay, by some hunters who had given him Notice of it the Night before tho he did not Suppose our party to be so large as it realy was. As soon as we had taken possession of the place Lt. Forqhars party joind us who had taken one Prisoner (who was a Capt. of Millitia) and fired at another who attempted to get off who was afterwards Said to be killed, but I beleive that is by no means certain. After having destroy'd all that was Near this place we proceeded on the road leading to fort Edward (a good Cart Road) destroying all that we found, except two houses which beloned to some Friends to Government, who begged they might be left. On the Road some of our Scouts took a prisoner Named Sherwood, Father to the Officer who Commanded Fort Ann. In the Afternoon we came to [a] place were there was two roads the one leading to fort Edward distance about three Miles the other to fort George distance about 13 Miles. Our party took the latter, and Slept that Night at a place Named Wings house about 7 Miles from fort George just by some

falls [Glens Falls?] on the Hudsons River which I am told were very beautyfull, which I did not know any thing of untill we had left the place.[42]

During the Night the Major Sent some partys of Roialists to destroy the
Country about Ford Edward, who on their return told us they had been
fourteen Miles below fort Edward on the Opposite shore and destroyd all they
could find the Inhabitants having left their houses on the first Alarm. Early
in the Morning on the *eleventh* we Marched towards fort George, And before
we had got within sight of the fort, Some of the Indians saw a Man who they
pursued without Success.[43] A Short time after our advanced party reported
that they Saw about fifty men come out of the fort, all the Indians Imediately
left their Packs and went in pursuit of them, but not being able to find them
were returning to the rear when some of our flanking party again discovered
them, and the Savages went a second time after them, who were now Supported by a party of royalists and fifty Men of the 34th Regt under the Command of Capt. [David] Forbes, & Lt. Roach [James Roche]. By this party they
were surrounded and defeated, whilst our line halted at a short distance from
them on the Road. After having Stayed in this position some short time we
proceeded and by the time we were Clear of the Wood all the fireing was over
and the Indians and Roialists were bringing in the Wounded & prisoners.
When we had got on the Clear land Called Gages Heights[44] we for the first
time got Sight of the fort. On their Seeing us very thick on the Hill they fired
three Shot from a Six pounder which was in the fort at us, without any effect.
Near this place was a Small hollow sufficiently large to cover our party from
the fire of the fort, in which we formed, and from thence the Major sent a flag
of truce to Summons the fort.

During the time the flag was at the fort we Saw some men leading in a
Wounded person whom we at first Supposed to be an Indian from his head
looking so Red and shining but on his Nearer approach found it to be one of
the Rebels who had been Scalped. This man had not been long brought into
us before Some of our Men reccolected him to be a deserter from our Regt
who had deserted from My party when Serving with the Artillery in 76. This

he at first denied but being questiond by a Man who had formerly been his Comrade he accknoledged it. Surely Never poor fellow Suffered more than this one did. He had one of his Arms broke by a Shot, a Violent contusion on his head and three very deep wounds with a tomahawk at the Back of his head Notwithstand all Which he lived for some days afterwards, and died on board of one of the Ships on lake Champlaine, after our party had returnd to them.

From some of the prisoners we soon found there were but Very few men in the fort therefore expected they would accept of the terms offered which they did in a very short time. By these terms they were allowed to send off one Waggon with some Baggage and one Married Officer was admitted to return on his parole.

Everything being Settled we Marched toward the place which the 34th Regt immediately took possession of, whilst the remainder of our party formed our Camp on the outside of the fort, it not being large enough to admit us all. As soon as every thing was setled according to the Articles the Garrison Marched out, and the Savages were admited to plunder the place a thing they always look upon as their undoubted Right. Whilst they were busy plundering, the Waggon was sent of according to agreement, and the Major sent to raise all the Boats belonging to the place which were Sunk in several different places, which was not finished untill near dark.[45] After the Indians had quit the fort all the prisoners were put into it in Charge of 34th and 53 Regts all the rest remaining as before mentioned on the outside.

This fort is Situated not more than two hundred yards from the place that fort William Henry formerly Stood (of which there is very little remains) and is part of a fort Intended to have been built during the latter part of last War.[46] But after having finished one Bastion it was found to be so commanded that they gave up the project which Bastion being closed up at the Gorge forms the present fort. The Walls are made of Stone with a thick earth parrapet and good Bomb proofs for the Garrison in case of a seige, togeather with a very good Well. They had also one six pounder Mounted on a feild Carriage and one not Mounted. From this account it may be Supposed the place might make a good defence, but the Walls from being burnt so often were in a very bad way, thro their Negligence they had Suffered the Well to be filled with all manner of filth so that it was impossible to drink the Water, and the Commanding Officer had so very much Weakened his Garrison by the party he had sent out in the Morning not one of which returned into the fort. They were also very ill found for any deffence as they had but 16 or 18 Rownds for their Gun and a few Rounds for their Small Arms, with not more than 3 or 4 day's provisions in the place. Such was the State of the place when it Surrendered.

Having Spent that Night very peaceably on the *12th* in the Morning all the boats being baled as dry as possible the best were Chose out for the Wounded which were immediately sent of under the care of our Surgeon, and the few boats which Remaind were given to some famillies who had followed us. By this time Lt. [Robert] McFarlane had arrived with his party and the Cohornes intended for the reduction of the place. On board of his boats were put the two good Six pounders, a bad one which we also found near the fort being broken, and all partys ready to Sett off, they Set fire to the fort which was soon consumed. The Commanding Officer of fort George Crossed the Lake in the Boats, all the rest set of by land by a path Called Rogers's Road.[47] It was near 12 OClock when we Marched and after having gone 7 or 8 Miles

13th we encamped for that Night. Early Next Morning we Marched meeting with nothing extraordinary during the course of that day at Night encamped at the head of the North Arm. Early on the *14th* we proceeded and about two in the afternoon came to the worst peice of Road I ever Saw, and which it is almost impossible to conceive. It is a very deep Gully Situated between two Mountains and is composed of an immence Number of large Rocks which have fallen from time to time from their Sides which are very Steep. You could hardly call it walking thro it as it was in general Sliding from Rock to Rock on our A–S. However this part is not very long as it is not More than ¾ or a Mile at Most long Notwithstanding which it took us so long in passing our party that we could not go much further that Night When we encamped within about 12 Miles of Ticonderoga. Next Morning [*15th*] we Marched very early and passing over a Mountain known commonly by the Name of Roger's Rock, from the top of which we had a most beautyfull prospect of Lake George from the Narrows on the one Side to the Landing at the End of the Lake on the other which is the place where the Late Lord Howe was killed.[48] After leaving this Mountain we Soon arrived at the landing where we found Lt. [Thomas] Booker of the 53 Regt with a party of Men which had been Sent by Capt. Fraser to Secure that pass. As soon as all our party had Crossed his party formed in our Rear, and we proceeded to Ticonderoga where we found all our Boats and Shiping, togeather with Capt. Frasers detachment very Safe.

16   The day was pretty far Advanced when we arrived at Ticonderoga, so that we did not proceed that Night, but next Morning we again embarked and went down to Crown point, where we lay all the *16th* and *17th*. On the *18th* the Savages finding they were not likely to get any more plunder resolved to Quit us, which they Accordingly did with some roialists who had leave to return. In the evening we all embarked and fell down the lake to Mill Bay where we lay untill the *23d,* before we had any Accounts from Capt Monro (who as I had already Mentioned left us on the 7 Inst). This evening a man Arrived from him Acquainting the Major that He would be at his Boats the Next day a place known by the Name of Sr. Johns Landing being the place where Sir John Johnson Landed and hid his Boats when he went to the Mohawk River last Spring.[49] On the *24th* we Moved to the abovementioned place to Meet him and as we Arrived long before him our men were employed in Making a sort of Abbatis Rownd the place our Boats lay in order to cover his retreat should he have been pursued by a Superior force. This did not however happen to be the case. He Arrived about one OClock without the loss of a Man or being harrased at all on his retreat, after having burnt the Greatest part of a town Called Balls town [Ballston Spa] and taken prisoners among Whom was one Lt. Coll. and two Capts. of Millitia.[50] As many of his party

were Much fatigued and some in Want of provisions we could not leave this place that Night but on the 25*th* we again return'd to Mill Bay.

On the 26 we all got under way to return to Canada but to our great disapointment had not gone more than two Leagues before we Met an express from the Commander in Chief Ordering us to keep on the Lake as long as possible, which Order however disagreeable to us all we were obliged to Comply with, for which purpose we again return'd to our old Station in Mill bay. As Soon as we had Arrived in our Camp one Capt. [Justus] Sherwood of the Roialists, was sent with a flag of truce to the State of Vert Mont [Vermont].[51] He was Accompany'd by Capt. [John] Chipman, the late Commander of Fort George who had received the Generals leave to return on his Parole. This evening some of the Officers on board of the Maria thought they saw two boats full of men Cross the Lake from the Scotsmans Bonmet [Scotch Bonnet] to Split Rock bay. A party of 100 Men under the Command of Capt. [Archibald] Campbell of our Regt were sent after them, and, the remainder of our party Moved our position from the Main land, to a Small Island which was on the Bay for the More ready embarkation, in case a large body had been passed in these and other boats in order to Surprize us. About two OClock Capt. Campbell returned after having made all possible Search to no purpose. I am apt to think they were no more than two large trees floting on the Water which I saw when we were under way in the Morning, which I then took for boats untill I was undeceived by an Officer who had a Spy Glass.

In the Morning we Again resumed our old Camp where we lay until the 29*th* when we again got under Way and rowed to a point Named three Mile point, because it is that Number of Miles from Teconderoga where we lay that Night. Next Morning we Moved to Mount Independant [Independence] where we stay'd some time and dined.[52] About 4 OClock in the evening we put off again and rowed about 7 or 8 Miles up South bay when it being dark we put about and returned to Crown point. When we left Mount Independant we had Set fire to a Quantity of brushwood and old dry Abbatis which was burn-

30*th*

ing at Night when we returned, which in the Dark had very much the appearance of a Great Illumination. The Northern lights were also remarkably Strong towards Morning. On the *31st* in the Morning two Roialists returned from a Scout towards Ticonderoga, and said they imagined the Rebels were coming after us as they had heard a drum at the above place.

As our present post was a bad one we Changed it to a point in a more secure Sittuation in case of an Atack. This drum at last proved to be no More than a Flag of truce from the Rebels, but we Still continued on the point. When we lay down to sleep at Night every thing appear'd perfectly Quiet and Calm which induced many of us to Sleep in our boats, but about the Midle of the Night there came on a Most Violent Storm, which soon drove us from our boats as the waves broke into them, and it was not without some dificulty we secured our boats from being hurt by the Surf which ran very high. All day on the *first* [Novr] we had very bad weather and remain in the same place. On the *Second* we Moved once more into Mill Bay, where we remain all togeather untill the fourth when the Commodore left us with Most of the Ships, leaving the Lee Sloop to lie of Crown point for the flag of truce and a long boat with us, on board of which was (an Naval Officer) and a Carpenter with some Stores to repair any damages that Might happen to our boats.[53] On the Arrived [Arrival?] another flag of truce from the Rebels commanded by a Major rosygrant [James Rosekrans] from Saratoga under a pretence of Settling a Mode of conveyance for some roialists famillies who where at that place to their husbands who were in Canada.[54]

For this purpose four boats were sent Man'd with a few of Sr. John Johnsons Corps and some Roialists as far as Skeensboro [Skenesborough][55] in order to receive them. On the *12th* we began our retreat for Canada and that Night got to River Bouquet but on attempting to enter it found it was froze so hard it was not possible which obliged us to lie at the Mouth of it. During the Night a Man came into Camp express from Genl. [Henry] Clinton at New York and was forwarded Imediately in a Cutter which we happened to have with us. On the *13th* before Day light we left this place and Rowed untill about ten OClock at which time we where all off Scuylers [Schuyler] Island where a Breeze or rather a Gall of Wind getting up in our favour we Crossed Cumberland Bay tho not without danger to some of our Rear Boats. We Made an excellent Run this day and could have Reached Isle aux Noix but as we were a good deal Scatered by the Gale of Wind in the Morning the Major chose to Stop at Ash Island,[56] about 5 miles from Isle aux Noix—where all our boats join'd us that Night except a boat or two of Roialists, which had been driven by the wind into the bottom of Cumberland bay, and Kept on the Island of Valcore. On the *14th* we got under way again and soon reached Isle aux Noix, at which place we left some of our party who belonged to that Garrison, and all the 34th detachment and the Rest of us proceeded to St. Johns where we found the remainder of our Regt.

Return of Prisoners taken at fort Ann *Octr 10th 1780*

Capt.	Lt.	Private
1	2	72

Return of the Killed Wounded and Prisoners of fort George *Octr 11th 1780*

	Capt.	Lt.	En.	Privats
Killed	1	2	1	23
Wound		1		1
Taken	1		1	42
On parole			1	
	2	3	3	66

Return of Killed Wounded &c. &c. under Major Carleton

34th Regt $\begin{cases} \text{one Private Killed} \\ \text{One Sergt. Wounded} \end{cases}$

Roialists one Wounded

Indians $\begin{cases} \text{one Killed} \\ \text{two Wounded} \end{cases}$

deserted $\begin{cases} \text{84th Regt one} \\ \text{Roialists one} \end{cases}$

Destroyd by the burning party

Saw Mills	6
Grist ditto	1
Large dwelling Houses	38
Barns	33
Tons of Hay	1500

togeather with a very great quantity of Wheat Indian Corn and Cattle of all Kinds

At which Place we remaind untill about the *20th* when we Marched into winter Quarters on the river Sorell [Sorel], when we were divided in the following manner at Belloile [Beloeil] two Companies, at St. Charles two Companys with the Music &c. attendant on Head Quarters, at St. Dennis [Denis] two Companies, and at St. Antoine the same Number. During this winter a Plan was formed of embodying a Light Company of which Dickson, Forquhar, and myself were to have been the Officers, but it was found imposible as we had at that time one Light Company atho they were Prisoners, and consequently laid asside for the time.

About the *latter part of Augt or begining of Sept 81* we got an account that our flank Compys were exchanged and the few remaining men, being draughted into the New York Regts, i[n] consequence of which we were ordered by the C M C [Commander-in-Chief?] to form New Companies which was accordingly done on the *first of October,* when I had the honor of being appointed to the Grenadier Company.[57] Soon after this (*about the 15th*) Genl. Heldemond [Frederick Haldimand] came up to St. Johns and a party was sent over the Lake under the command of Coll. St. Ledger [Barry St. Leger] consisting of the 29th, 31st and 44th Light Companies and a large detachment from the 29th and 34th Battalions with some Royalists who went and lay on Mount Independant Teconderoga and thereabouts untill the *15th of Novr* when they returnd bringing with them an account of Lord Cornwallis's defeat at York town which was communicated to them by a flag of truce sent by Lord Sterling [William Alexander]—the bearer of which said they would have had the News three day's sooner, But that on the receipt of the News Lord Sterling had got so Intolerably drunk that he was not capable of dispatching the flag but this News however Affirmed by these people was not believed in Canada till confirmed the following Spring. This party was no sooner returnd than our Regt Marched into Winter Quarters at the following Places, Grenadiers and Colls. Companies with Musick &c. &c. at Lachenaye [Lachine], Light Infantry & two Battalion companies at St. Henry de la Mascouch [Saint-Henry-de-Mascouche] wither I was sent to command, four companies at Terrebonne and one at Mascouch [Mascouche] le Page.[58]

In this state we remaind untill I got leave to return to England on the *28th* of *June* 82 which I had no sooner got, and learned that a Ship was to Sail in the begining of July than I Settled all my Affairs and proceeded immediately for Quebec at which place I arrived on the *4th of July* at which place I found a Young Officer Named Jaques [Ensign William Jacques] going up to Join the Regt with whom I staid, both of us receiving every Mark of civillity from the 31st Regt who were Quarterd in town.

On the *15th* we went to see the falls of Montmorency, with which we were both very much pleased. Near the top of the fall is a howse latly Built by General Holdemond[59] which not knowing it to be inhabited on our Arrival we passed and calling to a Soldier of the 31st Regt who I saw in the feild adjoining to the House desired he would shew us the fall, on which he conducted us to the top of it from whence we had but an imperfect View of it, on which we were returning to get some refreshment with an intention of coming again, when to our great Surprize we met Capt. Brehem [Diedrick Brehm][60] of the 60th Regt one of the Generals Aid du Camps who recd us with great civility telling us we had Seen Nothing as yet and if we would go with him to the House and refresh ourselves he would afterwards shew us the fall in all its different Veiws. This proposal we very readyly embraced and on our Arrival at the House began to unpack what Victuals and Wine we had brought in our Calash, which he observing said he was sorry he had it not in his power to offer us any dinner, as he had already dined, but that he had plenty of good wine which being cool out an Ice House, must be far better than ours which had been brought from town in the Seat of the Calash. This we refused for some time but Insisting on it he Leeped into the Cellar and soon returned with a Bottle of Madera and one of Claret. After having passed about an hour with him, during which time he treated us with the utmost politeness, he said he would then accompany us to the falls, and observing that we ought not to go to these places empty handed took a Bottle of Madera hemself and bid us take each a Glass and follow him. We did so and tho on the road I frequently begged he would suffer me to carry the wine, as I observed it was troublesome

12. A view of the Falls of Montmorenci, Gen. Haldimand's country house near it, taken on the ice May 1, 1781. Watercolor and ink drawing by James Peachey. *Courtesy of the Public Archives of Canada*

to him it being exceedingly hot weather and he being none of the youngest Men in the World, but this he refused saying he was the Master an must have his own Way.

In this Manner we Salied out, and revisted the place which the Soldier had before shewn us and passing it we proceeded about a Mile up the river to a place they call the Giant Steps, from its appearance which is beautyfully romantick. The Rocks on each side of the River are of Lime Stone though they have a very different appearance. On the one side the precipice being very high bears an exact resemblance to an old Castle Wall from the regularity of the Veins in which the Stones run, and on the Other side of the river which in some parts is not more than 15 or 16 yards wide, the rocks are so worn by the Water in the Spring that it forms a kind of Natural flight of Steps for the Space of Near half a Mile by which in some places you may Asend Nearly to the top of the rock, & from which it takes its Name. After having drank a Glass of wine to the King of the Giants we returned down the river and on our way saw what is known by the Name of the fishing place which is a Round deep Bason of Water in which I think it is very likly the fish lodge at sometimes of the Year, the Rocks round which are equaly Beautiful with those I have already spoke of.

Having seen this we once more returned to the top of the falls when we decended somthing lower than before from whence we had a much better View than the former being a few Yards lower than the shot of the fall we had a perfect View of the sheet of Water which roled over the Rock, which realy may be said to be Beautifully dreadfull. Here we had recourse again to our Wine after which we went round to the Bottom of the falls by a Road which the General has made for the purpose. By this we got as Near to the falls as the spray would permit us I suppose within about 30 yards which was Near enough to be Wetted by it and to have a very Sensible impression on our Breath from hence we had a full View of it. At the top I suppose the River to be from 40 to 50 feet wide which falls over a Rock, which according to Major

13. A view of the Montmorenci River a half-mile above the fall. Watercolor by James Peachey, 1783. *Courtesy of the Public Archives of Canada*

[Robert? Richard] Holland who lately Measured it is 240 feet high tho from its appearance I confess however astonishing does not appear to me to be so high.[61] About forty feet from the Grownd is a large Rock which Projects and on which the whole Body of Water falls and causing a break in the fall renders it more beautifull. Here Capt. Brehem called my Attention to a circumstance which had escaped my Eye, which is the different Strata's of Stone of which the Clift is composed, (Viz.) first from the top of the Clift down to the fall is of a lime stone through which the Water has Worked its way, down to a Bed of very hard Granite into which it has also worked some feet, and at the foot and all round the fall the most prevalent kind of stone is a Soft rotten kind of Slate.

The day being extreemly hot and this place from Various Causes being very cool we retired out the reach of the Spray and sat down to take a quiet View of the fall and to finish our Bottle of Wine. That done we again Asended the Hill to the house, which consists of one pretty good Room in the Center and two Smaller ones detached from it as Wings. It is not yet finished but as near as I can form an Idea of it, it will be a prety Neat place when it is finished. There is but one View of the fall from the house which is from the left hand Wing and that but a very imperfect one which I think a great pity. It was now getting so late that we were obliged to take leave of our hospitable entertainer to whom I was more obliged as I had heard a very different account of him, and before we reached Quebec it was so dark it was with the greatest dificulty the Man would take us over the ferry at St. Charles. However he was at last prevald on and we Arrived save at Quebec where I remained without any thing material hapenin untill the *18th* when we embarked on board of the Quebec, Capt. [William] Boyd, and at 4 OClock the same Evening left the Bason after being in some danger of getting on shore before the ship got Steerage Way.[62]

The wind was favourable all there was of it which was not much and we had in our Company an Armed Ship called the Harpooner[63] bound to Newfoundland and the West Indies, and a small Sloop bound to the Bay of Bradore.

In the Course of the Night the Wind became fresher which enabled us to Pass the Traverse at the North end of the Isle of Orleans about Day break, and

19th   about seven in the Morng spoke a Brig from the West Indies who gave us the first information of Rodney's Victory on the 12th of April.[64] About Noon we put our Pilot on shore on Green Island [Verte Isle] and the Wind being fair we passed the Isle of Bic about Nine at Night where we were join'd by another ship Named the Castle Cravie bound for Liverpool who Not being Armed had Waited for our Company and protection thro the River an Gulph. At Daylight

20th   Next Morng we had left them all out of Sight. The Wind being Still favourable we went under an easy Sail untill they over took us which they did in the course of the Morng. In the afternoon we discoverd a strange sail to the Southward of us, on which our Ship and the Harpooner Bore down on her whilst the Castle Cravie & Sloop who were at some distance kept their course. When we came up with her we found she was from the Madera's and had seen Nothing in the Gulph but a Small Yankee Prize belonging to some of our

21st   men of War. The Next Morng we again lost sight of the Castle Cravie, the Wind all day being light and Baffling, however we had made so good a Run the day before and in the Night that we were opposite the Bay of Seven Isles [Sept îles] by the Middle of the day during the Remainder of which Nothing material happened. In the course of the Night the Wind changed Round to

22d   the East and became right a head, Notwithstanding which about Noon we Made the West end of the Isle of Anticoste tho at a Great distance and in the Evening discovered a ship as far as we could distinguish to Windward which we supposed to be our lost partner who had taken a More Southern Course by which means she had found more favourable brezzees as she appeard to be going large whilst we were close hold upon the Wind, which again Changed

23d   in the Night so that we had a fine fair Wind all the Next day.

In the Evening we discoverd a ship to leeward near the east End of the Island of Anticoste and Bore down to see what she was, untill we got Near enough to find it was our lost partner on which we resumed our course, but she not Sailing so fast as we did was in the course of the Night left so far behind

July 24th that we could not perceive anything of her a day even from the Masthead. We had still a fine fair wind which gave us a good Run in the course of the day. About Six in the evening we could perceive a Sail to Windward on our Starbourd Bow which Bore down on us. In about two hours we could distinguish her to be a Square Rigged Vessle and in a short time after to be a Brig whch from the Cut of her Sails had the Appearance of a privateer. About this time She hauld her Wind and being so much to Windward of us it was impossible for us ever to get near her so we was obliged to be Sattisfied with looking at her as long as the day light permited us to See her. As we were now in the place where we expected to find privateers and our little Sloop a long way astern of us Capt. Boyd thought proper to shorten Sail to let her come up with us for fear of her being taken in the course of the Night. About Eleven at Night She came up with us, and was said to be under our stern when we tacked at one in the Morn after which we Never Saw her more tho we looked

25th for her from the Mast head next Morng.

The Wind was now blowing fresh against us with a very thick fog which came on about Six in the Morng and continued untill about five in the Evening when it began to Clear off and the Wind Shifting a Trifle at the same time enabled us to lay our Course tolerably Well. About Seven another Sail was Seen a head bearing somthing on our lee Bow at a Great distance. As we were stand in Contrary Way, we very soon Shortened our distance so far as to perceive her to be a large Sloop. When She got pretty Near us She would willingly have got away from us but it was now too late. We very soon got as we supposed within random shot of her when we fired a shot or to each according to custom to bring her too, the Harppooner standing in betwixt her and the shore and our ship keeping on the outside of her. At half past ten we got pretty near her and fired a shot that cut some of her runing rigging on which she struck. The Harpooner Boat was very soon alongside of her but the wind abating and Capt. Boyd not chusing to send his Boat far from the ship it was near half an hour before we got up to her, when she proved to be the Banter privateer (Capt. White) from Salim [Salem] Mounting ten Guns and forty men everything Quite New not having been to Sea more than Six Weeks.[65]

26th   The Numerous things which were to be settled rellative to the prize detaind us all Night and most part of Next day when at length having finished we parted the Men of the Prize between our too ships and Manned her from ours and the Harpooner, having determind that she should proceed with us to England. By this time it was far advanced in the Afternoon and being in Sight of the North part of the Iland of Newfoundland we accordingly took our

27th   departure there from. Next day finding the Sloop could not keep up with us we took her in tow. In the Middle of the Night we were all allarmed with a Monstrous Noise of which we could not conceive the Reason untill we were told the Sloop had Broke the tow Rope. This Occasion'd another delay as we were again obliged to wait for her in the Morng.

Having again made her fast and the Weather being very fine we passed our time very Agreably, and as we had now no longer any objects of either land or Ships to entertain us we were obliged to have recourse to our own Company which consisted of the following persons, besides the Captain and his Surgeon we had in the Cabbin, a Captain Bobbinson [Bobbenson?] who had been for many Years Commandant of Lake Ontario &c. &c., Mr. Charles Patterson [Paterson] a Merchant from Montreal, Mr. Le Blois [Deblois] a Merchant from Quebec whose family I suppose were originaly French but had been for a long While Settled at Boston untill driven from thence by the Rebells, a Canadian Lawyer Named Canete and a French Priest Named Du devent [Arnaud-Germain Dudevant],[66] a Merry Good natured Man who had formerly run away from his father who was a Merchant at Bourdaux [Bordeaux] and who was latly dead having left him a good fortune, Myself and a Lieut. [Maurice] Atkin of the 34th Regt who was going home on account of a Wound he got in his leg. With Such a Commical Company we could not be otherwise then Merry as we could reckon in the Cabbin all the Professions (Viz.) Army, Navy, Law, Physic, and Divinity, three different sorts of Religion, (Viz.) Church of Engd, of Scotld and Roman Catholick, Six Different Country men

(Viz.) English, Irish, Scotch, French, Bostonian and Canadian. Thus Our hours flew unperceived away eating drinking and playing at Cards for trifles or in Most for Nothing as we Never paid.

10th   Our tranquility however had like to have been disturbed on the *Ninth of August* by an alarm that our Prisoners had a mind to Rise, this however Improbable as it was every means was used to prevent by securing all the Arm Chests on the Quarter deck and the Mates with some of the most trusty of the Seamen on the Watch being always Armed.

Tranquility being thus restored and the Next day being very Calm we bent a New Suite of Sails our old ones being very bad and being now according to our Reckoning very Near land which we expected to make every day when to our great disapointment the Wind Changed and blowing hard from the East blew us off shore and kept us beating between the Lattitudes of 57 and 60 untill the *16th* in the Morng when Standing to the South East we Made Land

17th   and a Short time after could discern a Ship between it and us both being to Windward to which we Imediately Gave Chace and before Night had Gain'd very much on her. The Night was too Dark to keep Sight of her but as we Supposd her course to be westward we kept the Same and had the Satisfaction to See her Next Morng tho at a very great distance. It now blew pretty fresh against us however putting out all the Sail we could, about ten OClock as we Stood on Opposite Tacks we could discover a Dutch head on her Stern this convinced the Sailors the [she] was a Dutch Ship and being very large gave us all hopes of a good Prize. About Noon we got pretty Near her when we fired a Gun and hoisted the American Colours on which She hoisted a Swedish Ensigne still keeping her Course.[67] A little after two we got Near enough & fired a Shot at her on which She Backed her Main top Sail. We then fired another Gun to make her bear away to Leward of us which She obey'd. When Near here we sent our Boat and brought the Captain on board of us Still having the American Colours out and passing ourselves on him for Americans, myself and Atkin hiding our Uniforms, but after all our trouble and Cuning She proved to be a Ship from Liverpooll bound to Danzick

[Danzig] Loaded with Salt an a Small Quantity of Coffee and in the Course of my life I never saw so Ignorant a fellow. He could give us no sort of information nor had he any sort of refreshments to give us tho he had been but a few days from port.

Being thus disappointed we left her about three OClock and stood again toward the Island of St. Killda [St. Kilda] which having a favourable Wind we made and passed that evening. Having Made the Island we Stood to the Northward all Night the Wind blowing very hard. One of our top Sail Sheets Broke which caused great confusion on board for somtime but was soon set to Rights, and on the *18th* in the Morng some of the Men saw a Sail but we did not alter our course for her. About ½ past ten we Made a Small Island and in about a half an hour could See another which proved to be the Island of Borra [Barra] and Rona which lie about 16 Leagues West of Cape Wreath [Wrath] the Westernmost point in Scotland toward which we Stood. After having passed Borra and Rona which we also made in about two hours Nothing could be more agreable than the Sight of Cape Wreath. Desolate as it is it gave us pleasure to See even the most distant part of the Island we were Born in, and from which we had been so long absent. When leaving it we Stood along shore distance about four Leagues, untill about 5 OClock in the Evening when we Saw a Large Square Rigged Ship under the Shore Standing directly towards us, on which Capt. Boyd Cleard for Action and Stood towards it by which Means we got along side of her in about an hour, by which time every thing was Ready for Action & having previously ofered the Prisoners a Share of any Prize mony on condition of their assisting at the Guns which proposition they all agreed to provided it was not an American Ship. They Seemed equaly desirous of taking a Prize with ourselves, however precautions were taken to prevent their doing us any harm even if they should be so Inclined. You will easly conceive after all this preparation how we were disaponted to find She was a Ship from Dublin to Memell [Memel] a Small port in the Baltick. From a Pilot who was on board of her we found we was much Nearer the Orkney's than we Supposed ourselves to be, and as it was likly to Blow hard in the Night both Capts. agreed it was best to go a little further from Shore and lay too for the Night, which we did the Wind blowing very hard at West all *Augt 19th*   Night. Next Morng the Wind Still blowing fresh in our favour we again made Sail and about Eight OClock in the Morng passing the Hay [Hoy] Head we came to Anchor in the Bay of Stramness [Stromness] on Hay Island.

Here I made an agreement with Lt. Atkin who was Charged with Dispatches from Genl. Holdemand that we Should both land and make the best of our Way to London with them, and if Govemt paid his expences I was of course free but if not we were to bear our expences equaly. Having thus settled every thing Necessary we put up two or three Shirts each and proposed crossing the Pentland firth in the Evening and landing at Caithness to get Horses or what we could to convey us to fort George the first place where we expected to find Chaise's.[68] We Accordingly landed, Where to our great satisfaction we found a Small Custom House Cutter which was to Sail for Bamf [Banff] that evening and the Capt. asured us we should be at that place by Morng, by which Means as we had only to Cross a large Bay, we Should avoid all the highlands which if we went by land, would at least take us three or four days before we could arive at. This offer was too advantageous to be refused on our part, so after having refreshed ourselves as well as we could at such a Miserable place, which consisted only of a few very Ill built fishing Huts Distutute of every thing that could render Life comfortable. The only Manufacture of this place is Kniting of thread thackings [stockings] which they do extreemly well an Neat. As we had no inducements to stay in this dismal place we quit it without regret as soon as we had done Dinner, and Atkin myself and Mr. Patterson embarking on board of the Cutter we called on bord of the Quebec as we passed her and took a few more shirts as we were now sure of finding good Post Chaise's on our Landing, again put to Sea.

The wind still being fresh we Crossed the pentland firth and mad a tollerable good run during the Night but the Wind falling in the Night left *20th*   us somthing Short of the place we wished to Arrive at. However by Noon we Immagined ourselves within four or five miles of it, and Accordingly hoisted out our Small Boat (for Small it was I can asure you) and puting four Men into it embarked ourselves, the Sea being as Calm as a Mill Pond. After having Rowed three hours without apparently having got nearer the Shore we found we had been deceivd by the height of the Clift, and where [were] in a very disagreeable Situation. The tide now began to Ebb which caused a Small Motion in the Water when for the first time we began to perceive we had over loaded the Boat as every little Wave that came threw some Water into the Boat and examination found the Stern of our Boat was not More than two or three Inches out of the Water. In this Sittuation we at lenth got on shore tho I confess I think I was not without my fears during the whole time and to this time think that if the Wind had raised in the least degree we should all have perished togeather. The place we Arrived at was a Small fishing place Named Gairnstown, Where we made a dreadfull dinner on Some Salt Mackerell & Oat Cakes being the best we could Get, with some Nasty Sweet Ale and good B[r]andy and Water. After having refreshed us as well as we could finding our Sailors very much fateagued we enquired if we could get a horse to carry a Small Box or too which we had with us, but was told that was impossible but that we could get a Creell Woman who would carry as much as any Horse if we plase'd. This Method of making Slaves of their Woman surprized me at first nor could I beleive it possible untill I saw some of them carring Sea Weed on their Backs which I was told was to dress the Ground. Not liking this Method we prevaild on the Sailors with B[r]andy &c. &c. to take the Boat Round to Bamf about four or five Miles in which Atkin went but I, Mr. Patterson and Capt. Cooke of the Cutter proceeded by land where we Arrived after a pleasant walk about six in the evening when after having taken a View of the place which is a tollerable good town, and much better than I expected to See, and having made hearty Supper we retired to Bed.

    Adjoining to the town of Bamf is a Small place Called Dawn [Doune] and at a Small distance from these places stands Duff house a Noble Seat of the Earle of fifes [Fife], infinitely Superior to anything I ever expected to See *21st* in this part of the world. When we were in we were told that a very heavy firing had been heard early that Morng which we were afraid was our Ship that we had just left attacked, tho on our arrival at Edinburgh we found it was not. We were no Sooner up than we found a post Chase and four at the door which had been ordered over Night in which we proceeded and after a drive of five Miles Saw a pretty Seat [Forglen] of Lord Bamfs family sittuated in a beautyfull Valley, a little further we passed a Small place called Turreff [Turriff] and got to a Comon Inn Called Chaple Seggat [Chapel Segget] which is 15 Miles from Bamff where we got some breakfast. This place takes its name from a Chaple that Stood here said to be more than Six hundred Years old, of which there is at present but very little remains. Fifteen Miles further brought us to old Mildrum [Old Meldrum] and a short time more to New Mackar both of which are in themselves very small places, but have some very good houses in their Neighbourhood among which we took Notice of those of Genl. Gordon [Fyvie Castle], Mr. Ramsay [Barra Castle] & Mr. Dice [Dyce] to be the best, & about two OClock PM arrived at Abberdeen [Aberdeen], and having passed thro the old town which is the Seat of the University tho by no means well built we came to the New one which is much better built and Sittuated. It is on the Banks of a fine River and the Streets are very open and Airy. Having dined we proceeded thro Stonehaven to Laurence kirk [Laurence-kirk] about 30 Miles from Aberdeen where we put up for the Night. Early

22d next Morng we Set out and breakfasted at Brechin and passing thro farfar [Forfar] and Glamish [Glamis] we got to Cuppar Angus [Coupar Angus] to dinner. Near farfar is a most Noble Seat of Lord Strathmore & not far from it one of Sir Bayley [Baillie-Balruthrie House] with many others pleasantly Situated in all the different Valleys. In the afternoon passing thro Perth we arrived at Kinross. During this days Journey we found the country in General get much better than on the other side Aberdeen tho for the most part the top of the Hills are very Barren (for an account of Perth and the Road to Edinburgh togeather with an account of that place See our tour in 1783 Voll 2 page 16).[69]

23 Next day we left Kinross and passing thro Inverkeething [Inverkeithing]

got to Queens ferry where we embarked and soon reached the other side and in a short time got to Edinburgh to dinner. After dinner we left Mr. Patterson at Edinburgh at the Calledonian [Caledonian?] Hotell in princes street which I can venture to say is by far the dearest house I was ever in in my life, and passing thro Blacksheild [Blackshiels] we got to Lawder [Lauder] where we were obliged to stay for want of a Chase there being none. I wish I could add Sleep but it was too filthy for that in short they are most miserable places in a

24   country if possible worse than themselves. Next day we proceeded thro Kelso, Woolar [Wooler] and Rimside Moor during the whole of which Road I am sorry to say the Country altered but very little for the better. Near the latter place we had a Veiw of some of the Cheviot Hills, and passing the tweed [Tweed] we got on a Chain of hills very strongly Marked with old fortifications whereto had formerly been the Seat of war between the English and Scots on one of which is the Remains of an old Cross put up to the memory of one of the Percy family [Duke of Northumberland] but I could not hear when he lived.

After having Crossed these barren hills we were agreeably surprized all at once with a most extensive View of the Charming Country of Northumberland which my companion readyly acknoledged to be the finest he had ever Seen after which our difficulties being all over we got after a pleasant drive to Morpeth from whence we took the great Road to London for an account of which See our tour in 83, on which account I shall only Subjoin the Names of the places we went thro as we went too fast to make remarks.

Agut 24	Morpeth—slept
25	Newcastle
	Durham
	Darlington
	Northalerton [Northallerton]
	Borroughbridge [Boroughbridge]

26   Weatherby—slept [Wetherby]
      Ferry Bridge
      Doncaster
      Tuxford
      Newark
      Grantham
27   Whitham [Witham] Common (Chaise broke and obliged to sleep)
      Stamford
      Stilton
      Bugden
      Biggleswade
      Stevenage
      Hatfield
      Barnet
      London

Where we arriv'd about six oClock in the eveng on which Atkin went and delivered his dispatch to Mr. Towndsend [Thomas Townshend] and was Surprized to find that Major Carleton who Saild from Quebec a week after us had arrived the day before. However he alowed our expences which came to Near 50 pounds after which we each took his own Rout Atkin to Ireland and I to Richmond Green where I found my Uncle Aunt & Brother all well.

27

April

6

At which place we staid untill the latter end of March when my Brother and I went to Salisbury on a Visit to Mrs. Thorp[70] and after a week passed very agreeably we went to Bath where I found my Sister with whom we Staid untill the *21st of May* at which time we were called to Richmond by my Uncle being extreemly Ill of which he died on the *29th* inst. Having in the course of the winter planed an expedition to the North of England and Scotland after we had staid with my aunt untill Shee Saw Company we Set out on the *8th of July*.

RETURN TO CANADA—GARRISON DUTY

Oct 29, 1783   S OME TIME AFTER my Brother left me and went to Bath, but as I had been included in the late Reduction of the Additional Companys of the Army I staid behind in order to negotiate on exchange from half to full pay, and having at lenth put every thing as I thought in a fair way I went down to

Jany 20   Worcester with Major [David] St. Clair at which place I purposed staying for some time but was prevented by Reciving the disagreeable news of my sisters Death on which I sett off directly for Bath, where we Both remained with Miss Penrose until the *22d May,* when we went to make a Visit to Mr. [Henry] Eyre of Landford near Salisbury who had Lately married my Sister in Law.[1] We passed a fortnight in this place which I realy think to be the most agreeable time I ever spent in my life. Never did I to my knowledge see more genuine & true Country hospitality than in this family & the Reved. Mr. Eyre without losing any of that quality had added to it a polite and agreeable behaviour not often met with. During my stay at Bath I had tho with some deficulty procured an exchange into the Regt. I was formerly in which tho it gave me great

69

Map VI. A new and correct map of North America showing the places of the principal engagements during the Revolutionary War and the boundaries as settled by treaty in 1783. Engraved by John Lodge and published February 28, 1783, by J. Bew, London, in *Political Magazine* 43. *Courtesy of the Public Archives of Canada*

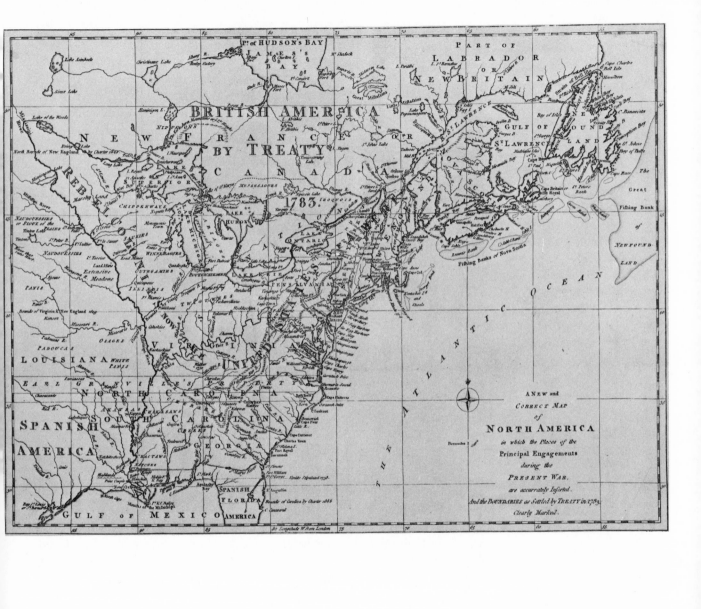

A NEW and
CORRECT MAP
of
NORTH AMERICA
in which the Places of the
Principal Engagements
during the
PRESENT WAR,
are accurately Inserted.
And the BOUNDARIES as Settled by TREATY in 1783,
Clearly Marked.

pleasure was still the means of defeating all our plan of Opperations for this summer.

On leaving Landford we again went to Richmond from whence we intended to go to Harrowgate [Harrogate] then to Buxton & Matlock and from thence on a tour through Wales in the Autum. On my Arrival in London General [William] Tryon who had now got our Regt. on General [William] Evelyns Death informed me that he expected a number of men would turn out Vollunteers for the 29th Regt. from the 70th, one which he had formerly Commanded and was then expected would be reduced, in consequence of which he wished I would keep myself in Readyness to go to Exeter in order to receive them on the shortest Notice. Having kept me in the State of suspence until the Middle of July he ended my expectation by a possetive order to join the Regt. in America. And having in Vain Attempted by every means I could to avoid a Voyage to which I had no Inclination was at lenth obliged to comply and having made all the preparations necessary and procured a passage on board the Speedy Packet then under Orders for Quebec I left Richmond in Company with my Brother the *2d. of Augt.* and took the Road to Bath where we passed a great part of a day in company with Miss Penrose and taken leave of her and some other friends at that place we proceeded towards Truro. On our Road at Crackington Well we saw the Duke of Northumberland who was just Ready to set off from the door of the Inn when one of his servants displeased him. He discharged him directly and ordering the other servants to tie the Saddle behind his Chaise set of with one servant only.

6   We arrived at Truro on the *5th* and next day went to Falmouth in hopes of seeing Capt. D'Auverne [Philip D'Auvergne][2] who commanded the Packet. In this we were however disapointed by his being out of town had however the pleasure to hear from Mr. Bell Agent of Packets and every one we spoke to that the Captain was a very agreeable young man and having learnd the Price was forty Guineas to be paid before embarkation we again return'd to Truro. In this place we staid not daring to go to the country to see any of my friends lest the express which brought down the despatches should pass without my

knowledge. I however intended to pay a Visit to Lady Vyvyan[3] who now lived at Enys in order to see my Native place but was disapointed by Mr. Houghton [William Haughton] of the 53d Regt. passing thro Truro in the Night of the *Ninth,* who wrote me by the Chaise which took him down that the Packet would sail in a Few hours. Being now obliged to set off directly I found great difficulty in Procuring a Chaise as they were all engaged to go to Bodmin on some trial about the Election. At lenth one Gentleman was so good as to let me have his Chaise and I was obliged to pass by Enys without calling.

On our Arrival at Falmouth we found Lt. Houghton & [Thomas] Hughes at that place but the wind coming foul just after I got there we did not sail until next day.[4] This evening we passed with our present party & Capt. Tidd of the Invalids. A little before supper being rather in Liquor I went to the other Inn when Mr. Brunstone who kept it accused me of going to the other house in preference to his who was a old Inhabitant of the town and a Native of the County whilst Palmer who kept the one we were at was as he calld him an east country man. This circumstance which I should not have cared for if I had been sober I thought a fault in my present state and endeavoured to pacifie him by calling for a great quanty of Punch and asking every one to drink that I could see. Among the Rest I got aquainted with Lt. Rose of the Invalids who I took back to our party to supper very much to the Disturbance of any head next day.

10   Early in the Morng Capt. D'Auverne came and told us the Wind was fair and he was going off. We got up instantly but it was Eleven OClock before we got into the Boat, when we all embarked togeather leaving my Brother at Falmouth.[5] As there were four Packets got under way at the same time and the wind being fair we had a pleasant sail for some hours, but before we had lost sight of Pendennis Castle[6] we found the wind came against us which obliged us to go over towards the french coast, but not so near as to see it. A calm succeded and we lay near 48 hours with very little motion, as it was supposed not far from Ushent [Ushant], from whence we got a favorable brezz that took us out of the Channel nor was the wind materialy against us until

the *24th* in the eveng when just at the Change of the moon it came directly against us. This was an unfavorable appearance and seemed to threaten what had been foretold at Falmouth that we should not make Quebec. Instead as of that part it was said by some that we should be driven to Hallifax [Halifax] others to New York and even some affirmed it was more likely we should go to the West Indies than to Quebec at that late season. But DAuverne never lost hopes and declared he would founder the ship but he would do all he could to get up to Quebec being induced to push by two Packets having faild in the attempt before to carry out a Mail at this advanced time [of] year the one of which landed her Mail at Hallifax. the other brought it back to falmouth tho these circumstances appear to me strange as Ships often sail from London to that Port Later than this. I am Rather lead to think that the sending Pakets to Quebec which was disagreeable to the Captains rather induced them on meeting with bad weather to give up their Voyage with more ease than they would have done had it been agreeable to their own taste, and represent the undertaking as more difficult than it realy is. This was however by no means the case of our Captain who never gave up the Idea of making his Voyage good.

The wind continued to blow hard until the *27th* in the Morng when it encreased so much as to Oblige us to lie to in the evening tho it still Blew yet the sea was not so high and we again made sail. Next day being more Moderate we were able to proceed tho the Wind being still foul we made but very little Longitudinal Distance. During the Night of the *30th* the wind became more favorable and we made a good slant of it. On Tuesday the *31st* we first got Sounding on the Edge of the great Bank in sixty four fathoms Water having been just three weeks from Falmouth. On Wednesday there was hardly any Wind and what there was against us we could make but little of it. About Eight in the Morng we saw a French Banker or Fishing Vessle and observing that she was taking fish very far we Brought to not far from her, as we had many men on board who were used to that business we had very soon two or three on board. Among the seamen was one old Fellow who had been in this kind of business a long while who directly began to cut open the fish with great

28

Sept 1st

eagerness and at lenth finding a Cuttle Fish and a few Kippling [capelin] in one of them said his fortune was made for the day, nor would he give anyone any of these Baits. He made his promise good for being provided with these Baits he Killed more fish than any one, but by these means he taught us all how to look after Bait as well as himself. The Cuttle Fish is as Ugly a looking fish as I ever saw nor am I able to describe it but as it is to be found in many parts of the English Sea it is pretty well known. Besides its strange shape it has a Large Bagg, containing a sort of black Liquor Like Ink which I am told it Emits when any large fish is in pursuit of it and by thus discolouring the water avoids the danger. The Kippling is a small Fish about six or Seven Inches long and very slender almost like an Eel but not near so long as [I] could not learn it ever exceeds the lenth abovmentiond. They are taken in great quantities on the Coasts of Newfoundland and being salted up in Barrels the Fishermen carry them off to the Banks where they throw them into the Sea by which means they draw the Cod Round them. Another good bait for Cod is the heart of that fish which is a small fleshy substance about as large as a Pidgeons Egg with a juice of very White Fat attached to it. There are many other kinds of Bait indeed almost anything will do.

This fishing is exceeding hard work, as the fish are in general at the Bottom in from 30 to 40 fathom water, so much so that a person who is not used to it is most likely to cut his hands with the line. I took a line with the Rest but was well contented by hauling in one. Finding it such disagreeable work I did not again attempt it. We lay in this place about four hours when having taken a fine Meridian observation, that day being very fine and Calm, we again made Sail, and tho we Proceeded but Slowly we passed a great many Bankers in the course of the afternoon during which time we also saw a great number of Grampuses or small Whales but was not near any of them. Having in the Morning Caught 59 fish we had fresh fish in plenty, which was by all agreed to be superior to those of the London Markets myself excepted, and I am very ready to belive that might not proceed from any fault in the fish but Rather from my not having so good an Appetite on bord ship as on Shore.

However as the day was Calm I was able to convince them that altho I could not agree they were better than those in London I still thought them exceedingly good. The Night being perfetly Calm the morng watch caught 27 more fish. About Eight o Clock we saw a vast number of Gulls and endeavourd to catch some by towing a small fish hook baited with a bit of meat after the Vessle but did not succed. Lt. Houghton shot some but could not get any on bord. About nine or ten oClock we saw a vast number of porpoises some of which came so near as to give us hopes of catching them and one of the men thought he has [had] once struck one with his harpoon which was confirmed by the Rest being seen to hunt him about a circumstance which I am told is common among these fish when anyone of them is wounded.

The wind now began to blow fresh from the Westward so that we could make no way by beating and the Captain said he would go look for a fair wind for which purpose he stood away to the Southward. Next Morning we was so fortunate as to find what we were in search of and before Night had made a considerable distance on our way.[7] In the Evening of the *4th* we saw somthing which had the appearance of Land which some of the men at first thought was the Island of St. Peter tho we was not within many Leagues of it by our Reconing. They were however soon undecevd by finding it to be only a Clowd.

Next morng a little before Breakfast there was a small Bird like a sand Lark flew on bord of us. As soon as Breakfast was over they sounded and the Lead brought up several strange Productions of Nature, one of which that stuck to a large stone was about the size of a Turkeys Egg of a fine flesh Colour had two openings like Mouths in it and was evidently Alive for some time after it was on bord until Captain D'Auverne put it in Spirits who told us he had seen these sort of things before and that the fishermen called them Whores Eggs.[8] This Day we almost all of us dined up on Chowder which tho it is a strange mixture (being composed of Fresh Fish, Salt Pork and Biscuit boild up togeather) is never the less extreemly good and the way I liked the best of any of dressing the Cod. We afterwards Repeated this dish frequently and every one seemed to continue their liking for it. In the evening the Breeze freshened and before day light we had got very near the Island of St. Peter.

6th   Early in the Morng the Wind again failed us and we lay all Day within sight of that Island distant 6 or 7 Leagues. I cannot help here remarking that tho it is a gen[er]al remark on the Banks that the weather is foggy and subject to hard Gales of Wind that we had experienced the opposite extreem the days bieng always Clear, and having had but one day that we could call even a fresh Wind, since we had been upon them. In the Evening we again got a fair Wind which soon Rose so as to drive us at the Rate of Eight, Nine and ten Knots an hour

7   for the whole of that Night and next day. This was a most agreeable Days sail as we were going extreemly fast at the same time had not much Sea to make it disagreeable and was running along within sight of the coast of Newfoundland. About 4 in the afternoon we passed the Island of St. Paul which stands at the entrance of the Gulph of St. Laurence between Cape North on the Island of Cape Breton and Cape Ray on that of Newfoundland. Had we now stood our Direct course towards the River St. Lawrence we must have fallen in with the Bird [Rocks] Islands during the Night which would be extreemly dangerous as they are extreemly Rocky and have been fatal to many Ships. Capt. D'Auverne therefore hauled his Wind and stood No[r]th towards St. Georges [St. George's] Bay until midnight when he again shaped his course to the Westward.

8   Next morning it is supposed they saw the East end of the Island of Anticosti but the wind came against us just at the time and prevented us from being certain however it is very probable as we by Beating was able to make that land about one in the afternoon, even 5 or 6 Leagues more to the West than the point we thought was seen in the Morng. Having assertained the Land they again Tacked and stood over towards Cape Rosiares [Rosiers], one of the Capes that form the Mouth of the River St. Lawrence, until about Midnight when they again altered their course and stood in towards Anticosti. This Island is Rather low land is said to be very Barren & to have no good harbours in it. I never heard that it was ever inhabited tho there was some

9   spots in shore that appeard like old abandoned Settlements. All this day was

very Clear so that we never lost sight of the Land but the wind being still against us we were obliged to keep beating in the Mouth of the River. Early on

10 the Next Day was within sight of the Island of Bona Ventura [Bonaventure] upon the South Shore not far from Gaspé Bay. About Eleven in the Morng we again stood back towards the Island and about sun set was near the same place we had be[en] on the evening of the 8th.

11th   Very Early in the Morng the Wind came fair and by Noon we had an excellent Breeze and were near abreast of Cape Rosiares. About 3 in the afternoon the mate came down in the Cabin and told us the ship was going 13 Knots. Capt. D'Auverne could not beleve this and went on deck himself to Look [at] the Logg when he made her Way to be twelve and half knots. At the same time we were so Steady that the Bottles and Glasses which were on the Table stood without the least Danger of falling. This was however the utmost she went during the passage. About six the same Evening she went but 10 Knots, and however strange to tell from that which is an immense Rate in the course of the Next half hour the wind had so much abated that she was found to go only two. A perfect Calm soon took place which was again about Midnight succeeded by a contrary wind. We were however so far up the strait that being about Midchannel we were enabled to weather the West end of

12 Anticoste in the morning and stood over towards the North shore. Altho we had been three days and four Nights off this Island it does [is?] not 34 or 35 Leagues in lenth. About 3 in the afternoon we were close in with the North shore and could see some smoke, some Indians I apprehend who were hunting in that Neighbourhood. As they are very seldom to be seen in that part I rather think they were a small party of the Labradore [Labrador] or Esqumaux [Esquimaux] which wonder about and are frequently on the Mingon [Mingan] Islands which are not far from hence.[9] I have been told that some fishermen have sometimes resided on these Islands during the fishing Season in the time of the French. The Principal fish which they catch are Seal and white porpoises from both of which they get a good deal of Oil as well as the Skins of the former.

Tho it is not so common for the English to go up the North shore as the South the French used generaly to do it for some distance, and as our Captain was of opinion the Current was not so Strong on this as the other shore he determend to try the french Rout. At sunset we could just distinguish the Bay of Seven Isles and having this under our Lea was a great point gaind as it is the only place where a ship can Ankor in the whole River until you come very near Bic & indeed you may say till you reach Bic itself as the places below it are much exposed. This however is not the case with the bay of seven Isles it being an excellent harbour when you are in but I fear the Entrance is but little known to the English. We had a small french mapp on bord that shewed the Bay to which had necessity required I beleive we might have trusted for altho it was on a small scale we found it by far more just than the Large English

13   one we had on bord. Before day light in the Morng the wind came fair but did not Remain so long. We could still however lay our course tollerably well. At ten in the Morng we had passed the Seven Isles, and before Noon could distinguish Cape Chat. So variable was the wind that about ½ past two in the afternoon it came directly against us. On our first Tack we made the west end of Egg Island and had not stood off from that shore very long before we perceived a exceeding Black Cloud to Leward.

The Weather still remaind Clear until about ten at Night when it began to Rain. Near Midnight the wind came to blow from the South East where we had before seen the Cloud. It was accompanied with hard Rain and a very thick

14   fogg. In the Morng the wind was quite fair and blew so hard that we were under Close Reefed Topsails The fogg and Rain still continuing as before so thick that tho we were within two Leagues of the south shore we could but just perceive it. As we passed along some of us thought we saw the Papps of Matone [Matane] one of the principal Landmarks but it was so indistinct that we could not be sure. The first land we saw distinctly was a very low Island about three in the afternoon and there was at first a dispute wither it was an Island or the main. I was very sure and so was almost every one that it could be no other than the Island of St. Barnaby [Ile de Saint-Barnabé] but as by our

Reckoning we were not within several Leauges of it we were nearly over ruled.

When the Fogg cleard of and gave us a not only a perfect sight of that Island but also of Bic which is not much more than a Leage distant. Capt. D'Auverne not liking to run in between the Island and Main without a Pilot, and as this is the place where they wait for Ships coming up cast Anchor of the Island it was not long befor a pilot came and having taken us over the Barr we again cast Anker after having been just five Weeks from the time we

15 Weighed at Falmouth to when we Ankerd again. Next day the wind was not fair but there being a tide in our favor we got under Wheigh but could get only 3 Leagues up the River. In this place our pilot missed a tide during the

16 Night altho he promised to proceed night and day. At Eleven next Morng we again got under wheigh and got up to Apple Island [Ile aux Pommes] where we again cast Ankor and some of our people went on shore where they found great quantitys of Cranberry but as they were mixed with a black sort of Berry which they did not know, they did not bring any on bord.

Whilst we lay here we saw a great many White Porpoises, and endeaverd all in our power to get one but could not. Tho I never Remember to have heard of this fish any where I cannot suppose it peculiar to this River. It has however a strange appearance in the water. They are in general seen in great numbers at a time like the common porpoises which they resemble in every

17 thing but Colour which is as White as Milk is. Next day was perfectly Calm until three in the afternoon, nor could we here make use of the tide which served before that hour on account of the very strong current which is here occasioned by the River Sagunay [Saguenay]. This is a very large and deep River but is still more Remarkable for the distance which it Runs into the Country which is certainly very near to the Bottom of Hudson Bay and has I beleve a communication with some Rivers which fall into that bay.[10] It is by this River by which the Traders who live at Quebec get thro furrs from the North, and tho they do not get [any]thing like the quantity of Furrs from hence that the Inhabitants of Montreal do by the grand River they are esteemed the best as coming from the more Northern Climate.

About ½ past three When we Wheighed this time the wind was by no means fair but the tide being with us had stopped the current so much that we could make somthing of Beating as the wind blew rather fresh. Our left[?] I had always Remarked had carried a great deal of Sail which was by no means wanting in this Instance, which induced the Pilot to ask him wither he meant of oversett the Ship or carry the Masts overboard. He replied Neither, Asked [asking?] him if there was any danger which could not be perceived, being answerd in the Negative he kept the same Press of Sail up as long as he could make anything of it. The wind favoring us a little we again got up the Anker and about eight at Night came to Anker a little above Green Island [Isle Verte]. About Midnight [the wind] again came round in our favor and having once more got up the Anker we proceeded on our Voyage. Our Pilot took us through the South Traverse at Caudre[11] which is not common. During the night the wind blew very fresh and just as we were in the most dangerous part they threw the Log and found the ship was going between Nine & ten Knots. The Pilot pretended this was a very great proof of his great skill and knowledge of the River at the same time declared it was not one Ship in a thousand he would atempt to bring up that way but he had conceived a very high opinion of the Working of the Ship from our passage between Bic and this place, and said he had never been on bord a ship that worked an answerd her helm so well but one, of which which he named the Capt. (Peirson) [Pearson] from which circumstance I beleve it was the Niger frigate that was crusing in the River at the time he mentiond.[12]

Tho our pilot had now been on bord more than three days he could not tell what to make of the ship. It was not a Man of War he could see by the Guns nor could he see any thing like Merchandize. At lenth his curiosity was raised to so high a pitch he could contain it no longer, and after making a great many apologys he begged to know what the ship was Loaded with. Capt. D'Auverne produced a small Mail containing about fifty Letters which he said was all his loading but that Lt. Houghton had five more which was the Only Reason for sending the ship. He Laughed at this nor was it easy to make him beleive this kind of loading was very common & that a great many ships was kept for no other purpose. Our passage this day was a very agreeable one having Settlements on each side of the River all the day which with Wind and tide we passed with a Velocity allmost incredible.[13] The wind was so hard and the Sea so high at the East end of the Island of Orleans that I was as sick as I had been the whole passage which prevented me in a great measure from enjoying the Prospect on that sweet spot. Having passed this Island we got a full View of the falls of Montmorency which were much mended by General Holdemand [Haldimand's] House which is a good object near them tho in itself rather a Whimsical Building. We proceeded directly towards the town and came time enough to deliver the dispatches before dinner and partake of what was going. As we found here the 31st and 44th Regts. our time passed agreeable enough tho with very little variety until the *24th* when I set off for Montreal in company with Houghton, Capt. John Mc. Donnal [McDonald] and his Sister, having left Hughes in Quebec as the 53d Regt. were under Orders to releve the 31st in that Garrison.[14]

A Journey from Quebec[15] to Montreal is at the very best of seasons extreemly tedeous and Disagreeable from the badness of the Roads and uneasyness of the Carriages. It is impossible to give any one an adequate Idea of these Infamous Veacles unless they have seen somthing of the kind. The[y] are somthing between a very bad sort of old fashiond one horse Chais or buggy and a small pleasure Cart. They have no sort of covering to keep of the Cold Wett or heat, none of them have any Springs but some have what they call Iron Cranks on which they are hung and many of them made so very Narrow that it is with very great uneasyness two people can sit in them, and as very few of the Calloshes or Carts in this Country have any Iron on there wheells the roads are made to sute the Carriages by removing all the stones out of them.[16] The only Repair these Roads get is by putting some brush wood into the deepest of the Rutts and throwing a little earth over it and as this is generaly done in wett weather, by the Inhabitants who want to pass over it so as it answers there own tempary purpose they care very little about any one else.

14. A view of the Cathedral, Jesuits' College, and Récollet Friars Church, taken from the gate of the Governor's House. Engraving by Pierre Charles Canot (1710–77) after R. Short, published 1761. *Courtesy of the Public Archives of Canada*

There are never theless very good Laws for the Roads and Officers called grand Vayers [Voyers] who have so large sallerys as 500 P[er] Annum to see them inforced but they seldom inforce the Laws except in the winter when the snow falls.[17] But to return to our Journey, on the *24th* about Eight in the Mong our party left Quebec. The Road for the first stage is not the same as that in the Margin[?]. Having taken the Road to Old Larrette [Lorette] in order to avoid a very bad Hill at Cape Rouge[18] the Road was intolerably bad and the first accident we met with was between Laraette and Point [Pointe] aux Trembles where the Calash in which Miss McDonnal was broke down.[19] Very fortunately for us we were able to procure another at the very next house tho not without some Difficulty and arguments of which the most forcable was the giving them more money than the usual Price.

At lenth every thing setled we proceeded to Point aux Trembles and from thence to Jacques Cartier and it was not without some difficulty we got across the River [probably the St. Lawrence] that night it being now quite dark. Having thus been employed a whole day without stopping except about an hour at Point Aux Tremble to dinner yet had we only advanced about 30 or 32 Miles. There is on this River [at Sillery] a very Remarkable Mill built by a Mr. Alsop of Quebec to which the Water is conveyed a very great distance in wooden troughs and is said to have cost him ten thousand pounds Building and many people think it will never answer his purpose.[20] It was so dark we could see nothing of it when we passed. Mrs. Alsop this Gentlemans Lady is the Celebrated Miss Arabella Harmar[21] mentioned in Emly [Emily] Montague.[22] The house on the west side of Jacques Cartier is far from a bad one for the Country and they got us some Tea for Breakfast next day, what I did not by any means expect and what we had provided for ourselves in case of failure. After Breakfast we proceeded by Cap Santé, Deschamboult & Grondines until we came to the River St. Anne. Here it was a long while before we could get over the River and in the meantime it Raind hard. There was no house near us but the Priest yet tho he saw us in that situation he never Offered to let us into his house, tho we had a Lady with us. However as we

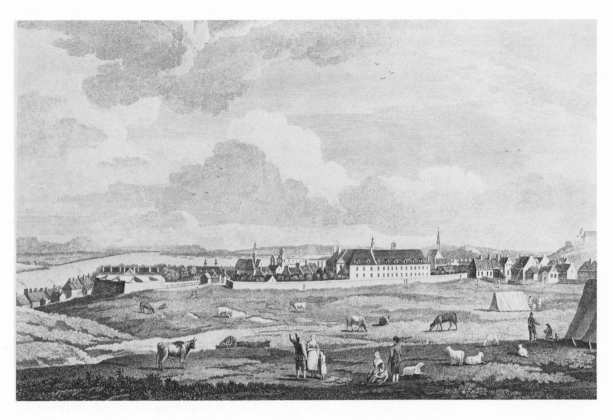

15. A view of the Orphan's or Ursuline Nunnery, taken from the Ramparts. Engraving by James Mason after R. Short, 1761. *Courtesy of the Public Archives of Canada*

had two large Umbrelas we contrived to keep ourselves tolerably dry & having at lenth got across the River we Proceeded by Batiscan & Champlain to Cap Madeleine. When we came here we found the Road betwext this and three Rivers was extreemly Bad and the men advised us to go in a Cannoe to that post which we accordingly did and arrived safe at three Rivers tho not before it was dark.

We had a great plenty of society at this place having found here a Company of the 31st Regt. who were on there way to St. Johns and an Offier of the 53d Mr. Robinson [Daniel Robertson?] who had a Guard in the town. This Gentleman had been here the whole summer and had the best Garden I Remember to have seen in the Country from which he supplied us with plenty of very fine Mellons. He had also in his garden a vere extraordinary Turnip. It was large and very Luxuriant in its leaves but what is most extraordinary when the leaves was lifted up it was so formed as to bear a very great Resemblance to the Private parts of the human speicies, on the one side those of an man, on the other of a Woman. The one was much more perfect than the other but having lost a Remark I made cannot remember which was the most so, but they were both very much like. The Barracks at this place are all gone to Ruin as well as the place itself. It[s] situation is very beautiful and pleasant and has several very good houses in it. Here is a Convent where they are remarkable for making all manner of things in Birch Bark wraught with Porcupine Quills. They are P[r]etty enough and some of them come to a high price. Many of these things are sent to England every year as presents.[23] The town was fortified during the french time with several Redoubts which are now in Ruins tho their foundation may easly be traced. Not far from hence up the River St. Maurice for it is only one River with three Mouths tho called the three Rivers, is an Iron foundery, the only one I know of in Canada where they make many Articles but the principal is Stoves. They are however so infinitely inferior to those brought here from Carron as not to bear any Comparrison.[24]

We did not leave this until about Noon on the *26th* when we proceeded through Point au Lac, Machiche, and River du Loup until we came to

Maskinenge [Maskinongé].[25] Here is the best house on the Road and we were in some doubt wither to stay here or go on to Berthier to sleep it being impossible to sleep at New Yorke [York] a place lately establised. But when we considered that if we staid here we could not get to Montreal next day it was determined we should go on. This was done with some difficulty. By the time we got to New Yorke it was dark and the Road was Extreemly Bad, but as the moon got up very shortly after we did tollerably well and what made the time pass so much the better was the Boy who drove Miss McDonnal and my self was one of those droll Characters which you seldom find. It was very late when we came to Berthier. Next day we were obliged to stay to breakfast with a Mr. Morrison an acquaintance of Miss McD.'s which prevented us from setting of so early as we otherwise should. The Road however was much better than we had formerly met with. We passed through (Dautray, or La Neray) La Valtrie, St. Suplice [Sulpice] and Repentigne. Here we had to cross a long ferry and a good way to carry our Baggage before we came to the Post house but as we were not much troubled with Baggage we soon got there and from thence to point Aux tremble. Here we did not go to the Post house as usual, but to a Public house kept by an English man where we got an excellent dinner and seemed to forget that we had still Nine [miles] of the worst Road of the whole Jouney to go. We however got an additional horse put to each Calash and proceded till we came within about 3 Miles of Montreal when the Callash I and Miss McDonnall was in broke down. As soon as She recoverd herself she exclaimed good God Capt. Enys how is it the Calashs I am in always break down and on my side to. This was a Qustion I did not wish to answer, but if She would have looked at herself she need not have asked. Having put her into the Calash with Houghton we sent them of as it was near dark whilst Capt. McDonall and myself with some difficulty got the Calash Repaird and got into town tho not until it was quite dark.

I was now come to the end of my Journey for sometime as this place was destined for the winter quarters of our Regt. I therefore took a Lodging for myself and waited for the Arrival of the Regt. which was not many days.[26]

16. A view of the City of Montreal, taken from the top of the mountain. Water-color by James Peachey, October 15, 1784, about a month after Enys' arrival there. *Courtesy of the Public Archives of Canada*

We were all soon very comfortably settled and the winter passed as agreeably as any I ever saw in thi[s] Country. The town and the Regt. being well acquainted entered jointly into all sorts of Amusements. We had an assembly[27] once a fortnight and a Concert in the Intermediate Week after which there was a Room lighted for Dancing for such as chose to partake of it, many Private Dances, and a great deal of feasting both of a Public and Private Nature. One of the most agreeable parties was that of the Bachelors Club so called from there admitting no one who was married. They also limited their number to thirteen nor would they admit any but such as were inhabitants of the town. They met once a fortnight and tho they were so strickt in making this society they by no means kept within themselves. Here you were sure to meet every stranger who was in town at the time and I hardly ever sat down to table there but the number of Officers was as great as that of themselves, and so cordial

Winter 1785 was the agreement of all parties there was hardly the trace of a party to bee seen tho this place has ever been more diveded than any I ever knew. Nor were our parties confind to the town alone. Several parties went to Laprarie [Laprairie] and Point aux Tremble but here I am sorry to say some party work [faction?] appeard tho it was of no consequence. Never was the usual diversion of Carrioling carried to such a height as this winter nor the Carrioles more Eligant tho there were not so many drove with pairs as I had before seen.²⁸

During the winter I had made an angagement to go on a fishing party on Lake Champlain with Major Campbell & Capt. Dickson [Hugh Dixon] of the Regt. tho we were very nearly putting it off on a Report of our going up to Releve [relieve] the 8th Regt. in the Back posts. However on the *Ninth of May* we got all ready and embarking in a batteaux went to Laprarie. On our way we passed the Island of St. Paul, one of the most Charming Spots in the Country, which Belongs to a Convent in montreal and is I think of all the places I ever saw in my life posesed of most capibillites as Mr. [Lancelot] Brown used to say.²⁹ We got to Laprarie early in the afternoon. The first thing which presented itself to us was a Coffin lying in a Canoe. In going into the Village we found a number of Indians and was informed in The Coffine we had seen was a Indian of there Nation (Caughnawaga) who had been killed by his Brother. Some were near Crown Point and they had brought him thus far to be buiried by a pri[e]st. The young man who had commited the murder was with them, nor did the crime seem to be thought anything of.³⁰ He said his Brother thought himself a better man than he, that they had fought and he convinced both him and the whole world to the contrary by gaining the Victory over him and as from what we could hear there was nothing unfair in the fight, it seemed to be thought very light of and it was not supposed that any thing more would be said about it.³¹

10 From hence we went to St. Johns where we slept, and next day went to Isle aux Noix. Here we again staid dinner and in the eveng got up to Windmill point as our intention was cheifly to go to the River Salanack [Saranac]. We next day made an attempt but the wind being very hard against us when we had got half way up Isle au [la] Matle [Motte] that we put before it and Run into River Chazee [Chazy].³² In this place we caught a few Salmon but not very many and having staid untill the *13th* in the morng we put out again and that evening got to Cumberland head. Here my Companions made great objections to our putting in and as many to pitching a Marquis [marquee] we had with us. Major Campbell observed I made use of every means. I soothed flattered and Bullied to get it done, however when done neather of them had

14   any reason to repent it as the Night was bad and Rainy. Next day we got off very early & by Eight in the morng we got to the River Salanak where we were destined. Here we found a Yankee Settlement.³³ The Inhabitants came to us on our landing wishing to know why we had come thither. On being told we came to fish for Salmon they laughed at us saying they never had seen any but there was plenty of other fish. Whilst most of us were employed fixing our Camp, Major Campbell took his Rod and very soon caught a fish. This was the first Salmon the people of the Settlement had seen here and they were equaly astonished to find those fish in the River and to see them caught with so Slender a Rod. They wished very much to see our Baits and it was not without some difficulty we made them believe that we caught them with the flies we shewed them.³⁴ This was said to be one of the best encouraging settlements on the Lake yet most of their comforts were in Idea. The poor people had subsisted on the fish entirely for three months and had been still longer without Bread or any sort of substitute. They seemed to be very Cheerfull. The Children said that dady was gone to fetch every thing they wanted but as Dady had been expected near two months it was not without some reason they began to fear that having taken care of himself he had forgotten his family. We had not very good success on the first day but it improved afterwards, so that we had as many Salmon as we could wish for ourselves, gave some to the Inhabitants and brought away twenty in Pickle.

During our stay there was a Man arrived in order to settle who had been a Lt. during the war. He brought with him a large family and the implements of his trade which was a Blacksmith, but the only hopes of subsistance was the fish they could get as he had brought only about a Bussle of Indian Corn and as many Potatoes which were for seed, but these people who you would suppose were almost starved mad[e] astonishing progress in clering their Land and seemed to be so Industrious that it in all probability will be a thriving settlement in a short time.

On the Morng of the *17th* we were all employed in our different ways for it was only at particular times of the day the fish would take. When at Breakfast Major Campbell had said it would not surprize him if we had an express sent after us, after which we all went to our work again repairing of our Tackle or shooting when about Eleven we saw a boat come round the Point of Cumberland head. This I at first supposed was Capt. [Thomas] Donaldson of the 31st who had promised to follow us if he could get Leave but [on?] its nearer approach could see plainly it was an express. When the corpl. came on shore he gave me a letter to Major Campbell who had just come in from the Woods containing orders for us to return to Montreal as soon as possible that the Regt. were orderd to the upper Posts. As the Wind was contrary we did not stirr that day but the next. In the Morng we left our Station and returned as far as Isle aux Noix where we slept. We left this as early as possible next day and being expected at St. Johns there we found carriages ready, and after having to [a?] bit of cold meat we proceeded to Laprarie, where we were again so fortunate as to procure a small boat that took us down as far as a point called point Charles about three Miles from Montreal and we got into town early in the Evening.

Here we found every thing confirmd and the Regt in such forwardness that the first part moved on the *24th* or *25th* but it was not my fate to be in this division, as we were to wait for the Arrival of the 44th Regt. from Quebec. We did not move until the *1st of June* at 5 oClock in the Morng and having Proceeded to the Kings store at LaChein [Lachine] about Eight Miles from Montreal we found Boats ready for our Baggage and selves.[35] The greatest part of our Baggage being on the spot we began loading directly and the remainder was come by the time we had done that. As soon as every thing was in our Boats they proceeded but as the current is still strong we had time to go by land to a Public house about two Miles further where we dined. By the time that was over our Boats were all arrived at the door and we again embarked and having Rowed up on this side of the Lake about a League to a small Island we crossed to a place called Chattau Gaye [Châteauguay]. It was dark when we got to the Mouth of the River after which being obliged to make the tour of an Island at the mouth of it it was past ten oClock when we came to the place we intended to stop. This was no less than a Nunnery.[36] Tho it is very common for passengers to stop at this place and the Canadians in particular are remarkably fond of doing it yet owing to the extreem Darkness of the Night and the Noise made by so many Men it was not without a good deal of perswasion that we could prevail on the sisterhood to open their doors to us. However when they did do it and found we were Realy Troops on the March they received us very civilly, gave us a large Room to ourselves and supplied us with Milk and any little thing we wanted. This can hardly be called a Convent tho it belongs to one being the principal Farm of the Convent of Grey Sisters in Montreal which is an excelent institution as has been already observed and resembling our Foundling.[37] It is here they send any of their sick either of the sisterhood or Children and from hence that Convent is supplied with Wood and every other Necessary in the Farming way.

2nd   The wind blew very hard all Night and Next Morng so that we could not move until about ten oClock when we again Crosed the Lake St. Louis and dined near the Church on the Point of Isle Perrot [Perot], and from hence after about an hours Row we came to the Cascades. Here we found the water so very high that we did not go through the 1st Lock but by Poles and Ropes got up to the Mill at the Sault da [du] Trou thro which Lock we were obliged to pass.[38] That being done we did not find much difficulty tho the water for about ½ a Mile is very strong and at some points there is danger of you[r] boats being turned Round by the current, when they are obliged in General to go down the Rapid it being but seldom they can gain the shore again. This is however dangerous if your Pilot is not a good one. After you have passed this strong water there is about a Mile which you can Row the greatest part of the way when you come to anothe[r] fall called Le Sault du Buisson where there is another Lock by which you easly pass this otherwise dangerous and difficult Point. Having passed this about a Mile we came to Point au Caulong [Coulange] not marked in the Map where we found a very difficult and strong current. The men who dragged the Boats were up to there middle in water and in that sittuation frequently obliged to Climb over Rocks and old Trees which had Lodged there. On the Rocks were to be seen the Remains of two Boats that had been lost before we arrived the same year, and to make it more disagreeable and difficult it was raining and the Bank being of a Clay soil when the men were out of the Water they could hardly stand on it. We were however fortunate enough to get up all our Boats before Night and having got the Officers Women and Children into the Neighbouring houses we stoped for the Night and ourselves being at the Lt. of Millitias got him to order Carts for us against Morning. Our men were but very Ill coverd at this place or indeed the whole Passage.

June 3   Early in the Morng we left Point au Coulange and after Proceeding about four Miles we came to the old Mill tho not without passing some points were the current Runs very strong. This being the foot of the Carrying place we immediately took out one third part of our lading which was directly taken across the Portage by the carts orderd for that purpose the Night before. This place is where Capt. Foster [George Forster] of the 8th Regt and some Indians in 1776 defeated the Americans taking a great many Prisoners and two peices of Brass Cannon.[39] The Rapid which you unload for is by the Canadians called the Grand Batture. It is a long shallow Rapid full of Rocks and the stream runs as swift or more so than in any of the others. The points the hardest to pass are those at the Mill and the point at the head of the Rapid. Only one of our Boats went round the former, having found means to get the Boats through the race of the Mill which was then in Ruins but is since repaird so that when I came up the same fall I could not do so. The space betwixt these points is not so strong close into the shore but is difficult from being extreemly Shallow. The Capt. of Millitia is said to be the best Pilot in this parish for these Rapids and says he can take a boat down either Night or day. I confess I should be sorry to trust to his skill however great it may be of a dark Night as he says he could only be guided by the sound of the Water. The price of Piloting a boat from the Church at the head of the Grand Bature [Batture] to the lower part of the Cascades is two Dollars. You can seldom want a good Pilot here as there are many who make it there profession and a great many others who can do it if required.

We stoped whilst our Boats was reloading at a Public house kept by an English man where we got a very good Dinner,[40] which being over we once more embarked and that Evening got up to the Coteau Du Lac.[41] On our way we passed several very strong points among the Rest one near the Cateau which they call Point [Pointe] au Diable, which tho it is certainly a divilish bad Point is not so bad as some which do not bear such very diabolical names.[42] At the Coteau Du Lac we found a small Garrison of our own regt which we were to take forward with us leaving in there place some invalids who were discharged in order to got [get] to England. At this place there is another Lock which is so long that it crosses the whole point of land. By the time our boats were got thro this place it was quite dark.[43]

The men encampted on the outside of the Fort whilst the Officers Procured an empty Room in the Fort to lie down in. As to sleeping that was out of the Question from the number of Muskeetoes that this place swarmed with, which were by far more than I ever met with in any other place.[44] Near this place in the middle of the River is a small Island so surrounded with Rapids that it is exceedingly difficult to get either off or on it. Its situation had during the Disturbances pointed it as a proper place to keep the most Violent of the American Prisoners on such as the Captains and Crews of Privateers and such people and Barrackes being built there for that purpose it was called prison Island.[45]

4   Here there was a man or to [two] kept still, which it was necessary to Releve in the Morng in doing which the boat in which was the Releve and the Wife and Child of one of the Soldiers, by some means got into the strong current and struck against a Rock by which the Child was by some means thrown out of the Womans hands and it was with difficulty the boat was got off without being overset. Tho this detained us some time yet they had begon so very early that we got of from hence about an hour after sun Rise and having got up the Rapid points for about a Mile above the Fort we came to the entrance of Lake St. Francois [Francis]. On our entering the Lake we found it blew so hard as to render it difficult proceeding further, and therefore following the example of a Brigade of Kings Boats which had put into a small Bay we did the same. Having refreshed ourselves and the Wind being somthing abated we again embarked but had not gone more than three Miles before it began to blow with greater force than ever which again obliged us to take shellter in the first Bay we could find. Here we found a Canadian house or two whose Inhabitants seemed to experience wretchedness in it[s] utmost extent of Dirt Poverty and Rags. Tho these Settelments had been ever since the French time they had hardly ground enough cleard to subsist themselves, and tho two or three miserable Cows found here were so starved as to be hardly able to stand. Indeed the poverty of these as well as all the Canadian Settlers on this Lake may be accounted for. The Men being all employed Navigating Bateaux on this communication receive their Wages in Montreal great part of which is spent before they come home to their familys. By this means they are not only deprived of the money the[y] so dearly earn, but of the time which should be employed in the cultivation of their Land, which joind to the other causes of Canadian poverty may well keep these poor creatures in a State of Wretchedness hardly to be concived. Here however we were now obliged to pass the Night and as the weather seemd to threaten Rain we preferred these Bad houses to the sheds we could make of our sails as we never took time to encamp to [the] whole passage. The Bugs, Fleas and Muskeetoes, here all seemd to unite in tormenting us, but so much was I worn

out from want of sleep for the two preceeding Nights and fateague during the day, that I got a sound sleep in spite of the whole combination.

5th   In the course of the Night the wind came fair and next day we sailed across the Lake. About four Miles from where we had slept is Point au Bodet where is the end of the Canadian settlements and the beginning of the Royalists who have been settled only since 1783 and many only in 1784 yet was these farms by far Better than those we had left. However the wind being fair we did not land at any of them. Not very far from Point au Bodet is Riviere au Raison [Riviere aux Raisins] where there are a great number of Scotch Roman Catholicks settled most of whose names are McDonnell [McDonald] who were formerly tenants of Sr. John Johnstone [Johnson] on the Mohawk River.[46] This River goes Back a good way from the Lake and I am told promises to be a fine Settlement. A little further on at the end of the Lake is a fine Point of Land apropriated to Sir John Johnston who was going to build a large house there at one time but the timber is still lying there in an unfinished state. This is a Beautifull place and said to be some of the best Land in the country which I think seems in some measure confirmed by the Garden stuff I have seen come from it and the looks of the crops as we passed by. On the Opposite side of the River is an Indian Village called St. Regis. I do not know to what Nation this Village properly belongs but belive the most part of its Inhabitants were originaly a Branch of the Hurons. It is now a considerable Village, can produce Warriors which are esteemd as good ones. The Last House in this Village is exactly on the 45th Parralel of Latitude.[47] Of course this is by treaty the last Settlement of the English. On the South Side the River as the boundery from hence runs up the center of the Lakes and Rivers go I only know where as to the Islands. They are all the Propperty of the Indians who will not part with them.

On these Islands all the way up the River and even above Cataruque [Cataraqui][48] the Indians grow all the corn the[y] make use of as we[ll] as Pumpkins Squashes and even a few Mellons. In the afternoon we came up to Point Maligne famous from being a place where Sr. Wm. Johnston defeated

17. Encampment of the Loyalists at Johnston, on the banks of the St. Lawrence in Canada. Watercolor by James Peachey, June 6, 1784. *Courtesy of the Public Archives of Canada*

the Canadian Indians.[49] At this point we again began our difficulties as the water is here so strong as to oblige us to drag the boats up by the Painters. Just above this Point is the town of Johnston [Johnstown] the capital of the new settlement.[50] Tho I have no doubt there may be good reasons for placing this town in the situation were it stands I confess I can by no means discover the shaddow of one. It is an old french settlement indeed, if we are obliged to follow them in all there follies, but appears to me to be the worst place for a town in the whole River being low swampy grownd, must of course have bad Water and be subject to those disorders which are inseparable from such a situation. Having passed this we got up to a place called Rapid Au Minerale [?] tho in the Map no such place is to be found it being called Isle aux deux tettes

[Têtes]. Here is a beautifull Point and on it one of the best Farms on the River. It belongs to a Mr. [Jeremiah] French.[51] Here was Industry and Cleanlyness as conspicuous as we had before seen at Lake St. Francois Dirt & Idleness. We were here very civily reced and passed a very comfortable Night which enabled us with better spirits to attempt the tremendous prospect that was before us.

6th

We had not proceeded more than two Miles before we came to the Mille Rockes [Roches]. Here the Rapid is extreemly strong and shallow and being very full of Rocks is tedeous to get up but as we were well mand [manned] and our Boats not much loaded we did not feel it so much as the common boats which come up heavy loaded with only 4 Men. Having passed this we very soon came to another Rapid called the Moulinett [Moulinette]. Tho this is not taken notice of in the Map it is little inferior to the former in point of difficulty being obliged to Dragg the boats thro it where the men are constantly in the Water.[52] Not far above this is another called the Batture which is not so bad as the two former tho a strong current. From hence it is about 3 Miles to the foot of the Long Sault the whole of which is strong water but is in general to be Poled up.[53] We at lenth got sight of the Long Sault the noise of which we had heard for a long while before. The sight is certainly beautifull to see the greatest part of the River St. Laurence at this place above a Mile across in one continued foam tumbling from Rock to Rock with a most dreadfull Noise. Indeed to look at it the most unobserving spectator must regard it as a Barrier designed by Nature to prevent the encrochment of strangers as its appearance cuts of every hopes of a Passage up it. This is in general immensly exaggerated by every one who has gone up it many of whose accounts I had been used to listen to with avidity. All these accounts concurring with the Appearance made it seem impossible to get up untill you examen close to the shore where you discover that however difficult and dangerous it may be it is nevertheless possible. The part of the Long Sault which you go up is a little more than a Mile in lenth. The great danger here more than at other places arrises from the strong Eddies which are found in several parts formed by large Rocks. These you are obliged to pass through which hurrys your Boat on a few yards with an increddible Velosity at the end of which meeting the current again if your men who are Dragging do not attend and keep the Drag Rope tight it is out of the Power of those who are in the boat to Prevent the Boat from turning Round with the current which if it once does your Boat is oftener lost than saved, and at any Rate in geneal filled with water.[54] In going up you have in geneal three or perhaps four men in the boat the Rest Dragging. A boat with 10 or twelve men can go up in a little more than an hour.

After we had got all the Boats up and taken some refreshment we again proceeded and that Night stopped in a Bay near Point aux Barbues [Barbue Point]. Here I was almost as much troubled with the Sandflies as I had before

7th been at the Mille Rockes which almost shut up one of my Eyes. Next day we again set of as early as possible and met no difficulty untill we came to Rapid Plat. This Rapid is of a very different kind from any of the others being as small as you can conceive anything to be and extreemly deep but at the same time so strong that we were obliged to dragg the Boats up it. It is about a Mile long and takes up about an hour to go up it including a strong point just at the head of it. After you pass this you meet with several strong points. Among the Rest is Point aux Iroquois called so by the french on account of an action they had near that place with the Indians of that name in which the latter were defeated, another called Point [Pointe] au Cardinal and the Presque Isle.[55] Tho these two last are not expressed in the Map they retard a boat very much by obliging them to dragg Round the points. The last explains its sittuation by its Name, and when the water is very high in the Spring and fall is a perfect Island, but even then you seldom find a pilot who knows the Channel but this will now soon be obviated as the Royalists who are every where settled will be able to take boats up and will most likely improve the Channel for their own convenience. The advantage of this short cut I could perceive very plainly by the Boat which was behind me taking it. We at first thought them going wrong but after we had got to the head of the Presque Isle could perceive them a great way before us. The Point[?] going round the Presque Isle is very strong at which we had some of our boats Emborded[?] but as the curren[t] is not very strong a little below the point they very soon got into there former sittuation. Among the Rest the Boat which Major Mansell [William Monsell] our Commanding Officer was in Emborded twice or thrice. I was told by the Officer who went the inside Passage that the Passage is itself very difficult and encumbered by Trees and that the water was even then extreemly shallow tho it was reconed very high for the season nor do I apprehend that this passage is passable except for about a Month in the Spring.

After you pass this you come [to] the lower Gallop which is a strong point but has nothing Remarkable about it. Having passed a small Bay you come to the upper Gallop. This is the last Rapid of any consequence going up and of a different kind from all the rest. It is formed by a long Barr projecting out into the River a long way. When we went up in the Spring this was all Coverd with Water and formed a kind of fall up which we should have found it very difficult to get up our Boats, had not Nature been a little assisted by Art, by forming a passage. Wither this is two sepparate Rocks or one with a passage cut thro it I cannot say but it is just large enough to admit a Boat through it. Altho there may not be quite water enough to float your Boat through this Cut when you press your Boat into it, the water by forcing itself under the Boat raises it so much as to admit of its passage. This is the common way but when I came up in October the same year [1785] I found the Barr quite Dry and the Nitch in the Rock so very shallow that I was afraid to attempt it so went Round the Barr. Tho the Water is very strong the greatest difficulty I found was the stones on the Barr being so slippery that the men who were dragging could hardly keep their Legs. Having got the whole of our party above this Rapid we conceived our difficultys all over as indeed they mostly are tho you may sometimes be kept by contrary winds in the Lake for so I think the River may be called after you pass Point de Barré. This evening we prepared our Boats for Rowing a thing not much attended to before as the whole of the way we were obliged either to dragg or sett with

8th   Poles. Next Morng we left this place and proceding along the Settlement of New Oswegatchee [Oswegatchie] were extreemly pleased to find the Progress the new Settlers had made in so short a time.[56]

About three Miles above the Gallop is the Remains of Fort Live [Lévis] which stand on an Island calld Isle Royale. This Island is very small and by no means high land tho I beleive it is higher than any near it. This place made a long defence against general Amherst when he came into this country tho it had only 600 Men in it. After it was taken it receved the name of Fort William Augustus.[57] It is now in appearance perfectly in Ruins. The Island is so grown up with Brush wood we can only see the Chimneys. The Cannon taken at this place are now lying on a point on the opposite side of the River, in a state truly Pacific as thear Muzzels are stoped with dirt, there Vents with Rust. As I was not on shore I can not say their Wheight of Mettle. Their Number is I think about thirty. Six Miles above this on the south shore is the Fort of Oswegatchee or as the French called it La Gallett. The Current of the River between these places is still strong tho nothing to what we had been used to. The Fort is Square with a Block house at each Angle. It has Bombproofs and every requisite was it [?] in good Repair to stand a small seige but is like almost every French work in this Country command within Musket shot. This fault in all the works of that Nation so famous for Enginneers appears strange at first, tho it is eassly accounted for when you come to consider that they intended them almost all against Indians who have no Artillery their principal intention being to cover their Boats, and facilliate the embarkation & debarkation of stores Provisions &c. They are built Close to the Waters Edge in places where the Protection and facillity of transport seem only to be considerd.

This was the place from whence the shipping emp[l]oyed on Lake Ontario used to sail before the year 1779 when it was found to be so very inconvenient that they were Orderd to Navigate from Carleton Island at the Entrance of the Lake.[58] From this Island to Niagara an ordinary passage is not more than three or four days. From Oswegathee it was common to be six weeks and one Vessle I think I have told was three Months but It has been know[n] that a Vessle has gone it in 48 hours. About 3 Miles above this Fort on the opposite side of the River is Point au Pin [Pointe aux Pins] near to which place when the ships saild from hence was the Dock yard. The last ship Launched from hence was the Snow Seneca in the Year 1777.[59] A little above this Point De Barrè a very beautiful point now the property of a Capt. Jones.[60] This is one of the Best farms in the whole River. The River just above this is Wide but it again Narrows about 7 or 8 Miles up where the current is again strong particularly in one place. There are settlements twenty Miles above Point De Barrè but they are not so forward as those below it. Having passed all the Inhabited Country and the 2d Narrows just below Isle Toniata [Tonianta][61] we proceeded to a small Island at the head of the last Mentioned one where we encamped as well as we could which was not very well as it was Rather wett and cold for the season.

June 9th   Next day we sett off at day light and on our way had the opportunity to see dame Nature in her perfect state. Could a person accustomed only to England be sett down in this place he would certainly say it was the most Charming place in the world, being there taught to think wood and water the only things worthy Praise they are lead to think Rocks at Plumbton, Hackfall, & Ledford [Lydford], the Lakes of Keswick Winander Meer [Windermere] and Lommond [Lomond] the greatest Beauties in Nature, but how would all these appear to a person placed in this situation.[62] Conceive a Lake about twenty Miles in lenth and seven in Breadth full of small Islands of Various sizes and kinds. To describe it is beyond my power. Rocks the most Romantic and beautifull, not like your Artificial ones quite Bare but the Trees of every Kind particularly Cedar growing from every Crack in them to diversifie the Scene. Many of these Islands appear to be one entire Rock yet are they in a great Measure covered with Trees.[63] Some seem as if they were cultivated by means of the swamps where the trees will not grow. These places being coverd with a coars kind of Grass have the appearance of fields. In short they continualy Present themselves to you in a different point of View some the most Beautiful others the most [difrent?] their sizes and shapes as

Various as there Numbers. The Prospects which every Moment succeed each other in Rapid succession are various. Some the Most extensive you can wish others that are more and more contracted form a Variety that is sure to please even tho you are sure the country you are in hardly gives subsistence to the wild beasts which frequent it in consequence of which they are but few in Number. But at some seasons this place abounds with wild fowl and fish from whence the Masapaga [Missisaugas] Indians take it to Cataraqui for sale. This place is called the Milles Isles or Lake of the thousand Islands and I have no doubt but there are as many as that number. As we passed through this place I could not but think this was the Country for Don Quixote to have come to have had he as many Squires as there are hours in the Year the[y?] might have given to each an Island where they might have governd with un-limited Authority nor would they have been troubled with either Doctors or subjects to cross their will or Appetites.

Having passed this place the River appears Wider and getting a Breeze of Wind we kept the Middle of the River and soon passed the Isle of Cauchais [Cauchois?] at the head of which about Nine Miles from Cataraqui is the first house in that settlement. The houses are however very thin there being only three in this distance. Having past there we came to Point Montreal about a Mile from Cataraqui[64] where we waited for our Rear Boats which having come up we went into that place where we arrived about 4 OClock in the Afternoon.

On our Arrival we found the first division of our Regt. had not yet left this place, and being again united in so poor a place we found it very difficult to get provisions for us all. A Sucking Pig was sold for two Dollars and no other kind of fresh meat could be gotten, so that Numerous as we were we were in general obliged to live uppon what fish we could catch for some time. On the *11th* Major [William] Potts of the 8th or Kings Regt. left. This and soon after the Lemnade [*Limniade*] arrived from Niagara but the wind was not fair until the *21st*.[65] When at Dark it came fair the 1st division of the Regt. were embarked during the Night and by day light on the *22d* were out of sight of the garrison. As soon as our friends had saild the party who were left began to think of some more Retired and Cheap way of life and on that day opened a little Mess of which I undertook to be Manager. About Noon I was very much allarmed. The Wind had Changed and we were informed the Lemnade was at Anchor about six or eight Miles from the place. I feard their return which would in a day or two [have] destroyed all the little stock we had collected to serve untill a supply could be got from Montreal. This fortunately did not happen and our small society proceeded th[r]o the summer with very little Variety.

I had often heard this place cried up for its plenty of Fish and foul. For my part cannot think it very plenty of the latter. The former in the Spring of the Year is in great abundance. Among the Rest is the Poisson Dorè or Pickerel which are taken near a Mill about a league and ½ from hence in a very Singular manner. In the Month of April they are at the Tail of this Mill in such abundance that, the people of the country get a Pole about fifteen feet long to which they fix two large Gafts [gaffs] in the manner of the double Eells Hooks. This they take at Night and go on the Water in a canoe. As soon as the[y] have fixed on there Stations they begin to Rake at the bottom of the water with this Instrument and when they feel any thing like a fish they give it a sudden jerk by which they hooke the fish. This is a strange mode of taking fish and one would suppose a very uncertain one yet such numbers have been taken by it as would surprise anyone. Two of our Solderes in the course of one Night Killed Forty Eight by this means and some people many more. Now I am on the Subject of fishing I cannot omit annother Mode which if I had not heard from several of the most undoubted veracity and seen the Instruments for that purpose I could hardly believe possible. The method of taking fish by a light and Spear is so well known to all the world as not to need mention of it. The Indians near this (Masapagas) are re-markable adroyt at this Work but the spearing I am going to speak of is of a Singular kind and done with a very long spear like that in the Margin. The handle of this is above twenty feet long of white Ash or some very light Wood. The lower part or fork of [it?] is made of Yellow Hickory, Iron Wood or some such thing bent nearly in the form you see so as to form the above fork which is fixed to the long hook in the end of which is a very fine small Spear. With this they go out at Night taking a light commonly made of a peice of Birch Bark. At a particular season of the year about June the Eels come to the surface of the water during the Night after a particular sort of fly which then abounds near this place when they strike them with the above mentiond spear. It appears to be well calculated for the purpose for if they once get within the fork they are guided directly on the spear. This is a plain proof that Eels do not keep always close to the bottom but that they swim like snakes at the top sometimes at least those of this country do which appear to be of the same kind with what I have seen in England.

On the *3d of October* I lef Cataraqui on my way to Montreal for stores for the winter. The first Night we slept at the first house in the eighth township,[66] and of all the places I was ever Crowded into this was the worst. The house consisted of but one Room about fourteen feet Square. In this we found a Man and his wife, his father and his Sister, and two servants or rather friends who having no house of there own acted in some measure in that state by helping to Clear the land for there House Room. This any one would suppose was full fammily enough for such a house, but our party was as many more, Capt. Bennist of the 8th, his wife and Child, her son by a former husband, her servant Maid, Mr. Pollard and myself, Mr. Southans chusing to sleep in the boats tho the Night was very bad. The p[e]ople were however very obliging to us not withstanding the trouble we gave them. We next day got down near Point aux Iroquois, from whence we got to Coteau du Lac and from there to Lachene. As we Crossed Lake St. Francois we had a hard breeze of wind in our faver untill just as we came to the Coteau when a Squall came of[f] land which very near overset the boat, and it was with great difficulty we got into the Locks at the Cateau which had we missed we must have gone down a very bad Channel with very evident danger. I got to Montreal on the *7th* and from the Civil reception I met with from every one soon forgot all the trouble I had met with coming down. During my stay here was what is called in this part of the world the Dark Sunday as per

Margin. I confess I was very much Alarmed for some time and expected no less than an earthquake.[67] Having fixed all my business on the 23 I left Montreal in Company with Mr. Brook [Thompson Brooke].

Octor 23, 1785   Brooks of the 34th and Mr. [Charles] Southouse of our Regt. and after a very disagreeable journey of fourteen days at length reached Cataraqui. Our winter in this place was almost as Dull as our Summer. We however continued to make up a Dance once a fortnight of from 10 to 16 Couples and lived in very tollerable Society with such few persons as are in this place. The winter here we found much milder than at Montral as we had only three or four

1786   days near the Queens birth day that could be called intensely cold.[68] The Spring was very forward. On the *5th April* a boat arrived from Oswegatchee [Oswegatchie] with corn to be grownd but could not get up to the Mill for Ice tho the River had been open some days before. On the *9th* we began to sow seed in the Natural Grownd in the Garden and on the *25th* of the same Month we had boats from Montreal. By these we got Orders to Change the Transport of Provisions and Merchandize which had the year before been carried on at Cataraqui to Carleton Island and I was orderd by General Hope to proceed to that post to take the Command and Charge thereof and ac-

April 26   cordingly sett of next day for that purpose.[69]

At this Place I may be said to have been alone as there was but one Officer with me and he being married of course we kept different houses. The society of this place is again less than that of Cataraqui but there is two or three families who made it tolerable and having the transport at that post we never wantd for Company. Indeed I had frequently more than I could well manage to get meat for. I had here also plenty of amusement. Being told I should remain here the winter I set to work in earnest at a Garden and Indian Corn field in one of which I spent all the time I had to spare from the duties of my Office or hospitality, which was no small part of my time. I had here the charge of not only the garrison but also of all the Kings Ships, the passing of all persons and propperty to the upper Country, and soon after my Arrival the Naval store keper being called away his business also fell to me and as

18. A view of Cataraqui on the entrance of Lake Ontario in Canada, taken from Capt. Brant's house. Watercolor by James Peachey, July 16, 1784. *Courtesy of the Public Archives of Canada*

there was no public house on the Island the home of the Commanding Officer was the only place where people of any sort of Rank could be accomodated. By this means my house was seldom empty and my time passed well enough until the *12th of Sept* when I reced Orders again by Name from General [Henry] Hope to proceed to Ford Ontairo [Ontario] to relieve the party of the 34th Regt. at that place. This was an order I had for some time expected and dreaded as I was so well fixed in my present quarters I had no sort of inclination to remove from them.

On the receipt of this Order I went directly over to Cataraqui and having setled every thing with Major Mansell returned home on the *14* and began to prepare for moving. The party who were to go with me arrived at the Island on the *16th*. Major Mansell who was ordered to take the command from me came on the *17th* and having got all ready I set of on the *18th* early in the morning in five Batteaux and one whole boat.[70] The day was favorable and the wind rather fair in the morng. Towards eveng the wind came more fair with hard Rain. We however was fortunate enough to make the long traverse to Grenadier Island that Night but the weather was too bad to attempt to cross again to the main Land so we put up for the night here. We had a prospect of a very Rainy Night but as soon as the Sun went down the weather Cleared up and the Rain ceased. At day light on the *19th* we again sett off with a fair wind and had I dared to keep out into the Lake believe I should have reached Fort Ontairo that Night but the wind did not seem settled and black Clouds rising above the Land made me fear the wind would come from that quarter which made me draw in shore lest a squall from the Land might drive me so far into the Lake that I could not get back again. About Noon the wind begain to freshen and come more on the Land so as to prevent all hopes of reaching Ontairio that Night, so I put into a small River they call Salmon Creek where there was a detachment of a Corpl. and two men from Ontario to prevent Cattle from being brought that way from the States.[71] This place takes its name from the number of Salmon which are found here at some seasons of the Year. During our stay here some Indians came and brought us several of those fish. They were large and looked very well before they were dressed but had neither the colour nor taste of good salmon after they were Boild. The wind blew very hard in the Night, which occasioned an exceeding high surf on the Barr which is off the Rivers mouth, so that altho the next day was as calm as could be it was not until near nine oClock that we could get out of the River. As soon as we got over the Barr we got out of the Breakers and tho there was a very heavy Long swell from the Lake we got on very well and arrived at Ontario about ½ past three to the no small joy of a Mr. [Capt. Alexander?] Fraser of the 34th who was not well at the place.

21s   The next day I received the Command from Capt. [David?] Forbes and on the 22d he left me to myself in the most loansome place I was ever quartered in.[72] This place is better known by the Name of Oswego than Fort Ontario but is by no means the same place, the old fort of Oswego being on the Opposite Side of the River Onandago which here empties itself into the Lake.[73] The present fort was built in the latter part of the late French War by General Haldemand and was let fall to Ruins during the peace but in 1781 was again refitted by Major [John] Ross of the 34th Regt. by Order of the above General. Oswego or the old fort is on the other side of the water & was built by the French. It appears to me to have been in a Triangular form with either Bastions or half Bastions or Probably a Bastion towards the land and half ones toward the water, however be that as it may it is now in utter Ruin. The Line of Pickets may be traced plainer than any other part. It was very small and all the store houses was on the outside near the Wharf.

Not far from the fort near the Banks of the Lake is a fine Cool Spring which was formerly much frequented on account of the goodness of its water. It is called the Punch Boul but Ill deserves its name as it is a small hole in the Rock which will not hold above a Pint of water nor does it appear to me at present to Run very fast. I am told it was spoild by the following Accident. An Englishman who was settled in the Province of New York was in the begining of the late disturbance supposed to be what was called a Tory for which among many others he was obliged to leave his house which he did with an intention of going to Canada by way of Crown Point, but near

20

Albany finding himself closely pursued Changed his Route and came by this place which was at that time uninhabited. When he came here he found himself quite exhasted and unable to carry all he had got. This was only sufficient Provision to take him to Niagara and 500£ in hard money which he had brough[t] away with him. A thought struk him of buring his Mony near this Punch Boul which he did and with out telling any one of it went to the West Indies. After the peace was concluded he wrote from thense to some of his friends to get the Money telling them where it was hid, who came and found it after having laid there from 1777 to 1785 with no other loss than spoiling the Spring which is sayd not to be near so prolific as it used to be before. Not far from the Fort is a kind of Flech [flèche] or Redoubt facing the wood which is call'd Fort Rascal but for what reason I cannot learn.

To speak of this place as a port for ships I should call it a very bad one tho I am told large ships formerly used to come into it. At present it is very difficult to enter on account of a Barr of large Beach which lies off it. This shifts every Year so that if a Man knews it ever so well one Year he may be perfectly Ignorant of it the Next. It is Occasioned by the River which is large and subject to very great land floods in the Spring of the Year, which being Naturaly very Rapid Rushes with great violence through a narrow Gutt at the Mouth. This place is also very subject at that season to Gales of Wind from the westward across the Lake so that when one of these Gales come it drives an imence surf into the Bay where meeting with the Current of the River it formes the Barr sometimes in one place sometimes in another. I sounded it in the *begining of May 1787* and found only Eleven feet water in some parts of the Channel. When you are once over the Barr there is water enough and after you enter the Gutt and pass it you find the River widen to a Considerable degree forming itself at the same time into two Basons one of each side. The one under the old fort is the Deepest and indeed the only one where any Vessle can be but the other formes a very comodious harbour for Boats. From hence to the present Fort (or Ontario) is near a quarter of a Mile apart. The grownd Round the fort is extreemly Broken which occasiond a number of small redoubts to be erected round it at convenient places to

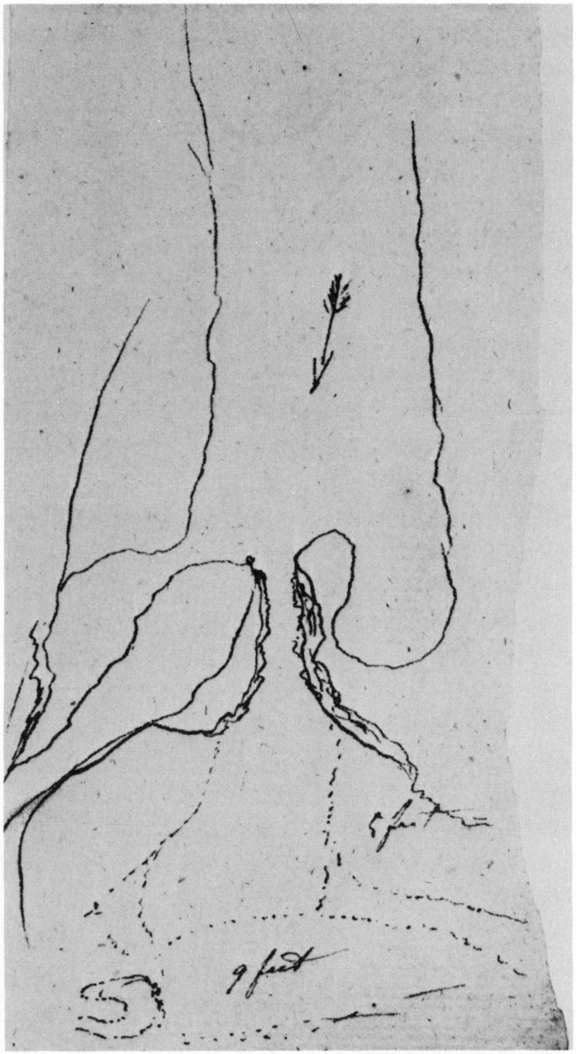

Map VII. Possibly the outlet of the Onondaga River into Lake Ontario. This map by John Enys faces journal material dated September 1786 in the original manuscript. Presumably, it illustrates the "Barr of a large Beach" which lies off the mouth of the river which "shifts every Year" and which is "subject to very great land floods in the Spring of the Year, which being Naturaly very Rapid Rushes with great violence through a narrow Gutt at the Mouth" of the river. *Courtesy of the Cornwall County Record Office, DD. EN 1809; photograph by Charles Woolf*

command the different Ravines one of which I have already taken notice of. These are now entirely in Ruins but may be traced as well as some parts of the Lines that were thrown up when they first took Possession of the place.

As you Enter the Fort on the Right of the first Bridge was the Battery that did most execcution against the old fort of Oswego when it was taken. Ontario itself is a handsom well built Earthfort of a Pentagonal form, the exterior Pollegon of which is about Ninty Yards. The Bastions are all full, each of which contains a Block house with Bomb proofs under it. Four of these were designed for the men, the fifth for the residence of the commanding Officer. On the curtains are also Buildings which were designed for Officers quarters, Storehouses, and Kitchens for the Blockhouses, which have no Chimneys in them except the Commanding Officers house.[74] On the Parade are two Wells of water and in one of the Bastions is a third but it is but very indiffent so that the Lake water is in general made use off. There is a very good Bomb proof Maggazeen. It has a Ravlin toward the land side, a Line of Pikets entirely Round in the Ditch and some part of the Covertway. Where there is no covert way and Pickets, I put an Abattis to strenthen it in the Winter 86–7. The soil is very good in general, and was it not for the Wind the Gardens might be extreemly forward, but of all the places I was ever at this is the most subject to hard Gales of Wind particularly in the fall of the Year, when it is seldom a boat can go out of the River, without danger, which makes it very difficult to supply the place with fuel for the Winter. The River Abounds with good fish of all kinds, and the contry Rownd except just near the fort, with Beaver, Bear, Otter, and all kinds of Game, so much so that Indians come from a great distance to hunt near it. It is about Eighty Miles South west of Cataraqui, 150 East of Niagara & 140 W by N of Albany.

I had not been long here before a Merchant Arrived from Mechelamackhuse [Michilimackinac] whose intention we soon found was to marry a Young Lady, Daughter of the Preventive or Customhouse Officr at this Post. Here I was obliged to take up a new trade and Officiate as Clergyman on the

Octor 1st 1786 Occasion. This will certainly sound very strange to an English Ear who are not used to such things but here Clergymen are so very scarce that Justices of the Peace, do their Office for them, and where, as in the present Instance, they are not to [be] gotten, the Commanding Officer is ex officio to act in both capacities. Never did I do any thing with a worse grace for besides that it was an office which I was wholey unaccquainted with I was sure we should lose the Young Lady who would have been a very great addition to our Winter Society had that not happened.

During the fall we had boats from time to time from the different ports on the Lake and the Sloop was here twice with stores. She left this in the *28 of November* after which we saw no one but what belonged to the fort until the *16th of Jany* when the first express arrived form Canada. Of these I had several in the course of the Winter which was here extreemly Mild. Our River was never frozen so as to walk over it nor was the Bay to stand more than 24 hours. And by the *Middle of march* there was hardly a bit of Ice to be seen near the place notwithstanding which the Spring was by far the latest I saw in my life.[75] We got a man from Albany on the *17th of Aprill* and a boat from the States on the *23d* of the same month but got no boat from Canada until the *3d of May*. Indeed that is as early as they can be expected. By these I got the first accounts that we were soon to be releived from hence but left the time undetermined. We learnt the party that was intended to releive us was gone to Niagara which left us in a more uncertain state than ever.[76]

1787

23

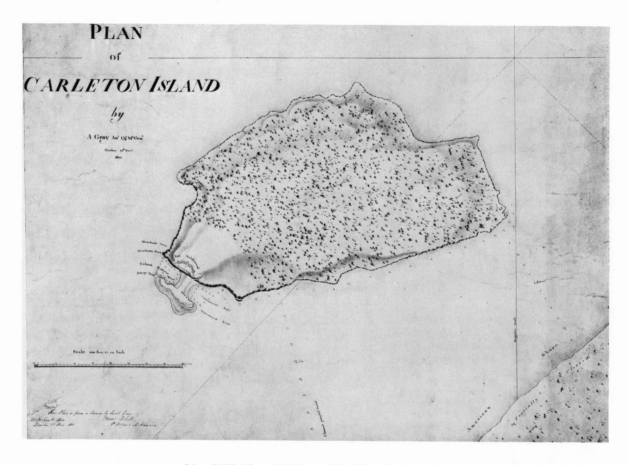

Map VIII. Plan of Carleton Island by A. Gray, 1810. No. III in a series on Upper Canada, prepared by the Assistant Quarter Master General, Quebec, December 29, 1810, and signed by James Kempt, Quarter Master General, North America, Quebec, June 1, 1811. Enys was at Carleton Island—one of the Thousand Islands at the head of the St. Lawrence River, between the present city of Kingston, Ontario, and Clayton, New York—during early July and August 1787. *Courtesy of the Public Archives of Canada*

NIAGARA FALLS AND A ROYAL VISIT

O<small>N THE</small> *26 of June* I was surprised on the return of a Boat I had sent to Carleton Island to find among the other passengers an Officer of the 65th Regt. who came to inform me that a detachment of that Regt. would be at my post that Eveng to releive me. The party Arrived a few hours after under the command of [Farman?] Close. On the *28th* I gave up the command but could not get all my Public Accounts finaly settled until the *30th* in the Afternoon. In the Morng of that day I sent off my party under the command of Lieut. McLeon [Allen Maclean] & Ensn. Swonne [Gilbert Swanne] with Orders to wait for me at Salmon Creek, a place about twenty Miles on our Way. The same afternoon I followed them and arrived at our rendezvous about Eight oClock that evening. Next Morng at day break we again set out. The wind Was fair but for some time very little of it. As the sun Rose the Wind encreased so that about Noon it was as much as ever our Boats could bear. Our little fleet were a good deal scatered, in crossing some of the deep Bays which obliged me to stop a full hour until the Rear Boat came up as

July 1

115

soon as I came in sight of the Fort at Carleton Island, not withstanding which delay, we got to the Fort to dinner after sailing near Sixty Miles that morning which I think I may esteem one of the most agreeable passages I ever made in a Boat. In the evening just as we got up from dinner we were informed there were some more boats in sight coming from Canada. On the arrival of which we were very much surprised to find they contained a detachment of the 60th Regt. under the command of Captain [William?] Porter, destined to releive the posts of Cataraqui and Carleton Island which party we had no reason to expect for some weeks to come.

All our posts below Niagara were now compleatly releaved and Major Mansell might if he pleased have set out for Montreal with his division of the Regt. But I was orderd to stay until Major Campbell Arrived with the Remainder, when I was to put myself under his command. With this intent I staid until the Morng of the *sixth* when the Seneca Snow Arrived from Niagara with the raminder of the Regt. We were now all togeather as Major Monsell had not yet moved from hence. Major Campbell no sooner found there were a sufficient number of boats to contain the whole than he Ordered them to disembark from the Ship into the Boats so that by half pas one oClock the whole sett off with a fine fair wind, Leaving me with some draughts from the Regt. who had turned out to remain with the 53d and 65th Regts who I was to see as far as Niagara, which charge I very gladly undertook as it gave me an opportunity of seeing the famous falls near that place. The Ship Limnade being ready to sail when I got my leave or Rather party I was in hopes of being at Niagara without further delay or difficulty. In this however I was dreadfully disappointed by the wind setting in very strong from the westward, which is very common in this place, occasioned in a great measure I conceive by its local Situation, it being placed in a kind of Funnel at the end of the Lake so that not only when the wind naturally blows directly down it, but whenever it blows any way near it we have a indraught of wind into the Narrow part near Carleton Island. Thus situated I was obliged to live upon my friends for five days without the least prospect of getting forward, during which time I was extreemly obliged to Capt. Porter of the 60th for his Polite attention to me.

In the afternoon of the *11th* the wind came round a little in our favor on which "Mr. [David] Betton or as he is more commonly called here Comadore Betton from having the command of all the Shipping on this Lake altho he is not in the Navy at all", came to me and desired I would come on board which we accordingly did.[1] We however had not got up the ships side before we found the wind had again shifted and was as contrary for us as ever. We however agreed to sleep on boad in hopes the wind should come fair in the Night or early in the morng. Day light however came but not a fair wind which continued as bad as before. We therefore passed the whole day on shore but in the evening when on board to sleep as before. In the course of the Night I [the?] wind came round to the NE which was just our wind so that before day light they had begun to Weigh the Anchor, which being in very deep water and deeply Buried in the Mudd from the Ship Riding so long at it in the late contrary winds it was with great difficulty we could get it up. It was at lenght accomplished about five in the Morng when we stood out towards the Lake with a fair wind tollerably fresh. At two in the afternoon we had cleared what are called the Duck Islands that lie in the mouth of the River and had stood to the Northward so as to be near what the Sailors call the false Ducks which are the outermost of all the Islands and in the Map called Les Isles des Couis when the wind failed us and became quite calm.[2] It was not long in that tranquil State for the wind again coming from the westward it began to blow hard which obliged us to stand across the Lake. As we crossed the mouth of the River some of our men said they could see the Senneca Snow coming out but She was at that time so far to Leward of us I could not discern her.

The Wind now blew so hard that most of the women and a good many of the Soldiers we had on board began to be sea sick if I may be allowed to call is [it] so upon a fresh water Lake and it was with some difficulty I could keep myself from being in the same situation by remaining a great deal upon Deck. In the course of the Night the Boatswain a remarkable fine seaman, Dreamed

12th (margin)

13th (margin)

that some accident had happened to the Ship which he directly communicated [to] a Serjeant Germain of the 65th Regt. then on board nor could he get the

14th least rest during the remainder of the Night. It was no sooner Day light than he made every possible search in every part of the ship without being able to find any thing amiss. We were now convinced the Man was Right who the evening before said he could see the Senneca as Now She was not only abreast of us but had in the course of the Night got to windward of us. In the Morng the wind abated and we got our Breakfast with tolerable comfort, and went upon Deck to walk. Still the Idea of the Night haunted the Boatswain so much that he set out upon another search, When on passing the Boltsprite [bowsprit] he perceived it had moved a little. Alarmed at this he proceeded to examen further when he found the Boltsprite Broken just before what is called the Bitts. This was immediately reported to the comodore who with myself and the mate went down to see it, and on a Nearer Veiw found some feet towards the Bottom or Heel of the Boltsprite perfectly Rotten.

Every thing was now done to secure it as well as time and place would permit but the wind being still contrary, and all on board agreing that they could not attempt to Beat to windward without danger, it was agreed that a signal should be made for the Senneca to come down to us. She no sooner saw our signal out then she came down and we all agreed it was best as the sea was now not very Rough to Shift the passengers and dispatches, from the Limnade, to the Seneca, and that the latter should proceed to Niagara with all dispatch, whilst the former putting before the Wind should go to Carleton Island to refit. This was no sooner determined upon than it was put in excecution. The boats of Both were Directly hoisted out and in about an hour the whole were shifted without any accident and about a half past two in the afternoon each took his own course. The remainder of the day we stood over toward the North shore, where the wind favoring us a little in the course of the Night we made a

15 good slant of it before Morng.

About noon next day the wind came fair and we ran before it until near Dark by which time we were within six Leagues of Niagara. It now once more

16

came round to the westward and bore so threatening an appearance I was very happy we had not attempted to come on in the Limnade. Captain [John?] Baker now got the Vessle under a snug sail and we continued Beating the whole Night in the midst of incessant Rain Thunder & Lightening but contrary to our expectations the wind never blew very hard. By day light we had gained our distance but were a good way out in the Lake, from hence we had good view of the Fort and the new Loyalist settlement to the westward of it, which made a good appearance.[3] Amongst other things Captain Baker made me take notice of a small black cloud which hung over the land a little to the westward of the Fort, in which I could perceive nothing worth notice until informed that however like to a Real Cloud it was nothing more than the Spray Arising from the Falls after which I could perceive it never varied its situation. The day was not so clear as I could have wished it to be. However we could distinguish the above Spray above twenty Miles, but of a Clear day I am told it may be seen at an immense distance, which from the clearness of the Atmosphire in that Neighbourhood in fine weather, I am inclined to believe. Having Beat up until we were a little to the westward of the Fort we made a fair wind of it and Ran into the River, and by about Noon Landed near the Fort.

On our Arrival I was most Hospitably received by Captain [Jonas] Watson of the 65th who commanded and the rest of the Garrison who wished I would take a Bed in the Fort. This however I declined as I found I could get a very excellent one at a public house in what they call the Bottom without the fort Gates, But accepted an invitation to dinner and supper whenever I was not otherwise engaged, by which my time was most agreeably taken up. The first day I of course dined with Captain Watson as Commanding Officer which is always expected from every one coming to any of these posts in the character of a Gentleman. By this I was introduced to all the Gentlemen of the Garrison, Captain Watson in the absence of his Lady being one of the General Mess.

I had also this evening an opportunity of seeing the Indian Squas to perfection. As both the Fame and infamy of these Ladies had reached my ears two or three Years before, I was prepared to see some thing extraordinary, and first it is but common justice to allow them more beauty than those copper coloured Ladies in general possess. But if they excell them in that good quality they also exceed them in a far greater degree in every kind of depravity. The day before my Arrival a famous Lady of that kind had returned from the Village to which She belongs. She is realy a very Charming looking Girl which has for some years past in general procured her the favor of whatever Officer has from time to time commanded at Fort Slosser [Schlosser],[4] which has obtained her the name of Countess of Slosser. Another quality of this aimable fair is that she can drink much more than any of her sisterhood by which means they are in general in a state of perfect drunkeness all the time she stays. The 65th Regt. had not been long here and wither it was out of curiosity or only for amusement I cannot say but after supper three or four of the Ladies were admitted into the Mess Room.

Having in the course of the day communicated by intention of visiting the falls as soon as possible to Mr. Humphry [John Humfrey?] of the Engineers he was so good as to offer to take me there in a one horse Chair [chaise], and it

17th   was agreed that we should sett out early next morng, and men were accordingly sent out at day light to find two horses which is sometimes very difficult to be done as thear are no enclosures on the side of the River the fort stands. Of course their horses straggle as far into the woods as they please. This happened to be the case in the present Instance for notwithstanding we had men out the whole day not a horse could be found. I was of course obliged to put up with the disappointment and making as good a use of my time as I could I delivered up the party of draughts which I had brought up for the 65th and 53d Regt. to the Officers appointed to receive them from me, and having thus got rid of that troublesome charge I passed the evening in the Fort without the Riot we had the evening before.

18   The men who were employed to find the horses were again disappointed and returned whilst we were at breakfast without any, and others were sent out in their place by different Routs. In the course of this Morng Capt. [Joseph]

Brant Arrived and not long after him Coll. [John] Butler the deputy super-intendant of Indians.[5] The Latter had received a letter from the deputy superintendant for the American States which contained nothing but that he had forwarded some official papers from the six Nations to Congress. But the Indian who brought this letter reported that As he passed a place called Venango which is on the same River that the French post called La Beuf [Le Boeuf] stood and which from its situation at the juntion of French Creek and the Allegheny River, which formes one of the communications with the Ohio at Fort Pit, is rendered an eligible place for a post, that the Americans had began to Erect a large fort, That he Enquired of them the cause of their build-ing it and Received the following Answer.[6] That he might remember there had been a War between them and the great King in which they had thrown the Great King on his back but that lately they had perceived that he was getting up again and might perhaps make another Attempt to conquer America. They therefore not only intended to build this but when that was finished to proceed with others until they got within a convenient distance of Niagara when they would proceed to take [it?] from the English.

This peice of news passed away the morning until near twelve oClock when the Men who had been out after horses again returned and told us they could not find any horses belonging to the fort but they had found two which they called Wild horses that they hoped would answer our purpose. As that term may require some explanation it may not be here amiss to say it is applied to all such as are not known, and as it is a Practice for the inhabitants who live on the other side of the River to send their cattle over on the Fort side during summer in order to save their own Pasturage these Wild cattle are not uncommon, And as the Officers Look upon this side as their Right they some-times take the liberty of Riding such stray horses as they can find by way of taking payment for their pasturage. Such was the case with the two they had now brought us. The strongest was directly put into the Chair and the other saddled. It was now near one oClock when Mr. Humphries and self got into our conveyance and Mr. Douglass of the 65th accompanied us on horse back.

It was now with the greatest difficulty we could make the Chair horse draw at all and when we had got him to do it he was so very bad that he fairly knocked up with us before we got to what is called the Landing only seven Miles and half from Niagara.[7] The country between Niagara and this place is in general flatt and not much Elevated above the banks of the River which altho it runs three Miles an hour or thereabouts is yet Navigable for the Largest ships on the Lake which sometimes if the wind is fair run past the Fort and discharge their Cargoes at this place but it is more commonly landed at the Fort and brought up here in boats. The view from hence is Romantic enough, for the River all at once becomes Narrow and extreemly Rapid. The Country is equaly altered from a flatt to an excessive steep Rugged Hill or Rather Ridge of Hills which cross the River at this place. Many speculative people seem to think from this appearance that the fall was once at this spot but I can by no means agree to this opinion. But to drop this subject for the present and return to the Landing which is so called from all the goods which are carried to the upper posts being Landed here and taken in Waggons across the Portage to Fort Slosser which is above the falls. Here are always a party of Troops quartered to protect the stores which is commanded by a serjeant only although an Officer has in fact the Charge and visits the place every day. As I do not remember to have seen in any other place the same conveyance for getting the goods from the waterside up to the place where they put them into the Waggons I shall here make a memorandum of it. The Bank is very steep and about forty or fifty feet high. This is sloped away a little and a Cradle Like that from whence they Launch a Ship is laid down on which a kind of Cart on Small Iron Rollers, which Run in Groovs, is placed. At the Top is a Capsterne [capstan] by which they hoist this Cart up, with a great Weight of goods in it, with a very small number of men. This is in general done by the Soldiers quartered here for which they are paid by the proprietors. This perquisite formes a considerable sum annualy to the Serjeant who has the charge of it as well as his being permitted to keep a small public house. So Lucrative is this place that I have heard a serjeant has made between 150£ and 200£ per Annum of it.[8]

19. Capt. John Montresor's tramway and cradles on the lower Niagara River. The drawing dates from 1902 or earlier and shows what is believed to have been the earliest railway in America, built in 1764. *Courtesy of the Buffalo and Erie County Historical Society*

It was our intention to have dined at this Little public house but upon our Arrival we found it so full of the Draughts for the 53d Regt that we were obliged to give up the Idea. It was however absolutely Necessary that we should get another horse ours being unable to proceed. Partys were therefore sent to look for some and proved more fortunate than formerly for they soon returned with several very good ones, from which we chose the two best we could and again set out. We had now no reason to complain of our Nag being Dull for so High was his Spirits for the first Mile or two I realy think we were fortunate in not being overturned. But by the time we had gone about three Miles he was quite Quiet and proved a very great acquisition to us. Having gained the sumit of the hill or as it is here called, the Mountain, we were charmed with the prospect which presented itself by Looking back on the plain beneath us, which presented us a most beautifull verdant prospect diversified by the Noble River with the Ships and Boats on it, the fort at a distance and the Lake in the Back Ground and on the opposite side of the River the new Loyalist Settlements. This Mountain or Hill may be said to be a high one but by no means so high as Pere [Pierre François Xavier] Charlevoix has said it is but what makes it appear extraordinary is its rising so very abrupt from the Plain.[9]

As soon as we were at Top of the Hill we found the Roads better and getting on at a good rate we soon reached a place called the Lions Den. This place has nothing very Remarkable in its appearance more than a very deep Ravine near the Road full of large stones, Trunks of Trees and all manner of things, but what renders it worthy notice it [is?] the Bloody Action which took place here in the latter part of the late French War of which I learnt the following particulars. As a Convoy of Waggons were passing near this place they were on a sudden attacked by a very numerous party of Indians. The small Guard of a serjeant and twelve men made all the resistance in their power. The noise of their firing Alarmed a Captain [George] Campbell who commanded about 100 Highlanders at the Landing, with these the[y] flew to releive the Convoy but the Indians aware of his approach had laid an ambuscade in a very judicious position in his way, into which he fell. They had so contrived the matter that he was admitted thro a great part of them before they fired at all then getting up all at once they poured in a most dreadfull fire upon them which very few are said to have survived. Then falling on them with their Spears and Tomahawks they Killed every one except one man who is said to have saved himself by getting down a Rock thought to be impracticable. The Waggoners with their horses and Guards next shared the same fate after which they wantonly tumbled the Waggons and the Bodies of Both horses and Men into this Deep Ravine where they left them and went off. The Bodies of the killed were afterwards taken out and Buried near the place. Captain Campbells Grave had formerly a Railing round it of which very little is now to be seen.[10]

Having left this Malencholy place we soon Arrived at a place called Saint Patericks [Patrick's] Lane. From hence in Winter you have a good view of The Top of the falls but the Leaves were now so thick that we could hardly discover any thing of them. This might according to my Opinion be rendered one of the most beautyful points of Veiw in which you can see the falls by Cutting an Avenue from hence towards them nor do I think it attended with so much Labour but that some curios Commanding Officer will one day or other do it. From hence to Fort Slosser is about a Mile & half or two Miles on a perfectly straight and good Road at which place we at lenth Arrived after being four hours on the Road from Niagara which is only fourteen Miles. On our Arrival we found Dinner over but we soon got a Mutton Chop, which we had no sooner swallowed than we all sat out to see the falls taking Mr. Hammilton [Thomas Hamilton?] of the 53d Regt for our Guide who having commanded Fort Slosser for some time knew his way. After passing through some feilds and a small peice of wood we came to the Riverside at an old Saw Mill about a quarter of a Mile from the Brink of the falls. This Veiw alone is worth going many Miles to see. The Current which is very strong more than three Miles above the Falls is here encreased by many Causes, for the River which grows Naturaly Narrower as it approaches the Brink of the Catteract is here divided by a Large Island in the Middle. It also begins to be shallow and Rocky, so that from hence quite down to the Brink of the Falls the water is in a continual foam and has in many parts of the distance Falls which would be much talked of were they in any other situation which may be easyly conceived from the perpendicular hight which the water falls in the course of this Quarter of a Mile previous to its reaching the Brink of the Catteract, which is at least Sixty feet. This many seem to think should be added to the Perpendicular height of the falls. Wither it should or no I shall not presume to determine. I already find my Pen or at least my Ideas inadequate to give any account of what is now before me as it is not only the Water which is beautyful but the Island also is covered with noble Trees down quite to the edge of the Water. To this we must add the many small Islands which have been severed time to time from the Larger one by the force of the Current and which still partake of their Parents Verdure and Beauty.

It was with difficulty we could prevail on ourselves to leave this place even tho we knew we were to go to parts infinitely more Beautiful. We at lenth however struck again into the wood and passing down its skirts Mr. H. brought us out a few Yards below the fall. Here I for one satt down for some time in silent Admiration and Astonishment at a sight which I am fully perswaded no pen or Pencil can ever convey across the Sea. In our present Situation we were too near to the highest part of the fall which in a kind of a sketch or Plan I have annexed is Marked 1 to enjoy its full beauty but we had a tolerable good view of the great or as it is in general called the horseshoe fall which is here Marked 4, 5, 6. To give any adequate Idea of the astonishing Variety which here crowds upon your mind is impossible and it may be well said to be the real sublime and beautifull conveyed in the Language of Nature infinitely more strong than the united Eloquence of Pitt, Fox and Burke even if we give them the Assistance of Loutherbaurgh [Philip James Loutherbourgh] to help them. As the water during its fall from Different parts meeting the Rays of the Sun in different directions takes an infinite number of different Colours and shades, to this we must add the numberless beautyfull breaks in the water, the delightfull verdure which covers the Islands and neighbouring shores, the

20. Plan of Niagara Falls. Sketch by John Enys, July 18, 1787. *Courtesy of the Cornwall County Record Office, DD. EN 1811; photograph by Charles Woolf*

beauty of the most Noble Rapid which can be conceived before it ever Reaches the Brink of the Precipice, the Astonishing Column of Spray which Rises from the great fall, the Thundering Noise which the Whole makes by its fall on the heap of Stones below from whence it Runs no longer like Water but Absolutely in such a state of foam as to appear like a perfect River of Milk for about 100 or 150 Yards after which it resumes at Natural state again altho it is still carried away by means of a Strong Rapid. To all this I must Add the loffty Banks which surround the Bason into which the Water falls the Tops of which are coverd with Noble Trees quite close to the Edge of their Clifts. Here I could not help remarking to Mr. Humphry that before my Arrival I expected to have been disappointed from having my Ideas raised too high by hearing so many people join in their praise but that I was sure from this Veiw alone no one can say to[o] much of it nor is there any fear of forestaling its beauty to any one who may afterwards visit it.

Here some of our party wished to go down to the bottom, a thing very seldom done on this side as well from the difficulty of the decent as that when down your Veiw is by no means so good as on the opposite side. It was however agreed upon to make the attempt, preparatory to which Mr. Hamilton made us all take of our Shoes as in many places it is so very slippery it would have been more dangerous to attempt with them on. Our party now consisted of Mr. H. our Guide, Mr. Douglass [Ensign Douglas?] of the 65th and Mr. Brunton [John Breynton] of the same Regt who had just releived Mr. H. in his command of Fort Slosser, Myself and last of all Mr. Humphry. We all with great difficulty got down about one third part of the way But when I saw the pass by which I was to decend further I gave it up telling Mr. Humphry that if he chose to go further I would get out of his way which I accordingly did and he decended as low as I had done where like me he gave up the point. The other three gentlemen compleated their design, and on their Return very candidly allowed although they were well pleased with what they had done now it was over they would by no means attempt it again until Ropes or something more secure was placed in the most dangerous parts as in some of the steepest parts they were obliged to let themselves down by means of a Twisted Stick in the manner of a Faggot Bond which was tied to an ole Stump above which Stick had been then in use for three Years. Mr. H. indeed went further and acknowledged then on Reflection when at the Bottom he entertained some doubts their being able to reassend. However they all got up safe with no other loss than the feet of their Stockings which were perfectly worn out. We next went back a few yards to the Brink of the Falls, And found to my surprise that we could not only approach close to the Top of the Falls but that the water was so nearly on a level with the Flat Rock on which we stood, Marked 1, that I could without the least danger stoop and take up the water with my hand after it had fallen over the precipice. The view which we have here straight over the fall is very fine but not so good as the one we had before left, except that we saw the pillar of spray to greater advantage as the fall from whence it proceeded appeard less in this direction than the former. I do not know how long we should have staid looking at the scene before us if the setting of the Sun had not reminded us that it was time to return on which we began our Retreat. After we had returned more than a Mile on looking back from a little eminence we could see the Spray of the fall rising to an immence Hight above the surrounding Woods like the large Column of smoke which assends from any large Building on fire but not of so Dark a Colour.

Having gone a little further we came to the house of Mr. Philip Stedman where we passed an agreeable hour in company with him and his Neice a good pretty Girl for this part of the world.[11] He very kindly invited us all to supper but we could not do that being engaged to Lieut. Brunton, however as Beds were not plenty at the Fort we accepted of three in Mr. Stedmans house, where he assured us we could not incomode his family at all for they would very soon be in bed in another part of the house but that we should find our candles lighted in the large Hall and the Room doors where we were [to?] sleep open, and that this was the custom of his house continualy when any gentlemen came that way. Indeed I am told this gentleman has ever been remarkable for his open frankness and hospitality. He is a Native of England, Yorkshire, I think he told us, whose family have had the exclusive privilidge of Transporting all the goods which pass and repass over this Portage ever since the English have had possession of the Country, by which they have made a great deal of mony, his Elder Brother having already retired to England with a good fortune, to which place I think this Gentleman will also retire for the same reasons in a very short time.

Among other curiositys of the place we were introduced to his principal Waggoner who has driven one of the Waggons of both Brothers ever since their first establishment and is now known by the Name of the Brigadier of whom they relate the following strange story as matter of fact. On the evening previous to the Attack which I have before mentioned as he returned from the Landing he said he could smell the Savages, on which all his companions laughed at him. He however persisted in what he said and when the convoy set out in the Morng Absolutely refused to accompany it nor could all the entreaties or Threats of his Master prevail on him to go. He still continues in the same story and vows to this day that he could smell them as plain as if he had been in their Wigwam and that if they had taken his advice they might have saved their lives and the convoy. At any rate he was fortunate enough to be saved by it wither it was realy so or only the production of his fancy.

As Mr. Humphry and myself had no business at the Fort we staid a short time after the rest of the party and were at last going in quest of our Supper without any hopes of seeing any thing more of the fall for the Night. Notwithstanding it was the very middle of summer and the day had been extreemly hot the Night was very cold so that we had run a good deal of the way when stopping just before the fort gate we saw the most beautyfull as well as strange appearance that can be well conceived. It was the Moon which was now just setting behind the Spray of the Falls. It appeard to rise to a very uncommon hight in likeness of a very dark Column but the Thinner parts of the Spray admitted the light thro it, which gave all the edge of the Collumn a Luminous appearance which looked more like a Pillar of smoak fringed Round with fire than any thing I can compare it to. Not wishing to keep this sight to ourselves we ran to call the rest who we found collected round a large fire from which we could with great difficulty draw them as they supposed it was only a story made for the purpose of drawing them from their seats by the fire that we might ourselves get possession of them by which means they were not out until the moon was very near gone, when from what they saw of it they sincerely lamented they had been so tenatious of their seats. This over we all returned to the Fort and after a hearty supper we retired to Mr. Stedmans again to Bed where we found the Candles & every thing as promised and being very much fatigued with the work of the preceeding day we all slept very sound until past

19th   seven oClock next Morning At which time from the orders which had been given to the servants over Night I was in hopes our Chair and horses were on the other side of the water. In this I was again disappointed as the first object that struck my Veiw was the Chair in the Court before the house just as it had been left over Night. I next hastened to the Fort with all expedition where I found both Officers and servants still in bed from whence they were soon Roused and a Boat and Party of men got to put the Chair and horses over which we soon sent off with orders to land them on the North side [of] the Chipaway [Chippawa] Creek whilst we having procured Mr. Stedmans light Boat remained behind to breakfast.

Whilst this was preparing we took a Veiw of the Fort which I have been so often lead to mention during this part of my tale that any person unacquainted with it might suppose it a place of some consequence which is however by no means the case at present as it consists of no more than two or three old houses surrounded by a Rotten Picketing which I conceive was originaly french work. The ordonance consists of one very small Iron Gun and a small Mortar of the same Metal, the Carriages of both being in a worse state than even the Pickets. In short I never saw any place which less deserved the name of a fort, Yet this is one of that Chain of strong posts which have been to guard the frontiers during the late War.

Breakfast being finished we left Mr. Brunton alone at his new government about ten in the forenoon and after having Rowed up a Mile or more under the East shore we Crossed to a very large Island that lies in the Middle,[12] which having gained we Rowed up under its western Bank for a considerable distance before we ventured to cross to the western side of the River. At lenth we made our crossing good and landed about four Miles above the falls at a farm of Mr. Stedmans. Here Mr. Hamilton left us and striking to the left went to Fort Erie[13] which I am informed is just such a fort as the one before described, whilst the rest of us taking the Right hand Road after a walk of two miles came to Chipaway Creek, where we found our horses at the house of a Mr. Birch [John Burch] one of the principal people in the settlement.[14] As the squire was not at home we were glad to wave the ceremony of a visit, so as soon as our Cavalry were ready we set out towards the falls. About another Mile brought us to the head of the Rapid, and a short way further we came to a Mill Mr. Birch has lately built. It appears to me to be a very Elegant peice of Workmanship and is to be both a Grist and Saw Mill but I am very much afraid from the Rapid above it he will find it difficult if not dangerous to bring down Boats and Rafts to it altho the man who superintends it says he thinks it may be done with ease when they become better acquainted with the Currents.

About one hundred yards below the Mill from a point that projects a little we had a most delightful veiw of the whole Rapid, which near a Mile in lenth and I should think three times as broad as that on the East side, the numerous falls are large in proportion which of course renders it infinitely more Grand than the one we had seen the evening before, but still it wanted those beautyfull little Islands with which the smaller one is adorned. In the course of this long Rapid I conceive the perpendicular fall of the water is not less than one hundred feet before it reaches the Brink of the fall and so full is it of Rocks and Cascades that I conceive it utterly impossible that any Boat can ever get down to the fall without being oversett. Indeed some of the 29th Regt whilst in these posts sent down an old boat for the purpose of seeing it go over the fall. They went themselves below the falls to look out for it whilst they left men on the different points to make signals when it passed them but some of those near the fall nor the Gentlemen at the bottom never saw anything more of it.

As the day was now advancing we could not stay so long here as I could have wished for fear of being stinted on time at the Fall itself, for which we now set off and very soon reached the nearest house to it and got permission from Mr. Elsworth [Francis Ellsworth] the owner to put our horses in his stable, but all the family being busy carring their Corn we could get no one to go with us.[15] However as Mr. Humphry had been here before, he undertook to guide us, and we accordingly set out under his directions. Not far from the house we came to the Edge of a very steep Bank which we decended through a very deep ravine or Gully not without some dread of Rattlesnakes for whose habitation this place seemed peculiarly adapted, and the pass being so very narrow and full of stones and stumps that had any such thing been there it would be difficult to avoid it. After going some distance we got to the bottom of

21. A view of Niagara Falls, from the bank near Birches' Mills. Engraving by Frederick Christian Lewis (1779–1856) after a drawing by George Heriot, in Heriot, *Travels through the Canadas* (London, 1807). *Courtesy of the Public Archives of Canada*

this nasty place and found ourselves again on level ground which took us to the brink of the Fall at a place from its Appearance calld the Table Rock, over a part of which the water Rolls. This being the nearest part to the great fall you are of course almost stunned with its noise and perfectly wet with the continual Mist Arising from the Bottom in form of the Pillar which having gaind a sufficient height is separated by the wind and falls like a small Rain or Mist. From hence we had a much better veiw of the falls than that which we had the preeeeding evening, but like that we were to near the object to see it to perfection. I am told many people think this is the best view in which you can place the fall, but I rather think it can only be such as have never given themselves the trouble to searce [search?] for any other. Here they say you can Likewise dip up the water after it has passed the brink of the precipice. However true this may be it is not so perfectly so as on the opposite side as here it is only a small branch of the fall you approach. On the other side it is Actualy the main body of water itself as may be seen in the little sketch of the Top of the fall before given, the former or Fort Slosser side being marked 1, the place I am now speaking of 8. The Table Rock is a very large flat Rock projecting from the Bank and overhanging its Base very much by which means it forms one of the best modes of determining the height of the Fall, being exactly upon the same level and projecting so much that a line let down from its summit will drop very nearly at the Waters Edge at the bottom. But whatever methods may have been taken to assertain its height that of both sides is very well determined being agreed by all hands to be 170 feet on the East or Fort Slosser side whilst from the Table Rock it is only 140. But this thirty feet if it is taken from the perpendicular of the fall adds to the Noble Rapid that is above it.[16]

Having staid a long while we at lenth set off from hence hoping to find a way to a point not many hundred yards below where we now [w]ere with out returning to the Top of the bank again. In this however we were disappointed finding the Brake to Thick and the grownd to swampy to admit of our passage, altho I hear there is a possibility of going to those who are accquainted with the place. This was not our case so we were obliged to assend

22. A view of the western branch of Niagara Falls, taken from the Table Rock, looking up the river, over the rapids. Engraving by Frederick Christian Lewis (1779–1856), after the 1802 painting by John Vanderlyn (1775–1852), the first painting of Niagara Falls by an American artist; published at London in 1804. *Courtesy of the Public Archives of Canada*

the Gully by which we came, at the Top of which we turned off to the right
and soon found a Path leading to another Gully of the same kind through
which we a second time decended the Bank. Having got down to the level
ground we could find no kind of path, we therefore marked the Trees as we
went thinking they might serve us as a guide on our Return. Thus guided by
the noise of the Falls more than anything else we soon came to the brink of
the Clift and striking off a little to our left found the place we were in search
of, and which I beleive is now called Painters Point from a man of that Name
in whose Ground it is.[17] Here we found a spot which had been in some measure cleard (by Lieutenant Tinling [William Tingling] of the 29th when he
was Acting Engineer at Niagara) on purpose to give you a good view of the
whole of this Grand object at once, and it most certainly is the best Veiw of
any on a level with the fall as here every part is by far more equidistant than
in any other point you can look at it from. From hence you look directly against
the Island which is in the center having the great fall to the right and the
smaller one to the left. From this place you have also a better View of a small
fall on the east side of Goat Island which is called the Montmorrency [Mont-
morency] fall and which is said to disembogue more water in the course of a
year than the famous fall of that name near Quebec which perhaps it may but
I do not think it is so broad as that fall. Perhaps its very diminative appearance
here may be only occasioned by its being placed in the midst of such astoninsh-
ing large ones, as the nearest computation that has ever been made allowes
the breadth of the fall from one side to the other to be 1300 yards including
all the turns which there are in its summit and the Island in the Center which
last may be something more than one hundred yards broad. I could have willingly have staid here much longer than we did but having determined to [go?]
down to the Bottom we were obliged to hasten towards the place where you
decend. This place lies some hundred yards to the left of Painters point from
which you pass all the way on the brink of the precipice. Nor is it easy to find
the opening unless you are acquainted with it as you pass round a small Bush
where you find some stumps and roots which assist you for the first three or

four yards of a very steep Bank when you come to a place quite perpendicular for perhaps about twelve feet. Here they have put what they call Indian Ladders which is no more than a Tree about a foot in diameter with notches cut in its side that is placed rather slantwise to answer the purpose of going down. Not far after you pass the first of these ladders you come to a second not quite so long after which you decend through a very steep Gully full of Rocks and stumps, most part of the way being assisted by the Branches of the Neighbouring Trees.

It surprised me to find that this decent was so easy to what I had always [been] led to think it which I conceive proceeds from many who have never tried it but speak from hearsay. Indeed I am fully perswaded that many who say they have been at the bottom never have been there as they frequently betray by the Erroneous accounts they give of this lower Region, which in fact is I believe visited by but few. Once Arrived at the bottom you receive Ample reward for the pains the decent has occasioned you. If this noble scene inspires you with awe when above it may be easyly conceived how much it must be augmented when you get to the bottom absolutely into the very bason where all this shot of water falls. You are no sooner clear of the wood than you have a full and compleat veiw of all this magnificent scene in which all the various shades which the water receives in its fall either from the Projecting Rocks or from the intersections of the rays of the Sun appear to the greatest of all possible advantage, besides which you here see nothing of the Rapid above, your prospect being confined to the perpendicular fall and the bason which receives it but then that fall appears to much greater advantage & much higher than it does from any of the views above. Having sat down a few minutes to rest after our decent and drank a glass or two of wine we proceeded to get as near the fall as we conveniently could. This is by far the most difficult and I may add dangerous part of the days journey. The distance from hence to the fall is very considerable and you have no kind of Road, they [the?] way lying along the beach which is formed of huge stones which have from time to time fallen from the high Clifts which overhang most part of the way. These Rocks lie just as they happen to have fallen so that sometimes you are obliged to climb over them at others to creep under them whilst they seem to threaten your destruction every step you take. Many of them appear as if they would fall every moment being only ballanced on a point, others seem to have no other support than Trees which have fallen at the same time with themselves which appear very slight supporters for such immence Masses of stone. Then as the appertures among these Rocks are not large enough to admit of your walking through you are obliged to creep through them on your hands and knees or slide thro them on your back every moment in danger of meeting with either a Water or Rattlesnake for both of which this place is very remarkable particularly the latter. And the very best part of the Road lies over a parcell of large Round Stones that slide under your feet. Notwithstanding all these dangers such is the beauty of the surrounding prospect and such the pleasing kind of awe which I felt at the time that it never once struck my mind that I was in the least danger until the whole was over and we had got back again to the entrance of the wood.

But to return to my tale. Having scrambled over these Rocks until we got pretty near the fall we found the spray begin to fall like hard rain. Here Mr. Humphry stoped, but Mr. Douglass and myself went on untill we got within about twenty yards of the Falls. Here we were in some doubt wither or no we should strip and go as far as we could under the fall. This we however at lenth rejected as we never found any one pretends to have gone further than under the first small shoot which we thought unworthy the trouble of undressing for. The[r]e are reports of people that have gone under the great shoot but who they were I could not learn altho I have examined several who asserted they had been under the falls of Niagara yet when questioned closely upon the subject it appeared to have been only the small spout they had been under.[18] Yet I by no means mean to assert there is not that kind of cavity betwixt the under part of the Rock and the fall itself that would admit of a man going under for some distance. On the contrary from the Table Rock being so very much undermined near its base, I conceve it to be highly probable the rock over which the Fall rolls is the same, but as the falling of the Spray is so very thick and troublesome as to prevent your seeing and almost to prevent your breathing even where we were, I do not conceive it is possible for a man to exsist under the great shoot itself.

However we did not advance thus far without finding something which had as far as I could find never been spoken of before. Within a few yards of the place we turned round I could perceive a very strong smell of Sulphur, which I remarked to Mr. Douglass & on a further examenation we perceived a small Rill which decended from the rocks above and all the stones over which it passed seemed covered with a whiteesh kind of slime. This induced me to taste the water which I found to be exactly the same as the Waters at Harrow-gate [Harrogate] in Yorkshire.[19] Mr. Douglass also tasted of the same water and directly exclaimed good God it is just like the washings of a Gun Barrell, although he declares he had never heard the Harrowgate water compared to that mixture. Having staid here for some time contemplating the granduer of the object before us our time passed away insensibly until we found by our watches that it was high time we should turn our backs upon the scene from which we had received so much delight.

On our return we employed ourselves in picking up a kind of stone which is said to be the Spray of the Fall Petrified but wither it is or no I will not pretend to determine.[20] This much I can say that it grows or forms itself in cavities in the Clift about half way to the Top from whence it falls from time to time. Its composition is a good deal like a piece of White Marble which has been burned in the fire so that it may be pulverized with ease. Whatever may be its composition it does not appear that it will bear to be exposed to the Air as some peices which seem to haven fallen longer than the Rest are quite soft whilst such as have lately fallen are of a much harder nature. Having again made our way back to the edge of the Wood where we were to reassend we sat down to take some refreshment, very well satisfied to have seen every thing worth our Notice except the Rainbow which very often formes itself in the spray. During the time we were lamenting the loss of this object it made its appearance in a most perfect state across the highest part of the fall which made our sight of this place as compleat as possible. We now began our Assent and after again visiting Painters point in our way we came to the place where we had marked the Trees. We found one or two of the first but had done it so very Ill that we could not trace our way back by them. We therefore struck into the wood and endeavoured to keep the sound of the Falls directly behind us by which means we found our way by a much nearer Rout than the one we had decended, from whence we again soon reached the house we had left our horses at after an absence of Five hours and half from which time we had been employed walking about this place which for one I can say I quitted with regret at last.

The land above the Fall is very good and seems to have fallen into good hands. It is one of the best improved places I have seen in this part and although he has been here only three years I am told he has been already offered one Thousand pounds for it. What is very extraordinary there are several women who live in this house and the next who have never had the curiosity to look at it yet.[21] And what is still more so I am told a Captain of the Tenth Regt. on their way to Detroit and back passed as he must have done within a half a Mile of the fall and would not go out of his way to see it.

It was near Six in the evening before we could get every thing ready to set off on our return, by which means we could not stay to examen the Channell of the River which is most romanticaly beautifull all the way from the falls to the Landing. Amongst the rest I am told there is a very singular wirlpool which is worthy of notice but if we had time to have gone to it we had no guide that knew the way so passing it we arrived at the Landing about seven in the evening where we found Mr. Pidgeon of the 65th who had a most excellent dinner ready to put upon the table when we got there, for having heard the time of our departure from Fort Slosser he well knew we could not return sooner than we did. As soon as we got here our companion Mr. Douglass had ordered the horse which he took from hence on our way to the Falls should be turned loose intending to ride to Niagara on the one he brought from thence which as it happened had also gain'd its liberty the day before. This mistake we did not find out until Dinner was over and we were about to return when on examination of our Cavalry we found one wanting. Thus were we again at a loss how to act. In the meantime it began to get Dark. At lenth it was agreed that Mr. Pidgeon who was a very little man should get into the Chair with the Engineer and myself and Mr. Douglass should Ride his horse. In this manner we again set out and had to find our way through a very bad dirty woody Road with only the light of a very Young Moon just before it set. In the course of our ride we very often got off the Road when we were obliged to wait quietly in the Chair until Mr. D. could find it out for us again. In this manner after a great many very narrow escapes of being overset we again reached Niagara about ten or Eleven oClock at night with no other Injury than a slight Cold and being extreemly fategued with the labour of the day

20th   which had been very great.

It may not be improper here to take notice of an Opinion which is held by some people of this place who seem to think The Original situation of the Fall was at the Landing which as before observed is seven Miles from where they now are and that thro a Series of Years the water has worn away the Channel that distance. Among those who favor this Opinion is a Mr. Hamilton[22] a Merchant at Niagara and a man of very good understanding who says also that he has examened the face of the adjacent country which has confirmed his Opinion, and in particular conceives the place which has before been taken notice of by the Name of the Leons Den to have been made by a Chanel of the River formerly passing thro it. How far this may be true I do not know. I did not he[a]r this Opinion until after I had seen the place at which time no such Idea ever entered my head. The principal Reasons they seem to give for this Opinion are two. First, from the abrupt Rise of the Banks of the River at the Landing which from being of a moderate height and almost every [very?] Accessable from the waters edge they became at once very high and perpendicular Clifts at the same time the River becomes much more Narrow and Rapid than before. The second reason seems to have more reason in it and is that according to thear language the falls have altered their position or retreated since the memory of Men. Having made all the enquiry I could concerning this movement I found that about twenty years since there was a Projecting Rock at the end of the center Island which had fallen and seems to be the only grownd work for this strong contested Opinion.

One thing I must grant that it is possible that in a very long series of Years they may alter a little and for this Reason the Spray Arising from the bottom continualy striking against the Clift wears it away and forms a kind of cavity over which a large Rock projects as the Table Rock already mentioned, which when it becomes so under mined that it is not able to sustain the wheight of Water which overflows it in great floods must naturally fall. How long it may take the Water to excavate its Clift in this manner I cannot determine. All I can say is the place from wence the Rock fell twenty years ago does not yet appear to be the least worn by its influence, nor does any one pretend to remember the table Rock any other than it now is projecting very far over its Base By which I conceive we may fairly conclude it will take many centuries to bring about this revolution which when done only alters one small part of the fall for a yard or two.[23] At [this?] Rate how long it would have taken to have Retreated from the Landing I shall leave to those who pretend from such like causes to ascertain the age of our Terrestial Globe. But even if we should for a moment grant the possibility of their favorite maxim, What is become of the immense quantity of stone which must from time to time have fallen during its movement, this seems to me to be a question none can answer. Certain a great quanty of stone must have been in a Chanell above Seven miles long and from ½ to a whole Mile broad and from Seventy to Eighty feet deep. Had it fallen in such quantity as it is natural to suppose, it is very strange the fall should keep its present perpendicular form. It is by far more Natural to think had this been the case that these immence Rocks remaining where the[y] fell would have altered the fall from a perpendicular to a strong Rapid. But say the Advocates for this opinion the force of the water has driven them away from its food [foot]. This may also be true in a small measure, for where [were] it so the Rocky part of the River would no[t] break of so abrupt just at the same place where the Mountain ends, which is at present the case, for not more than two hundred yards from the End of this Rocky Rapid part which is the spot they say the falls Originaly Occupied.

The River expands itself and becomes deep, Muddy, and Tranquil, which course it continues for about 9 Miles by the Water to the mouth the outside of which is encumbered with a Barr of sand. I also when at the Fall observed another circumstance which seems to be against their having been once so far down the River. Below the present situation of them is a Circle of more than a ½ perhaps a Mile or more in diameter whilst the outlet is not so wide. I conceive this part has been widened by the same means the falls have retired as when you get beyond the influence of the spray the River assumes its natural breadth. Speaking to Mr. Birch who lives at the mouth of the Chipaway Creek he said he had perceived a regular flux and reflux in the creek resembling the tide in the sea. Mr. Hamilton who I have before mentioned says it is not a regular flux & reflux at all but that occasionaly the Current runs up instead of down, and what appears at first more extraordinary is that the Creek has its source to the West and runs to the Eastward yet is it a Westerly or a wind directly down the creek which occasions the current to Run up it to the Westward. This he accounted for in some measure to my satisfaction. It is well known that Lake Erie is to the westward of this place on which a Westerly wind has great powers and driving its waters into this its outlet meets with no resistance until it comes to the falls where not being able to empty itself so fast as it comes from the Lake it causes the waters above the Rapids to Rise. Now this Creek being a dead swampy Creek just above the Rapid some of the Repulsed water forces itself into it and conteracting it[s] own current formes one of the contrary way.[24]

All day the *21st* was taken up by an Indian Council as unentertaining a thing as can well be to any but the Indians who generaly get presents and Liquor enough to make them all drunk. Joseph Brent spoke in this council and as well as I could judge seem[s] to give himself great Airs, speaking in

English which the Cheifs could not understand but as they did not take Offence at it I conceive it was agreed among themselves he should do so.[25] Here I had the pleasure to see old Schyanderacta [Sayenqueraghta] who is the only Crowned head in America I ever heard of he having inherrited a Crown from his Ancestors which was sent by our Queen Ann to them as Kings of the Seneca Nation.[26] He is a sensible old man and has been a very good Warrior in his day but like all the rest is very much adicted to Liquor, for no sooner was the council over than his Majesty was dead drunk rolling in an Outhouse amongst Indians, Squaws, Pigs, Dogs, &c. &c.

The Fort itself is the next thing I shall take notice of. It is situated on the east side of the River or Rather straights which communicate from Lake Erie to Lake Ontario, directly on the point which forms its Mouth By which it is in a triangular form with only one side regularly fortified one end of which joins the Lake the other the River or Rather their respective Banks. This is a very regular earth work with two Bastions & a Ravlin [ravelin] before them whilst those sides next the water are only surrounded with very large high Pickets so placed that every part of it is flanked by Artillery. In each of the Bastions is a square stone Tower with a Block house on the top of it which are divided from the inside of the fort by high strong Pickets. But the most remarkable building by far is what they call the Large house of which I was given the following account. The French thinking this a very proper place for a post [were] yet fearfull the Indians would not like to give them permission to build a fort in the very heart of their country. Having gathered a large Council of the Neighbouring Indians to whom they represented the damage done continualy to their goods for the want of good stone houses, at the end asking permission to build one at the mouth of this River this was agreed to by the Natives provided that it should have but one door. Having gained their point

23. French Castle at Old Fort Niagara. Modern photograph. *Courtesy Old For* *Niagara Association, Inc.*

to work they went and built a very large stone house three stories high capable of containing a whole Regt. with wells and every convenience for a good defence, at the same time keeping their word with the Indians, there being but one door to this day on the grown floor and those which are now at each end on the second story seem to be of a later date.[27] On the Top of the house is a very large Glass Lanthorn which is used as a Light House to prevent Ships running to the Westward of the fort in the Night, in whch they always keep a light whenever they expect ships. As the Fort contains a good deal of ground there are a great many other building[s] within it many of which have very comfortable gardens belonging to them which make good Quarters for the Officers. The Gardens within the Fort are not only sufficient to supply the garison with Cheries, Peaches &c, but also to send a good many to Cataraqui & Carleton Island. Indeed I have known Peaches sent from thence to Quebec. They are surely not worth sending so far being very small and of very little flavor but as there is no such Fruit in Quebec they go down very well and are esteemed a rarity. There is no Public House or shop within the Fort they being all gathered togeather in what is called the Bottom, a flat peice of land between the Fort and the River, and all these holding thear permission only during the pleasure of the Commanding Officer they are able in a great measure to prevent drunkeness among the men.[28]

The Settlements near this place are all on the Opposite side of the River as the side the Fort stands on is by the Late Treaty with the Americans within their Limits, the house of Mr. P. Steadman and one or two small Huts near the landing only except. The Inhabitants are Cheifly composed of Butlers Rangers and their Relations who have come to settle among them.[29] But of late a great many more have offered to come in, and a good many have come at the hazard of being sent back again. Many of these people have left good farms in the States and come here to a very precarious settlement as from what I can find they go on their Lands without any Title from Government and are liable to be turned of them again if it may be hereafter proved they have born Armes or acted against us during the late Warr. Notwithstanding these hard termes

July 22

so much are they Opressed on the American Frontiers that they come to the English Settlements in vast numbers. Such vast progress have these New Settlements made already that they are not only able to supply themselves with corn but to supply govenment also with enough to support the Troops & Indians, which is an immense quantity.[30]

Opposite to Niagara near what is called Navy Hall is a large Barrow or Tumulus with a Pit in the Middle of it not unlike a Cock Pit, which is supposed to be an old Buirying place of the Chipaways but no account of it or of any Battle being fought near it is to be found among the Indian traditions.[31] Yet no one likes to open it least it may give offence to the Indians, however I dare say at some future period they may get leave to open it which may in some measure assertain its purpose. We asked Joseph Brent if there would be any harm in opening it. He thought not but could not answer there would not. The Idea was therefore droped for the present. I am told also that near the Chipaway Creek there are two others of the same kind which are said to contain the Bodies Slain in a very great Battle between the Chipaways and Senecas or some of the Southern tribes. They are at a small distance assunder and on small Eminences which may be well supposed the posts occupied by the adverse partys. It seems very uncertain how long it is since this Battle was fought but by the accounts I recevd it must have been since the introduction of fire Armes among them as there are a number of Balls found on the Adjacent Trees, from which some of the knowing ones pretend to tell you its date which they say is not more than seventy years Back.[32] But I should suppose that if it was no longer ago than that the tradition would be more perfect, as the Indians are in general very exact in those things.

23d   On Monday the Vessle was Reported to be ready but the wind was foul. This was a very mortifing circumstance as it confined me to the place, having promised to return in the vessle I came in and she liable to sail in a half an hour after the wind shifted I could make no more trips into the country, and prevented my taking another Veiw of the Falls which I would surely have done had I known I should have been kept so long by contrary winds. On the 24th we had another Indian Council rellative to the Americans Advancing and settling in the Indian country at the Mouth of the Miamis or Rocky River, which like most others come to nothing altho Brent boasted a good deal and went off to his Village to collect his Warriors. But they never marched a foot from thence. The *25th* was a very wet day but produced no change in the Wind nor was there any until *Monday the 30th* when the wind was fair about Breakfast time. Every thing was accordingly prepared and we went on board but before we could get under weigh the wind shifted and blew fresh in a contrary direction which obliged us to return to the Fort again. On Our return we found the whole Garrison Assembled in the Plains without the Fort and found them entertained with a Race of four Men in sacks in which there was nothing either new or entertaining. This was followed by another amusement which was New at least to me. A space of Forty yards square was measured out and enclosed with Ropes into which Thirteen men were placed twelve of whom were Blindfold. The thirteenth was not but had in his hand a small Bell which he was to keep ringing and endeavouring to elude the twelve others who on their part were to strive to catch him. The Bet was wither or no they would be able to accomplish it within an hour. The Match from the very begining appeard to be unequal, as the exercise of evading so many within so small distance was to much for one man. The man who undertook it was both strong and active and did more than any one could have expected he would after the first five minutes notwithstanding which he was taken in about a half an hour. This sort of Game of [if] rendered more Equal by making the space Larger and circular or by reducing the number of pursuers might afford good amusement but it should by all means be a circular space as they by their numbers have the opportunity of hemming him up in one of the corners in the Square.[33]

31st   The next day a large party went on a visit to Mr. Steadman and very sorry I was that the uncertainty when the vessel would sail deprived me of accompanying them. They staid part of two days yet on their return found me still at the Fort. In the course of thear visit [they?] crossed the River to Mr.

Steadmans farm which has lately [been] settled, where they were shewed a very remarkable spring of Water of which I received the following account from Mr. Edward Pollard a London Merchant who was one of the party. A small distance behind the Farm house is the Spring which has two apertures or Mouths, one of which appears to have been enlarged, the other in its natural state. In the enlarged one the water appeard covered with a white scum and smelt very disagreable, whilst that which was in the smaller one was extreemly clear, however on examination they found the small one to be of the same kind of water as the other and even the strongest of the two. Some of those who tasted it at the Spring said it was sour as vinegar, however it was not so when I got it but as much so as you would make Lemonade. What the cause of its being so is I cannot determine but most people seem to think it strongly impregnated with Vitriol. Another circumstance is that the Farmers say the snow will not lay near its mouth altho some feet deep else where.[34] What is likewise to be remarked is that at a very small distance from this Acid Spring is one of uncommon good fresh water with out having the smalest taste of Acid in it. I thought this so extraordinary that I begged a Bottle of each kind from Mr. P. who was good enough to grant my request.

I think in speaking of Carleton Island I have before observed that the wind is four fiths of the year from the Westward on this Lake yet it so happened that we had been now confined a fortnight for want of that wind a circumstance hardly ever known here.

At last on the *first of August* the wind changed a little in our favor so that could we but once get over the Barr we could make our course tolerably good. The Limnade and Mohawk Sloop were both in this Harbour by the help of whose boats we were towed over the Barr about two in the Afternoon. When out here we found the wind more favorable than we expected it was but still so very light that we went very slow through the water. Our party consisted of A Lady and her Child, Lieut. [George] Oliver of the 65th Regt. and myself.[35] After dinner we found the water very warm and wishing for some cooler the Capt. said he would soon procure that for us. He accordingly left us and making fast a Bottle to a long line lett it Corked down to such a depth as that the wheight of water should press in the cork which done, it was drawn up and proved to be as cold as if just brought from an Ice house. This Liquor was so gratefull to our tastes that we wished to repeat the experiment, but it was too late. A Breeze had sprung up and we were going to fast

2nd   for the Bottle to sink. By Eight next Morng we were opposite what they call the 50 Mile Hill. Here the wind again faild us so that we did not get sight of the Islands until the Morng of *the third*. This day was again extreemly Hot, so much so that we were fearfull the Sun would quite overpower the wind. However we still moved Slowly on and as our passage now lay among Islands and in sight of some of the New Settlements in the Bay of Quenty [Quinte] we found our time pass off more agreable than it had done the preceeding day for the Lady we had on board was a miserable bad sailor. As the Sun went down the Breeze freshened so that we reached Carleton Island by ten at Night.

On our Arrival we had the mortification to hear that a Brigade of Boats had just gone from thence. This was bad news to my Companions but was of small consequence to me, as I had a Whole Boat with a compleat crew left by Major [Archibald] Campbell to wait for me. But I could not accomodate them, as My Boat would not carry one more than the number I had

4th   got in her. It was not until three in the next afternoon that I could get all my business over at which time I embarked with a fair wind but so very little of it that we made use of our Oars. On our Way down this communication after you enter the Narrows about twenty Miles below Carleton Island you have a favorable current the whole way into Lake St. Francis and as I could not reach any dan[g]erous part of the Rapids before daylight, I was resolved to keep on all night, that is to keep two men Rowing whilst the rest slept in the Boat.[36] In this I was disappointed for my men had neglected the directions I had given them early in the morng to cook two days provission. In this state neither of us having eaten anything since Breakfast I was obliged to put on shore at the first place I could find any Indian fires where we might find the means of dressing our meat.

Soon after I got out of the Narrows I saw some fires on the Island called Toniata [Tonianta] to which we immediately went and found two Indians and ther wifes who received us vere civilly and gave us plenty of fish in return for which and the use of their fire and Utensils we gave them some Bread and a Bottle of Rum. Soon after our Arrival one of the Indians and his Squaw went out in their Cannoe to spear Eells as I have before described them to be taken at Cataraqui on the Top of the water. The others remained with us. This young man soon claimed Acquaintance with me from having been one of the party with us at the taking Fort Ann and George in the year 1780. His wife as far as I could see from the light of the fire was pretty and could speak French very well but seemed extreemly shy and would hardly give an answer when spoken with, except with our Guide a very old man with whom she conversed freely, and who afterwards gave me the following history of her. That although she now dressed like a Squaw and by leading that kind of life had contracted a good deal of the manners and appearance of one, he remembered her [as] one of the prettyer Canadian Girls in the parish where he lived not far from the Cateau du Lac on the South side of the river. That she had very young been debautched by a Mons. Beron an Indian Trader of the Village of St. Regis who a very short time after enjoyment quit her for some other Game. Thus thrown on the world at a very early age and fearing to go back again to her parents she determined to live the rest of her life among the Indians and was soon married to the young man we now found her with. They had been married four Years when we saw them and she says her husband always has used her very well and that as he is one of the best hunters in the Village they are in general well supplied with every thing, but could not deny that notwithstanding all their endeavours they had been sometimes in want. She seemed to Lament the precarious method by which they were obliged to seek their food but in all other respects seemed contented with her sittuation in life. Having cooked our Meat we took leave of our Indian friend and his wife about eleven at Night.

Having proceeded about a mile on our turning a Point of land we saw a great number of lights before us, all moving about upon the water which as the night was Dark had a very pretty effect. Our Boat rowed well and curiosity prompting us to see what they were we soon got up to them and found they were all Indian Cannoes fishing, each containing a man & Woman and some of them a Child or two. They were Cheifly Messasagus [Messassagnes][37] whose Torches are very Artless consisting of only a peice of Birch Bark stuck in a Cleft Stick which neither burn so long nor give so good a light as those which I had seen used by the Caughnawaga but for fear by any Accident their light should be put out they have always a kind of Platform in the center of the cannoe in which they have a fire burning. This Indian Regatta if I may be allowed to call it so was so numerous and extended that it was in sight for near two hours the Novelty of which entertained us so much that we did not go to sleep until we lost sight of it when we took to the plan I had before proposed to keep two Oars Rowing whilst the other five slept. In this state we got about an hour or two of rest but I was very glad to see day light, the situation in which I lay being very uneasy.

5th   By day light we had got clear of most of the Islands and about nine were at Point du Barré. About Noon we entered the Rapids at the Gallop [Galop]. Between three & four we passed the Long Sault in all its Beauty. The water this season was extreemly low which occasioned the waves at the foot of the Sault to be higher than common. To this was added a violent Storm of Thunder & Lightening and a strong wind up the River the whole making one of the most picturesque scenes that can be well conceived and added very much to the terific granduer of the place. About Six in the evening we reached Johnston when I would willingly have gone down to the point of the Lake but a very Black Cloud at that time appearing and the Men of my party extreemly fatigued for want of rest the night before, I was now afraid to encounter such a gust of contrary wind so put up for the night altho it is a very inconvenient place owing to the public house being so far from the

6th   water. The inconvenience of this we found next day as we were so long loading our Boat that we lost near two hours of daylight. And the wind in Lake St. Francis being rather against us it was one oClock before we passed the coteau du Lac. This is a Rapid I never was down before as in 85 we had slept at this place and put our Boats through the Locks. It is one of the swiftest of all the Rapids and as you Approach the upper end of Prison Island you seem to stand so directly towards it that your Boat must run on shore but here as in the Long Sault you find an Eddy or rather division of the current just before you reach the Island which guides you to the one side. The Chanell lies close to the North shore of Prison Island which you have no sooner passed than you Row across the foot of the Rapid towards the Cedars. Having determined to go down all the Rapids in the Boat I took in another Pilot a little above the Church at the Cedars, who took us down very well altho we struck rather hard on a flat Rock just at the last pitch of the cascades but it did us no harm. We came down both the falls at Le Buisson and La Sault du Trou without taking in a drop of water. Having put our pilot on shore at the foot of the Cascades we went as far as La Chene that night but it was very dark before we got there. It was impossible to think of going further until daylight. I however sent and procured a Pilot named La Pensè [Pensée?] who is accustomed to take the Merchants Cannoes down

7th   the next Rapid who was with me by five next morng. The Rapids between La Chene & Montreal or as they are called La Sault de St. Louis is by no means so tremenduous as most of the others but is full as dangerous as any of them, being so very shallow and the Chanell so extreemly Crooked, for which reason the ordinary Pilots of the River although they will bring you down all the other falls seldom attempt this, but as there are plenty of Men in La Chene who know it you can never be at a loss for a guide.

Having passed all the Rapids I got to Montreal to Breakfast where I learnt the 5th and 26th Regt. were Arrived at Quebec and that His Royal Highness Prince William Henry [William IV] was dayly expected. This inteligence togeather with my being charged with dispatches for General Hope made me wish to hasten to Quebec by the most expeditious Rout, which on consulting my friends I found would be to take the regular post leaving my Boat to come after me, which plan I accordingly adopted and having done

8th   all my business left Montreal at 5 in the evening. This Night I slept about two hours at Dautray and the next about the same time at St. Anns and reached Quebec about four in the afternoon of the *Ninth* and gave the papers with which I was charged to General Hope without any accident worth relating on the road unless that the heat was intence the whole way.

On my Arrival I found the 29th: 31st: & 34: Regts. on garrison at Quebec whilst the 5th & 26th Regiments occupied the Villages in its Neighbourhood. In the Bason before the Town were the following Men of War, The Leander of 50 Guns, Comodore [Herbert] Sawyer, the Resourse [*Resource*], Capt. [Paul] Minchin, and the Ariadne 20 which with a great many Transports and Merchant ships made a very beautiful sight.[38] I now found that I had taken the shortest way by coming from Montreal by land as my Boat was three days after me, owing to some Wind on Lake St. Peter. Nothing happened worth notice until the *13th* when we received an account

14th   that the Prince was in the River, and early the next Morning his Royal Highness Arrived in the Pegasus of 28 Guns accompanied by the Thisbe, Captain [Isaac] Coffin. I presume it took all this day to fix the ettiquette of his Landing for he did not come on shore until the *15th,* when he came on shore not as a Captain in the Navy but as a Prince of the Blood, when as near as I could observe the following form was observed. About half past ten AM he left the Pegasus and went on board the Leander, when the Royal standard was hauled at the fore top Gallant Mast head, the yards manned and a salute fired. A little after Eleven he left the Leander in his own Boat which had the Royal Standard flying in the Bow. He was followed by the Comodore with his Broad pendant [pennant?] in the same manner, after which came the different captains in their respective Boats with pendants hoisted in the same manner. In this Order he visited every Ship in the fleet & received a salute from each of them, after which he rowed on shore where he was received at the waters edge by the governor & Council, all the principal Clergy & four Officers who had been previously appointed to attend him whilst he s[t]aid on shore and who were called Aid de Camps but never wore any other uniform than that of their respective Regmts. They were Colonel

[Thomas?] Davis of the Artillery, Captain [Adam] Hay 31st, Captain Dickson [Hugh Dixon] 29th & Captain [William] Kemble of the 34th Regiments. The instant he landed a salute was fired from the grand Battery, and the Troops in Garrison being previously drawn out formed a Lane thro which he passed from the water side to the grand Parade where the 31st & 34th Regiments with some Guns were drawn up. Whilst he passed the Parade the Guns fired another salute and on his entering the Castle Gates he was received by the Flank companies of the 29th Regiment as a personal guard & on his entering the Castle a third salute was fired from the Battery on Cape Diamond. He was now conducted to the council chamber where all the principal Officers & all the council, Clergy & many of the first inhabitants were presented to him & where he likewise received an adress from the council.

In the afternoon he dined with Lord Dorchester [Guy Carleton] the Governer, where were assembled many of the principal people in town. At Seven in the evening The Troops and the Militia again Paraded forming a circle round most part of the town. At a little past Eight the Grand Battery fired a Salute, when the Troops on the left of it took up the fire after the manner of a feu de joie until it came to the next Battery, when another salute was fired, when the Troops on its left took up the fire in the same manner until it had passed three times round the Garrison.[39] When it ceased The Troops were dismissed and the whole town Illuminated. I cannot say there were many Transparencys but among the rest were the following ones. Over The Cheateau Gate was a very large & good Star of the order of the Garter with the Letters PWH. At the house of Mr. Alsop was a Design of a Crown & two Anchors with the Motto of Regio Gloria Nautico.[40] There were some others particularly at the Recolet Convent, but it was so high and so complicate that I could not find out what it was intended for. Unfortunately the day proved very wett so that all the troops were wet thro twice but that did not prevent many Ladies particularly french ones from parading the streets to see the show until it was quite over. The Prince returned on board at ten oClock at Night I beleive without any form.

16th   The next day he came on shore but not in form. In the evening he walked in the Thuleries [Tuileries] with the officers of the navy and such of the Garrison as he was acquainted with. On the *17th* Lord Dorchester when [went?] on board to pay his Royal Highness a visit where they had a Breakfast & Cold collation. He saluted Lord Dorchester both on his going on board [and] on return. At half past two the Prince again landed and was received by a Guard and the four Officers who attended him. In the evening a great many Ladies were presented to him after which they went into the Thuleries Garden where they Danced, carpets being spread on the gravel walks for that purpose.[41] During the dance the party were served with coffe, Tea, cakes, sweet meats &c. &c. The company were numerous and I may say by far the smartest I ever saw in this Province. Indeed the display was such as would not be found fault with in a more Pollished part of the world. From hence to the *21st* we had no form for altho the Prince was generaly on shore every day it was only in a private Character But as that day was the Prince's Birth day the same was observed with every testimony of Joy throughout the town.[42] Between Ten & Eleven he came on shore and had a Guard &c. appointed. By Noon The Troops were all Drawn up on the grand Parade when a Salute was begon by the Leander and on her firing her second Gun taken up by all the rest of the fleet together, which I am told by those who saw it had a very good effect. When that was over the Grand Battery fired a salute and after that the troop Three Volleys, which over, there was a Grand Levy at the Chateau where he received addresses from the Clergy, the English & French Merchants &c. &c.[43] This day he dined at Comodore Sawyers with many of the principal Officers. At Night there was a very Grand Supper & Ball at the Chateau where all the principal people civil & Military were invited. No Ladies were asked but such as had been presented on the former day. The Officers were also cercumscribed, owing to their number, to the Public departments, commanding offcers of Corps & an Captain & one Lieut. per Regiment. The whole was conducted by Coll. [George?] Beckwith Aid de Camp to Lord Dorchester and went of extreemly well. The company consisted of more than 150 persons. There were some fire works prepared for the occasion but the Night proved so very wet they were obliged to omitt them. At Night the whole Town was again Iluminated in the same manner as before.

From this time until the *29th* was taken up in preparing for a grand Review of all the Troops in this part of the Province but the Prince was on shore almost every day. The *29th* proved a very fine day and the Revew went of extreemly well for an account of which see the proposals.[44] The Troops were all collected in time most of whom were under Armes from five in the Morning until Noon when it was over, when all the Officers & most of the Principal inhabitants partook of a very elegant public Breakfast given by Lord Dorchester at the Cheateau upon the occasion.[45] For several days after this nothing particular happened except that his Royal Highness dined with the several corps in Garrison in their turn, also with Lord Dorchester, Admirl Sawyer, Coll. [Alexander?] Dundas &c. &c. Lord Dorchester set out for

Sept. 3d   Montreal and on the *4th* the Prince attended by the General Hope & his Aid de Camps went to see Indian Larrette [Lorette] where there is a Tribe of the Huron Indians settled and returned by way of the falls of Montmorency where they dined. They were received by the Indians with all the pomp and ceremony in there power, firing, Dancing &c. &c. In the latter from what I heard they rather departed from their original character as I am told they danced double Minuets & cotillons, but it must be said in their favor that they are so much connected with the Canadians that they are now almost Frenchmen.[46]

On the *sixth* in the Morning his Royal Highness accompanied by Coll. Dundas set out for Montreal and left us a little more at our ease. On the *Eight* myself and four other Officers of the Regiment went to see the Falls of Cheadeere [Chaudière].[47] On our Arrival at the Water side we found we were too early for the Tide, which runs extreemly strong particularly down, the common Rise of the River being from 16: to 18 Feet perpendicular and considerably narrower in this part than it is either above or below the town. We however embarked and went a small distance but finding we made very little way we stopped at the wharf of a Mr. [John] Fraser, commonly known by the appellation of Bon Homme Fraser, who is one of the principal Merchants in the province and is now employed in carrying on very large Warfs and works which when compleat will be a very considerable improvement to the town.[48] But what attracted our particular attention was an Esquimaux Canoe lately brought from the coast of Labradore. To any stranger who considered only the distance betwixt Labradore & Quebec it will seem strange that one of their Canoes should be a curiosity but I was assured this was only the third of the kind ever seen in Quebec. It is most certainly a most extraordinary Boat. Many have been seen in England but the form in the Margin is nearly correct. It is about 22 feet in length and as many Inches in breadth and not more than Ten Inches deep. The Bottom of it is perfectly flat until it becomes so narrow to be of no use, when it is rounded off a little. Its Deck is perfectly Level so that it has a small Rake upwards both at head and stern. It is formed of Ribs of very tough wood covered with seals skin, which encloses the whole Deck & all except a small hole just large enough for a man to thrust his Legs down who works the Canoe. This hole lies rather obliquily across the canoe as in Figure A. This hole is strengthend by a good strong wooden hoop and rises about three Inches above the Deck which serves to keep out the water. But I am told in bad weather they sew a skin all round this hoop which the[y] fasten up under their Arms so that no water can possibly enter altho a wave may break over them. I am also told that however small these things may seem even to carry one person they often carry their Squaws with them the manner of doing which is rather singular. The man being once seated in the Canoe [t]he Squaw Seats herself behind him with her back to his and ties her ancles to the two loops placed for that purpose (B) in which situation she holds fast by the Man. We were so fortunate as to find the man who had brought it up & who had resided for some years among the Esquimeaux. He got into it and paddled it about both up and down the stream with incredible velocity. Up the stream one of the Man of War Boats had no chance with it, down they were nearly equal. It is wrought with a double Paddle like those used about Oxford. This man did not seem to agree in the common storey of the Indians going a long way out to sea in them but says the[y] are only intended for seal fishing and any expedition that does not lead them far from the shore, But that when they go to any great distance or after Whales &c. it is in larger ones which are made in the same Manner & materials but large & in the shape of a Boat and worked with single Paddles in the manner of common cannoes. He also says it is quite a mistaken Idea that these Indians are more ferocios than any other which notion he thinks originated from the improper manner formerly used by by [*sic*] the Traders who went into their country who never traded with them but at the point of the halbert which suspicious mode [of?] dealing often occasioned allarms that proved in turn fatal to both parties but that now a more frendly intercourse had been used for some time and it was hoped they also will lay asside their fears.[49]

Having still time to spare we went to see a large Biscuit Bakery in which the men seemed very expert. At length we again embarked But the tide not yet being in our favor we Rowed up the shore passing in our way the place of General Wolfs [Wolfe's] Landing now called Wolfs [Wolfe's] Cove. This place is in general supposed by people in England to be a place of difficult access which is however by no means the case as the Landing although but small is very good and the Road to the plains of Abraham winding up a Ravine betwixt two hills is of an easy Assent. This Mistake I conceive takes its rise from an accident of the Light Infantry who when they attempted to gain this cove were driven down by the tide a little nearer Quebec among some very steep rugged rocks up which they Assended with great difficulty, which cercumstance is however said to have been in a great measure the reason the English Troops gain'd the heights so easy as they did, for when they had gained the plains they found themselves in the rear of the post intended for the defence to the passage from Wolfs cove. It was nearly dark & the french taking them for a reinforcement coming to them were off thear guard and suffered them to come so near that they took the post with very little loss, and by that means the body of the Army had nothing to impede their March from the cove.[50]

Not far from hence up the River we passed Sillery the so much extolled ressidence of Mrs. Brooke in ther [her?] Emly Montague. In vain did I look for these beauties which induc almost every reader to envy her or wish themselves for a moment at Quebec. Not one of thes charming beauties could I find but in there place was an old shabby canadian farm house situated in a hollow with hardly any trees about it, and its v[i]ew perfectly confined to the River which is in its front and the opposite Banks which are very high and woody.[51] These would in England be called fine, But near Quebec are by no means equal to many things in its neighbourhood.

The tide now began to favor us and getting out into the Stream we soon reached the Mouth of the River Chaudier which is on the opposite or south side of the River St. Lawrence. Having entered the mouth of the River we disembarked and leaving a party of men with our Boat we followed a small path up the Hill which in about a Mile brought us to a house from whence we took a canadian Guide to shew us the way to the falls which are about three Miles from his house. The road is very bad the whole way but it is possible to go in a Cart or Calash for about two Miles of the distance after which every one must walk. This renders it very disagreable and difficult for Ladies. There are however many who get over them all. The Road or path led us directly to the top of the fall from whence we decended a little to a small point which projected in front of the falls and gives you a very fine View of them. The season of the Year was too far advanced and too dry to see them in full perfection, as our Guide informed us that in the Spring or after heavy rains a large Rock over which we passed was covered with water, which must make it full as large again as it now is. But to proceed. The Fall as we saw it is about 200 Yards wide and about Sixty feet high. It is a very different kind of Fall from those of Niagara or Montmorency as those are quite perpendicular Falls, This being far more variegated altho very small in comparrison with them. It is most beautyfuly broken in its course by many large Rocks. Over some of them it pours forming beautyfull cascades, forces its passage thro others like a very strong Mill race. In this manner it desends until it meets a very large Rock on the east side of the River which breaks

24. Fall of the Grande Chaudière, on the Outauais River. Aquatint engraving
by Frederick Christian Lewis (1779–1856) after a drawing by George Heriot, in
Heriot, *Travels through the Canadas* (London, 1807). *Courtesy of the Public Archives
of Canada*

the fall entirely after which the whole stream unites and falls in a perpendicular body to the bottom which is a considerable height. A little to the westward rather upon the flank of this Fall is another channel of the same River which comes in an immense torrent pouring over a large Rock in the form of a cascade. This Fall or rather two falls unite below in a semicercular Bason, and on the whole altho it is not so high as Montomorency has more variety and has a more pleasing effect, and if I can form any Idea of it when full in the spring of the Year and pouring over the high Rock before mentioned I should conceive it deserved to be ranked among the first falls in the World, and seems only infereor to Niagara by not bieng so large. It is nevertheless very large and has the same kind of Column of Spray which is found at Niagara which rises above its own surface, & of course in the right time of the day would shew the Rainbow the same as that fall does, but the day was very cloudy that we could see no such thing. Having satisfied our curiosity we returned to our boat during which time it began to rain so that we were both wet and dirty before we reached it. This induced us to cross the river to a house we saw on the opposite bank. On our arrival we found it was empty but we soon gathered wood enough to make a good fire and having dried ourselves we dined very heartyly on the cold meat we had brought, and the evening clearing up a little we reached Quebec about sun set.

On the *19* The Prince returned from his excursion to Montreal and on the *24th* he went to see two young Ladies take the White Veil at the General Hospital. As this was a sight which exited every bodys curiosity it was necessary to go very early to get a good place, in which I was fortunate enough to succeed very well.[52] On the Rails of the communion were placed two long wax Candles adorned with flowers near to which the two Young Ladies took their seats without the rail. The cerrimony commenced by a solemn Mass after which the Young Ladies received the sacrament by the hands of the Grand Vicar who officiated upon the Occasion assisted by two other Priests whose dresses were all very magnificent who after adminastring the Sacrament retired and a third Priest dressed in a Common white Surplice assended the Pulpit began a long Oration in which after paying a great number of Compliments to Prince William he complimented the Ladies upon thear peculear happiness in having the honor to make their Vows in presence of such a destinguished Personage.[53] Then after entering into a long explanation of the Nature of the Vows they were about to make, commending them for their Virtue and the choise they were about to make, at the same time hoping that thear good example might prevail on many others to do the same. Then pointing out the instability and Vanity of a Wordly life, he drew a very flattering prospect of a Religeous one, as the only one Worthy of our attention and Choise. This over the Young Ladies each taking the Candle wcth stood before them went into the Convent by a small Wicket in the Grating within the Communion Railing which seperated the Private Chapel of the Convent from the Public Church and in which the Nuns of the Convent were assembled. The Prince and his Suite now were admitted behind into this Chapel behind the Grate, and seated himself on an elevated seat placed for that purpose. The rest of the Audience were now permitted to pass the Communion Rail and assemble round the Grate opposite to the entrance of which the three Priests again seated themselves. Very soon after, the Nuns began a Procession by advancing two & two with each a Candle in their hands up close to the Wicket door where the Priests were seated to whom they made a most Profound Bow then turning towards the Prince did the same to him. The two Young Ladies came in last and instead of making their Bow and filing off to the side of the Chapel as all the rest did the[y] made their Courtesy and Kneeld down facing the Preists at a short distance from the Grate. Very soon one of them arose and going up to the Grate kneeld down close to the Wicket. The Grand Vicar then Asked her what she had to demand? She replied she was desirous of being admitted into the Religeous Sisterhood of that Convent. He then Asked her if she could forego the World, and all its enjoyments to take upon herself a life full of Fasting and pennance? To which she replied in the affirmative. He then told her request was granted, when she returned and kneeled down in the place from whence she had come and the second came up to the Grate and went through the same ceremony. When this was over they Arose, Courteseyed to the Grand Vicar and then to the Prince and retired. During all this time they were dressed in their usual dress. After they had retired some Prayers were said in Latin and the Nuns continued to sing for some time during which a Table was brought in and placed near the Wicket on which was placed part of the Dress of their Order among which were their Veils, the whole of which was consecrated and sprinkled with Holy water. The Young Ladies now again entered still holding the Ornamented Candles but every part of their dress was changed for that of the Sisterhood except such parts as were on the before mentioned Table, still having common Veils over their heads. They now once more came up to the Wicket but I did not hear any words pass before they again retired to the Table where the remainder of their dress was put on (by one who I conceive to have been the Superior) exept the Veil. They now again advanced to the Wicket followed by the Superior with their Veils where Kneeling down their Veils were put on by the Grand Vicar assisted by the Superior. This done they retired from the Wicket leaving their Candles behind them & going into the Middle of the Chapel they stood there whilst the[y] Sang several Verses of an Hymn or Pslam which was Answerd by all the Nuns in full choir, after which they again came forward to the Wicket and were sprinkled with Holy Water, and appeard to receive benediction from the Grand Vicar which completed the Ceremony as they now on return made their Bow like the other Nuns. They then went to the Superior and appeard to receive her benediction to whom they also Bowed. They appeared to be about 17 or 18 Years of Age and neither remarkable for their Beauty or the opposite extreeme. But I thought they looked better in their Nuns dress than in all their finery.[54]

In the evening the Officers of the Garrison performed Lethe and the Padlock &c. &c. for his Royal Highness's Amusement the Profits of which were given to a Party of distressed Players who came in town and whose Scenes and Dresses were used upon the Occasion.[55] On the morning of the

25th I went to see a Review of the 26th Regiment with which everyone was very much pleased as they were realy a very fine steady Corps. On the *29th* Lord Dorchester gave the Prince another Ball at the Chateau but like the former it was too ceremoneous to be agreable. On the *4th of October* his Royal Highness came on shore in state to take leave being the last time he meant to lånd in his Princly Character, On which Occasion he had a Guard of honer and a grand Dinner prepared for him at the Chateau which over, there was a Drawing Room attended by almost every one who had been introduced to the Prince, from whence we adjourned to a Gallery on the House to see a display of fireworks, which being uncommon in this Country were much admired though for my own Part I did not think them worth the pain we sufferd from the Cold during their exhibition. On our return into the House there was a dance which was only called a hop but it was as formal as the Balls had been which proceeded it. At Midnight we were shewn up into a kind of Garret where there was a very excellent Supper, to which as usual the French Ladies did very great Justice. After Supper they again danced for a short time but the whole was over by two oClock in the morning. On the *5th,* the 29th and 34th Regiments embarked and on the *6th,* the 31st and Artillery did the same, the 29th being on board of the General Elliot & Jane Transports. They however remained at Anchor off the Town until the

8th   [time?] when all the Transports droped down to St. Patricks Hole except the General Elliot which Joined them on the following morning when the whole sailed for England.

During the stay of the fleet at Quebec a poor Midshipman or rather a Masters Mate had been tried by a Court Martial and found Guilty of Mutiny for which he was condemned to die, and this was the day appointed for his execution, as a Signal for which a Yellow Flag was hoisted on board the Resourse Frigate to which he belonged. This Poor mans fate seemed to intrest the whole town as he was said to have been a very worthy good Character and on this occasion happened to be in Liquor when he committed the fault. When every thing was ready he was brought up to the Cat Head where he was informed that he was Pardoned when immediately the Yellow Flag was hauled down to the General Joy and satisfaction of every one present.

On the morning of the *9th* hearing that two Nuns were to take the Black Veil, I went as early as I could to the Hotel Dieu to enquire whether it was so or not and it was realy so and by which means I again got a very good Situation to see the cerremony.[56] You may suppose it resembled very much that of taking the White Veil, but at any rate I shall relate the cercumstances as well as I can remember them. This Cerremony like the former began With a Solemn High Mass in which the Young Nuns were seated behind a kind of temporary Alter within the Chapel & fronting to the Grate. Byside each of them was an Ornamented Candle, ("which however were not adorned with flowers &c. like those used in taking the white veil, but only a plain Crimson Ribon rolled round each of them"). On this alter were Books, Pens, Ink & paper. By the side of them on a small Table lay the Black Veils of the Order, and behind them on the Floor lay a large Black Pall. When the Mass was finished they advanced to the grate and received the Sacrament from the Preists who had officiated therein, when they retired and formed with the other Nuns round the Chapel. It was not very long before Bishop or rather the Coajuter dressed as Bishop came in to the outer Chapel and seated himself opposite to the Grate, where one of the Preists having previously kneeled down before him and Received his Benediction assended the Pulpit and Preached what appeard to me a discourse very proper upon the Occasion, That is he endeavoured to prove the superior merret of these Young Ladies scluding themselves from all intercourse with Mankind, Highly commended their resolution in prefering a Religeous life to all others, And defied the whole World to say they could find the same pleasures in the Sensual World that are to be found in the Retirement of a Convent. He then observed that these Young Ladies who had at first been drawn within these sacred Walls by a love of Religeon alone, were now from a Special call from the Almighty about to renounce the World altogether and become a part of the Holy Sisterhood, Proving from Texts in the Holy Scripture that as this World is nothing more than a probationary prelude to that which is to come there could be no doubt but that a Religeous life was the only true & proper preparation for the future state. Then after having inveighed bitterly Against Ambition, Avarice, Vanity and all the Sensual pleasures of this World, after which he drew a comparrison between the two in which you may be sure he did not fail to make the Balance very much in favor of a Conventual Life. Having finished he left the Pulpit and placed himself with the Coajuter opposite to the Wicket in the Grate when as on the former Occasion the Rail of the Communion Table was thrown open and the Audience admitted round him. One of the Young Nuns now advanced to the Wicket with her White Veil on, And on being asked by the Coajuter what she Wished? replied to be admitted into the Sisterhood and remain within the Walls of that Convent. He then asked her Whether she understood all the Rules, Regulations and duties of such a life and was still desirous of taking upon herself the hardships and duties which such a life imposed upon her? She replied by the Grace of God she was. He then informed her request was granted upon which she left her Ornamented Candle by the side of the Wicket and retired behind the tempory alter before mentioned, when the second Young Nun came forward and went though exactly the same cerremony. They now each in her turn took a paper from under the Book which was on the Table, when reading it aloud it proved to be written Copy of the Vow which they then made, From henceforth to consecrate the remainder of their lives to the Service of God, in Poverty, Chastity and perpetual confinement together with a faithfull attention and care of such Sick persons as might be brought to the Hospital according to the Rules & regulations of their Order. Havin[g] each Read the paper and signed it the[y] delivered it to the Superior of the Convent who was seated on one side of the Chapel. Whilst this was doing two other Nuns brought the Table on which the Black Veils lay forward to the Wicket where the Coajuter after having said some Prayers over them and sprinkled them with Holy Water they were replaced in their former Situation. The Young Nuns now advancing to the Grate their White Veils were taken from them and the Black ones put on by the Superior assisted by the Coajuter, as in the taking of the White Veil when they retired and sung some Hymns or Psalms after which they once more advanced to the Wicket and were again Sprinkled with Holy Water by the Coajuter. The Temporary alter was now removed and the two Young Nuns placed themselves in the Middle of the Chapel just in front of the Black Pall where they sang several very Solemn Hymns Accompanied by the Whole Choir of the Sisterhood, during which time they Bowed themselves so low that their heads very near touched the Floor, at last having Bowed as usual instead of rising again as before the[y] fell prostrate on the Floor of the Chapel, at the same instant four of the Sisterhood taking up the Black Pall which was behind them spread it completely over them Both. A great many Prayers were now said and the Whole Community Sung or rather Chaunted what I was told was a Solemn invocation to all the Saints in the Calender after which the Black Pall was removed and Nuns Arose from the Ground and standing in the Middle of the Chapel again Sang a Hymn or two after which they each in turn advanced to the Wicket where they received the Coajuters Benediction then retiring appeared to receive the same from the Superior and from each of the Sisterhood in succession which finished the Cerremony. Thus were immured two Young Ladies of about 17 or 18 Years of Age one of which appeared to be very handsome and the other far from plain.

On my return to Town I heard a great deal of firing and could not think what it could mean until I was told Lord Dorchester had been on board the Fleet in form to take leave of the Prince and the Admial who were to sail early next morning. Having before said that the 29th Regiment had sailed it may appear strange that I should remain at Quebec But this was Occasioned by my having obtained leave to return to England by way of New York which I wished to do that I might see something of the American States before I returned to Europe And herein I was so furtunate as to meet at Quebec Doctor [George Muirson] Muireson of New York,[57] who was going to return immediately as we had each of us Business to transact at Montreal.

We agreed to meet at that place and set out from thence, And as I had now nothing more to keep me at this place I set out for Montreal that very evening and slept at Point aux Tremble which is about Seven Leagues on my way.[58]

Next day the *10th* I set out early and after a very agreeable drive considering the kind of Carriages I got in good time to three Rivers. Having now a good house over my head and a prospect of getting something to Eat for my Supper I put up for the Night being very certain that if I went further I should be worse lodged and get nothing I could eat. It is remarkable that notwithstanding the advanced state of the season and the hard frosts which we already had felt I saw them making Hay on two different farms during this days Journey. I again set out early in the Morng in hopes to reac[h] Montreal before Night but was disappointed and obliged to lie at a place of the same name as that where I had slept two days before [Pointe aux Trembles]. I afterwards found it was fortunate I did not attempt to go into town that night for having Promised to go to a Merchants house on coming to town I should certainly have gone there wher at that time was one of the Partners at Point of Death; he did not survive my arrival long as he died the next Night. On the *12th* in the evening the Gentleman Doctor Muireson who was to accompany me to New York arrived by whom I found the fleet had saild as they proposed on the *10th* in the Morng.[59] Being now both in town we began to prepare for our journey but I had the Mortification to find his business was likely to detain him longer than he first thought it would. However as I was aquainted with all the town my time passed agreeable enough. On the *15th* we had a heavy fall of Snow so that a great deal of it lay on the grownd the whole of the next day.

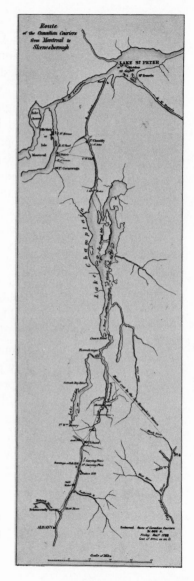

Map IX. Route of the Canadian Couriers from Montreal to Skenes-borough. Copied October 1908 by J. H. Brigly for the British Museum from a map by Finlay, New York, 1788. *Courtesy of the Public Archives of Canada*

VISIT TO THE UNITED STATES

IT WAS NOT UNTIL the *25th of October* that Mr. Muirsom was ready to proceed on the journey when we began to prepare for it by procuring from Coll. [Richard] St. George an order for a Collash and Cart at Laprarie which I sent over by a Butcher of that place engaging the same man to come to town again on the morng of the *27th* with a light Batteau to take us to the above place. However when the day came he disappointed us and having waited until two in the afternoon I engaged a canoe to take us to Laprarie [Laprairie], at which place we Arrived just before Dark. Next day we set out for St. Johns and the Road being very good we got there in about 3 hours and ½ where the first thing we did was to enquire for a conveyance across the Lake, and were very happy to find a very fine Marthas Vanyard [Vineyard] Pilot Boat which had just Arrived from Ticonderoga, to which place one of the men agreed to take us at the Rate of two Dollars each, promising at the same time to set off next day by Noon. This done we went to the fort to pay our Respects to Major Murray [Philip Maurage] of the 60th who commanded

28th

171

the Garrison at whose house we found Miss Delisle [de Lisle] and Miss Jordan of Montreal, and a Miss [Maria?] Livingston who they had accompanied thus far on her Road to Albany. We all dined togeather at the Mess and at Tea were joined by a young french Lady named Fortier.[1] In the evening notwithstanding it was sunday some of our party insisted on Dancing. The Music was accordingly called for and a Dance or two Danced by the whole party (the Gentlemen standing up with each other) Except Miss Delisle who expecting her father the Revd. Mr. Delisle would not join us, And fortunate it was She did not as in the middle of our Mirth who should come in but the Parson which of course stopped our dance for that Eveng.

29   The next day the wind blew so hard down the lake we could not move, so we again repeated our diversions at the fort being joind by Captain [Marcus?] Pictet of the same Regt who commanded at the Isle aux Noix. Our party being to sepperate next Morning he requested my companion and I would accompany him to his post in his Boat which being better manned than ours I readly accepted directing the men who was [to] take us across 30th the Lake to call for us at that place. Next day when we came to embark I was surprised to find that Miss Livingstone was also to be of our party. This was an addition to our party we did not wish for as it was sure to divide our party when we came to the Island Capt. Pictet having a Girl living with him at that place to whom we could not introduce our companion. Wether or no 31 Miss L. found out this or no I cannot say but the next day she set of early in the Morning with two Gentlemen who came with her to a farm about three Miles further up the Lake kept by one Barron who also kept a Public house and where she could be infinitely better entertained than where we were the woman of the house being a very Decent Genteel Woman. This left us more at our ease Yet I could not conceive what kept our Boat which we expected every hour. On the *first of Novr* the Schooner in which Miss Livingstone was to cross the Lake passed from whom we learnt that our boat was just behind. This inteligence however afterwards proved to be false and I rather think was only intended to prevent our wishing to go on board with them.

2*d*   The Next Morng the Snow was three Inches Deep on the ground, and being quite tired of waiting for our boat we procured a Canoe from Capt. Pictet in whch Mr. M. set out to find the Reason of our disappointment, he had not however gone above four Miles before he met the boat and returned in her. It was now to late in the day to think of getting further than Barrons that Night and the wind being contrary we feared we should fall in with the party who were in the Schooner, and by that means not be able to get Beds for us all. We therefore accepted of the civil offers we receved to stay where

3*d*   we were until the next day when about ½ past seven in the Morng we embarked and found our party to consist of the following persons (Viz.) one Coll. [Stephen] Pearl from the state of Vermont to whom we afterwards found the boat belonged, a Mr. Roe [Jack Rowe] a young Lawyer from Boston whose father lived in Quebec, One Potang [Mathew Potan] a french man who said he was an officer in the American Army during the War, one Stewart who was the man that engaged to take us to Ticonderoga and some others whose names I do not know.[2] The wind being against us we Rowed as far as Barrons farm where we stopped to breakfast and were entertaind with very excelent Tea and sausages. The owner of the house was an old aquaintance of mine having been a Sergeant in the 29th Regt many Years. His house is extreemly neat and clean and is by far the best Public house on the whole Communication between Albany and Montreal.

After we had done we again Set out but by the time we had gone about Eight Miles we found the wind so hard against us that we were obliged to give it up and Stopped at a house about two hundred Yards from the Line of 45th which in this place is the boundary between the English and American Settlements, the English however keep posts beyond it at present. At this house we were soon after joined by Mr. Rogers of the Artillery who was on his way to visit the post of Point aux fer but like us prevented by the Wind. About two hundred yards North of this house are two Stones Erected in a direct line at a little distance from each other and an Avenue cut thro the Woods into Misessquai [Missisquoi] Bay to point out the direction of the

Boundary Line. The Stone next the Lake is incribed as Per Margin.[3] The Wind rather increased as the Sun went down which obliged us to stay the

4th Night And next day the wind being still contrary Mr. Rogers return'd to Isle aux Noix, and we were obliged to wait all day in our present situation tho a very disagreeable one. In the evening we were joined by Mr. Cockran [Alexander F. Cochrane] Brother to Lord Dundonald who was just arrived from

5th England who passed the evening with us. Next day as soon as it was light we set out he for Quebec and our party for New York. The weather being moderate we got on tolerably well and having called on board the Maria[4] and seen Capt. Barnsfair we continued our Rout as far as Point au Roche [Rock] where General Hazzen [Moses Hazen] is settled in a dismall poor house in a very bad situation. It is however much the same to him as he is so Ill they are now obliged to left [lift] him on and of his horse. This Gentleman was formerly an Officer in the British Army and on leaving it settled in Canada near St. Johns but on the commencement of the late disputes, took part with the Americans and after the Peace settled at this wretched place.

When we came here we found the Boat we were in belonged to Coll. Pearl who told us he was obliged to call at two or three places in the State of Vermont that might detain us a day or perhaps two, that if we chose to go with him he would be very glad of our company, but if we did not chuse [to] do that there was a boat at this place belonging to Stewart the man who had engaged to take us across the Lakes, in which we could proceed directly to Ticenderoga. The Change of Boats was dreadfull the one we had come thus far in being an elegant fine Boat the one belonging to Stewart a heavy crazzy old thing fit only to carry Dung in. The Wind about this time changed a little in our favor and seemed to promise us a speedy passage. This induced us to take the old Boat and proceed directly on our Rout. The wind was fair and we made a good run of it up to Cumberland head, where it was agreed we should run over to the grand Isle as the Safest passage and go on all Night No one having any Idea but our Boat man knew the Lake well enough to perform his proposal. However when we got over on the east side it was extreemly dark and the Night seemed to threaten bad weather. Mr. Stewart then began to shew his Ignorance of the Lake saying there were he was told Rocks in our course but for his part he did not know where they were and I tho well aquainted with the West side of the Lake could not inform him tho I had every Reason to think his information true. For these reasons it was agreed we should Sleep upon Grand Isle and accordingly made towards a light we saw up in a small Bay just after we had passed the small Island that lies opposite to Valcore. Here we found an excellent harbour and a small house belonging to one Captain [Jedediah?] Hyde who[s]e wife receved us very civily he being absent. This place was so very small that there was hardly Room for us all to sleep upon the floor. The poor Woman however was willing to do all in her power to please us, gave us some Beer made of Pumpkins. This drink was so extreemly sour that I could not drink it by itself but when mixed with Rum & sugar it made a Liquor not unlike Punch which I thought agreeable enough, they

Novr 6th called it Flipp. At Six next Morning we again got under weigh with a fair wind but very little of it. I was in hopes to have found it encrease as the Sun got up But it had the contrary effect and when we had got as far as Schylers [Schuyler] Island it failed us entirely so that [?] and obliged us to take to our Oars with which it was with a good deal of difficulty we reached a small Bay about a Mile Southward of Split Rock called Gragg harbour. Never did I see a stronger proff that riches are not necessary to our happiness than in this place. The house we were now lodged in was extreemly Open the Poor people had not any thing to eat but a little very bad bread nor had they any kind of furniture to their house even to dogs meat when fortune threw it in their way. Their Cloathing was of the same cast as the rest and the poor Woman was employed weaving a Kind of Cloath from the refuse of what comes from the flax when it is dressed which was the only covering they seemed to look up to to shelter them from the inclemency of the weather. Yet did these people seem perfectly happy and content with their situation.

7   The wind blew so hard the next Morning that we did not attempt to get off until Noon when finding the wind did not encrease we agreed to attempt

proceeding. It was not without very hard work that we gained the east side of the Lake, about five Miles South of the place where we slept at a place they call Bason harbour [Basin Harbor]. Here having refreshed ourselves with such things as we had with us and replenished our Rum Bottle, with some very bad Rum we found for sale at this place we again set off and by dark reached Ferries's Bay the place where Arnold burnt his fleet in October 1776.[5] The Wrecks of this fleet are still to be seen and had like to have made me break my Arm next Morng for going carelessly down a very steep Bank from the house with my mind full of the Business of those two days which drove him to the necessity of Runing his Ships onshore, my foot slipt and down I fell from the top to the Bottom near 30 feet but fortunately mett with no harm except tearing the sleeve of my Coat in a most horrid manner. I[t] was about Sun rise when we left this place the wind being still very hard against us it was not without difficulty we reached Chimney point where finding at one Paynes good accomodation we were in no humor to encounter the wind again this day particularly as it was now joined by a little current against us. We therefore put up for the Night, and by sun rise next day were again in our Boat and after Rowing 15 Miles arrived at Ticenderoga. Here the house seemed to promise but poor entertainment, and being fully perswaded it would be better to get our Baggage over the carring place to the South landing [Landing] that Night if we could I sett of in Quest of a Waggon whilst Mr. Muirson went in the boat to the Mills. I was fortunate enough to meet with one very handy so that we took leave of Mr. Roe who went, by Skenesbor [Skenesboro] and lodged that Night at the South Landing which is the place Coll. [John] Brown took the 4 Companies of the 53d in 1777.[6]

At this place we found a Schooner which they said was to sail next day for fort George if the wind permitted, But as we had been so long accustomed to be disappointed by the wind we would not trust to it so engaged a small Boat to take us across the Lake, On board of which we embarked a little after daylight. This was the first open boat I had ever seen a Pump in which we however found very usefull in the course of our voyage as the boat not having

8

9th

10th

been much used in the summer all her upper Seams were open and admitted the water so fast that it would have kept one of us constantly at work to keep her dry if we had not been fortunate enough to have this contrivance which was no more than four Boards of about four Inches wide Nailed togeather in the form of a Base in which there was a kind of sucker that was used in the manner of a hand Churn.[7]

About Noon we reached Sabath day point [Sabbath Day Point] where we stopped and got a good Vennison Stake for dinner after which we again proceeded on our way, but we had not gone more than two Miles before the wind came to blow so Violent that we were obliged to put back to the Point in which House or Rather Hovel we were obliged to pass the Night. I wish I could say Sleep, but that was out of the Question. The house was extreemly small a part of which was divided of for the family the remainder a space of near about twelve feet Square was divided between our party that now consisted of five and two hunters who happened also to lodge there that Night. This party when we laid down coverd the whole floor and a good fire kept us warm instead of Bedcloaths of which we had none. In the Middle of the Night I was awaked by one of these Hunters and one of our boatmen who occasionally followed that business who were in strong argument on the best manner of taking the Hives of the wild Bees that are found in this part of the country, yet so very insignificent was their information that altho deprived of my rest I could learn nothing by it, but have since learnt the common mode is this. These Insects allways flying in a direct line to their Hive, as soon as they have got the quantity of honey, the hunters place a little of that Arti[c]le in a place where they find the Bees frequent watching the direction the Bees take after they have filled themselves, then at some distance they repeat the same and where these two Directions intersect each other they in general find

11th   the Hive.[8] Next day we again embarked and tho the wind was fair it was not in our power to make use of it the Lake being here very Narrow and enclosed between two high ridges of Mountains the wind striking against them forms so many eddy winds that unless the wind is either in a direct Line up or down it never blows five Minutes in the same direction. This Narrow part continues about 8 Miles after which the Lake widens. Having Rowed down to the place where the Lake gets wider we found the wind fair and having hoisted Sail we Ran with a fine Breeze for the last fourteen Miles when we Arrived at fort George in good time for Dinner. It was however too late, to sett of from hence this evening we threfore took this opportunity of Cleaning ourselves which was now become necessary which being done we were invited to drink Tea with a Mrs. Hay the Lady of Coll. [Udny] Hay an American Offcer who lives at this place. This Lady is extreemly Chatty which With the company of two very pretty Girls made the evening pass away very well.

Novr 12th   My Companion Mr. Muirson had in the course of the evening engaged a Waggon to take us to Albany into which after a very good nights rest we got about nine oClock in the Morng. This was a very uneasy Carriage as ever I was in but being the best we could procure were obliged to put up with it. About two Miles from fort George we passed a small Pond to the left of our Road called the Bloody Pond, on account of some Action which happened near it in the french war.[9] About four Miles further we came to a small space which had formerly been Cleared and where there was still a small heap of stones lieing. This they told us was the remains of fort Amherst.[10] Having gone four Miles further we stopped at Wings house and leaving our Waggon went about a quarter of a Mile to the right of the road to see the falls of the North River at this place [Glens Falls].[11] This is at some times when the water is high a very beautifull sight. At present owing to the very dry season it had lost greatest part of its beauty the water being confined within two or three chanells. It's strange how great a variety there is in things of this kind, for as I have never formerly mett with any two I could call simmilar so this differs from all the rest. It is formed by a large bed of Rock which extends from side to side of the River at least 150 yards. This Rock lies in a very rough state and has many Chanells cut by the water thro it to which as I have before said the water was at present confined altho there are plain signs that when the water is high it overflows the whole when it must be extreemly Picturesque and beautyfull.[12] There is a Saw Mill on each side of the river that on the west belonging to Mr. Glenn who married Miss Southouse.[13] It is most remarkable for its height for was the whole height taken it would not I think exceed 50 feet but as it now decends from stage to stage I do not remember to have seen any one more than 20 feet high in itself.

After having traveled fourteen Miles we stopped to dinner at Fort Edward.[14] This fort is now in ruins but when it was in good order was a neat little Square work, of sod & Logs and was defended by two Whole and two Demi Bastians with a small Ravlin to cover the gate way, but what renders this place more worthy of notice is its being the place where the unfortunate Miss McRea [Jane McCrea] was Killed by the Indians in 1777 which was done on a Hill a little north of the fort.[15] After dinner we again sett out and after a ride of seven Miles we saw the House of a Coll. [William] Duer of New York. It stands on a hill a little to the left of the road surrounded by woods, appears to be prettyly finished in the English style but is very seldom visited by its owner.[16] Near the water side is one of the finest Saw Mills in the State of New York. As I had never seen what is called a Gang of Saws we went to it. It is wrought exactly in the same manner as a single one being fixed in a very strong frame, in this Gang there were no less than 14—which wrought extreemly well and cut very handsome boards.[17] Eleven Miles below Fort Edward we crossed to the west side and put up for the Night at the house of a Mr. McNeal.[18]

13th   At daylight next day we again got into our Waggon and in about 6 or 7 Miles came to Sorratoga [Saratoga] so much talked of as the place where General Burgoine [John Burgoyne] was taken. The day was by no means fine nor had we time or spirits to examine this place. The Block house which the British Army had is still standing. That on the opposite side of the creek is destroyed. What kind of defence the general had towards the wood I do not know, but the Spot where they Piled their Arms is extreemly low and commanded by the opposite side of the Creek, where General [Philip] Schyler has a very good house near some very excellent Mills which stand just where you cross the River.[19] As there was no one with us who knew any thing of the different Actions we could learn but very few particulars but could see every now and then the remains of a redoubt, but found Nothing remarkable to atract our notice untill our Driver pointed out the House where General Burgoyne lived just before he retreated, not far from whence on the summit of a little hill we saw the remains of an old redoubt, in the middle of which were a few Rails standing, which we were then told was General [Simon] Frasers Grave.[20] The Hills to our right were now almost all coverd with Lines and Redoubts of that unfortunate little Army. About two Miles back in the woods from hence is Freemans farm where the Battle of the 19th of September & 7 of October were fought, but the place which particularly struck me was the height where the American Army were posted called Breams [Bemis] hight. This Hill is much higher than those where the British Army were & does not rise in one Slope but is formed in three different ones, one over the other, on all of which they had Lines and Battery's. The work at the top of the Hill seems to be very strong indeed from what I could see as we passed this seems to be as good a fort as any one would wish for. We did not go back into the woods to look at it, but as far as we could see this hill seems to have the command of all round it.[21]

It was with the greatest satisfaction I quit the sight of these places which spread a Gloom over my mind in spite of all I could do to prevent it and which I hardly got the better of the whole day. To speak of this country it must certainly be called a rough strong country but it is not near so much so as I expected it to be and the Road when we passed was as good as any one could

Map X. The northeastern states. Detail from the first map of the United States to be engraved in America following the Revolution. "A New and correct Map of the United States of North America Layd down from the Latest Observations and best Authorities agreeable to the Peace of 1783," by Abel Buell, New Haven, March 31 1784. *Courtesy of the New Jersey Historical Society; photograph by Joseph Crilley*

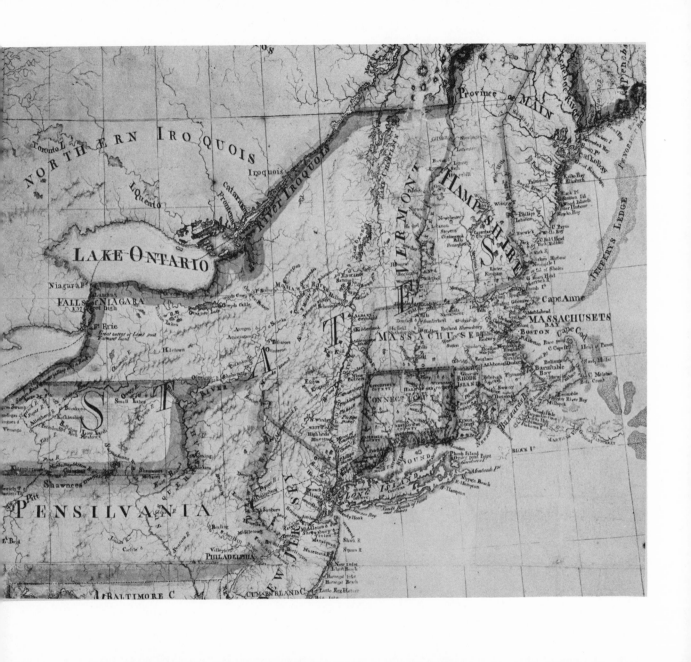

25. State Street, Albany, New York, 1805. Lithograph by Hoffman, Knickerbocker & Co., Albany, probably about 1857 or 1858, after a sketch by James Eights (1798–1882). The view is to the east toward the old Dutch Church, which was demolished in 1806, at the intersection of Broadway and State Street. To the right, near the lamp post, is the location of the City Tavern. *Courtesy of the Albany Institute of History and Art*

reasonably expect, indeed it must be owned the weather had been very dry previous to my Visit which might make them better than ordinary. We dined this day at Half Moon Point [Waterford]. The common Road from hence to Albany is to cross the North River and go down about Six miles on the opposite side through what they call Lansingburgh [Lansingburg-Troy] or the new City. This place is nearly opposite to the Half Moon and has been built from the ground since the late peace. It is situated as high up the River as any Sloop can ever come nor is it often they can come so high. It contains about one hundred houses some of which are tolerably good, but I do not think it a good situation for trade nor do I think it will answer the end of its Inhabitants.

We were however not obliged to take this Road as what they calld the Sprouts were so shallow that our Waggon could ford them. This is no more than the Mohawk River which here empties itself into the Hudsons in four Branches or Sprouts as they are called, from the Northermost to the Southermost of these Branches is not less than four Miles.[22] The Country had been gradualy improving all this day as we came along and when we came within about four or six Miles of Albany it may be called tollerable. About three or four Miles before we came to town I perceived a very large stump of a Tree the Trunk of which had fallen. On my pointing it out to our driver he said it was the remains of the Largest Tree that was ever known in this part of the country, that when it was standing Eight men could stand up within the hollow of it. In the course of this days journey we passed a vast number of Mills altho from the many Rafts we saw upon the rapids the navigation to Half moon must be very bad, but what surprised me the most was the number of Public houses we found on the Road there not being hardly a decent house without its being a tavern most of which were kept by either justices of the peace or Captains. It was very near Dark before we got to Albany where we found ourselves well lodged and got plenty of very good Oysters which to us were a great treat at the City Tavern. What they call the Coffee house was kept in this house which all over this country signifies no more than a place where the people of the town meet every evening to do business and drink Punch,

26. The Van Rensselaer manor house. Drawing by Thomas Cole (1801–48), 1839, done prior to the major changes made by architect Richard Upjohn in the 1840s. At the time of Enys' visit, this was the home of Stephen Van Rensselaer. *Courtesy of the Detroit Institute of Art; photograph by the Albany Institute of History and Art*

Porter &c. &c. Smoke their pipes.²³ Having nothing to do I thought I would go and see what sort of people there were in this place, but the very instant I opened the door I realy thought I should have fell down with the intollerable smell produced by the smoking the worst tobacco spitting on the stoves and every thing which is bad. In short tho well accustomed to such places I was obliged in an instant to shut the door again and go up stairs.

Novr 14   After a good Nights sleep I arose very much refreshed and as we were not to move this day as soon as we had cleaned ourselves a little we went to see the town. This is a very Ancient it having been founded before New York. It is very large and Poppolous and appears to carry on a very considerable trade by the number of small sloops & schooners we saw at its Quay's. This place seems to be improving very fast a great many very good new houses having been lately built in a very pretty style, as to the old part of the place it is perfectly german like its inhabitants. It is chiefly built of Brick but the old part looks dreadfully Ill as they only present the Gable end of the house to the street and in general keep all the Doors and windows shutt.²⁴ I am also informed it is a custom here to make but very little use of the front Door, but keeping that shut to oblige every one to go round by the Back door. The town is situated in a low Spot near the water side surrounded with Hills towards the Land on one of which just out of the town stands the remains of an old fort which is at present in ruins.²⁵ There are here several Churches for the Church of England that of Scotland and a Dutch one togeather with a very handsome Gaol. As well as several good houses in the town there are some in the Neighbourhood of Which that of Mr. Van Ranselwark [Stephen Rensselaer] the Patroon as they call him or Lord of the manner situated just as you enter the place from the Northward and those of General Schuyler and a Mr. Yaetes [Peter Waldron Yates] situated on the Rise of a hill to your right hand as you go out of town on the opposite side may be called by far the best. The latter was built by the Late general Broadstreet [John Bradstreet].²⁶ Altho this place is 165 Miles from New York yet it has the advantage of a very strong tide which not only comes here but goes up near to the New City. When tired

27. A view of Bryans Place, formerly the Schuyler mansion. Watercolor by Philip Hooker (1766–1836), about 1818. Owned by James Bryan when drawn, the former Schuyler mansion includes a portico, added long after Enys' visit, and a kitchen house and carriage barn in the back. *Courtesy of the New-York Historical Society; photograph by the Albany Institute of History and Art*

of walking we returnd to Dinner after which we crossed the ferry and Mr. Muirson introduced me to the house of a Mr. [Abraham? Henry?] Cuyler who had formerly been an Officer in the British Army. His house is a very Genteel Building on the east side of the Hudsons River nearly opposite to that of General Schuyler. Here we passed some hours very agreeably in company

28. The Peter Waldron Yates mansion, First Ward, Albany, about 1795. Water-color by St. John Honeywood. *Courtesy of the Albany Institute of History and Art*

with Mr. & Mrs. Cuyler & the two Miss Ranselwarks after which we returned to Albany having engaged our passage in a Stage Waggon that was to sett out for New York next Morng.

Novr 15   We were accordingly called by daylight and by sun rise were seated in our waggon the seats of this being upon kind of Springs it was somthing easyer than the one that brought us from Fort George but was still very bad. We had now another difficulty as the wind blew very strong up the River, we were afraid they would not have been able to get the Waggon and four horses over in one Scow whch would have detained us very much. It was agreed to make the attempt which succeded with less difficulty than we expected, tho it took us a great deal longer in our passage than usual. Being once more placed in our Stage we set off. Our first halting place was 20 Miles the Road to which was very good but the Land very bad being cheifly Pine land. There are however a few farms scatered here and there. This place is called Kinderhook and as I was sitting at Breakfast there came in a man who I was sure I had seen before but I could not recollect when or where until enquiring his name I found it to be a Mr. Van Seciek[?] who I had met at Crugars [Henry Cruger] Election for Bristol. From hence we got of after about an hour stop and soon came to Claverak [Claverack] the Cappital of Collumbia [Columbia] County. Here are in this place several good handsome houses with a New Court house & Gaol. Here we got an addition to our party in a Gentleman who came from Hudson. This place like the New City above Albany has been entirely built since the peace, and as that is placed as high as any sloop can go so is this as high as any large ship can go and by what I can learn is in a good situation for trade and likely to do well. They say that at some season they catch Herrings in great quantities as high up as this place. This Town was Settled by a party of Masters of Ships from Rhode Island. The Road all this day was very excellent and the country after the first stage became gradualy better & better with very good houses belonging to different Gentlemen at no great distance from each other most of which were in very pretty situations.

16th   We slept this Night at a place calld Rynbeck [Rhinebeck] and next day

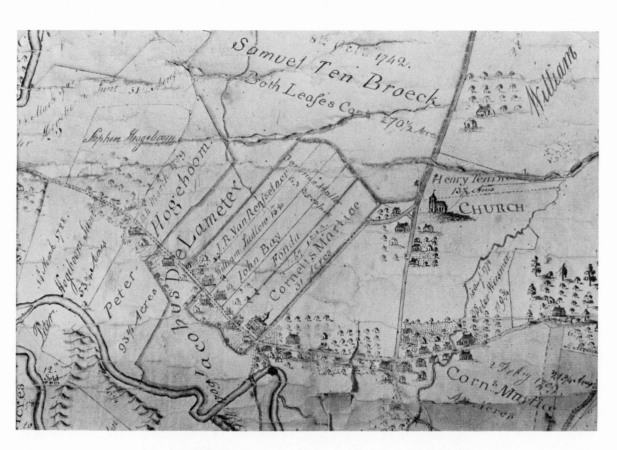

Map XI. A map of the several farms and unappropriated lands in the Town of
Claverack and Corporation of Hudson belonging to Daniel Panfield Esq. Manuscript
map showing survey by William Cockburn, Fred Hauser, and William Cockburn, Jr.,
1799. *Courtesy of the Columbia County Historical Society, Kinderhook, New York;
photograph by the Albany Institute of History and Art*

set of by day light and traveld thro Dutchess County which seems to me to be a very fruitfull well settled country. After going 17 Miles we came to Pough-keepse [Poughkeepsie] a very pretty little place with a good many good houses in it, among the Rest two very good Taverns set up opposite to each other quite in the English Style. From hence we went to Fish Kiln [Fishkill] to dinner where we mett the Stage from York. As soon as Dinner was over we sett off to pass the Highlands which are 19 Miles over thro a very Rough Montanous country and to make our situation still worse we had the most uneasy Waggon this Stage that we found on the whole Road. Soon after we began to Climb these Hills we met two Continental Soldiers who we found were a Part of the Garrison of West Point. This Place is well known from its being the one which was the cause of the unfortunate Major [John] André's Death, and is I believe the only one where the Americans keep any regular Garrison unless they may have a few in the western country but I believe they have not.[27] It is a very strong Post which Commands the North River. I do not find that it is regular fortification but a number of strong Redoubts which defend each other reciprocaly are well mounted with cannon and casemated [?], and fur-nished with Magazeens and stores of all kinds. This is the grand Arsenal for all sorts of Millitary Stores and here I am told among the rest are kept the trains of Artillery taken at Sorratoga [Saratoga] and York town [Yorktown]. Altho these hills are very steep & Rocky yet the land that is capable of cultiva-tion is so good that a number of people are settled among these Mountains. It was rather late before we arrived at Peaks Killn [Peekskill] but when once there we received very civil treatment a Clean hous and good Beds. Our Land-lord was one of the proprietors of the Stage and has one of the provincial Troops of Dragoons. He had been the day before Parading and Mustering his troop which he told us as he waited at supper he thought would be equal to any in the state. I confess I thought it rather out of Character to see a Captain of Dragoons wait at table but was informed his dignity never prevented him from attending to his business And a person with whom we breakfasted told us that he was at this house just as the Captain was setting off to meet his troop and altho he was dressed in full uniform he condescended to go to the stable and fetch the horses of a party of farmers who were about to leave his house.

Novr 17   We were all Seated in our Waggon before day light next morning and after a ride of about nine Miles stopped to Breakfast about ½ a Mile from Croton ferry [Croton-on-Hudson]. We Staid here no longer than was necessary, but proceeding to the ferry embarked on board of the Scow. This ferry is not very Broad and the boat is worked backward and forward by means of a Rope. The Man who took us across the water had two Thombs one one of his hands. On the opposite side of the River we found another Waggon waiting for us into which we got and having gone about two Miles and half we came to a small Run of water famous for being the place where Major Andre was taken. A man who lives near the Spot gave us the following account of that unfortunate affair. He was well aquainted with the three Men who took the Major. They were some of those men who used to go beyond the bounds allowed without leave, where they laid in wait for any one they should find bringing their goods to Market, which they plundered indiscriminately wither friend or foe. They were upon one of these excurtions in the present instance the proper bounds being the Croton River And were hidden behind a large Tree and some brush wood at a small distance from the South s[h]ore of the creek and about a ½ a Mile from a small Village called Tarry town [Tarry-town]. At this Brook the Major stopped to water his horse on which they chalenged him demanding who he was. He replied friend. They then demande[d] to whom, he returnd to the King, on which they advanced towards him and entered into a conversation, and as they came from the South Side of the creek and had taken thear post fronting towards the American posts, he unfortunately mistook the side to which they were attached and in the course of this conversation gave them so much information of who he was as to lead them to think him a propper Prize which they accordingly seized and took back to the American Camp notwithstanding all the Offers he made them. These men have often told the man who gave us this information that had the

Major shewn them his pass from Arnold at first they would have very gladly let him pass and been happy to get rid of him for fear of his informing against them for having gone beyond the limits allowed them.[28]

This Mornings Drive had hitherto been thro what is called Courtlands Manner [Cortland Manor] which tho not so Montanous as the Highlands is still Hilly and bad Roads.[29] Near this place we came into Phillips's Mannor [Phillipse Manor] the Estate of Coll. Phillips [Frederick Phillipse], whose propperty was confiscated and sold on account of his attachment to the Royal cause in the late disputes.[30] I[t] was one of the finest Estates in the Country and attended with some peculiar terms in the grants. In the first place it was like a good many others in this Part let out on three lives in failure of which it again reverted to the Landlord. Second if any Sale took place he was to have the refusal of the Bargain and if he did not chuse to take it was to have the fourth part of the Value of the improvements made there in by the late possessor. And lastly he had a right on the death of any of his Tennants If he thought the eldest Son was an impropper person to reject him and give the Estate to either of the Younger Brothers even tho the Parent had left it by Will to the Elder one. This was a priviledge we did not find that Mr. Phillips ever had made use of altho they did not deny his right to do so if he thought propper. This Estate is now sold out in different Lots by the State & held in fee Simple by the present Possessors. The house of the Phillips family is a good old building with the best Gardens hot houses & Green houses in the country but the Person who now inhabits it being by no means in such affluent circumstances as Mr. Phillips it is not kept in so good a state as could be wished. Our Road this days Journey being near the Banks of the North River we got several very beautyfull views of it which with the number of small craft employed upon it made a charming appearance.

The day being very fine we arrived after a pleasant Ride at Kingsbridge where we Stoped to dinner at a very good house.[31] I cannot say much for the beauty of the bridge. It is rather a stone cause way with a wooden Arch in the center over a branch of the East river which here divides York Island from the

Main. There are several small heights which have small redoubts upon them to the North of the Bridge but the principal works are on the Island. They are formed on a chain of high grownd which seems designed for being fortified extending from side to side of the Island, but the evening was getting too dark to see any thing of them more than that the Hills seemed to be coverd with strong redoubts with Lines of communication between them all of which are now in perfect Ruins.³² These were once very strong and served as the advanced post of the British Army when they were on the Island. On our Road from hence to town we passed over the Plains of Haarlem and saw by the light of the Moon a good many Elegant houses belonging chiefly to people of the City. It was late before we got to town and not thinking it worth while to seek for Lodgings until next day contented myself with the house where the Waggon put up and confess I was not a little surprised to be awaked by a number of people in the middle of the Night singing the Corronation Anthem as loud as they could Bawl.

Next day I got myself Lodged and boarded in the house of a Mr. [Verdine] Elsworth in Maiden Lane.³³ Our party consisted of five Members of the Congress, a Gentleman and his daughter from Boston, the Widow of Coll. [A. Hawkes] Hay of the Artillery, a Gentleman from the west Indies and myself, with whom I passed all the time my other engagements would admit of. This was however not a vast deal as I found several people here which I had known before and having brought a number of letters I was a great deal engaged. This City stands at the South end of York Island and was originaly a Dutch settlement a great number of its present inhabitants being decended from the first Settlers. It is a very handsome Poppolous place and by a computation made before the two late great fires in the years *1776* & *1778* contained about 4200 houses and near 30,00 Inhabitants.³⁴ These were certainly great misfortunes but it is recovering very fast and is now almost entirely built up again. There are a great many very Elegant houses in town belonging not only to Merchants resident in the place but to Gentlemen who come here from the country to pass the winter as well as those where the Ambassadors, Envoys &c.

live. This is at present the place where Congress Assemble and the Port to which both English and french Packets resort. Its Principal Public Buildings are two Epi[s]copal Churches. Besides these is one dedicated to the Trinity which has not been rebuilt since the fire and from its Ruins must have been a most Elegant building. There is also a Chaple for the Roman Catholics and Meetings for Presbetereans, Moravians and all sorts of Religions. A handsome University formerly called Kings now Collumbia [Columbia] Colledge which is well provided with professors of all sorts, and a good Library, a handsome City Hall where the Congress Assemble, a very good Hospital, Workhouse and Gaol with a variety of other public Institutions, too Numerous to mention. I cannot help however remarking that there is a Large Charity School supported by only two Annual Sermons. There is in St. Pauls Church a new Monument lately Erected in honor of General Montgomery who was killed before Quebec. The Design was I am told neat at first but some part of it being either lost or broken in its passage from France they have in replacing it added too much Gilding and finerey.[35]

I had brought so many letters to different people in this place that my time was very much engaged in agreeable partys. Among the rest on the 22*d* I went to the Assembly. It was said not to be a full one there being only 48 Ladies. The whole however danced and to speak of the place in general I had often heard that for their numbers the New York Assembly excelled all others in Beauty and Dancing and must say I was by no means disappointed. The party were divided into three setts two of which danced at a time alternately. The Ball by its rules breaks up at two in the Morng.[36]

On the 26*th* I went with Capt. Bibby of the Fusiliers to see the works at Kingsbridge. It is about 13 Miles distant. On our Road we passed a vast number Eligant country houses and had a great variety of Charming prospects of the North River, east River, Sound, Hell Gate and Long Island as well as the Romantic Rocks on the coast of New Jersey which are extreemly high and perfectly perpendicular. We drove beyond the old Lines when turning Round the ground exhibited as strong a natural defence as I ever saw. The Hills Rise

29. Monument to Gen. Richard Montgomery, St. Paul's Church, New York. Engraving by Augustin de Saint-Aubin (1736–1807) of design executed in 1777 by the sculptor Jean Jacques Caffieri (1725–92); engraving published at Paris, probably in 1779. *Courtesy of the I. N. Phelps Stokes Collection, Prints Division, the New York Public Library, Astor, Lenox, and Tilden Foundations*

to the Right and left of you forming a deep Ravine thro which the Road passes, at the termination of which is rugged high grownd. All these Hills are occupied by Redoubts, that on the right by Fort Washington.[37] They are all in Ruins but may be plainly traced. All these were connected by a very strong Line running from one to the other with high Pickets round the Conterscarp of the Ditch, besides which there were on the other side of the water small detached Redoubts on all the Heights as outposts. This as I have before observed was the advanced posts of the Army on York Island. When we had returned about four Miles we came to a peice of Low ground that which seems to form a Natural ditch across the Island with a Creek into which the tide flows runing a great way into it. This on the side towards the City is bounded by a Montanous Ridge which like the former is approachd only thro a Ravine the heights of which were also occupied by Redoubts but not so strong as those at Kingsbridge. This place is called Mac Gowens [McGowan's—McGown's] Pass and is Naturaly as strong ground as can be wished for.[38] Behind this is Haarlem Heights where the German Troops used in general to be. In the course of our Ride the weather Changed and was very cold and unpleasant which lessend the pleasure which the delightfull Veiws must give at a more favorable season. Just before we got into the outermost parts of the town we came to another Line of fortification which extends from side to side of the Island, the whole of which is commanded by two Rising grounds one of which is called Bunkes Hill [?] but for what reason I cannot tell.

We had no sooner entered the town than we found a vast number of people flanking towards what is called I think Delaneys [DeLancey] Square. On enquiry we found they were going to see the Millitia who were then under Arms. Curiosity of course led us back as well as the Rest and we arrived just as the Governor [George] Clinton assisted by General [William?] Maxwell, Coll. [Nicholas] Fish and many others has [had?] gone along the Line and were placing themselvs to see them pass by divisions. We accordingly took post behind them. The Numbers on the feild consisted of near four thousand but not one fou[r]th of them were in uniform. Here Coll. Fish did me the honor to introduce me to Governor Clinton who was not at home when we called on him. The first part which passed was the Artillery with two Brass Six pounders. They were all in uniform and Looked very well. Then came the remainder of that corps with a good Band of Musick which I am told are all germans from the Troops who were sent out to this country. The Artillery Uniform is Blue and Red. The Next was the Corps of Grenadiers with there Drums & Colours a fine Body of men Cloathed in Blue and White. After these came the Light Infantry in Cloathing of the same Colour, which looked very Neat and Clean. They had a Variety of Colours which I thought very Neat but what struck me most was the corps of Riflemen in there propper Dress who looked very Neat had the Neatest Colour I think I ever saw but thear Dress being only White Shirts fringed looked something to Airey for the present season. After these followed the corps who were not in Uniform and as our Dinner time was near at hand we left these Gentlemen to pass unnoticed by us. As I was going to Dinner I heard some Platoons fired very well & others as badly.

On the *27th* I told Mr. Griffeth a gentleman from the west Indies who lodged in the same house with me that I intended to go to Boston the next day when to my great surprise he told me he would accompany me, if it was agreeable. A proposal so consonant to my wishes you may be sure was not declined on my part and we accordingly that very day began our preparations.[39] It was however not until the Morng of the *29th* that we sett out when at about Eight in the Morng we embarked on board of the General Green Paket a Sloop of about Sixty Tons Burthen bound to Providence. Our accomodations on board were very good and having only two other passengers who were both agreeable men we passed the short time we were on board pleasant enough. We had not been long embarked before we got under Weigh with the wind and tide in our favor. The former was however more nominal than real but as the latter ran very strong we went at a good rate up the East River, whilst the beauty of the two Banks that of York Island to the west & Long Island to the Eastward, beautyfully interspersed with Villages and Country seats presented new prospects every Moment to our Vews and made us forget the want of Wind. About Noon we entered into the Narrow place which is here called Hell Gate which is esteemed a very dangerous place for Shiping to pass through. It is situated at the West End of Long Island just where the Sound turns off to the eastward. It is full of small Islands & I am told there is an Indian tradition that one could formerly pass it on foot. The Channel at this place is not only contracted by these Islands but is also very Shallow which makes the tide Run very Rapid and leaves only one Channel by which Vessels can pass. In this dangerous pass there are several Shoots which go by different Names, as the Hogs Back, the Grediron, the Frying pan, &c. But the worst place of all is called the Pot. This is situated very near the Channel and has been fatal to many Ships among the rest a frigate Huzzar during the late War as I am told tho I could not learn her Name.[40] I conceive it is occasioned by a Steep Clift under water over which the flood tide rolling with great rapidity forms a kind of Wirlpool, which if a Vessel is so unfortunate as to get into they are in danger of being thrown upon the Rocks on the Long Island shore. This place is not as bad in the Ebb tide at which time they tell me a Vessel may go through the pot without danger provided she does not draw too much Water.

The little wind we had here began to baffle us and we ran some risk of getting into the Pot but by an exsertion of all our force at the Oars we got clear of it. Having passed this we went pleasanly down the Sound, and in a short time had a little Breeze in our favor. We had now Long Island to the South and the East part of the State of New York to the Northward both of which was ornamented by a great number of good houses and now and then a Village, this added to a vast number of small Sloops who were in company with us added to the beauty of the Scene. As Night came on the wind began to freshen which gave us a fine run during the Night. Before I went to bed I could not help walking on deck for some time as it was a Charming Moonlight Night, in order to enjoy the Idea of our Sloops Sailing as we came with almost every thing we saw. About three in the Morng we passed what is called the race which is no more than a Narrow part of the Sound betwen Long Island

and the State of Conecticut [Connecticut] "which was now to the northward of us" in which stands Fish or Fishers Island which contracting the Channel renders it more Rapid than at the broader parts of the Sound.

Novr 30th   When we got up about seven in the morng we had again changed the State to the Northward of us from Conecticut for that of Rhode Island and to the Southward of us was the open Sea having passed Long Island altogeather. Whilst at Breakfast we came up with and passed Block Island, and runing along what is called the Narraganset [Narragansett] Coast which is famous for a Breed of Racing horses known in the West Indies by the Name of Narraganset Ponies we came about Eleven OClock to Point Judith, which is the western most Point of the Bay in which Providence lies.⁴¹ As soon as we came up with this we hauld our wind and stood for the Light house near the town of Newport with an intention of stopping at that place, But our Capt. one Godfrey told us if we went into Newport we could not reach Providence that Night, when on the contrary by keeping our course we most likely should. It was at lenth agreed upon to Leave Newport behind us. This place was the Capital of the State of Rhode Island before the war [and] is situated on the Island of Rhode Island, but from its suffering during the war is very much impoverished and most people of property are moved from thence to Providence which is I believe now called the capital.⁴² The Wind now began to blow very hard which obliged us to shorten sail after which we continued to Run at an astonishing Rate by Rhode Island which is very beautifull and well cultivated, and having gained the North end of it we got a view of the town Bristol at a distance. The wind now blew extreemly hard and we run like Lightening by several small Islands called Faith, Hope, Prudence, &c. &c. from some Young Ladies of those Names who were Daughters to one of the first Proprietors.⁴³ We now saw the wind which continued as hard as ever take up the dust in Wirlwinds which induced our Captain to Run under a high point called Marleborough head to reef his Mainsail. Having gone about four miles further the River takes a different course for a short distance which bringing the wind directly in our teeth obliged us to attempt to Beat but this was in vain against so hard a Gale so that after trying for an hour we were at lenth obliged to go back to Marleborough head, and Ankor. Here one of our Passengers left us and went up by land. About Nine at Night the wind abated and the tide which had been against us before now came in our favor. They again got up the Ankor and about one in the Morning We arrived safe at our destined

Decemb 1st   Port. In the morning having paid Capt. Godfrey six Dollars and half each for our passage, eating and drinking whilst on board we took our time and went to a Public house kept by one Rice.[44] This town is situated at the bottom of a Deep Bay & occupies both the Banks of a small River over which there is a tolerably handsome bridge. There are some very good houses in this place and three Churches for different Sects. The one which struck me most was that of the Annabaptists [Anabaptist] which is a very Large handsome wooden building the Spire of which is by far the Neatest I have Seen in America. There are also in this town a University, Public Schools, Workhouses &c. and it has a good trade to the west Indies for Lumber, Horses and Provisions of all Kinds.[45] By the time we had done our Breakfast we had a coach and four ready at the door. This was the first stage coach I saw in America which I am told does not go regular but only when passengers offer. Into this Mr. Griffeth, Mr. Dawse [Thomas or William Dawes?] our fellow passenger who is related to Sir John Temple the English Consul at New York, and myself got. We were not so fortunate as to make the whole of the company for they put a Woman & Child in with us whose company we should not have requested had we had an Option. Our fare was three Dollars, the Coach was decent and the Horses very tollerable. The Country through which we passed is agreeable and the roads far from Bad. The Hills it is true are rather Rocky but the Vallies appear to be very fruitfull, and even amongst the rocks there is good pasturage for Cattle. We passed thro three or four small Villages at one of which we were so fortunate as to find a Dinner ready dressed which had been done for a party who did not come, and which we did not fail to take the advantage of.

We arrived about six in the evening at Boston where we put up at Mrs. Lorrings Boarding house in Hanover Street, after a journey of 45 Miles.[46]

30. A view of the bridge over the Charles River. Engraved for the *Massachusetts Magazine* 1 (9) (September 1789). *Courtesy of the American Antiquarian Society; photograph by Marvin Richmond*

Next day being Sunday which I had been told was observed very strictly in this place I did not make any Visits altho we afterwards Learnt that we might have done it without giving the least Offence. We however walked out before Dinner and saw some part of the town among the rest the New Bridge from Boston to Charlestown. This is a very Neat wooden building of fifteen hundred feet in lenth has a draw Bridge in the Middle to admit Ships up the River and I am told in the Middle Arches the Water is twenty seven feet deep at Low water. The whole cost about Sixteen thousand pounds Currency.[47] After Dinner we took a walk on the Mall as it is called which is a very excellent Gravel walk about half a Mile in Lenth with Trees on each side which is kept in very good order and is by far the best thing of the kind I have yet seen in america, but the weather was too cold to tempt any of the Belles of the place from the fire side. From hence we went to Beacon Hill from whence we had a Charming View of the town and harbour.[48]

Decemb 3   Early on Monday Morning Mr. Dowse who came from York with us came to our Lodging to conduct us to the Governor Mr. John Hancock of famous Memory who received us with great politeness. From hence we went to the Late Governors a Mr. Bodaine [James Bowdoin] father to Lady Temple but was not fortunate enought to find him at home. However as our conductor was a Relation of the family we were admitted to the Garden from whence we had a View of the town and harbour much the same as we had seen the Night before Beacon Hill but more beautifull as the tide was full which had not been the case before. From hence we went and delivered our Letters of introduction to a number of Gentlemen, after which we found our

4th   time pass as agreeable as possible. On Tuesday we dined at the house of Mr. David Sears one of the principal Merchants of the place where we met a very Large and a very fashonable party of Both Sexes among the rest was the family of Governor Bodain and Mrs. Jefferies [Mrs. Patrick Jeffery] so well known in England as Mrs. [Mary] Hayley sister to John Wilks [Wilkes] Esqr.

Decemb 5th   On Wednesday Morng we took a walk to Prospect Hill which was the principal work of the Americans when they lay before this place. From hence we had a beautyfull Veiw of the town harbour and all the adjacent country. The fortifications here as well as those on Winter hill, Cable hill [Cobble Hill] and Letchmores [Lechmeres'] Point are in utter Ruins. Those on the latter I think must have Galled the town very much, the rest are at too great a distance to do much harm but are effectual guards to the communication with the country towards Cambridge. Having satisfied our curiosity here we returned towards the town but on our way paid a Visit to Bunkers [Bunker] hill. This famous hill is situated just above the little town of Charles town. The works on this hill are in rather better condition than those I have before spoken of tho very little. From hence we had also a great many very fine prospects, among the rest a full view of a New Bridge built this Year over the Mistick [Mystic] River just beyond Charlestown Neck. This Bridge is one third longer than the one over the Charles River but not so wide nor is the water so deep, and so much were they improved that it did not cost more than one fourth of the sum which the former one did.[49] One circumstance which I learnt this day surprised me a good deal which was that the Action in general called the Battle of Bunkers Hill was not fought on that Hill at all nor had the Americans any works on it, the one where their Lines were being calld Breads [Breed's] Hill on which and a small one adjoining called Millars Hill the Battle was fought, the works now to be seen on Bunkers hill being wholly erected by the English to defend Charlestown Neck. The thoughts of that mismanaged days work gave me as little pleasure as I had felt in passing Saratoga so we left it and passed thro Charlestown. This is a Pretty little town entirely new as the one which formerly stood here was burned on the day of that action and the day after except a very few houses which were afterwards burned by the Americans. The town formerly had 500 houses in it, at present about 2 or 300.[50]

An odd circumstance happened to us this day. A Gentleman Named of Doctor [Abiel?] Smith was so good as to ask us to drink Tea and pass the evening at his house but not Speaking very loud and I not being used to such Lady like invitations from one of the Male Sex thought he had asked us to Dine and pass the evening. Accordingly about three we waited on him but to our surprise found he had dined two hours before. He very Politely offered to get us Dinner which we however declined telling him we should be time enough for Dinner at our Boarding table but not wishing to go back again after we had once come out we went and got Dinner at a tavern and in the evening repaired a second time to the house of the Doctor where we found a very numerous and agreeable party assembled and passed a most pleasing Evening. On Thursday we again resumed our Ramble to see the Rope Walks Markets and some parts of the town which took us till Dinner when we Dined with a Mr. Cuttler [Benjamin Clark Cutler] who had Married a Miss Sheaf [Mary Sheafe] sister to Mr. Sheaf [Roger Hale Sheafe] of the 5th Regt. and to Mrs. Moldsworth [Molesworth], Lady of Capt. Pansandby [Ponsonby] Moldsworth [Molesworth].[51] This Gentleman gave us tickets to the town Assembly which was held that evening, to which we went and found it Brilliant beyond our expectations there being near Sixty Ladies many of whom were justly cellebrated as Belles. The number of the Gentlemen was Superior to that of the Ladies. The whole was conducted with a regularity seldom met with in these kind of Amusements by a Lt. Coll. [Gamaliel] Bradford who was without compliment one of the most attentive Masters of the Cerrimones I ever beheld. The party broke up a little after Midnight when every one went home to all appearance well pleased, at least I can answer for one who did.

6th

7th   Next Morng Mr. Cutler and a Mr. Beaton called on us with each a one horse chair to go to see the University of Cambridge [Harvard College] which is about three Miles from town. The day was rather cold for riding in such kind of Carriages but our horses being good we soon Arrived. The University or Colledges consist[ing] of three very handsome Brick buildings is the place where most young gentlemen in this country receive their Education. There are about 80 here at present. This Colledge confers all kinds of degrees the same as Oxford or Cambridge and has professors of all kinds, a good Library and a Museum in which there are many Curiosities among the rest one of the large Teeth which have been lately found near the Ohio, and a vast number of other things too numerous for me to mention.[52] I cannot however pass over a pair of Globes which were shewn us in the Library which were drawn with a Pen and Ink and were as neat as any I ever saw printed.[53] Having passed through the Colledge we returnd to town and Dined with a Mr. [Thomas] Russell a Merchant who formerly lived at Charlestown before it was destroyed and who with his father lost forty thousand pounds sterling by that event. On *Decemb 8* Saturday we intended to go to see Dorchester heights [Heights] which was the last Post occupied by the Americans before the town and which obliged the English to leave the place but we were prevented from seeing this by a fall of Snow which lasted the whole day. We this day dined with Mr. [Samuel] **9** Breck where we again met a very agreeable party.[54] On Sunday Mr. Cutler again waited on us in company with Coll. Bradford with each a one horse chair into which we got and after a very agreeable Mornings Ride in which we saw a great many Elegant Gentlemens Seats and beautifull views and passing thro the Villages of Cambridge and water town [Watertown] we stoped at little Cambridge at the house of Mrs. Beeton [Beaton] Mother to a Lt. Beeton late of the 64th Regt. who had asked us to dine with him.[55] This house stands very pleasantly and well sheltered from all the cold winds, and is in every particular and Elegant & comfortable Seat. Whilst dinner was getting we took a walk about two hundred yards behind the house where from a hill we had a[s] beautifull a prospect as any one can well conceive. The owner says he thinks it equal to Richmond Hill, but I cannot agree to that altho I allow it to be very fine and abounds with very great Variety. In the evening we returned to Boston and began to prepare for our return to New York.

To speak of the town of Boston in General I think its Inhabitants the most Hospitable social people I have ever met with and from whom I certainly received more civilities than I ever did any where else. It contains between 2 & 3,000 houses a great part of which are built of wood but there are a good many Eligant ones both of Brick and stone, and tho a good deal of the town lies very low yet there are a number of houses situated on Beacon hill which stand high and command eligant prospects particularly at high water. That of Governor Hancock stands the most conspicuous just at the top of the common with a full view of the Mall before it besides its distant views of the harbour and adjacent country. There are also a great many good publick buildings, besides the two Bridges before spoken of such as churches for all kinds of Religions, the state house, Fanuel [Faneuil] Hall and the Long Warf [Wharf] which is by far the Longest thing of its kind I ever saw. It is 2 or 300 yards in Lenth projected out into the harbour so that Ships can Lie on each side of it.[56] It is also broad enough to contain stone houses upon it with Ample Room for landing or Shipping of goods before them, at the end of which a frigate may lie afloat at low water. There are also here large Hospitals, Workhouses and Public Schools.[57] These last are found in great plenty almost all over America But most particularly in the New England States for which reason you seldom find a man from them however low his Station may be who cannot at least read and write. The country at large round Boston corresponds with what I have already said of that near Cambridge abounding with beauty and váriety and I am told as you go towards Portsmouth in New hampshire it is again Better. This however not coming within my Plan I was obliged to leave it.

Decemb 10   On Monday Morning at five oClock we set out from Boston I confess with regret. We were put seven in a Coach not bigger than usual altho we were told it frequently carried nine by means of placing a center seat across from Door to Door. Crowded in this manner we had a very unpleasant ride of it for Eight Miles to Watertown where we Breakfasted, when a Lady who was of our party proposed taking out the middle seat and placing a small Box for the seventh person to sit on. By this Alteration we were something better tho far from being in a pleasant situation. We this day dined at a place called Marleborrough [Marlboro] and in the afternoon got to another called Worcester. The former was not even a Village that I could perceive, the latter a very pretty little place with a very decent Inn. The country thro which we passed this day was a good deal like that between Providence & Boston Rather Stoney but upon the whole a good country. We did not leave this place until *11th* about nine next day and after we had gone about Seven Miles we lost our Lady. We this day dined at a Place called Spencer and slept at another called Palmer both very hot houses. The face of the country continued much the same as before. As soon as breakfast was over we again set off from this place and very soon reached Springfiel [Springfield] plains which is the grand Arsenal for the State of Massachusets and where there are a great many fine

Cannon and a vast number of small Armes deposited.[58] This is the place which was attacked by one Shay [Daniel Shays], last winter who behaved in a most dastardly manner or he must have got posession of it as it is on a plain without any defence.[59] Near this place is a Small neat Village but the principal town of Springfeild is on the other side of the Connecticut River. We stopped here to Bait our horses which done we went to the usual ferry but found the Ice had blocked up the passage which obliged us to go down the River about Eight Miles to another ferry where we got over with great ease. A little distance from the River we came to the town of Suffield where we dined. This part of the country now began to be delightfull, so after dinner, I quit the inside of the Carriage and took to the Box, and thought myself well paid by the prospect for the cold which I suffered on the occasion the whole way thro New Windsor being a continued Village. About five Miles before we reached Hartford it got dark so I got into the Carriage again and arrived at that place about Six in the Afternoon where we got into a very good House but unfortunately we offended the Landlord by wishing to have a Room to ourselves after whch we could get nothing from him but Insolence and Ill treatment. Hartford is a very pretty well built town and has a State house, Gaol and College, with three good Churches in it. The courts of jutice are held here & at Newhaven [New Haven] Alternately.[60]

Decr 13   We left this place as soon as Breakfast was over and passing thro a Charming Country particularly near Weathersfield [Wethersfield] and Middletown we dined at Durham and in the evening got to Newhaven the country still continuing to be equly beautifull. On our Arrival finding ourselves very much fatigued with being jolted all the way from Boston and being now on the Banks of the Sound we wished to take a Packet from hence to New York but unfortunately the wind was hard against us which obliged us to be content with our old method of conveyance. In the mean time we found ourselves well lodged in a comfortable house with civil treatment a rare thing to be met with in this Country from Inn keepers who being the first people in the place think they do you an honor when they admit you into their houses.[61] The town of

Newhaven is a pretty large place and a great many of the houses are perfectly New having been burnt in the begining of the late Disputes as well as its Neighbouring place fairfeild [Fairfield.][62] It has a good many public Buildings such as Churches, state house, Gaol and a very Elegant College [Yale], Schools

Decr 14 &c. Next Day we again set off and having dined at a place called Stratford we got to Norwalk about Eight in the evening without any thing material happening except that our horses knocked up which occasioned us to be so late. Indeed it was no wonder they did so for the poor Creatures had gone 48 Miles that day with a Waggon and we had half the distance seven people in it as for the other half I believe they came empty. We were obliged to stop & feed them on the Road otherwise I dont think we could have got in at all, and when we told the man of what we had done he said that was the reason they could not do their work that they were too high fed. We left this Brutes house

15th at 4 oClock in the Morng and got our Breakfast about 8 Miles further the road begining to be very bad. Our Meal was no sooner over than we got into the Waggon and was jolted over what is called Horse Neck [Horseneck] one of the worst peices of Road I eversaw in my [life?].[63] When we got to Rye our driver told us one of the hinder wheels had been broken for some time but he would not tell us of it as we were to Change our Waggon here and he thought it would bring us in. The house where we stopped in this place was a very good one kept by a Widow who had a most Charming Daughter who honored us with her company. A few Miles after we left this place the Road became better and the country more agreeable than the former part of this day but we met with nothing worth Notice unless that seven Miles from New York where we stoped to dinner they gave us nothing that was eatable and a Room as cold as if we had been out of doors. From such entertainment we found no reluctance in leaving the place as soon as possible but our misfortunes were not over for before we got within three Miles of New York one of our fore wheels actualy Broke so that I and most of the passengers got out and walked into town where the Waggon arrived about a half an hour after us and I once more got to my old Lodging at Mr. Elsworths in Maiden Lane where we found the same party we had left with the addition of two more Members of Congress.

I now remained in town for some days passing my time very agreeably with my numerous acquaintance which I had now got, from whom particularly from Capt. Bibby, Doctor [George] Draper, Mr. Constable, Mr. Kennon, Mr. Seton [William Seaton?] and Mr. Chapman I got letters of Introduction to almost every part of the Continent.[64] Thus prepared at all points I sett off on the 28*th* Inst and got across the ferry to Pauls [Paulus] Hook, before I found out that the next day being Saturday the Stages did not Run from Elizabeth town. Finding from this information that I should not forward myself by going to Newark I resolved to return to New York and wait until Sunday afternoon which I accordingly did, returning in the same Pettyagar [pirogue] which took me over. These Pettyagar are a kind of Boat very much used in this part of the world tho seldom met with in any other. They are perfectly flat bottomed and make use of Lee Boards by means of which they Beat to windward very well. Their Masts are lofty but as their sails are what are Called Shoulder of Mutton Sails, they have not too much upper Sail, and very seldom overset which one would think from their construction they would be very liable to do as they are as I have before observed flat bottomed and their sides perpendicular. As you cross this ferry from Pawls Hook the town of [New] York has a very beautifull appearance as you have a full view of most of the principal objects particularly of the Hospital which stands a little to the North of the place on a small eminence, and a Row of good New houses at the South end of the town built by Mr. Macomb [John McComb] and some other gentlemen.[65] The other Public Buildings presenting only their gable ends to you are not seen in so good a point of Veiw. On my return the wind being fair we were only twelve minutes on our Passage by which means I got to my old lodgings at Mrs. Elsworth time enough to take my dinner with the Rest of my old Companions with whom I remained two days longer. For this detention I was well repaid by the Company of Coll. [Edward] Carrington one of the Members in Congress for Virginia, and formerly a Coll. of Artillery in the Continental Army who went as far as Philadelphia with me.

30*th*   We accordingly got all ready and set out in Company about 3 PM on Sunday, and had a fine favorable passage to Pawls Hook as far as rapidity was

31. The Bay of New York from Paulus Hook. Watercolor drawing by Archibald Robertson (1765–1835), March 1796. *Courtesy of the I. N. Phelps Stokes Collection, Prints Division, the New York Public Library, Astor, Lenox and Tilden Foundations*

concerned but it began to snow whilst we were on the water which threatened to be deep before the next day. On our Arrival at the Hook we found the Waggon was not ready to set out, which gave me an oppetunity of looking at the old works on this point. This was a post of the English the whole war and was once in the early part of it surprised and about 150 Men taken in it most of whom were I am tole Invalids.[66] This post seems to me to be a very good one for a small party. It stands on a point projecting into the mouth of the North River two sides of which are washed by the water and Round the remainder is a swamp overflowed by the tide. The point itself is tolerably high and consists of several small rising grounds each of which were occupied by a redoubt with a Line of communication from one to the other, and appears to have been a place of some strenth in the latter part of the war. On my return from my Walk the stage was ready into which we got in company with two french men, a young Gentleman of New York, a Young Woman and our party. This Company promised to be a very merry one but we soon lost a principal member of it by our female companion quiting us after a Ride of little more than a mile. When we had gone about four Miles we arrived at the Banks of Hackinsack [Hackensack] River where we left the Stage and Crossed the river in a Skow or flatbottomed Boat.[67] When we reached the other side of this river our prospect was a bad one. It was now sun set, the stage we expected was not come to meet us and we had another Ferry to cross. The stage at lenth arrived and having all got in to it we were Jolted over a Causeway for about three fourths of a Mile of intolerable bad Road when we came to the Banks of the Pissiace [Passaic] River where embarked Waggon horses and all on board of another Skow and just before dark landed on the other side, after which our Road begun to mend and having gone about two Miles further we got to the Village of Newark. This is a very pretty little Village situated in a well cultivatated country, but it was not only a bad time of the Year to enjoy its beauty but we had only Moonlight to see them by. Here we were obliged to stop a few Minuts to pay our Stage fair to Philedelpia which done we proceeded to Elizabeth town where we slept. The Rout which I have here spoken of from New York to this place is a very tedeous one on account of the two ferrys before mentioned so that when the wind will permit and more particularly in the summer time it is best to take a boat from New York directly here several of which are constantly going between the two places. We left this

Decembr 31st

place at about Sun Rise next day and got after a very pleasant Ride (the Snow having blown off) to the Banks of the Rariton [Raritan] River opposite to Brunswik [New Brunswick] where we got out of the Waggon and crossed upon the Ice whilst the waiters of the Tavern brought our Baggage across during our Breakfast which was no sooner over than we again got into our Stage and proceeded. The town of Brunswick appears to me to be a very pleasant place in Summer, has several very very good Brick houses and a very large Building which was formerly Barracks now occupied by a number of poor families.[68]

From hence we went thro a very well cultivated country through a small Village calld Kingston which seems to be going to decay very much at which place we Crossed Millstone Creek and arrived at Princetown [Princeton] by dinner time where we got a most dreadfull dinner and some Wine we absolutely could not drink. The town of Princetown stands very agreably on an emminence the whole Country round it being open a great distance and is esteemed a fine post for a large body of Men. The Aclivity of the Hill is by no means steep in any part but there is no grownd that commands it in any part nor can it as far as I could se be approached by any Ravines. This place is famous for an Action or Rather Cannonade on the *2d* of January 1777 in which the English were obliged to Quit the place.[69] It is a Pretty little town, has many good houses and a large Coledge which has in general from 80 to 150 Young Gentlemen at it. They here go through every Branch of Education from the Grammar upwards. This Coledge is much frequented on account of its healthy situation the Country Round it not being Remarkable for the Salubrity of its Air. I heard a circumstance which I hope for the honer of our Nation is not true, that the English on leaving this place plundered the Colledge Library of its most Valuable Books.[70] From hence we went to

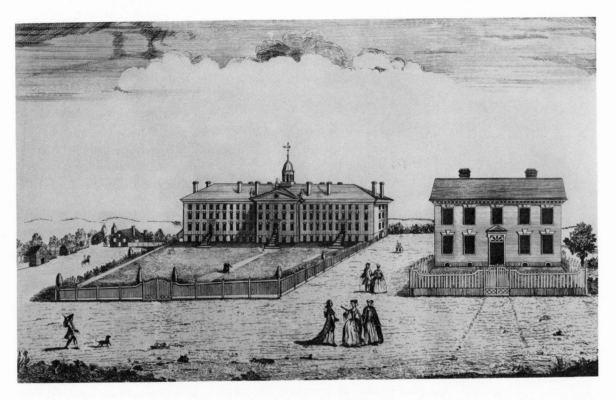

32. A northwest prospect of Nassau Hall, with a front view of the President's House, Princeton, New Jersey. Engraving by Henry Dawkins (before 1754, after 1785) after a drawing by W. Tennant, issued 1764. *Courtesy of the I. N. Phelps Stokes Collection, Prints Division, the New York Public Library, Astor, Lenox, and Tilden Foundations*

Jany 1st, 1788

Trenton where we again slept. This place is famous for the taking of the Hessians under Col. Rholl [Johann Gottlieb Rall]. It is a considerable town, has a good many good houses in it, is situated Near the Banks of the River Delaware, seems to me to be a place which does not bear the smallest appearance of any thing like a defenseble post. This being New Years Eve we were Amused the whole Night by Bonfires, Beating Drums, firing Guns &c. and by Eight oClock next Morning we were once more seated in our Waggon. Having gone about three Quarters of a Mile to a ferry we found it had frozen so hard during the Night that the Ferry was impassable at that place. We from hence returned to the town again and after some dispute ordered Breakfast whilst we sent to some other ferrys to learn wither or no we could pass.[71] Our Messenger came back by the time we had done our Meal with accounts that we could cross upon the Ice at a small place called Lambarton [Lamberton] about two Miles down the River. To this place we accordingly drove. On our Arrival we found the Ice very good in the middle but very weak at the sides so that we were obliged to drive into a Skow that Lay at the Bank in order to get on to the Strong Ice. This gave us some difficulty as the fellow missed the Skow with one of his hinder wheels and obliged us to lift the Waggon by force in to it. This done we got over very well near the other side when we found we could not use the Skow on this side for the same purpose as we had done that on the other it being frozen so hard we could not place it in a propper possition, which delaid us near an hour. At lenth it was agreed to Break the Edge of the Ice and pass the horses one by one after which with some difficulty we got the Waggon on shore and pursued our Rout. Before we had got to Bristol we had to encounter another disagreeable [occurence?] attendant on Stage traveling in this country which was that of Meeting the Stage from Philedelphia when the Drivers insisted it was necessary that we should Change Waggons. This after doing all we could to prevent it we were obliged to comply with for there is no reasoning with these fellows who are as obstinate as Ignorant. Having at lenth shifted all our Baggage &c. we continued our Journey three Miles further when we arrived at the town of Bristol which is likewise a tollerable little place. Here I thought we should again have been obliged to undergo the trouble changing, but with some perswasion the Stage that brought us was suffered to go on. When we got within Eight Miles of this City we again had to shift our Articles in which I was very Near lossing my Umbrella. As it could not be found for some time at lenth I resolved to search the Waggon we came in where I found it conceald under one of the seats and apt to think it was intended by the driver as a fund to keep Christmas upon. About two Miles from where we Changed our Waggon this time from a Rising ground we got a distant View of this City.

During our Ride from hence we passed a few Genteel Houses but not near so many as are found near New York and passing through what is called Kensington we Arrived in town about three in the Afternoon and fixed ourselves at the Old Indian Queen Inn where I found a Mr. Coan [Coon?] who had formerly lodged in the same house with me in Boston.[72] I also found that Mr. Griffeth who I expected to have found here had gone to Baltimore only the day before. The whole day of the 2d I was taken up in finding out the different people for whom I had brought letters which I found Rather difficult to find on account of the Largeness of the City and the sameness of its streets. On the Morng of the 3d a Mr. George Meade for whom I had brought Letters waited on me and introduced me to the famous Doctor Franklin now President or Governor of this State, who is a very fine hearty old man of more than Eighty notwithstanding which he is indefatigueable in the necessary duty's of his imployment.[73] He is however so infirm in his feet that he is generaly carried about in a Sedan Chair. This old Gentleman received us very politely but the Morng was so far advanced our visit was obliged to be but short. On the same Evening I went and drank Tea with Mr. Meades family who had a Wife and two very agreeable daughters after which we went to the City Concert where I met with Mr. [David] Franks who I remembered to have seen in England and lives at Islesworth in Middlesex.[74] The concert was no very great thing not having any Number of

33. A view of the City of Philadelphia. Etching by Gilbert Fox (1776–c. 1806) after a drawing by John Joseph Holland (c. 1776–1820), about 1797. *Courtesy of the I. N. Phelps Stokes Collection, Prints Division, the New York Public Library, Astor, Lenox, and Tilden Foundations*

performers some of them however as Mrs. Brown on the Flute and a Chap[?] on the Violin are esteemed capital in their way. I was told the display of Beauty on this occasion was but very indifferent. The number of Ladies did not exceed thirty and the Room being extreemly cold all these were crowded round the fire so that it was impossible to see them. There were however many who deserved the appellation of very Beautyfull, others of very Pretty Women in the Room. The Evening of the *4th* I passed at a Mr. [John?] Ross's where we had only a family party, himself Mrs. Ross and her daughter, until joined late in the Evening by Mr. Franks. They appear to be a Genteel family.

On the *fifth* after passing by Morng as usual in roving about the town I dined with General [Walter] Stewart a genteel agreeable young man a Native of Ireland who had entered into the American service early in war But who now as indeed most of the American Officers have done is in Business in this place. Gentlemans Lady is daughter to Mr. Blair Mac Clonagan [McClenachan] who is the present posessor of the famous House at German town [Germantown] into which Coll. [Thomas] Musgrave threw himself **6th** and made so good a defence in the Action of that Place.[75] The next day I was introduced to Mrs. [Anne Willing] Bingham the most fashonable as well as one of the most beautifull Ladies in this place. Her husband [William Bingham] is a person of a very large private fortune most of which he gaind by fortunate speculation during the war, among the rest by purchasing up the notes of La Caisse disconmpte [d'Escompte] in Paris when it had stoped payment.[76] This day I also found out that a Coll. [John Eager] Howard of Baltimore was in town for whom I had letters of introduction which I accordingly presented which procured me an introduction to the family of Mr. [Benjamin] Chew his father in law.[77] This old Gentleman has a great many Aimable and Elegant young Ladies for his daughters. He himself was I am told rather attached to the Royal cause during the late Revolution in this Country But his Son in Law Coll. Howard was on the contrary side and one of the most distinguished officers at the famous Battle of the Cowpens for which he was voted a Medal by Congress as an acknowlegement of his service.[78]

Jany 7th   On the following day I was favored with a visit from this Gentleman and his Brother in Law the Young Mr. Chew who invited me to be a partaker of what they were pleased to Call a Childrens Dance at Mr. Chew's which

8th   I accordingly gladly accepted. The day after I dined with Mr. Ross where I met Mr. [Phineas] Bond the English Consul for this state and several other Gentlemen.[79] Mr. Bond is a Native of this place and a very agreable Cheerfull man. I found he was engaged at the same place with myself where we went about seven oClock and found a great number of the first Ladies in town Assembled. It is true there were a great proportion of Young Ladies under the age of thirteen, at the same time there were a very good Set for a Country dance of Grown Ladies and Gentlemen, with whom I readyly joined dancing with Miss Bond the Consuls Sister. We had here in addition to the Agreeable family of the house which is most certainly one of the most pleasing I ever met with, several of the most Beautifull of the fair Sex both married and single which the place afords, among which I cannot help mentioning of Mrs. Bingham and Miss Allen.[80] The Room was large enough to admit of two Sets the one of which consisted of the Grown the other of the Younger Ladies. During the intervals between the Country dances the Young Ladies danced several Cotillons & figure dances in a most Capital manner particularly two who were not more than ten or Eleven Years old the one Miss Harriet Chew the other a young Miss Allen sister to the Lady before mentiond who I really think would do honor to the first dancing Masters in Europe. The Cotillons were all well danced among the rest. Whilst the Younger part of the Company were at supper a Cotillon was formed by the Elder performers two Couple of which danced inommitally [inimitably?] well. The top Couple was Miss Allen and Mr. Franklin Nephew to the famous doctor of that Name and the Bottom was Miss Maria Chew and Le Marquis de Chappidelaine [Chappedelaine].[81] These two Couples danced so remarkable well that they hurt the appearance of the side Couples altho they both danced very well. At ½ past Eleven there was a Cold Collation for the company below stairs after which the dance recommenced and was continued until near One oClock when the whole parted, tho I beleive very few without regret. The whole of this little party was as New to me as it was pleasing, and conducted with that easy politeness by the whole of Mr. Chews family that I shall never forget it and hope to see a similar party frequently among your [i.e., Francis Enys'] Truro society on my return from this Country.

9th
10th   The Next day was so cold that I hardly went out of the house but the very extreem Cold abating a little the day after I went with intention of taking a long walk on the Germantown Road. The day was very fine but Rather Cold so that in order [to] keep myself warm it was necessary to walk fast by this means I soon found I was near four Miles from town and not more than three from German town [Germantown]. I now determind to proceed on to the town before me to see the field of Action where the Armys were engaged on the 4th of October 1777. I had no one with me who could give me any account of the matter so must pass it over in silence. I passed through the whole town which is near two miles long consisting of only one street. The houses are not in general very good but are substantial Stone Buildings & appear to me to be cheifly Occupied by Tanners and Coach makers. The Inhabitants are Cheifly but not altogeather Germans. At the farther end of the town a little to the right of the Road as you go from Philadelphia stands the House famous for turning the fate of that day in favor of the English. It was before the War the Propperty of Mr. Chews family and is as I have before observed now in posession of Mr. Blair Mac Clanagon. It is a very strong Stone house about thirty five or forty feet Square with small Offices rather behind it which are connected by kind of Circular passages. It stands high and appears to be well calculated for defence. There are however several Stone houses near it and in particular a large Stone Barn which belongs to it, nor do I think its Situation so high as some ground about 300 Yards beyond it on the same Road. It is lastly a very pretty country house, seems to have a very excellent prospect, the country round it being open and

34. Lt. Gen. Thomas Musgrave, Governor of Gravesend and Tilbury Fort, Col. of the 76th Regiment of Foot, with a view of the Chew House, Germantown, Pennsylvania, 1777. Engraving by G. Facius, 1797, after a painting by Lemuel Francis Abbott (1760–1803), 1786. *Courtesy of the Trustees of the British Museum*

prettly laid out.[82] This being the only thing I had to see I return'd to the other end of the town where I had previously orderd an old Dutch Woman to get me some dinner. On my return I found she had got me nothing but Smoaked Sassages which she fried with some slices of Apple. However as I wanted no Sauce to my meat my walk having provided me with the very best sort, I eat my Dinner with a good Glee and found the old Lady had some most excellent English Porter which I paid my respects to after which I returned into the City again.

On my return I found an invitation from Mr. Mead to drink Tea at his house to which I accordingly repaird where I found a good many Ladies Assembled. I have before mentioned this Gentlemans family as a very agreable one. His Second daughter this evening played on the Guittar and Sung, to which I must add that a Beautyfull young Lady Miss Markoe played upon the Harpsecord and sung most Charmingly.[83] Thus our Evening passed off

Jany 11th
12
and I was again very sorry when the party Broke up. The next day was again a very bad one so that I hardly went out of the house and on the day following after having paid a number of Morning Visits and was sitting after dinner I saw a Gentleman alight from the Southern Stage whose face I thought I knew and who I soon found out to be a Mr. [Joseph] Hadfield who I had seen once at Cataraqui when he was making a tour of that part of the

13
Country, whose principal residence is now at Baltimore.[84] Being Sunday I went to the Roman Catholic Chaple with several Gentlemen and found they did not go thro any thing like so much ceremony as I had seen done in Canada and even said one Prayer, sung their Hyms and Read the Epistle for the day in English.[85]

14
On Monday being the day appointed for the Ball I went at about Eight in the Evening to Mrs. Binghams, where I found a most Brilliant Assembly of all the most fashonable persons in town. It consisted of about 60 or 70 Ladies and from 90 to 100 Gentlemen. Here I found almost all those which I had before seen at Mr. Chews except Mr. Bonds family and connections who were prevented by the death of an old Lady who was nearly related to them.

The display of Beauty and dress here was far superior to any I have seen except in the Rooms at Bath. Among a vast number of Ladies whose names I could not learn & have forgotten I remember to have Noticed Mrs. Bingham, Mrs. Craig, Miss Allen, Miss Juliana, & Sophia Chew, Miss Hammilton [Hamilton], Miss Sue, & Miss Markoe.[86] The House is a most Elegant one the Chimney peices and furniture in a most superb style. The Room where we danced which is intended for the Withdrawing Room is an Elegant Oblong Octagon if I may be allowed the expression in short Like the duke of Queensburys Large Room on Chalmondby [Chalmondeley] Walk.[87] It was long enough to dance fifteen Couples with ease but not being quite finished was rather cold in the beginning of the Evening. The dancing was conducted by Major [William] Jackson but as every one was let do as they pleased he had not a vast deal of trouble more particularly as the whole party seemed to wish to please. There were two Cotillons danced by two Setts the one consisting of four Gentlemen and as many Ladies the other of Eight Ladies which surprised me not a little on account of the number of Young Gentlemen who were present. Among the Gentlemen who I was introduced to this evening was a Young Mr. Penn who said he thought he remembered me at Eton but I rather think it must have been you [Francis Enys] he meant as I do not remember any such name among my acquaintance.[88] About twelve we had a most Elegant Supper served in the Lower appartments where an old French Marquis Named I think Le Marquis De La Bouverie distinguished particularly in enjoing the Supper which he was frequently recomending as most excellent & served in a very pretty taste. In this point he was certainly right but seated as he was between two fine Women I conceived from the universal gallantry of his Nation that he would have found some other topic to have descanted upon. As soon as supper was ended the dance recommenced and lasted until about two oClock when every one parted as far as I could perceive well pleased with the reciprocal endeavours of the whole Company to please each other. In fine it was certainly one of the most Brilliant and at the same time agreeable Assemblies that I conceive could be collected on the Continent.

35. Landsdown, the seat of William Bingham Esq., Pennsylvania. Built by John
Penn, Governor of Pennsylvania, 1763 to 1776. Drawn, engraved, and published by
William Russell Birch (1755–1834) in *The Country Seats of the United States of
North America* (Springland, Pennsylvania, 1808), plate 3. *Courtesy of the Historical
Society of Pennsylvania*

15   The next day was employed in taking leave of the Gentlemen & Ladies who had favord me with their Attentions and on the *16th* I left Philadelphia. Before I leave this place it will be Necessary to give some slight account of this City. It is the Capital of the State of Pennsylvania situated at the head of the Navigation of the River Delaware and about 150 Miles from the Mouth of that River. It is Situated betwixt the Rivers Delaware and Skuylkill [Schuylkill] and according to the Proposed Plan is to extend from the one to the other. This distance is near two Miles but the Present City does not extend much more than half a Mile from the Banks of the Delaware. The whole is laid out in regular streets of a very convenient breadth which Intersect each other at Right Angles whch Plan as far as they have yet built is strictly followed. These are Numberd from the Delaware by the Names of Water Street first, Second, third and so on to Ninth Streets. On the other hand the Intersecting Streets are named in general after some kind of Tree as Pine Street, Chestnut Street, Wallnut Street &c. Th[e]re are however some exceptions to this Rule as Market Street which is one of those Cross Streets in the Center of the town which is much broader than the rest, and has in the Middle of it the Market house which extends for more than a Quarter of a Mile and is one of the Neatest as well as best supplied Markets I ever Saw in my life.[89] The extent of the town along the Banks of the Delaware is including what is called Kensington and Southwark which are the Suburbs to the City very near two Miles in lenth and contains about five thousand houses among the rest a great many Churches for every kind of Religion but

Map XII. Plan of the city and suburbs of Philadelphia, 1794. Engraved by Robert Scot (?–after 1805) and Samuel Allardice (?–1798) from a drawing by A. P. Folie and published at Philadelphia probably to accompany Benjamin Davis, *Some Account of the City of Philadelphia* (Philadelphia, 1794). *Courtesy of the I. N. Phelps Stokes Collection, Prints Division, the New York Public Library, Astor, Lenox, and Tilden Foundations*

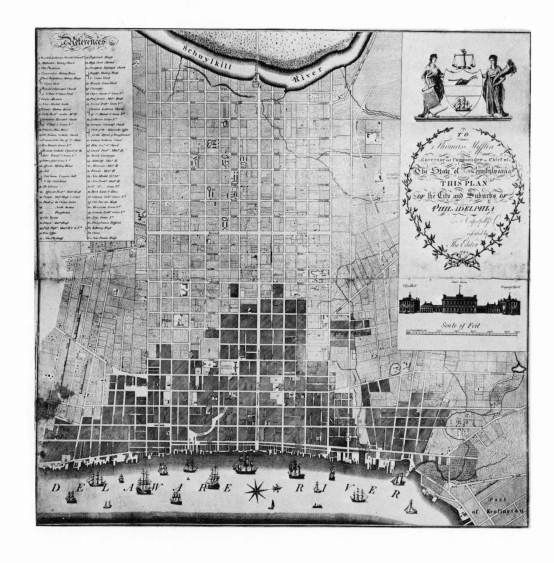

the one which is esteemed the most beautifull is a new one built by the Dutch Calvinists which is said to have cost ten thousand pounds building.[90] Near to this is the University [of Pennsylvania] which does not make any great show and is in the hands of the Presbiterians. This has occasioned a New foundation to be formed under the title of the Protestant Episcopal Accademy which I am told is in a very thriving way. The Building belonging to this society is not yet quite compleated but appears to be very Neat.[91] Among the other Public buildings are the state house which has an Elegant garden belonging to it. Near the outskirts of the Present town also stand three very fine Buildings, the Hospital, the Poor house, and the Prison, the two former built with Brick the latter with Stone.[92] There is also in fourth Street a large Pile of buildings belonging to the Quakers who are the most Numerous Sect in this place but it presents nothing either grand or Elegant to the Eye. This place used to build a great many ships before the War but that business appears to be nearly at a stand at present there being several on the stocks which seem to have been on hand a long while. I have already observed that a great many of the Inhabitants of this place are Quakers and the Rest being in general of a very Sedate cast more occupied by Mercantile pursuites than by pleasure that a Stranger does not find that ready admittance into society that he does in many other places on the continent and altho there are certainly some very genteel agreable families in town yet the society is not so general as in the smaller places. I have before observed that their Concert was not sufficiently full. I must also remark that this Year they have not even a Public Assembly altho several gentlemen did all in their Power to promote one and as to Play's they are actualy prohibited by an act of the Legislature although I am told the people of the place are particularly fond of such representations.[93]

ON TO VIRGINIA AND HOME

Jany Having taken leave of every one as before mentioned I left Philadelphia on the *16th* in the morng & was fortunate enough to have for a companion the Young Mr. Seton of New York whose father was among those who had favord me with their acquaintance at that Place. The Morning was extreemly bad and rained very hard the whole day, this we however did not feel in the begining of the day. We crossed the Skuylkill at the lower ferry about four Miles from town on the opposite bank of which stands a Place of Public entertainment Called the Green Room which is in the manner of our Tea Gardens which I am told is frequented in Summer. The Room from all appearance is a good one but as it was not in season I did not go into it.[1] From hence we went to Chester to Breakfast after which we again set off. The Rain still continuing & freezing as it fell made the Roads very slippery and in some parts quite one sheet of Ice. This was a very great Inconvenience to us as the horses were not shod for the Ice they were falling continualy which rendered our Journey tedious as well as disagreeable. The Next place of any kind of

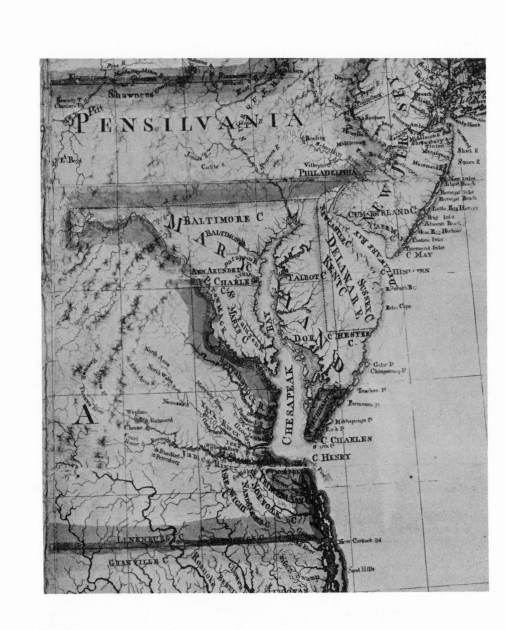

Note is Brandywine. This place is not only famous for giving the name to the action of the 11th of September 1777 which was fought about twelve Miles above this place at or near Chadsford [Chadds Ford] on the Brandywine Creek, but Likwise for having some of the finest Mills in America.[2] They are so situated that the tide flows up to the Mill Tails so as to admit the small Sloops close to the Mills to bring Wheat and take away the flower when grownd. These buildings are not very large or Elegant nor do any of them by what I could learn contain more than three pair of Stones, but they are very numerous, I believe about ten of them. These are supplied with diffent [different?] streams by being Situated below a place where there is a considerable fall, at the head of which the water is diverted from its Natural course and conveyed in small Channels along each Bank of the River till by the time it arrives at the Mills it has obtained a sufficient fall to turn an overshot Wheell. These Mills as well as the goodness of their Situation are said to make the best flower on the Continent from whence the City of Philadelphia is supplied where they certainly have the best bread in the world, at least I think so.[3]

About a Mile beyond this Creek we came to the town of Willmington [Wilmington], where we again stopped to Change Horses. This little place altho it has hardly a good house in it is nevertheless the Cappital of the State of Delaware.[4] It is said to have about 400 houses which here as well as in Philadelphia being built with Brick look neat enough tho small. Before we left this place our Driver told us he was very much afraid we should find it difficult to get over Elk Creek which made us determine to push on as fast we could in hopes to reach it before the force of the Land flood should have

Map XIII. The Middle Atlantic states. Detail from "A New and Correct Map of the United States of North America," by Abel Buell, New Haven, 1784. *Courtesy of the New Jersey Historical Society; photograph by Joseph Crilley*

augmented its waters for which reason we defered Dining here and pushed off as soon as the horses were ready. As we advanced our difficulty's became greater. The Road from hence to Elk [river] was one entire sheet of Ice and our Horses were smoother than those we had from Chester, by which we did not reach the Banks of the Elk until very nearly Dark at Night. When we arrived we found it much worse than we even expected it was, as we had no sort of doubt but we ourselves would be able to get across by the help of an old Bridge which was not however Strong enough to drive the Waggon over. But even this expedient was found to be impracticable on account of the water and floating Ice that ran between us and the old bridge. At lenth after having done all in our Power we were obliged to turn back. On our return it was with the utmost difficulty we could get up the Hill by all of us getting out and Walking up it, in doing which Mr. Seton got so severe a fall that when we got him into a small house at the top of the hill I was affraid he would have fainted away. Here we were at first in hopes of staying the Night but on enquiry found we could get Neither entertainment for ourselves or horses which obliged us to return four Miles and half further, where we obtained a wretched Supper of Bacon & Eggs Tea Coffee &c. It was however the best we could get & having had no dinner we could eat anything in our way. We here got very Clean Beds but from the dampness of the Room I

17th   got a violent Cold and next day after Breakfast we again set out. On our Arrival at the Banks of the Creek we found it was not so high as it had been the Night before and were able by means of throwing some Rails across the Stream which ran between us and the Bridge we got to the opposite Shore and after a walk of about a Quarter of a Mile reached the place called the head of Elk [Elkton], near to which General Howe disembarked his troops in 1777 before the Action of Brandywine.[5] This is a small straggling town but has a tollerable good Inn in it. From hence we sent people to assist in getting over the Waggon, which was done by taking out the Horses and passing them sepperately over the Bridge and then Bringing the Waggon over by hand. This however detained us so long that it was past one oClock when we left the head of Elk, and after going only seven Miles we came to [a] Creek which they Call North East [Northeast], where we were obliged to drive the Waggon over large heaps of Ice which were piled up on each Side of the ford which was done with no small danger of oversetting the Waggon. Otherwise the water here was not deep enough to be dangerous, but what we were most afraid of was that the floods might have broke up the River Susquehanna which was nine Miles further. We Arrived at its Banks about Sun Set and had the pleasure to find it was not only unbroken but remarkably fine Ice. This River is here a Mile and Quarter wide, and having left the Waggon our Baggage was transported by the man who keeps the ferry here in summer to whom we paid the usual rate of ferryage. On our Arrival on the other side we found another Waggon ready for us into which we got and it being a very fine Moonlight Night and the Roads good we very soon drove twelve Miles further to a little place called Bush [Harford] where we found a Comfortable Clean public house kept by very civil people who are the owners of the line of stages betwixt the Rivers Susquehanna and Potomack [Potomac].

Jany 18th   We left this place a little after sun rise next Morning and had hardly got out of town before we got to a small Run of water which we found some difficulty to get over on account of the Ice.[6] When we had gone about four Miles we came to a small Creek they Call Winters Run. This we with great difficulty got into and found it very deep but when we got to the other side the Edge of the Ice was so Strong that it would bear the horses at the Edge of which there was near two feet Water and how to get the Waggon out of it we could not tell. Our Leading Horses were very Spirited and no sooner found us entangled in the Run than they Sprang forward Broke the Swingle Barr [swinglebar] and draged the Reins out of the drivers hands. Very fortunately for us our Wheel horses were very steady and stood fast tho in a very uneasy position with their fore feet upon the Ice and ther hinder ones in the Water until we all got out of the Waggon detached the Leaders from the Pole by which means their Burthen was so much Lightened that they were able to drag it up themselves which was very fortunately done with no other loss than that of the Drivers Whip which he Lamented very bitterly. We got Breakfast this day at a place where we Changed horses. It is only a single house kept by one Skerret [Skerett?][7] where, as the Stage was out of the usual time, we got but a very Indifferent meal after which we again proceeded passing on our way several disagreeable Runs of Water particularly one about four Miles from Baltimore whch was very Broad and Deep with a great many large Stones or holes at the bottom and I realy think it was owing to the Spirit and Skill of our driver who was a Hessian that we escaped being overset in the Middle of it.

On My Arrival at Baltimore I put up at the Fountain Inn kept by Mr. [Daniel] Grant by far the best I ever was in on the Continent.[8] Here I found Mr. Griffeth who had left me at New York. To speak of the face of the Country between this and Philadelphia in general termes it may be said that from Philadelphia to the head of Elk is some of it very good but is by no means so well settled as the Jerseys and that betwixt head of Elk and Baltimore is very bad and has very few Settlers on it. This may be accounted for by its being carried along a Ridge of Hills which have very fertile plains to the Westward of them nor are they wanting in Riches being full of Iron Ore which is worked with great Profit at some forges about Seven Miles from Baltimore.[9] I had hardly done dinner and was debating within myself wither I should dress myself or let it alone until the next Morning when the Waiter came and told me two Gentlemen wanted to speak with me. On my going to them I found one to be Mr. Seton who came with me in the Stage and A Mr. Curson Uncle to the above young gentleman.[10] Mr. Seton I found had informed his Grandfather that I had letters of introduction to him, who very

Map XIV. Plan of the Town of Baltimore and its environs by A. P. Folie. Engraved by James Poupard, Philadelphia, about 1792. *Courtesy of the I. N. Phelps Stokes Collection, Prints Division, the New York Public Library, Astor, Lenox, and Tilden Foundations*

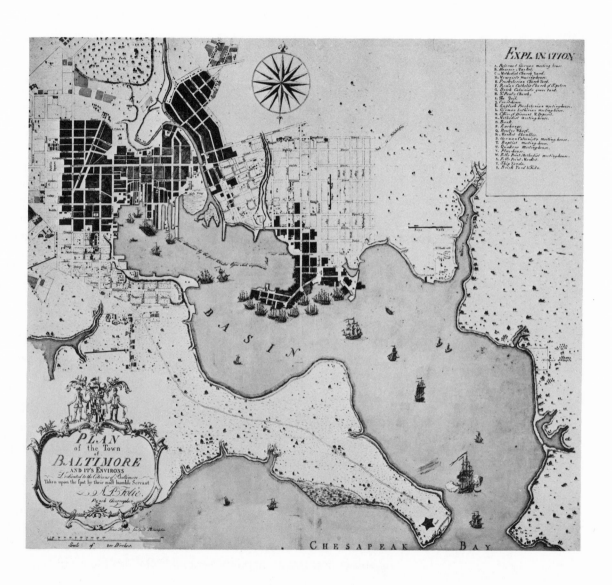

PLAN
of the Town
of
BALTIMORE
AND IT'S ENVIRONS

CHESAPEAK BAY

BASIN

obligingly sent his Son and Mr. S. to let me know there was a private Dance in town that evening and that a Card would be sent me if I would go. This was to[o] agreeable [a] party to be rejected altho I was very much fatigued, I threfore accepted the Offer and in a very short time received a Card from a Mr. [Luther] Martin Attorney General of the State to pass the evening at his house. By the time I was dressed Mr. Curson again came and we went togeather to this party. Here I found about thirty Ladies and a great many more of the other Sex Collected Among the Ladies. Here as at Mrs. Bingham the Mistress of the feast was amongst the finest women in the Room as well as the two Miss Smiths, Miss Seton, Miss Ireland and a Miss Williamson.[11] Miss Ireland dances extreemly well and does great honor to Miss More's of Bristol where she was Educated. If this party was not quite so Numerous and Brilliant as the one I had partook of four days before it was not less agreeable as there was far less form. They danced Minuets, Contry dances & Cotillons until Eleven when we had an Elegant Supper after which the dancing again went on until near two oClock when the greatest part of the party went away but Mrs. Martin told me afterwards they continued to dance Jiggs & Reels and to sing far above an hour afterwards.[12] These latter Dances I always thought were peculiar to Canada, that is I mean on this side the Atlantic, as I never saw or heard of them since I came into the States before now.

Jany 19
20   All day Saturday I was employed delivering my letters of introduction and on Sunday passed a very agreable day at Mr. Cursons. I was now fully introduced to the society of this place which like Boston is general so that I was engaged every day and frequently obliged to dine at one house and drink Tea at another. Dancing here seems very much the fashion. They have an Assembly once every Week. It is alternately called by the Names of the Baltimore Assembly and the Amicable Society. This latter was at first instituted by a number of young gentlemen who were not old enough to be admitted to the town Assembly, but as their Rules do not proscribe the elder ones from becoming subscribers it is now pretty general.[13] Besides these public meetings

they have a Number of Private ones such as I have before spoken of at Mr. Martins, another of the like on the *23d* at a Mr. Holingsworths [Jesse? Hollingsworth] and again on the *24th* at a Mrs. Buckanans [William? Buchanan].[14] The *25th* was the Amicable society, thus we had four Dances in Eight days.

    The Town of Baltimore contains more than two thousand Houses. The streets are built at right Angles to each other the same as in Philadelphia. The houses if not very large are well built in Brick. The main Street is near a Mile Long of well built houses each side of the way and is on the whole as neat as any I have seen.[15] The others are not so compleat nor are they likely to become so on account of the very heavy grownd rent which is demanded by the Landholders. There is now before me a large Methodist Meeting house the Grownd rent alone of which is fifteen shillings sterling per foot Square which amounts to about Twenty Pounds per Annum & I am told in other parts of the town it is so high that the Grownd Rent is more than the Buildings are worth and that if any person was to purchase one for one shilling he would have a bad Bargain. There is a handsome State house and churches for all kinds of Religions.[16] This place carries on a considerable trade but the port cannot well be considered as part of Baltimore. It is called the Point and stands at a small distance from the town on the other Side of a small

Jany 26

River. The land Round the town is far from being Rich but there are some very Charming prospects from some of the Hills, among the rest from the Seat of Colol. Howard which is situated on an eminence but is well coverd by trees from all the cold winds, has a charming View of a Water fall at a Mill, a long Rapid below it, a full View of the town of Baltimore and the Point with the shiping in the harbour, the Bason and all the Small craft, with a very distant prospect down the river towards the Chasapeak Bay. The whole terminated by the surrounding Hills forms a fine Picture.[17] On the *27th* I began to prepare for leaving this place but to my great disapointment was told in the evening that the Waggon had broken down and thre was no possibility of my getting a conveyance. Pressed as I was for time this detention was very

36. Old Light Street M.E. Church, Baltimore. Lithograph by A. Hoen & Co. after a drawing by Thomas Coke Ruckle (1811–91). *Courtesy of the Maryland Historical Society*

37. Belvidere, Howard family home. Built between 1786 and 1794, the Howard mansion was torn down about 1875. Oil painting by August Weidenbach (active at Baltimore 1858–69). *Courtesy of the Maryland Historical Society*

disagreeable but I had at least the consolation to think that it could not have happened to me in a more agreeable or hospitable place. This accident Proved more tedeous than was at first expected for by the time the Waggon was mended there had been a considerable Thaw which had swelled the Runs of Water so much as to Render the Roads impassible.

Jany 29th

31st

This detention gave me an opportunity of seeing another prospect nearly equal to the one at Colo. Howards from a Hill about two Miles from town on the opposite side to the former. On the Last day of the Month I was present at the Baltimore Assembly where we had again all the Belles of the place collected to the number of about forty. The evening passed off very agreeably and concluded with a tollerable Supper which all entertainments of this Nature do in Baltimore. Next day took a Ride in Company with several Gentlemen to see the fortification which had been erected on a Point about four Miles from town during the War to prevent the English fleet from coming up the River. It consisted of two very strong half Moon Batterys one of them close to the water edge the other a little raised from it both of which seem to be well constructed for the purpose designed which was to cover a Boom and betwen them I conceve when compleat (for they are now in a very ruinous state) mounted about thirty Guns of different sizes many of which are now lyeing near the place but the Carriages are secured some where else. Behind these works was a small pentagonal Star fort which I conceve had [been] formerly Barracks for the troops to man these works altho no remains of even the Chimneys are now to be found.[18]

Feby 1st

2nd

Feby 3rd

4th

At lenth on Saturday evening the Stage arrived which opened a prospect of moving. My time however was still engaged every day as before. On Sunday it thawed all day and rained at Night so that we had but a bad prospect before us, however as Monday Morng proved very fine and we had a good party we determined to push forward at all events. Mr. Griffeth who accompanied me to Boston was to have been one of our Party but when we had got to the Stage and ready to embark he gave it up on account of the Cold which began to be rather severe.[19] At About nine in the Morning we got into the Stage and found our Party consisted of Le Marquis de Chappedelaine, a

Captain in the first Regt of french Dragoons, a Mr. Clow [Clough?] a Merchant in Philadelphia, a Mr. Jordan of Baltimore and Myself. It was to be remarked that we had not a Native of the Country with us nor had we any two of the same Nation being an English, a french, a Scots & an Irishman. Our time passed very merryly and after having gone about Eight Miles we crossed the Patossco [Patapsco] ferry on the Ice and met with no accident until we stopped to dinner, but whilst we were eating our dinner someone took away a bottle of Cherry Brandy which Mr. Grant of Baltimore had given us. Having again fixed ourselves in the Waggon we Proceeded some Miles when our driver turned out of the common Road and went through feilds for two Miles which he told us he was obliged to do to cross at a ford below the ordinary one which was so clogged up with Ice that we could not cross at it. Here after some difficulty we arrived and it was for some time a matter of doubt wether or not we should attempt to cross it the water being much higher than our driver had ever seen it before. It was at lenth determined to try it, in whch we succeeded but our horses very near swam and the water came into the Waggon very much. This difficulty over we were in good hopes we should get on until our driver told us that this water which we found so deep was by far the shallowest Creek on the road and that he did not think we could get on to Bladensburgh [Bladensburg]. It was near dark when we got to a small house kept by one Willet where we changed horses, and contrary to the opinion of every one in the house determined to go on. As the Sun Sett it began to freeze extreemly hard and the wind blew a hard Gale which encreased the cold so as to make it very disagreeable. We had not gone more than a Quarter of a mile from the house before we came to a Run of water which obliged our driver to leave the main road and drive some distance through the wood whilst we all got out to lighten the Stage. Having got in again we proceeded about five Miles when we came near another run of Water but to our Surprise when within about two hundred yards of the Stream the whole wood was so overflowed as to render it very dangerous to attempt passing it.

We had now no alternative but were obliged to return to the Wretched hovel we had just left. On our return it being Quite dark we found a great deal of difficulty in getting through the swamp in the Wood, but the Poor Marquis who remain in the Stage was in a worse State than ourselves as he was very near overset several different times. At lenth we arrived once more at the Miserable House we were obliged to lodge at. This house like all the rest in this part of the country seemed calculated only for the Summer, being Situated on a high Hill, open at every seam and a vast number of doors and Windows to create a free Current of Air in the hot season of the Year, which no doubt is in that season very pleasing but to us was dreadfull for the Wind encrasing as Night came on blew almost a hurricane and might have perhaps shook down the old fabreck had not the openings of its Joints admitted the Air freely thro every part of it. Our Supper was the best thing we found in the house which consisted of some Bacon and a few Quails fried, but as to Liquor we could get nothing but very bad common Rum. Such as it was we put up with it and making the best of our bad bargain, with the assistance of a very large fire contrived to keep ourselves tolerably warm, but when bed time aproached we found another difficulty. There was only two in the house and none of us chose to sleep two in a bed.[20] I therefore offered to Sleep on the Floor and Mr. Clow took possession of four chairs for his bed. Wither the Marquis conceived that I had chosen the warmest Birth or did it out of compliment I cannot say but he collected all his Cloathes and laid himself down before the fire whilst I was out of the Room which place all my arguments could not make him relinguish so I was obliged to take to one of the beds On which I laid myself wraped up in all the Cloathes I could muster. As the Night passed off so the Wind encreased and towards Morng it blew so hard that the house shook very much and I Rather think we are indebted to a strong stone Chimney that it was not blown away. About day light our fire was almost out and Mr. Clow was obliged to creep into bed with Mr. Jordan. The Marquis stood out a short time longer but at lenth was forced to get up and Call the people of the house to make up the fire which done he was so digusted with his Bed that he satt until we all arose by the fire side. About Eight oClock our

Feby 5th

Driver told us he would prepare his horses to proceed and we of course prepard for our Journey. As we had not taken off our Cloaths we had only to get up and shake ourselves as the dogs do and we were dressed after whch we took a Biscuit and a little Rum and Milk for Breakfast and once more embarked in our Crazy Waggon.

When we got to the bottom of the Hill we were obliged to walk thro the Swamp as before and having gone to the place we turned back from the Night before, we had the satisfaction to find the water had sunk very much so that we passed without difficulty over the Stream which is called the Point Branch, or Run. We now proceeded until we got within sight of the town of Bladensburgh where we found another Creek equaly swelled with the former. Our driver however at lenth pushed through it and we got over it very well. Here we Stopped at a house almost as bad as the one we had left where we got some bad Tea and worse Coffee for Breakfast in a Room where we were almost frozen, the whole time we staid the cold being very intense.[21] This Morng whilst we were here one of our party, Mr. Jordan, found he had left his purse containing near ten pounds sterling in the house where we slept, and altho from appearances he had very little reason to hope ever to see it again he nevertheless sent a man back for it with orders to bring it to George Town [Georgetown]. In the mean time we pursued our Rout towards that place. We again recrossed the River at the end of this town with good success but we had not gone above two hundred yards before we came to another Creek which we got through with great difficulty as the Ice formed on each Bank was almost Strong enough to bear our horses, and being the first who had crossed were obliged to break our way through it. We were hardly out of this water before the Pin came out which fastens the hind to the fore Wheels. Had this happened when we were in the water we should have been in great danger. This took us near an hour before we could repair it sufficiently to get the Waggon to the next house which was about half a Mile, where we got the pin put in. It was however done so badly that we had not gone more than half a Mile before the same accedent happened again and we were again obliged to have recourse to the Assistance of some Negroes from a Neighbouring Plantation who again set us to Right. It now seemed to be well done and I was in good hopes we should have got into George town but just as we got within two Miles of that place when a sudden jerk broke it again worse than ever. We were however again fortunate by being near to a house where we went to warm ourselves and got the man from thence to mend our Waggon for we were now so very cold we could be but little use ourselves. This repair took longer time than any other but as we were warm in the house we thought the least of it. Being thus a third time reinstated we moved slowly on with fear and Trembling least the same accedent should again happen which would have been fatal as we could expect no kind of help. We however got very well to within about a quarter of a Mile of George town where we came to a small Creek called Rocky Run [Rock Creek] which we found in such a State that we could not get the Waggon over. It was nevertheless frozen hard enough to bear ourselves and quite tired out with fatigue and Cold we left the Waggon to go round by another ford and walked into town on foot. Our way lay over a very bleak Hill on one side of whch the town stands. Here I realy think I felt the cold as sharp as I ever did in Canada being often in the course of the quarter of Mile to turn round and take my Breath which the Cold wind had nearly deprived me of.

At lenth we arrived and got into a tolerable house where we got a very good dinner and after having waited about two hours for the Stage fearing it could not get over the ford we sent a Cart to bring our Baggage and it was fortunate we did as our horses were not strong enough to bring it up the Hill although they had got across the ford. Thus we had been from Eight in the Morng until Near Seven in the afternoon hard at work and only advanced Sixteen Miles on our Journey, and to add to our misfortunes we found the Southern Stage tired of waiting for us had sett off some hours, and we were now left within Eight Miles of Alexandria without a possibility of getting to it. We could indeed have walked ourselves but then we must have left our Baggage in a very precarious State which we did not like to do everyone of us having large Sums of Money in change to carry to a Merchant in Alexandria.

Feby 6th

By this means we were obliged to stay at George town the whole of the Next day. Next Morng after a more than usual indulgence in Bed we took a Walk to see the town which is agreeably situated at the head of the Navigation of the Potomack [Potomac] of which it commands a very fine and extensive View. It is a place now just rising into Note, does not contain more than two hundred houses, but it is one of the Ports from whence a good deal of Tobacco is shipped, having what is called a Tobacco warehouse for the Inspection of that Article. As this was the only curiosity to be seen we went directly to it and was fortunate enough to find the inspector employed in the Line of his office. The Warehouse is a Square Shed open to the inside of the Qadrangle in which the planters deposit their Tobacco until it is inspected. The Quantity here at present was not great, thre being only about 200 Hogsheads which I am told are Valued on the Spot at about ten Guineas Pr Hogshead. Altho the day was very severely cold we waitd to see the ceremony preformed which was simply thus. The Tobacco being Pressed so very hard into the Hogshead that when the hoops are started it comes off and leaves the Tobacco standing in a hard Mass, into whch it is with difficulty they can drive a Crow Barr. This must however be done in three different places so that he may see the center of the Hogshead, in Presence of the public Inspector who is an Offcer paid for that purpose by the State and who is the Judge wither or no it is Marketable Tobacco. If he finds it is not it is rejected, if it is, it is Passed and from that time becomes Saleable. This ceremony over, the Hogshead is again put over the Tobacco and the hoops whch had been before started replaced. The Hogshead is then Turned upon its other end, the Tobacco again Pressed into it, when it is headed and hooped as before.[22] When we return'd to our little Tavern we found the Man who Mr. Jordan had sent from Bladensburgh to enquire after his Purse had returned but no tidings of either Purse or Money.

Feby 7th

The whole of this day passed off without any kind of intelligene of our Stage, but about Eight in the Next Morng we had the Pleasure to hear it was on the other side of the River. We threfore once more prepared to proceed. It was not however without some difficulty that we could procure a Cart to take our Baggage across the River At lenth however having got one we crossed the Potomack and of course entered the State of Verginia. This River is here called ¾ of a Mile broad but I conceive about if we call it half a Mile we shall be nearer the Mark, yet had these people the consience to demand a dollar for the hire of their Cart. Having once more got into the Stage after a ride of Eight Miles without any accedent we Arrived at Alexandria where we put up at the bunch of Grapes Tavern.²³ This house is by no means so good as Grants at Baltimore tho tollerably good for an American Inn. It has one disadvantage in common with all the Rest whch is that a common Table is kept where you find Dinner at two oClock at which all the strangers in the house of every denomination are expected to Dine. This inconvenience was in some measure made up for by an acquaintance I formed with Colo. Harry [Henry, "Light-Horse Harry"] Lee who was famous as a Partizan the whole War having the command of an American Legion.

I was now within ten Miles of one great object of my Tour, General Washington, and having Letters to Coll. Fiztgerrald [John Fitzgerald] formerly one of his Aid de Camps and a Mr. [William] Hunter the Mayor of the place who was one of the generals intimate friends,²⁴ I immediately thought of paying him a visit and it was agreed that we should go on *Monday the 11th* whch was the anniversary of that Illustrious Mans Birth on whch day he had compleated his 56th year.²⁵ We had made a Large party to congratulate him on this occasion but unfortunately the Morng Proved so very bad that we could not go.²⁶ In the course of the Morng I reced a Card from a Society of Gentlemen requesting my Company at a Ball in the Evening which was given in honor of the day.²⁷ It was held in the house where I lodged, where by about seven we had thirty Ladies assembled, and great many more Gentlemen but the latter in this part of America are so fond [of] Cards it was with some difficulty we could find as many who would dance as there were Ladies, for every one of the latter Sex Danced. I cannot say much for the Elegance of the Ladies dress altho one of them assured the Marquis that there was a very great improvement since that day twelve months. At Eleven we had a cold collation in another Room after whch we Again danced until two oClock, at whch time they all left the room.

Feby 12th   Next day was the day appointed for the Election of the Mayor and Aldermen of the Corporation, whch put of our visit to the General until the *13th* when we set out for Mount Vernon, about Eleven in the fore noon.[28] Our party consisted of Mr. Hunter, Colol. Fitzegerald, Mr. Nelson, son to the General [Thomas Nelson] of that Name, the Marquis de Chappedelaine, and myself.[29] The frost having just broke up, the roads were of course very bad. Just as we got out of the town of Alexandria we had a Charming Vew of that place & the River Potomack which is here about a Mile Wide togeather with the hills on the opposite side which are everywhere interspersed with good houses belonging to the Neighbouring planters, for so every farmer in Virginia is called. On a Hill a little to the right is a house belonging to a Colol. Lyons [James? Lyon] which commands this prospect in all its beauty. In the course of Eight miles riding we got one or two other tollerable prospects, when we got a sight of the Generals House, and soon after entered his grownds by a new Road he is making. He seems to be laying out his grownds with great tast in the English fashion. Brown was he alive and here would certainly say this spot had great Capabilities but he could never call it good soil.[30] After riding about a Mile or not quite so much thro the grownds on rising a small hill we came to Mount Vernon. This house I am told came to the General by the death of a Brother of his who being very much attached to the late Admiral Vernon had named his seat after that Admiral. The front by which we entered had a Gras plot before it with a road round it for Carriages planted on each side with a number of different kinds of Trees among the rest some Weeping Willows which seem to flourish very well. On the one side of this stands the Garden, green house &c. and on the other the Stables &c. very well hidden from the vew of the house.

We had no sooner alighted than the Immortal General came to receive us at the door and conducted us into his Parlour where we found Mrs. Wash-inton, a Mrs. Stewart [Eleanor Stuart] her daughter by a former husband,[31] and a Colonel Humfreys [David Humphreys] formerly one of his Aid de Camps. We were hardly seated before the mildness and affabillity of this great man had removed all restraint, and our conversation became generall. It turned on the adoption of the New federal plan of government which he appears to be very much attached to. He said he had read with attention every publica-tion both for and against it, in order to see wither there could be any new objections, or that it could be placed in any other light than what it had been in the general convention, for whch as well as I could hear him he said he had saught in vain. As the Dinner was not quite ready we took a walk out into his grownds on the other side of the house. This front is placed towards the south in front of which is a Portico supported with Pillars near thirty feet high and Paved with flagg stones which must form a Charming shade in warm weather.[32] From hence is one of the most delightfull Prospects I ever beheld. It had the Command of a View each way of some Miles up and down the River Potowmack whch is here about two Miles broad On which during the Summer there are constantly ships moving. The Hills arrownd it are coverd with plantations some of which have Elegant houses standing on them all of which being situated on Eminences form very beautifull Objects for each other. Among the rest the General pointed out one whch I undertood belonged to Mr. [William?] Digges that we know in Richmond which is now inhabited by his Brother and is said to command a more beautyfull prospect than even Mount Vernon itself, from which it must receive a very considerable share of its beauty, having a full Veiw at about three Miles distant.[33] Digges's is on the Maryland shore of the River. But to return to Mount Vernon, before the South front is a peice of Ground kept as a Park in which thre are about forty Deer, some English, some Natives of this country but among the rest one very singular one whch he lately got as a present from the Back country called Kentucky. It is the size and shape of the American Deer and its Spots are of the same Colour but the rest of its Body is as white as the Driven Snow.[34] They

38. Mount Vernon, Virginia. Drawn, engraved, and published by William Russell Birch (1755–1834) in *The Country Seats of the United States of North America* (Springland, Pennsylvania, 1808), plate 15. *Courtesy of the Historical Society of Pennsylvania*

39. Dove with olive branch weather-vane, Mount Vernon. Modern Photograph. *Courtesy of the Mount Vernon Ladies' Association of the Union*

are all extreemly tame, come to be fed when they are called and will suffer you to play with them.

The next place we visited were the Stables whch are rather good than handsome. The first thing we were shewed was a Spanish Ass fourteen hands three inches high, whose head was of an enormous size and had Ears fourteen inches long. It was by far the largest Animal of the kind I ever had seen, and his Joints were all very large and Clumsey but extreemly strong. He gave us a Specimane of his song as soon as he was led out which appears to me to be the same as his kindred in England make use of. He was then led into his Stable again and one of the same kind of Animals from Malta brought out. This Animal was as delicate as the other was Clumsey. His head and Ears were indeed very large and long but his make was extreemly fine. He was not near so tall as the Spanish one but his coat much finer. The Spanish one was of a Light Colour the Maltese of a Dark. This Exhibition of Asses over we were shewen a very fine Stallion called Magnolio. He was above Sixteen hands high, of a very beautyfull shape, it supposed to be I am told as fine a horse as any born in this country. He is however from English parents tho I did not hear his genealogy. By these Animals it may be presumed the General is very fond of breeding horses whch I am told is his turn as well as that of a great many other Gentlemen of this country. He seems however to think that the Introduction and use of Mules will be usefull to the country for which reason he makes it his study to raise as many of that usefull Species of Animal as he can. He has hitherto been very very unfortunate having lost a good many before they were old enough to work. He however shewed us some of about a year and half or two years old from the Spanish Ass which were at that Age as large as common Mules when full grown. These he intends to make use of in his Carriage as soon as they are old enough, but his Attention in this way does not seem confined to horses and Mules Alone.[35] It is the compleatest farm Yard and he appears to be the compleatest Gentleman farmer I have ever met in America and perhaps I may Add England.

Having gone thro the farm yard we again returned to the Parlour where

40. Advertisement offering stud services of the jackasses Royal Gift, Knight of Malta, and Magnolio, dated Mount Vernon, March 6, 1788. From the *Annapolis Maryland Gazette*, March 13, 1788. *Courtesy of the Maryland Historical Society*

Mount Vernon, March 6, 1788.

ROYAL GIFT,

and the

KNIGHT of MALTA,

Two valuable imported jack-asses,

WILL cover mares and jennies at Mount Vernon the ensuing spring, for (on account of the scarcity of cash) three guineas the season, and two shillings and six-pence to the groom, for his care of, and attention to, the females.

The first is of the most valuable race in the kingdom of Spain—the other is of the best breed in the Islands of Malta.

ROYAL GIFT (now 6 years old) has increased in size since he covered last season, and not a jenny, and hardly a mare to which he went, missed.

The KNIGHT of MALTA will be four years old this spring, about fourteen hands high, most beautifully formed for an ass, and extremely light, active and sprightly; comparatively speaking resembling a fine courier.

These two jacks seem as if designed for different purposes, but equally valuable; the first, by his weight and great strength, to get mules for slow and heavy draught; the other, by his activity and sprightliness, for quicker movements. The value of mules on account of their longevity, strength, hardiness and cheap keeping, is too well known to need description.

MAGNOLIO,

STANDS at the same place for two guineas the season, and two shillings and six-pence to the groom—The money, in both cases, to be paid before the jennies or mares are taken way, as no accounts will be kept.

Good pasture, well enclosed, will be provided at half a dollar per week, for the convenience of those who incline to leave their mares or jennies, and every reasonable care will be taken of them, but they will not be ensured against thefts, escapes, or accidents.

JOHN FAIRFAX, Overseer.

we found the party Augmented by the Arrival of Major [George Augustine] Washington, Nephew to the General, and a Mr. Ingram [Ingraham] who I had before seen in Alexandria.[36] Soon after our return [we] were joined by a Miss Stewart [Stuart] sister to Mrs. Stewarts husband.[37] As soon as all the party were Assembled Dinner was Announced. It was a very good one but the part of the entertainment I liked best was the affable easy manners of the whole family which continued thro out the whole. The Ladies left the room soon after Dinner but the Gentlemen continued for some time longer. There were no public toasts of any kind given, the General himself introducing a round of Ladies as soon as the Cloath was removed, by saying he had always a very great esteem for the Ladies, and therefore drank them in preference to any thing else.

After we rose from table we again went to enjoy the Prospect before the South front of the house which I have before said was beautifull beyond description and the Mildness of the day left us nothing to regret but the want of Verdure which the season of the Year had Naturaly deprived us of. We were now obliged to think of returning But before we set out again joined the Ladies and drank Tea. I am sure my dear Frank you will expect me to give you some account of this family of whom we have so often spoken and for whom from the General public character I know you have so high an esteem. As to his Public Character it is above my Pen so I shall only endeavour to give a few particulars which perhaps may not be so well known. He is decended from an English family from the north of England, I could not find what County from whence his Grandfather came to this Country.[38] His father lived on the River Rapahannak [Rappahannock] almost Opposite to the Town of Fredrickbg [Fredericksburg] in which town his Mother and Sister now live. His Paternal Estate was not very great, he however by good Management, by his Marriage with a Rich Widow named Custis, her Maiden Name was Dondridge [Dandridge] and by the Addition of his Brothers fortune to his own has now a very good one, which he appears to me to be cultivating with very superior taste. The House at Mount Vernon is a good one about Sixty feet long exclusive of the Wings which are Joined to it by a light Collonade.³⁹ It has however the misfortune to have been built at a great many different times, for which reason like a great many others it has very few good Rooms in it, except one which is lately added that I am told is a good one, for I did not see it. The House however does not to look at it appear to be a patched affair like a good many we could mention, being reduced to two regular fronts. But to return to the family, His person is by no means like any Picture I have ever seen of him nor do I know how to give a juster Idea of this great man's person than in the words of Le Marquis De Chastelleux [Chastellux], whch I shall therefore transcribe in the Margin.⁴⁰ As to his Lady she appears to me to be a Plain good Woman very much resembling the Character of Lady Bountyfull, is very cheerfull and seems most happy when contributing towards the happiness of others. Mrs. Stewart is a very lively agreeable Woman, & Lastly Major Washington seems to be a very Genteel Young Man of perhaps five & twenty who is lately Married to a Miss Basset [Frances Bassett] whose family I am told are Originaly from England.⁴¹

It was near dark when we left this agreeable party but tho [thro?] having a fine Moon we got very safe home to Alexandria which place I left the Next

Feby 14th   day on my way to Frederiksburgh.⁴² It was late in the afternoon before I set out so that I was again obliged to the Moon the greatest part of my Journey to Dumfrees [Dumfries] where I arrived about Eleven oClock at Night, having passed on our Road a small place named Colchester. Both these places are situated on Creeks that communicate with Potowmack River. Dumfries tho not a large place is a place of considerable trade. Having staid here all Night I

Feby 15th   again set out in the Morng and after Breakfasting at Stafford Court house I reached Fredricksbugh in good time to dinner.⁴³ Here I met with Mr. [Josiah] Watson of Alexandria & Mr. Clow who had come from Baltimore with me.⁴⁴ This place is situated at the head of the Navigation of the Rapahonack, has a good many houses but is not so large as Alexandria. Its situation is very fine and is surrounded by a great many very fine houses belonging to different Planters. In short the Banks of all these Rivers are extreemly beautifull. I her also met with an Irish Gentleman named OConnor who is about to Publish an history of America.[45] Having a good many letters of Introduction to this place I could have spent some time very agreeably but that I wished to hasten my departure for England. I threfore staid here only two days one of which I dined with

Feby 16th General [George] Weedon, with whom I met a Coll. Heath [William Heth] who had been Prisoner at Quebec on our coming there in 1776, who pleased me very much by very publicly doing justice to Lord Dorchester and his Brother Thomas [Carleton] for the treatment they then received.[46] The next

17th 18th day I dined with a Mr. Patton, a Merchant, and on the day following late in the afternoon being joined by my old fellow Traveler the Marquis de Chappedelaine we again set out and that evening slept at a house called the Bowling Green about 22 Miles and from thence proceeded on our Journey. In

19th the course of the Morng we crossed the heads of the Mathapony [Mattaponi] River but finding Bridges we had no difficulty altho when we came to the Pammunkey [Pamunkey] we found it so much overflowed that altho we passed dry over the Bridge we were obliged to drive a considerable distance up to the Horses Bellys in water, and a Waggon whch had crossed just before us not knowing the road had been in danger of being lost.[47] After this we crossed the heads of the Chickahammony [Chickahominy] River where we found Bridges as in the former one and we arrived at Richmond about Sun Set in the evening and put up at Andersons Tavern which is a very tolerable American Inn.[48]

This place is at present the seat of Government where we were very civily received by Governor [Edmund] Randolph. It is situated at the head of the Navigation of the James River just abreast of a very Beautyfull Rapid intersperced with small Islands which to look at it from the lower end of the town appears not unlike the Coteau du Lac above Montreal tho on a smaler Scale. The Town may be said to be situated in a low situation close to the Banks of the River. Altho thre is a great many houses on the Hill this upper town is I am told much more healthy than the lower. They are almost all wooden houses and were I am told entirely so until last Winter when a dreadfull fire swept away almost half the Town which has induced them to build them up with

41. A view of Richmond, Virginia, about 1804. Etching, probably issued before 1807, by Charles Balthazar Julien Fêvret de Saint-Mémin (1770–1852). The large building with columns on the hill in the distance is the Virginia State Capitol which was built between 1785 and 1796. *Courtesy of the I. N. Phelps Stokes Collection, Prints Division, the New York Public Library, Astor, Lenox, and Tilden Foundations*

Brick to the great Ornament of the place. But the principal Building is the State House or, as it is Called, the Capital. This is not yet finished, but if they compleat it agreeable to the Model it will be the most Elegant building in America. It is built after the Model of the Maison Quarre [Carrée] at Neomes [Nîmes] in france. It is a Brick building of amazing strenth. I am told the Walls at the foundation are six feet thick And so on in proportion upwards. In its present situation without the Portico or Roof it looks rather heavey so that a gentleman the other day compared it to a Square Iron Box. There is also here a handsome Hall belonging to the free Masons and many Light pretty houses upon the different Emminences near the Town.⁴⁹ On the opposite side of the water stands the small Town of Manchester which adds very much to the beauty of the Landscape. These places carry on a very large trade for Tobacco which is now almost the only export from this state. Of this Article however they export Annualy Sixty Thousand Hogsheads which valued at ten pounds sterling pr Hogshead Amounts to Six hundred Thousand pounds sterling.⁵⁰ I'am told also that before the War their Trade with the West Indies and the Mediteranean [Mediterranean] was nearly of equal Value. The one is lost by their seperation from England the other by means of the Algereens [Algerines or Algerians]. The Loss of the West India Trade has very deeply hurt all the States as well as this of which you hear constant complaint where ever you go.⁵¹ It is now some time since I spoke of the face of the country which has been occasioned from a want of Variety. To pass thro Virginia by the common Road any one will Wonder where the Inhabitants live, as you may very often go several Miles without seeing any kind of habitation better than a small Hutt for Negroes who cultivate the small patches of Tobacco land that you find near the Road. The reason is this. The Planters Possess very large Tracts of land which they cultivate by Negroes who live in small huts while they themselves live in the more agreeable parts of the Country on the Banks of the Large Rivers, which are every where extreemly beautifull. The Negroes in this State are computed to be as Numerous as the Whites.⁵² In this particular part more so.⁵³

On the *21st* we dined with a Mr. [William] Donald after which we went to the Governor. This day turned out very bad, a heavy fall of snow for the greatest part, so as to prevent my going to Petersburgh [Petersburg] as I at first intended, but from what I can learn no great loss was sustained by this disappointment, particularly as it gave me the pleasure of passing most part of *22nd* the next day with the Governor and his family.⁵⁴ Both he and Mrs. Randolph are very agreeable people. He is very much like General [Henry] Hope both in person and manners. He seems very anxious for the success of a Navigable Canal they have in hand in order to pass the falls near this place. It is about five miles in lenth and in great forwardness. This done and some other small obstacles removed whch does not amount to more than three miles more they will have intercourse by water up beyond what they call the Blue Ridge where the River takes its Rise by which they will be enabled to bring down the greatest part of the produce of the back part of the Country.[55] It will also be of great service in suppling the town with fuel there being very fine Coal mines up the River. This coal does not appear to me to make a very cheerfull fire altho is [it] cokes very well, and burns very long. A Gentleman of the place told me some experiments had been made between it and some Coal brought from England in Blacksmiths work in which it was found to go further by an fourth than the English Coal.[56] On Sunday the *24th* I was to have dined with Mr. [William] Alexander formerly a partner with the famous Robt Morris but tho [thro?] his house being four Miles in the country I could not go without a Carriage on account of the bad roads and being Sunday all the Carriages were engaged.[57]

This evening I took leave of the Marquis and left Andersons Tavern, to lodge at the house from whence the Stage went. On my Arrival I found the house in confusion owing to a Young man who was by trade a Carpenter, a relation of the Landlord, who had got up in his sleep and getting out of an end window had got up on the Top of the house where he was walking backward and forward on the Sharp Ridge for some time then supposing himself at work in the line of his business took of his Coat and sitting down appeard as if he was at work shingling the house finding fault with some one who he supposed was at work with him and snoring all the while. I [He?] would then take a walk again which he repeated for when he came down the same way he went up but when he came to the window he could not open it which some of the people seing did for him very gently then taking hold of him draged him in to the Room and put him to bed. He had hurt his hands very much by knocking against the Roof of the House but did not awake until they had taken hold of him and almost got him in at the window. Altho this was all over before my getting to the house Yet it made such a noise I could get but little sleep before *Feby 25th* day light when the Coachman came and called me to set out on our Journey.

We went Seventeen Miles to Breakfast at a house kept by one Fraser, the place where Lord Cornwallis halted the first days March of his fatal retreat towards York town [Yorktown].[58] Indeed each Stage as we went was one of his days march towards that place. Our next stage was to New Kent Court house 14 Miles where we Changed horses and in fourteen further came to Bird's ordnary[59] where we dined after which 16 further brought us to Williamsburg the former Capital of the State when under the English govrnment. This place seems to me to look more like an English town than almost any I have seen in this State. It consists principaly of one long strait Street which I was told was a Measured Mile in lenth. I confess it did not appear to me to be so long. At one end of this is placed the Colledge of William & Mary whch is a very handsome building. The front towards the town is by far the best which has a spacious Yard before it in which are two very handsome houses detached from the principal building in which the Professors live. The other front towards the Country is spoild by the wings being made too deep for the Center of the building which gives it something the appearance of the

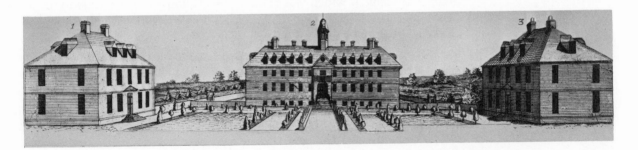

42. William and Mary College, Williamsburg, Virginia. Copperplate engraving possibly after a drawing by John Bartram or Mark Catesby, about 1740. (1) Brafferton Building (1723), the Indian School of the College of William and Mary. (2) The east front of the Sir Christopher Wren Building, the principal building of the College. (3) The President's House (1732). *Courtesy of Colonial Williamsburg*

Pallace of Hamilton in Scotland.[60] This Coledge is endowed well, has a Noble Library and very able Professors notwithstanding which it cannot by what I could learn be said to be in a flourishing state. A very large number of the students prefer Boarding out in the town.[61] On the Opposite end of this long Street is the Capital or State house which is a very handsome building adorned by a very handsome Marble Statue of Lord Bardintown [Botetourt] formerly governor of this state for whom the people of Virginia have a very great regard even to this moment besides which there is a handsome Church and a small but neat County Court house.[62] Altho I speak of this street in particular thre are many others which form a pretty town in all of which there are many good houses which I am sorry to say, that a great number of them are going to Ruin for want of inhabitants since the seat of government has been removed to Richmond. This place cannot be called a seaport in itself as no Stream comes up to the town but there are Creeks on each side within a half mile one from York River the other from James River which gives it free communication with both.[63]

About Six Miles from hence on the Banks of James River is Jamestown the first Settlement which was made in this Country. I did not go to see it as I could not hear it had thing[s] worthy of notice except its antiquity and I was rather hurried by hearing of a Sloop being advertized at Norfolk to sail in a few days for Charlestown to which place I wished to go. This induced me to

Feby 26th take the Stage the next day and Proceed to York town. This place rendered so famous from the fate of Lord Conwallis's Army was of too much consequence to be left unseen which induced me to stay. If I could have kept the Stage two hours it would have been as much as I could wish but that was impossible so I was obliged to let it go and to remain here two days. My time however passed very agreeably as I found here a Mr. McColly [Alexander McCauley] whom I had seen at Mr. Cursons at Baltimore with whom I passed that day, with whom I took a walk in the evening to see some part of the works, but as he had not been here during the war he could give me no kind of account

Feby 27th of the place. In the course of Breakfast next morning I found my host had been

43. Statue of the Right Honorable Norborne Berkeley. Drawing by Benjamin Henry Latrobe (1764–1820), about 1796, showing the Williamsburg Capitol portico with the statue of Berkeley, Lord Botetourt. *Courtesy of the Papers of Benjamin Henry Latrobe and the Maryland Historical Society*

44. Bruton Parish Church and William and Mary College. Watercolor by Thomas Millington, about 1836. *Courtesy of the Earl Gregg Swem Library, The College of William and Mary*

an Officer in the American Army, who I got to go round with me. The first thing that will strike anyone in the town is the ruins of the once Elegant house of Secretary [Thomas] Nelson. This was Lord Cornwallis's Qarters for the three first days of the seige when he was obliged to quit it and from that time lived in a small house under a high bank by the River side.[64] The Town of York is Situated on the Banks of a River of the same Name very near the mouth where it empties itself into Chesepeeke [Chesapeake] Bay. The situation of the town cannot well be called high altho the Bank of the River in which most of the place stands is rather so. Under this Bank where [were] a few houses which proved usefull in the seige as it was the only place of safty in town and those not even safe from Shells which were thrown in great abundance. Not far from each end of the town are two Marshes which very nearly encircle the place. On each side of these are extreemly high Banks and where on the whole if not inaccessable difficult of access. It seems to me that the keeping the Command of these Marshes and the Neck of Land between them should have been the principal object but his Lordship, as his Engineers, thought otherwise as they had made their marks on a more contracted Plan. He had indeed some small detached redoubts at first upon Pidgeon [Pigeon] Hill and the adjacent heights but these were left so soon as the Enimy were before the place.[65] They however had still a very Strong Line of works round the town and some good redoubts without it but it is now so much of it thrown down, and other parts altered and added to by the french Troops that it is now impossible to form any judgement what the works then were. By what I could make out the attack was only made upon one side of the town which was defended by a kind of Hornwork which occupied most part of the Neck of Land betwen the two Marshes with two Strong redoubts without it. One of these on a point near the River was called Point of Rock and was so Situated as to be inaccessable on two sides. The other was a Strong square on the open grownd. These after the Seige had been carried on some time were attacked and carried, the Point of Rock by the Americans, who took it with little or no Loss, the other by the French, who suffered very considerably altho they car-

To His Excellency Genl. Washington Commander in Chief of the Armies of the United States of America.

This Plan of the investment of York and Gloucester has been surveyed and laid down, and is Most humbly dedicated to his Excellency Published in every State in Servant.

Sebas. R. Bauman, Major of Artillery, New York, 1782.

YORK RIVER

References to the British Lines.

No. Battery of 2 guns and 2 howitz.
1. 1 do 24 Pr.
2. 1 do 6 or 8 Pr.
3. 1 do 9 Pr.
4. 1 do 9 Pr.
5. 2 do 24 Pr.
6. 2 do 24 & 18 Pr.
7. 2 do 18 Pr.
8. 2 do 24 & 18 Mor.
9. 2 do 24 Pr.
10. 1 do 4 In. Howitz.
11. 2 do 4 In. Howitz.
12. 3 Pr.
13. 6 Pr.

Gloucester side.

14. Battery of 2 Guns, 1 18 do 1 cohit.
15. Part of the British ships
16. Part of the British fleet, 2 night of 3.
17. Guadaloupe Frigate
18. Fowey Sloop of War
19. British Shipping as they appeared sunk
20. a do in. Ship set on fire
21. The Church set on fire by hot shot

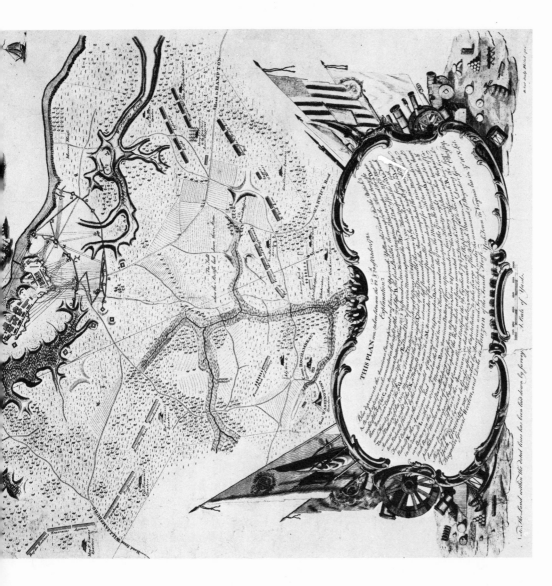

Map XV. Plan of the investment of York and Gloucester, between October 22 and 28, 1781. Dedicated to General Washington, this plan was prepared by Sebastian Bauman, Major of the New York or 2d Regiment of Artillery, engraved by Robert Scot, and published at Philadelphia in 1782. *Courtesy of the I. N. Phelps Stokes Collection, Prints Division, the New York Public Library, Astor, Lenox, and Tilden Foundations*

ried their point. These Works once taken the Americans immediately formed a communication between them and made them their second Parralel. It was now evidently over with his Lordship as these works were on as high or rather Higher grownd than his remaining ones were not many Yards distant from them, but above all the Point of Rock was so Situated as to command the Town in every part even under the Hill where they had before had some little saftey. The Americans had no sooner altered these works than a Negotiotion for the surrender of the place was begun.[66] The sequel is to well known to need repeating. My guide told me a circumstance of Collonel [Thomas] Dundas who was one who brought out the Articles, which by the agreement were to be the same as those at Charlestown in which it was agreed the Troops should march out with their Colours Cased, which Article Dundas wanted to have altered and after having in vain done his utmost to procure an alteration he deliverd the Articles ratified by Lord Cornwallis and burst into Tears.[67]

The most part of this day I passed with General Nelson son to Secretary Nelson of whom We have before spoken.[68] This gentleman has more the appearance of an English Country Squire than any one I ever met with in America. He had just returned from Riding when I delivered my letters of Introduction to him which I had got from Col. [Edward] Carrington And his conversation like those Gentlemen whom I have compared him to turn a good deal on horses and Dogs, Sporting &c. His family is very large and would have been very agreeable had there been less reserve on the part of the female part of it, who seemed to take hardly any part of the conversation and dinner once gone they went with it and we never saw more of them until Supper, not having joined us in the card Room, when they shewed the same inclination to silence. Among the company was a Mr. [Mann] Page from Gloscester [Gloucester] on the other side of York River who I think is son-in-Law to the General who seems to be a very sensible man & it is expected he will be one of the Convention for this State.[69] Having taken my leave of every one in this place I set *Feby 28th* out next day at Nine oClock in the Stage for Hampton. The road thro this part of the Country lies in very bad grownd along the Top of the Hills although you find excellent land near the Rivers on each side of you. It has however one advantage that being sandy grownd the road was extreemly good even at this season of the Year, as a Proof of which one set of horses took us 24 Miles. We got to Hampton about two PM where we got some Dinner.[70] By this I began to be a little aquainted with my fellow Travelers one of whom was named Reed who lived near the Mouth of Rapahannak the other, [Robert?] Boyd lived at Richmond and was brother to Capt. Boyd, of the Quebec with whom I went to England in 1782.

We had no sooner got our dinner than we agreed to set out for Norfolk. This is Eighteen Miles distant by water, and having procurd a boat we set off with a fair wind. The boat we were on board was not one of the regular ferry Boats but a Pilot boat borrowed for the purpose. She Saild extreemly well so that we crossed Hampton Road and got to Norfolk in two hours and half. The boys told us they had often gone in the same boat in one hour and a quarter. A little below the town of Norfolk on the opposite shore is the Remains of Fort Nelson,[71] which stands on the Spot whre Lord Dunmore first entrenched himself with his Regimented Negroes, nearly opposite to which is the remains of a very fine building which I was told was a distillery burned in the begining of the War and not yet rebuilt. This however was but a Prelude to what I was to see on my Arrival at Norfolk. Every twenty Yards presented the ruin of some house many of which appeard to be very good ones. Having heard this place was wantonly burnt in the commencement of the war I expected to have also heard it was the work of the British. In this however I was agreeably disappointed by learning from one of the Principal inhabitants that the English had only set fire to a store house or two near the waterside and which would have done but little dammage to the place, had not the Inhabitants set fire to all the Rest. On my expressing a wish to know what could induce them to commit such an act I was informed that it had been done, with an idea to prevent Lord Dunmore from forming a Garrison town of it, a pretty effectual means you will say of effecting their ends.[72] It enjoys a very excllent Port in common with Portsmouth whch is situated opposite to it a little higher up the

Bay. It is a place where a considerable quantity of Produce is Annualy Shiped. The town is now just rising from its Ruins but the houses are by no means so good as the old ones seem to have been. I put up at the Borrough [Borough] Tavern[73] kept by one Smith a Native of England but found it a very bad house and to my great disappointment found the Sloop for Charlestown which I expected to have found here had sail'd only a few hours before my Arrival. I had now no Alternative left but was obliged to wait with this determination that if any Vessle sailed for that part in a week or ten days I would go, if not that I would embark on board of one that was to sail about that time and return to England.

My stay here was extreemly disagreeable to me particularly the first week which happened to be very bad weather with hard frost and Snow notwithstanding the advanced state of the Season and the Latitude of about 36 degrees.

March We had on the *3d* of a Snow Storm which fell a foot or a foot and half Deep upon an average that confined every one very much at home, but after a few days hot weather it cleared of and we could again walk about. I now in a Short time made some aquaintance which helped to pass away the time, among the rest a Mr. Gilbert Robertson, lately of the west Indies, a Mr. [Benjamin] Pollard, Mayor of the place, to whom I had a letter from Philadelphia, a Doctor [James] Taylor & Doctor [John?] Ramsay who are aquaintance of Mr. Riddle. To these I soon added a Capt. Bolton of the Ship Union Island from Bristol, and for a day or two had the pleasure of Collel. Elegoods company with whom I had been aquainted in England.[74] This made my time toward the latter part pass infinitely more agreeable than the former. On the *9th* I took a walk to see the little town of Portsmouth which tho not so large as Norfolk is still a place of very considerable trade. They are both situated on a dead flat so that you can get no good prospect. The best is from on borad ship in the harbour when you see both places, togeather with a little place which is adorned with the name of Washington. In the course of my stay I saw Lord Dunmores [Dunmore's] Lines which have nothing remarkable in them. They extended from the head of one Creek to that of another and were simple Lines defended with small flat Bastions now very near level with the grownd. On the

12th I met my old aquantance the Marquis De Chappedelaine by whom I was introduced to Coll. [Josiah] Parker an American Officer of note who commanded in this part of the Country all the Latter part of the war and was I am told a principal in taking the Hessians at Trenton. He was extreemly civil to me and would have made my stay very agreeable if I had remained longer but tired of waiting I had taken my passage on board of the Brig Abby for Liverpool which was to sail on the *14th,* which prevented my leaving Norfolk after that time as I could not tell at what hour I should be called for. I [It] was not however before the *17th* that we got under sail and after some difficulty got into Hampton Road that evening but the wind altho such as would bring us down the River would not take us to Sea so we were obliged to come too where we remained until the *19th* in the Morng the wind being foul all day of the *18th,* nor could we get on shore the whole day as the wind blew very fresh and we were in the open Road, otherwise we should have been very glad to have gone to Hampton to get some Piggs having been disappointed by the person who was to suply us with them at Norfolk but as we could not leave the Ship we were obliged to put to Sea Next day without them tho very much against my will but as we had very remarkable success with all our Poultry we had no occasion for them as it turned out in the end.[75]

Day of Month	Latitude	Longitude	Remarks
March	d m	d m	
19	36..50	75..50	Saild from Hampton road at day Break with a pleasant breeze. At 11 A M passed Cape Henry. Left the land in the afternoon.
20	36..41	73..48	
21	36..16	70..50	
22	36..23	69..20	Spoke to the Brig Fame[?] of Washington which was known to one of our sailors before I could see the men on her deck.

Days of Month	Latitude	Longitude	Remarks
March	d m	d m	
23	37..2	66..42	
24	38..10	64..12	} Blew hard but fair.
25	38..47	61..42	
26	39..34	59..13	Moderate.
27	40..23	56..37	Blew hard.
28	41..9	54..7	
29	42..1	51..49	A Boy belonging to the Ship died. Supposed from the Colour of the Water and number of Birds that we
30	43..18	48..49	were on the Banks but found no soundings.
31	44..18	46..32	
April	d m	d m	
1	45..36	44..6	
2	45..35	41..14	
3	44..53	39..46	Here our difference of Latitude was nine miles more
4	45..27	37..53	than the distance on the Log Board supposed. A Northerly current.
5	46..32	37..37	
6	47..53	36..18	
7	48..41	34..3	
8	49..12	30..13	
9	49..31	26..31	
10	49..40	23..17	
11	50..8	20..3	
12	50..54	16..29	
13	51..0	14..31	In the morng early saw two french Luggers fishing. Could not speak to.

Days of Month	Latitude	Longitude	Remarks
April	d m	d m	
14	50 . 58	11 . 12	At noon hove the Lead in 60 Fathoms. Found white sand [and] small black specks. At One P M made the old head of Kinsale bearing North.
15	" "	" "	In the Evening passed the Saltees Rocks.
16	" "	" "	Passed Holy Head in Night, Midnight saw the Skerry [Skerries] Light.
17	" "	" "	Came to Anker of[f] Liverpool about Noon but was obliged to wait the next Tide before we could get into the River.

April 17   In the Evening the Tide serving we got up to the town where we had no small difficulty to get into the Dock having got a ground at the entrance but the weather being tolerable altho it blew fresh and the tide rising we at last got in very safe but it was still some time before we could get into a proper Birth for which purpose it was necessary to move several other Vessels. Whilst this was doing I was Surprised to see several men come on board with Strong Chains with which the[y] fastened down the Hatches without appearing to take notice of any one on board who on their part made no objections to its being done. On Enquiry I found this was a precaution taken with every Ship that came in loaded either wholly or in part with Tobacco which was our case. This took up more time than we expected so that it was quite Dark before we got on shore when Capt Brathwaite conducted me to the Hotel where I remain during my stay and which I found a very excellent house but very

18th   extravagant. The whole of the next morning was taken up in getting my Baggage Cleared at the Custom house, when having taken an early dinner I took a Walk to see as much of the town as my time would permit me to do. I found it very extensive and abounding in Public buildings of all kinds many of which were very handsome particularly the Royal Exchange. Having lodged my Baggage in the Waggon Warehouse to be sent to London and taken my place in the Mail Coach which to me was a New Conveyance. We set out therin at Eight oClock in the evening and was surprised at the Rapidity of our

April 19
20th

Journey, as we Breakfasted at Stone, Dined at Coventry and Arrived in London the day following at Eight in the morning but not without my being extremely fatigued and from my having been so long on board Ship my Feet and Ancles Swelled so much that I was obliged to cut off my Boots before I got to town where a little rest soon set all to rights again.

NOTES

ENYS' INTERPOLATIONS, here treated as notes, are indented. All other notes are by the Editor.

INTRODUCTION

1. Daniel Lysons and Samuel Lysons, *Magna Brittania; Being a Concise Topographical Account of the Several Counties of Great Britain–Cornwall,* III (London, 1814), 103: 119. "The Creation of the Universe" is a manuscript in the Bodleian Library. Reference to the second play is in "Notes," compiled by the late Sarah Louise Enys (1867–1952). Mrs. Enys wrote: "A parchment rent-roll goes back to Edward III, and there are documents of John's reign. Hals, the Cornish Historian says the Enys family is British and this means of course that they were here before the Saxons came to Cornwall. In an ancient play written in the Cornish language Enys is given as a present to King Solomon!" Regarding the Enys library, Mrs. Enys wrote that it contains "the usual collection of books found in any gentleman's country house in England—Poetry, History, and many volumes of Buffon's Natural History, Gentleman's Magazine, Annual Register, Herbals and Bestiaries, and a great many leather-bound Tomes—among them a

'Vinegar' Bible and a volume hand-printed in Latin with the date 1482. . . . Here and there on the shelves are volumes published at the time of the Revolutionary War.

"Between the long Victorian windows in this room are low cupboards with books above. . . . " Here "I came upon a pile of what looked like eighteenth century exercise books—The covers were faded pink and green, and the writing inside was fine and almost illegible. I got a magnifying glass and read, to my amazement 'Ticonderoga,' 'Lake Champlain,' 'Quebec,' 'Montreal' with sketch-maps here and there. Then I saw Diary and 'John Enys, Ensign, 1774.' "

2. Burke, *Landed Gentry* (1939), p. 705.

3. Enys, "Notes," no pagination. The *Eton College Register* (pp. 182–83), which contains incomplete information for the years 1750–90, lists Francis (1766–70) and Samuel (1766–67) Enys, but not John Enys. Major H. Everard, *History of Thos. Farrington Regiment, subsequently Designated the 29th (Worcestershire) Foot 1694 to 1891* (Worcester, England, 1891), p. 71.

4. For an excellent, definitive account of the Boston Massacre, see Hiller B. Zobel, *The Boston Massacre* (New York: Norton, 1970). Everard, *29th,* pp. 62–71. Other, less important sources of information on the 29th Regiment: *Short Histories of the Territorial Regiments of the British Army,* edited by R. de M. Rudolf (London, n.d.), pp. 285–93; Richard Gale, *The Worcestershire Regiment* (London: Leo Cooper, 1970); Richard Cannon, *Historical Records of the British Army* . . . (London, 1836); "MSS Records of the 29th Foot (Worcestershire)," Ministry of Defence Library, Whitehall, London.

5. John Enys, "History of the 29th Regiment of Foot 1702–1800," MSS in the archives of Cornwall County Council, Truro.

6. J. W. Fortescue, *A History of the British Army,* 4 vols. (London: Macmillan, 1935), vol. 3. For more detailed accounts of American operations, see Benson J. Lossing, *The Pictorial Field-Book of the Revolution,* 2 vols. (New York, 1860); William J. Morgan, ed., *Naval Documents of the American Revolution,* 6 vols. Washington, 1964–); Christopher Ward, *The War of the Revolution,* edited by John R. Alden, 2 vols. (New York: Macmillan, 1952); Piers Mackesy, *The War for America 1775–1783* (Cambridge, Mass.: Harvard University Press, 1965).

7. Everard, *29th,* p. 77; Enys, 29th.

8. Lossing, *Field-Book,* I: 168–99; Ward, *Revolution,* I: 150–80; Mackesy, *War for America,* p. 79; Fortescue, *History,* III: 164.

9. Fortescue, *History,* III: 165–67; Alfred L. Burt, *The Old Province of Quebec* (Toronto:

Ryerson Press, 1933), pp. 224–30; Gustave Lanctot, *Canada and the American Revolution* (Cambridge, Mass.: Harvard University Press, 1967), p. 102 and passim; Ward, *Revolution*, I: 181–201; Lossing, *Field-Book*, I: 190–202. Data on troop strength vary. In 1776 General Burgoyne organized his troops in an advanced Corps and three brigades. The 29th, along with the 21st and 62nd, composed the third brigade commanded by the General Gordon mentioned in Enys' journal. C. T. Atkinson, "British Forces in North America, 1774–1781: Their Distribution and Strength," *Journal of the Society for Army Historical Research* 16 (61) (Spring 1937): 3–23.

10.   Everard, *29th,* p. 78; Fortescue, *History,* III: 180–82.

11.   Meticulous coverage of the Valcour engagement is given in *Naval Documents of Revolution,* especially VI: 1197–1262, 1272–79; names and armaments of American vessels, p. 1258; British vessels, p. 1244. See also pp. 1272–79; Ward, *War of the Revolution,* I: 384–97.

12.   Everard, *29th,* p. 93.

13.   Ibid., pp. 94–96; Enys, 29th.

14.   Everard, *29th,* pp. 97–98.

15.   Ibid., p. 100.

16.   This manuscript is also in archives of Cornwall County Council, Truro.

17.   *A Journal by Thos: Hughes,* edited by E. A. Benians (Port Washington, N.Y.: Kennikat, 1970), pp. 134–35.

18.   Enys, 29th.

19.   Everard, *29th,* pp. 107, 127–31.

20.   Ibid., p. 136.

21.   Ibid., pp. 138, 158–61, 185–210; Enys, 29th.

22.   Everard, *29th,* pp. 163–66.

23.   Ibid., pp. 167–71.

24.   Ibid., pp. 177–78.

25.   Ibid., pp. 178–79; Enys, 29th.

26.   Everard, *29th,* pp. 179–81.

27. Enys, 29th; Everard, *29th,* pp. 213–14.

28. Everard, *29th,* pp. 221–22, 560.

29. Ibid., pp. 218–27; Fortescue, *History,* IV: 516–19, 570–79.

30. Fortescue, *History,* IV: 589–91; Everard, *29th,* p. 227; Enys, 29th.

31. Fortescue, *History,* IV: 591–98; Everard, *29th,* pp. 227–29.

32. Enys, 29th; Everard, *29th,* pp. 230–31.

33. "The Helder Expedition," Public Records Office (London) W. O. 1/179, pp. 144–45, 168. Everard, *29th,* pp. 232–33; Fortescue, *History,* IV: 650–53.

34. Everard, *29th,* pp. 232–36; Enys, 29th.

35. Fortescue, *History,* IV: 657.

36. Ibid., IV: 665; Enys, 29th.

37. Everard, *29th,* pp. 239–42.

38. Extensive coverage of the Sept. 19 and Oct. 2 operations is in Fortescue, *History,* IV: 670–700. The peace terms were favorable to the British considering the fact that they had but three days' bread supply left on Oct. 20.

39. Everard, *29th,* pp. 243–44; Enys, 29th.

40. Everard, *29th,* pp. 246–48.

41. *Bath Chronicle,* Aug. 6, 1818; Street Directories, 1809, 1812.

42. Pierre Francois Xavier De Charlevoix, *Journal of a Voyage to North America . . .* 2 vols. (London, 1761); William Guthrie, *A New Geographical, Historical, and Commercial Grammar; . . .* (London, 1777); Marquis De Chastellux, *Travels in North-America in the Years 1780, 1781, and 1782* (London, 1787). Since there is no evidence that Enys knew the French language, the English editions of the travels of Charlevoix and of Chastellux have been given.

THE AMERICAN REBELLION, 1776–1782

1. A sandbank in the Thames estuary.

2. William Evelyn was commissioned Lieutenant-General of the 29th (or Worcestershire) Regiment of Foot, Canada. War-Office, 1783, *A List of the Officers of the Army,* p. 9. Unless otherwise noted, identifications of British Officers are based on this work.

3. *Surprize,* frigate of 28 guns; *Martin,* sloop of 14 guns. James J. Colledge, *Ships of the Royal Navy* (New York: Augustus M. Kelley, 1969), pp. 535, 349.

4. The *Isis* was a ship of 50 guns. Ibid., p. 286. In reaching Quebec the *Isis* had great difficulty with ice. "Journal of H. M. S. *Isis,* Captain Charles Douglas," *Naval Documents of the American Revolution,* edited by William J. Morgan, 6 vols. to date (Washington, D.C.: USGPO, 1964–), IV: 1211–12. Thomas Hughes, who reached the Banks of Newfoundland at about the same time as Enys, wrote: "One of these mountains [of ice] was so large and high, that our largest ships near it appear'd like boats, the tops of their masts did not reach a tenth part to the summit." Hughes, *Journal,* p. 3.

5. This was a very slow, yet correct, way of distilling fresh water.

6. "Anticosti Island was surveyed in 1767 by Thomas Wright under Sir Guy Carleton's instructions. This surveyor may very well have made such a statement [concerning the goats] in view of the disastrous incidence, for many years, of shipwrecks in the Island's waters. The Island remained undeveloped until 1874 when the first attempts at colonization were initiated." Information provided by Miss G. D. Beauvais, Public Archives of Canada.

7. On Gaspé Peninsula.

8. Linzee was Captain of the *Surprize. Naval Documents of Revolution,* V: 1364.

9. Ibid., p. 1364.

10. This number is highly exaggerated. In reporting on the engagement at the Cedars, Capt. Charles Douglas, R. N. stated, May 25, 1776: "if my information be true, a Triumvirate, consisting of Doctor [Benjamin] Franklin and other members of the Rebel Congress, went away in a great hurry, on hearing of the flight of their Army (of 3000 Men) from before Quebec." *Naval Documents of Revolution,* V: 243–45. Richard Montgomery's column had consisted of 300 men; Benedict Arnold's forces

had numbered about 600. Carleton had 1,800 men. Mark M. Boatner, *Encyclopedia of the American Revolution* (New York: McKay, 1966), pp. 907–908. On April 2 Major General David Wooster came to the American camp at Quebec with troops that brought up the American force to 2,000 men. He took command and Arnold withdrew to Montreal. In May Gen. John Thomas superseded Wooster. The army that had reached a strength of 2,500 was reduced to 1,900, of whom no more than 1,000 were fit for duty. Ward, *Revolution,* I: 196. See also Burt, *Quebec,* pp. 224, 233; Lanctot, *Canada and the American Revolution.*

11.   Either Capt. Robert Douglas, then serving under Carleton, or Charles Douglas, Captain of the *Isis.*

12.   During this critical period Quebec was not devoid of judicial machinery. On April 26 Carleton had issued a proclamation announcing the appointment of six conservators of the Peace. Burt, *Quebec,* p. 249.

13.   Enys was probably referring to Colonel Allen Maclean (1725–84), who commanded the 84th Regiment in the Revolution. Thomas Anburey, *With Burgoyne from Quebec* (Toronto: Macmillan, 1963), pp. 45, 203n.

14.   Vessel of 28 guns, built in 1757. Colledge, *Ships,* p. 323. Mackenzie was also spelled McKinzie. Morgan, ed., *Naval Documents of Revolution,* V: 1440, index.

15.   See C. T. Atkinson "British Forces in North America, 1774–1781: Their Distribution and Strength," *Journal of the Society for Army Historical Research* 16 (61) (Spring 1937): 3–23.

16.   Harvey's report from Three Rivers to Capt. Charles Douglas regarding the action of June 8 is in *Naval Documents of Revolution,* V: 433, 467–69.

17.   The *British Queen* was a British Army victualer. Ibid., p. 1397.

18.   Irvine was exchanged 6 May 1778; Thompson was exchanged 25 October 1780. F. B. Heitman, *Historical Register of Officers of the Continental Army during the War of the Revolution* (Washington, 1893), pp. 238, 398. Major Griffith Williams wrote to Lord George Germain, 23 June 1776, "We took General Thompson, Colo. Irwin, their Aids du Camp, & I know not what number of them more prisoners." *Naval Documents of Revolution* V: 692–95. Ward, *Revolution,* I: 198.

19.   Gen. William Thompson had a force of 2,000 musketmen. Brigadier John Sullivan led a brigade of 3,300. But insurmountable difficulties again met the Americans in this second attempt to capture Quebec. Ward, *Revolution,* I: 198.

20.   Sir John Johnson (1742–1830) was the son of Sir William Johnson to whose baronetcy
and estates at Johnstown, N.Y., he succeeded. In May 1776, Johnson, with several
hundred followers, fled to Canada. He was soon commissioned a Colonel, commanding
a regiment composed mainly of loyal German and Scot settlers on his New York
estates, which were confiscated during the Revolution. After the war, Johnson settled
Loyalists on Canadian lands and himself built a temporary house, still standing, at
present Williamstown, Ont. He became Superintendent of Indian affairs in British
North America and was also a member of the Legislative Council of Canada. Lorenzo
Sabine, *The American Loyalists,* 2 vols. (Boston, 1847), I: 577–82. William L. Stone,
Border Wars of the American Revolution, 2 vols. (New York, 1846), I: 109–26.

   In the spring of 1776, Colonel Timothy Bedel of New Hampshire, "with smallpox
in his veins and fear in his heart," took command of a stockade recently constructed at
Cedars. He had 390 provincial troops and two cannons to hold the place. Captain
George Forster had forty of his own unit drawn from Niagara, about a hundred
Canadians, and four or five hundred Indians led by Joseph Brant. When Bedel heard
that this party was forming he went to Montreal and left Major Isaac Butterfield, who
was also coming down with smallpox and was fearful of Indians, to hold the place.
When Forster appeared on May 18, constructed breastwork in front of the fort, and
initiated an attack, Bedel and his men, only one of whom had been wounded, surrendered. Bedel and Butterfield were both cashiered 1 August 1776. Burt, *Quebec,*
pp. 234–35; Ward, *Revolution,* I: 198; Stone, *Border Wars,* I: 131–36.

21.   For official reports of these operations, see *Naval Documents of Revolution,* V: 694–
749.

22.   General Gordon had been far within Canadian territory. Arthur G. Bradley, *Sir Guy
Carleton* (Toronto: University of Toronto Press, 1966), p. 152. Although Whitcomb's
deed was denounced by some Americans, he was promoted to Captain in October 1776.
Heitman, *Historical Register,* p. 430. Zadock Thompson, *History of the State of
Vermont* (Burlington, Vt., 1833), p. 162, wrote that Whitcomb robbed Gordon of his
watch and sword. This charge is also found in Bradley, *Carleton,* p. 152.

23.   A list of British vessels engaged on Lake Champlain is in *Naval Documents of Revolution,* VI: 857–58. Those mentioned specifically by Enys include the *Inflexible,* a sloop
built at St. Johns, and the schooners *Maria* and *Carleton.* Colledge, *Ships,* pp. 282,
345. The gondola, or gunboat, was named *Loyal Convert,* and the radeau was named
Thunderer. Philip K. Lundeberg, *The Continental Gunboat* Philadelphia *and the
Northern Campaign of 1776* (Washington, D.C.: Smithsonian Institution, 1966),
pp. 8, 13.

24.   The American fleet under Arnold included three schooners, one sloop, five galleys, and
eight gondolas. Besides the schooner *Royal Savage,* Enys also specifically mentions the

galleys *Washington* and *Lee* and the gondola *Jersey*. Not mentioned by him is the gondola *Philadelphia* which was sunk near Valcour Island at dusk on October 11. The wreck of the *Royal Savage* was raised from Lake Champlain by L. F. Hagglund in 1934. The *Philadelphia* was raised the following year and since 1965 has been on exhibit at the Museum of History and Technology of the Smithsonian Institution at Washington. Lundeberg, *The Continental Gunboat* Philadelphia, passim.

25.   British losses, it was reported, consisted of two armed boats, about ten men killed, and sixteen wounded. "Diary of Joshua Pell," *Naval Documents of Revolution*, VI: 1198.

26.   With the remnant of their fleet consisting of two schooners, two galleys, one sloop, and one gondola, the Americans retreated to Ticonderoga. Lossing, *Field-Book*, I: 164–65. A list of "Rebel" vessels taken by the British on Lake Champlain is found in *Naval Documents of Revolution*, VI: 1245.

27.   The detachment under Brown captured a vessel containing provisions and took possession of Mount Hope and Mount Defiance. The Americans also took 293 prisoners. Lossing, *Field-Book*, I: 50. Helen I. Gilchrist, *Fort Ticonderoga in History* (Fort Ticonderoga, N.Y., 1923), pp. 82–86; Harrison Bird, *Navies in the Mountains* (New York: Oxford University Press, 1962), pp. 244–48.

28.   Richard Haughton and William Haughton were both lieutenants in the 53rd.

29.   See H. P. Smith, *History of Addison County Vermont* (Syracuse, N.Y., 1886), pp. 251–52, 364, 524, 643; Walter H. Crockett, *A History of Lake Champlain* (Burlington, Vt.: McAuliffe, 1937), p. 20.

30.   The "large Creek" was probably Middlebury River. Before fleeing from their homes, the Vermonters buried the effects they could not take with them, such as staples and pewter. For brief accounts of the British incursion in Vermont, see *The Vermont Historical Gazetteer*, edited by Abby Maria Hemenway, 5 vols. (Burlington, Vt., 1868–91), I: 50–51; Hiland Hall, *The History of Vermont* (Albany, N.Y., 1868), pp. 272–73.

31.   In the summer of 1773, Asa Blodget took possession of a lot in the South part of Middlebury on Otter Creek. After the defeat of the Americans in Canada, the Vermont frontier became exposed to depredations from the British and Indians, and most of the inhabitants in the western part of the state abandoned their possessions. At the close of the Revolutionary War, most of the pioneers returned to their former holdings. Merrill Thomas, *History of Middlebury* (Middlebury, 1841), pp. 8–10.

32.   Chambers, recently promoted to the rank of commodore, was in command of the British Lake Champlain fleet. Bird, *Navies in Mountains*, p. 255.

33. A biographical sketch of Daniel Claus, Sir William Johnson's son-in-law, is in James Sullivan, et al., eds., *The Papers of Sir William Johnson,* 14 vols. (Albany, N.Y.: University of the State of New York, 1921–65), I: 489n. His likeness is in Barbara Graymont, *The Iroquois in the American Revolution* (Syracuse, N.Y.: Syracuse University Press, 1972), p. 119. See also ibid., pp. 157–58, and Thomas Jones, *History of New York during the Revolutionary War,* 2 vols. (New York, 1879), I: 216; II: 269, 285, 274. Capt. John Munro served in the King's Royal Regiment of New York during the Revolution. After the war he settled in Canada; he was originally from Scotland. Patrick Campbell, *Travels in the Inhabited Parts of North America . . . ,* edited by H. H. Langton and W. F. Ganong (Toronto: Champlain Society, 1937), pp. 129, 129n.

34. A brief account of this October (1780) campaign is in Louis F. Hyde, *History of Glens Falls, New York, and Its Settlement* (Glens Falls, N.Y.: Privately printed, 1936), pp. 152–53; Graymont, *Iroquois,* p. 69.

35. In May, 1780, John Johnson with a force of 500 Tories and Indians marched across country from Crown Point, burned Caughnawaga, and raided and burned Johnstown. Lossing, *Field-Book,* I: 288–89; Gilchrist, *Ticonderoga,* pp. 89–90.

36. The Americans threw a floating bridge across the lake to maintain communications between Ticonderoga and Mount Independence. The bridge was supported by twenty-two sunken piers of large timber at nearly equal distances. Gilchrist, *Ticonderoga,* pp. 77–78; Lossing, *Field-Book,* I: 128–29.

37. Lake George flows north into Lake Champlain via a creek several miles long.

38. A coehorn was a small grenade-throwing mortar.

39. Enys was probably referring to the blockhouse and sawmill described and illustrated in Thomas Anburey, *Travels through the Interior Parts of America,* 2 vols. (London, 1791), pp. 123–24, 306–308. Blockhouses, he wrote, "are constructed of timbers, placed one on the other, of a sufficient thickness to resist a musket shot . . .; there are two apartments in them, one above the other, in the upper of which is a division for the officers. In both the lower and upper apartments are two pieces of cannon and four port-holes, for the purpose of pointing these cannon on any side of the blockhouse on which it may be attacked." The farm mentioned by Enys belonged to Daniel Parks. Benjamin F. De Costa, *Notes on the History of Fort George* (New York, 1871), pp. 13–14.

40. Fort Ann, rather than "Anne," is the correct spelling for this post according to French's *Gazetteer* (1860). Lossing writes that it was built in 1757, but David L. Salay, of the New York State Historical Association, states that it was built in 1709 as one

of a chain of forts. The fort was a small outpost and was never the scene of important hostility. Lossing, *Field-Book,* I: 139, 141; Gilchrist, *Ticonderoga,* pp. 89–90. See also William H. Hill, *Old Fort Edward before 1800* (Fort Edward, N.Y.: Privately printed, 1929).

41. Capt. Adiel Sherwood was the commander at Fort Ann. With him were seventy-five "idle Militiamen, whom he had given up trying to make into soldiers." Bird, *Navies in the Mountains,* p. 256.

42. Abraham Wing and Ichabod Merritt had moved into Queensbury with their families in 1763. Wing kept an inn. Hill, *Old Fort Edward,* p. 247.

43. During the French and Indian War, Sir William Johnson built a fort on the bank of Lake George which he named Fort William Henry. In 1757 when General Montcalm retired to the North, he left the fort a heap of smoldering ruins. In June 1759, General Amherst reached Lake George and encamped on its banks. With the assistance of Colonel Montresor, Chief Engineer, he drew a plan for the erection of a fort, which received the name of Fort George. De Costa, *Fort George,* pp. 2–14. An account of Major Carleton's raid in 1780 is in ibid., pp. 49–61.

44. Enys may have been referring to "Fort Gage," a little to the south of Fort George. Lossing, *Field-Book,* I: 111–13.

45. Bateaux and small sailing craft were often sunk in shallow water at the conclusion of a campaign. Thus they were safe from destruction by raiding parties or damage from ice. In the spring they were raised and refitted. An example of a French and Indian War bateau which was so scuttled was raised from Lake George in 1960 and is on exhibit at the Adirondack Museum. See John Gardner, "Relics of 'Ghost Fleet' Are Small Craft Bonanza," *National Fisherman* (October 1966): 8A, 9A, 14A, and further articles by the same author on this subject in monthly issues of the same periodical, April through August 1967.

46. Lossing estimated that Fort George was about one mile southeast from Fort William Henry. *Field-Book,* I: 111–13.

47. This road ran north along the west side of Lake George. The road was probably named after Major Robert Rogers. Bird, *Navies in the Mountains,* p. 63 and passim; Francis Parkman, *The Conspiracy of Pontiac,* 2 vols. (Boston, 1913), I: 168–70.

48. Lord Howe, an able commander much loved by his troops, was killed July 6, 1758, in a sharp skirmish at Ticonderoga under General James Abercromby. "The British loss in this affair was trifling in numbers but none the less fatal to the expedition; for Lord Howe lay dead with a bullet through his heart, and with his death the whole soul of the army expired." Fortescue, *History,* II: 330–32.

49. See above, n. 35. The Landing is on the west side of the lake.

50. Munro had led a diversionary force against Ballston Spa. Hyde, *Glens Falls,* pp. 152–53.

51. Justus Sherwood was a prominent Vermont loyalist. Ostensibly Sherwood went to Vermont to arrange an exchange of prisoners. Sabine, *Loyalists,* II: 297; *Vermont Gazetteer,* I: 71.

52. Mount Independence, situated in the southwest corner of Orwell, Vermont, was fortified by the Americans in 1776. They were dislodged by Burgoyne in July 1777. Lossing, *Field-Book,* I: 129, 135, 147–48; Ward, *Revolution,* I: 406–407.

53. The *Lee* was a sloop of eight guns and was in service on the Canadian lakes. Colledge, *Ships,* p. 314.

54. The name is also spelled Rosenkrans. Heitman, *Historical Register,* p. 351.

55. Whitehall was incorporated 31 March 1765 as Skenesborough; the name was changed in 1786.

56. Schuyler's Island is near Valcour on Lake Champlain. Cumberland Bay is near Plattsburgh. Ash Island is mentioned in Frederick F. Van De Water, *Lake Champlain and Lake George* (Indianapolis: Bobbs-Merrill, 1946), pp. 64, 255–56, 284.

57. Grenadiers companies were traditionally made up of the tallest and strongest men of the regiment. This was a hang-over from their original function of throwing grenades into fortifications on the attack. The Grenadier company was stationed on the right of the regiment when it was drawn together on line. Grenadiers and Light Infantry Companies were known as "flank" companies but were part of the regimental rather than the battalion structure; each regiment was made up initially of light battalions, one Grenadier Company and one Light Company. Information provided by Ministry of Defence Library (Central and Army).

58. The editor is indebted to Miss G. D. Beauvais, Public Archives of Canada, and Ms. Elizabeth Silvester, McGill University Library, for the location and correct spelling of many Canadian places.

59. Isaac Weld thus described Haldimand's house: "This house is supported by large beams of timber, fixed into the sides of the chasm, and in order to get to it you have to pass over several flights of steps, and one or two wooden galleries, which are supported in the same manner. The view from hence is tremendously grand." Isaac Weld, Jr., *Travels through the States of North America and the Provinces of Upper and Lower Canada during the Years 1795, 1796, 1797,* 2 vols. (New York: Augustus M. Kelley, 1970), I: 359. Joseph Hadfield wrote that Haldimand's house was "most

advantageously situated on the declivity of a hill commanding a most extensive view of the Isle of Orleans, the river, Quebec, and the country for some distance on all sides." *An Englishman in America 1785, Being the Diary of Joseph Hadfield,* edited by Douglas S. Robertson (Toronto: Hunter-Rose, 1933), p. 135. Haldimand's cottage, which he called "Henry Lodge," is now commonly known as the "Kent House" and was the property of the Dominican Fathers until it was sold in December 1974 to the Government of the Province of Quebec. *La Maison Montmorency* (Courville, Quebec: La Maison Montmorency [1960]).

60. Brehm was a capable engineer officer, who fought at Ticonderoga 1758–59.

61. The height of the falls is currently measured at 274 feet. *La Maison Montmorency,* pp. [3], [5]. There are a number of references to a Major Holland, no first name given, who was the commander of a red-coated corps of pioneers which in the spring of 1777 had at least fifty men stationed at New York. War-Office (Great Britain), 1783, *A List of the Officers of the Army* and information provided by the Ministry of Defence Library (Central and Army).

62. *The Quebec Gazette,* July 18, 1782, reports the departure of the *Quebec* but does not give the passenger list.

63. The British ships *Harpooner* and *Castle Cravie* (mentioned below) were probably privateers.

64. Admiral George Rodney's fleet fought the famous action of the Saints, which brought de Grasse a prisoner to England, saved the important island of Jamaica, and greatly reduced French Naval power in the West Indies. Fortescue, *History,* III: 416.

65. The *Banter* was a Massachusetts privateer sloop of eight guns and fifty men. Her captain was Henry White of Salem, and she was captured in the Straits of Belle Isle in July, 1782. Information provided by Gordon Bowen-Hassell, Naval Historical Center.

66. In 1780, Charles Paterson and his brother, Allan, became partners in the fur trade. They lost over £3,000 during the first three years, but after that they cleared a good profit. Charles was drowned in Lake Michigan in 1788. Campbell, *Travels,* pp. 132, 132n. Either Gilbert or John Deblois, loyalists, sons of Stephen Deblois, who settled in Boston in 1720. Hadfield, *Diary,* p. 191n.

67. Falsification of a ship's nationality was not uncommon at this time.

68. Fort George was built at the time of the second Jacobite uprising (1745). The uprising sought to procure the British throne for Prince Charles Edward Stuart, the "Young Pretender."

69.   Enys' reference is to his manuscript "Tour of Scotland." See pp. xxiv–xxv.

70.   The first husband of Mrs. Thorpe, nee Sarah Penrose, had been Samuel Enys, brother of John Enys.

RETURN TO CANADA

1.   This was probably a daughter of the Rev. Thomas Penrose, rector of Newbury, whose daughter, Sarah, had married Samuel Enys, the older brother of John Enys. Burke, *Landed Gentry* (1939), p. 705.

2.   Philip D'Auvergne, Prince of Bouillon, was made a captain 22 January 1784. *A List of the Flag-Officers of His Majesty's Fleet; With the Dates of Their First Commissions as Admirals, Vice-Admirals, Rear Admirals, and Captains* (London, 1795), p. 10.

3.   Lady Vyvyan, presumably a widow, was one of the Vyvyans of Trelowarren to whom the Enys home, furnished, was let. This information has been kindly provided by Miss Elizabeth Enys. For the family of Richard H. Vivan of Truro, see George E. Cokayne, *The Complete Peerage* (London: St. Catherine, 1959), p. 289.

4.   Thomas Hughes, who also kept a journal of the voyage in the *Speedy:* "We did not arrive at Falmouth till 3 o'clock in the Morning of the 9th and on the 10th sailed in the Speedy packet Captain D'Auvergne. . . . Several packets sailed from the harbor with a fair wind, which soon failing us, we were the next day off the French Coast. On the 12th our companions separated for their different ports. There were but three passengers in our ship, Capt. Ennis, 29th, Houghton and myself; we paid forty guineas each, and lived as well as people on board a ship could. The Captain keeping a table fit for an alderman, gave all sorts of wines and had every convenience. The Speedy is one of the largest packets in the service, has two cabins which we called the drawing room and parlour, and were used as such, and we had small cabins for a dozen passengers." Hughes, *Journal*, p. 134.

5.   This was his brother, Francis, also an officer of the 29th Foot, then on half-pay.

6.   In the harbor of Falmouth. The castle was constructed in the reign of Henry VIII.

7.   Nothing happened that day to put down in my Memorandum that I had like to have forgot the day altogeather.

8.   Eggs of one of the family of sea urchins.

9.   Labrador Indians should probably read "Labrador (or Eastern) Eskimos." These Eskimos are by far the most numerous of Labrador's native peoples.

10. Probably there are still a fair number of marine mammals in the area of Ile-aux-Pommes, as the Zoological Society of Canada organizes annual sighting trips there. The porpoise prefers bays, estuaries, and coasts to the open sea.

     The Saguenay River, in Quebec, is the outlet of Lake St. John where drainage of a large area in the northwest part of the province is collected. From Chicoutimi to the St. Lawrence River the Saguenay Channel is in the nature of a fiord rather than a river.

11. When referring to "South Traverse at Caudre," Enys may mean the channel between Ile-aux-Coudres and the mainland.

12. Alexander or Robert Pearson, probably the latter, since his lieutenancy, January 1, 1781, antedates that of the former, March 8, 1783. *List of Flag-Officers,* pp. 15, 184.

13. Thomas Hughes wrote: "A fair wind on the 18th September blew so hard that our ship in spite of a rapid current brought us to Quebec (forty leagues) in twelve hours; we saw the settlements, villages, churches, etc. in such a rapid succession that the country appeared much better settled than it really is." *Journal,* p. 135.

14. McDonald belonged to the 84th Regiment Foot or Royal Highland Emigrants, Second Battalion, Canada. The editor could not find the name of his sister.

15.   The Town of Quebec stands at the upper end of a Round Bason about Six Miles in diameter. The View for this piece of water is Remarkably fine. The first object that strikes you is the fall of Montmorency to the left of which is a fine fertile Country Rising gradualy from the waters edge untill lost in the Clouds. It is cultivated for a great distance back from the River. Many other objects [and?] the Villages of Beauport and Charlebourg [Charlesbourg] make a very beautyfull appearance. The former is situated near the Water, the latter on a rising Ground at some distance. The opposite side presents you a different View. The Rocks are high and Rugged tho the land is in most parts cultivated. At the top you have here also the entrance of the River St. Laurence. This is here contracted so as to be little more than a Mile Wide and the Current and tide comes down with united Violence at the Rate of 8 Miles pr hour. It Runs up near Six Miles Pr hour. The town lies directly before you on a point formed by the Rivers St. Charles and St. Laurence. St. Charles is in itself but a small River but is wide at the Mouth from the influx of the tide. This point formes itself in a very high Cape and many seem to think the top of it now called Cape Diamond from the small Bright Spars found in it is like a hawks Bill. I have heard the Name of the place accounted for in the following

manner. As soon as your ship comes Round Point Live [Lévis] this Cape Presents itself all at once to your Veiw. When the first Ships came up this River the Officer on deck on seeing such an immence Rock Present itself at once to his sight exclaimed with astonishment the two Words, Que, Bec, (what a Bec or Bill) and having afterwards determind to build here they gave it that Name from the exclaimation of its first discoverer. The town itself is built on the side of this Rock, and one part of it where the Vessles lie and the Principal Quays are is under the Precipice fragments of which sometimes fall, to the great damage of the houses. This precipice Runs quite across the point which with some assistance of Art done by the french devedes the town effectvely into the upper and lower town, one of which might be burn'd without communicating the Flams to the other. The only communication betwen the two towns is up an exceeding steep hill and in one place so steep is the assent that they have been obliged to cut thro the Rock to ease it. In this spot General Carleton placed a Barrier in 1775 but after the danger was over it was soon Removed. Both towns are well built almost all the houses with Stone. The lower town is inhabited chifly by Merchants or indeed may be said to be wholy so. In the upper town is the Castle of St. Louis where the Governor Resides. Here are now very little Remains of that Regular and beautiful Cittadel which Mr. Guthery [William Guthrie] mentions to be the Residence of the Governor. There is still the Remans of a Wall which had formerly a towr at each Angle but it is now almost a Ruin. The house itself has several good Rooms in it and commands a fine View down the Bason and over point Live. General Holdemand about the year 1779 built a large Addition to it not adjoining to the old house but on the opposite Side of the court yard on the foundation of the old wall or fortification. Before the Chatteau is a Square where the Guards and common parrades of the Garrison are formed. Of this the Chateau forms one side. Another is formed by the Recollet Colledge and Church, the latter of which is appropiated to the service of the English Liturgy. On the third side are several private houses and on the fourth which is not so wide as the Rest is the Road leading up the cape Diamond. This is near the Center of the town and has some of the principal streets terminate themselves in it. The Large Church is situated somthing lower than the former and forms one side of the Market place. This is a handsome Church and was near being burned in the seige of 1759 by a shell bursting in it. On the opposite side of the Market Place is one square of Barracks large enough to contain a Rgt. A little lower down the Hill is the Jesuits College. This order as well as that of the Recollet is now allmost extinct and on there failure there lands fall to the Crown. At the Bottom of the upper town is another large Range of Barracks which extend from the Pallace gate to the works of the town. In this the

American Prisoners were kept during the Seige 1775–6. [I] do not know how many it may be able to contain. Besides these Public Buildings there is in Port Louis Street a convent of Noulines [Ursulines] and a Pallace for the Bishop but the latter is now in private hands and the Bishop lives in the Jesuit College where there is also a seminary of the young men of the Country from whence since the English have been in possession of the country the priests of the different Parishes have been appointed tho some are appointed from a simmilar institution in Montreal. The fortification of the town are by no means Regular and tho they have frequently been spoken of as very strong are by no means so formidable as the accounts make them. Very large additions have been made since the year 1777 by Deepening the Ditch making a Covert way and mines and some Out works before Cape diamond but still there are without all they have done some Spots af Ground as high or higher than the works themselves. But what will ever Render an attack of this difficult is the Rocky situation of the hights of Abraham in that part in some parts of which ther is hardly any earth at all. At the Top of Cape Diamond there was formerly a Cittadel of stone which is now in Ruins but in place of this there are some Batterys made on the Rock and some Block Houses Erected which will contain a good many more. On the outside of the town in the Suburbs of St. Rock was the Intendents Pallace which gave the Name to the gate of the town which still retains it but this was burnd [in] the Seige 1775–6 by the garrison as was all the subburb of that Name either by one or the other party. Not far from the town near the River St. Charles is the Convent call'd the General Hospital which is an excellent institution and answers its Name by its Actions. This was a great advantage to the Americans in the above Seige as they made it their Hospital and from a regard to the place and the sisterhood the garrison never fired upon it during the Seige by intention tho I have heard tho I cannot say from good authority it was once done by some person without orders.

Cape Diamond derives its name from the numerous transparent crystals which are found upon it and which are so abundant that, after a shower of rain, the ground glitters with them. William Bingley, *Travels in North America from Modern Writers* (London, 1821), p. 267.

Another visitor to Quebec stated that the situation of every cottage at Beauport was "enviable" and that Charlesbourg had nothing to recommend it but "its neatness and situation." Hadfield, *Diary*, pp. 130, 153.

Peter Kalm repeats Enys' account of the naming of Quebec, then he adds: "Others derive it from the Algonquin word Quebégo or Quebec signifying that which grows narrow because the river becomes narrowed as it comes nearer to the town. The pronunciation of 'Quebec' by the French was 'Kebäk' almost without accent." *Peter Kalm's Travels in North America—The English Version of 1770*, edited by Adolph B. Benson, 2 vols. (New York: Wilson-Erickson, 1937), II: 433–34.

For an account of the effectiveness of the barriers, see Burt, *Quebec,* pp. 226–27.

William Guthrie wrote: "The town is covered with a regular and beautiful citadel, in which the governor resides." *A New Geographical Historical and Commercial Grammar. . .* (London,1777), p. 646. Enys probably used this or the 1776 edition of this popular work.

Haldimand began to replace the rotting French fortifications at Quebec with stone and ordered that secrecy be maintained about this work. The orders were sent to England in 1784. Hadfield, *Diary,* p. 140n.

Bingley wrote that the most important public building in Quebec was the "government-house, or Castle of St. Louis, a large, plain stone edifice, which forms one side of an open space or square called the parade." *Travels,* p. 269. See, also, Weld, *Travels Through the States of North America,* I: 351–52.

The Ursuline Convent was founded by Madame de la Peltrie, in 1639, for the education of girls. The nuns wore black dress and were renowned for their piety. Bingley, *Travels,* p. 270; Hadfield, *Diary,* p. 158. For a good description of the convent, see Kalm, *Travels,* II: 470.

"The building the Jesuits live in is magnificently built and looks exceedingly fine, both without and within. . . . It consists of stone, is three stories high, exclusive of the garret, is covered with slate and built in a square form." Kalm, *Travels,* II: 448–49.

The Intendant's Palace stood to the east of the suburb of St. Rock. Bingley, *Travels,* p. 270; Kalm, *Travels,* II: 429; Burt, *Quebec,* p. 7.

The hospital consisted of two large halls and some rooms near the apothecary's shop. The beds were furnished clean bedding and curtains. The nuns attended the sick, including soldiers, who were commonly admitted. Kalm, *Travels,* II: 446.

16. The Canadian calash (caleche) was "a two-wheeled light carriage with a seat on the splashboard for the driver." Hadfield, *Diary,* p. 127n. This type of carriage was in general use in Lower Canada. For a detailed description see, Weld, *Travels,* I: 306–307.

17. The grand voyer, or surveyor general of the highways, commanded "the fences to be removed in winter wherever they might cause drifts of snow to block the way. In the fall, before the ground was frozen, the sides of each road had to be marked every 24 feet by poles 8 feet long, usually driven into the soil"; and during the winter, "after every snowfall or drifting, the people had to get out and beat a smooth passage wide enough for two sleighs." "Each owner or occupier was responsible for maintaining the roads, bridges, and ditches adjoining his land, except when the burden was so great that it had to be spread over others as well." Burt, *Quebec,* pp. 40, 263–64. See also Frances M. Brooke, *The History of Emily Montague,* edited by Lawrence J. Burpee, *The Canada Series,* edited by F. P. Grove (Ottawa: Graphic, 1931), p. 93.

18. The Lorette Indians, the chief inhabitants of the village of that name, belonged to the Huron nation. They had been converted to Catholicism and had adopted French customs. Kalm, *Travels,* II: 462–63.

19.

Post Road from Quebec to Montreal with the Distance

Names of the Posts	Leagues	Names of the Posts	Leagues
Cap Rouge [Cap-Rouge]	3	Champlain	2½
St. Augustin [de Quebec]	3½	Cap Madeleine [Cap-de-la-Madeleine]	2
Point aux Tremble [Pointe-aux-Trembles]	1½	Three Rivers [Trois Rivières]	2½
2d	2	Point au Lac [Pointe-du-Lac]	3
To the River Jaques [Jacques] Cartier	2½	Machiche	3
To Jaques Cartier Post house	2	Rivera Du Loup [Riviere-de-Loup]	3
Cape Sante [Cap-Santé]	2½	Maskinenge [Maskinongé]	2
2d	2	New Yorke [York?]	3¼
Deschembault [Deschambault]	3	Berthier[ville]	4
Grondines	2½	Dautray [Dautrai? Dautré? Dautray?]	2½
2d	2	La Valtrie [Lavaltrie]	3½
River St. [Ste.] Anne	2	St. Suplice [St. Sulpice]	2½
St. Ann Post house	2	Repentigne [Repentigny]	2
Batiscan	2	Point aux Tremble [Pointe-aux-Trembles]	2½
2d	2	Montreal	3
	34½		41¼
			34½
			75¾

Such are the distances which a Traveler pay[s] for betwixt the two places by which they make it 225 Miles, that is allowing 3 miles to the canadean League which is not 3 English Miles in fact, but in speaking of the distance it is seldom thought to be more than 180 Miles. Mr. Guthery in his Gazetteer makes it no more than 120 but he must certainly be short of the truth. The Rate you pay is one Shilling Halifax pr. League if you have but one horse. If you order two you pay 1s. 6d. One person is allowed to carry 100 Ct. of Baggage but if there are two persons and [?] 35 Ct. each, and by the Ordinance no post house is to keep you waiting more than a quarter of an hour in the day or half an hour in the night but this Article is frequently infrindged. By another part of the Ordinance they are obliged to drive you at the Rate of two Leagues an hour, but there is here a Clause of (when the Roads will permit) which the[y] take care to make use of on most occasions. For every offence against the Ordinance they forfeit ten shillings on the Oath of one or more Credible Witnesses. The posts from Quebec and Montreal are called Posts Royal and are paid for by custom more than the Ordinary Allowance. That from Quebec is 7/6 tho only three Leagues and that from Montreal 5/ shillings tho only the same distance. The rasons given for this is the Badness of the Road which near those places is certainly the worst on the Road and the great expence of keeping horses in the town. The Post from Point au Lac to Three Rivers we paid 4 Shillings for three Leagues tho I cannot see the same Reason. *Rates of the Post 1786.*

There are 2½ miles to a Canadian league. The distance between Quebec and Montreal along the North Shore of the St. Lawrence is 180 miles.

Enys cited Guthrie incorrectly. The latter wrote that the distance from Quebec to Montreal was about 170 miles. *Geographical Grammar,* p. 647.

"An Ordinance for regulating all such persons as keep horses and carriages to let and hire for the accommodation of travelers, commonly called and known by the name of maîtres de poste," *Ordinances Made and Passed by the Governor and Legislative Council of the Province of Quebec* (1780), pp. 63–69, 99, in effect until 1787. It provided that postmen should charge one shilling for the hire of a horse and carriage and an additional six pence for each additional horse; that one person could carry baggage weighing one hundred pounds and two, seventy pounds; that postmen should not delay a person demanding transportation for more than a quarter of an hour in the day or half an hour in the night; that postmen should drive "at the rate and distance of two leagues for every hour at the least, provided the roads will permit"; those neglecting this last provision should forfeit ten shillings; maîtres de poste in the towns of Quebec and Montreal should receive twenty pence per league for the hire of a horse and carriage, and from the town of Three Rivers one shilling and four pence per league. *Encyclopedia Canadiana,* III: 175, states that in 1777 the Spanish dollar was given a rating of five shillings which meant the establishment of the Halifax currency as the standard for the colony.

20.   Probably George Allsop, a merchant of Quebec. Burt, *Quebec,* passim.

21.   I do not know her maiden name.

22.   [Frances Brooke], *The History of Emily Montague,* 4 vols. (London, 1777). Enys doubtless meant "Arabella Fermor." This first novel descriptive of Canadian conditions was written by the wife of the Rev. John Brooke, Chaplain to the garrison at Quebec. Thomas Hughes had this to say about Sillery: "The place itself so far from being a paradise is the vilest hole I was ever at; it shews the fertility of Dr. Brooke's fancy

and I give him great credit not only for his picturesque landscape of Sillery but for his portrait of Bell Fermor, who is now transformed into a stiff gawky old woman, at least if as the world says he meant the character for Mrs. A——P [Mrs. Alsop]." Hughes was, of course, wrong in attributing authorship of the novel to the Rev. Brooke. *Journal,* 140. *Emily Montague* was first published in London in 1769.

23.   Hadfield wrote that the nunnery was famous for the number of girls who were educated there and that the nuns were "very ingenious" in all kinds of needle work. *Diary,* p. 119; Kalm, *Travels,* II: 419.

24.   The Carron Iron Works, near Fallkirk, Scotland, were quite extensive. Enys had visited them on Oct. 3, 1783, and described them in his "Tour of Scotland." Erected by the king of France, the Trois Rivières works became the property of the British government after the conquest. The works consisted of a forge and a foundry, and the principal articles manufactured there were iron stoves. Weld, *Journal,* I: 377–78.

25.   Maskinenge so called from in [an] Indian word synifying a fish [Muskellunge] which resembles a Pike very much but grows in geneal [general] much larger. I cannot say the difference between these fish nor am I even sure that if both [were] put before me I could distinguish one from the other. The taste is however materialy different, the Maskinenge being infinitely better as well. As I remember the head of it is not so flatt as that of a Pike and the spots on its Back are very small instead of large as those of a Pike. This place is remarkable for this fish which they frequently send to montreal market. It is not at all uncommon to give a Guinea a peice for them and some times more.

26.   About the 27th or 28th of this Month died the famous St. Luke La Carne [Luc de Chapet de La Corne St. Luc] the french partizan. As his actions are on Record in many Books it is needless to say anything of him. I am told that in 1777 when near 80 years of Age he Danced the Indian War Dance for near a Mile, an excursion that would be thought very hard even to a young man. He had a great deal of influence on the remote Indians and when they were in town it was not uncommon to see him driving Round the town in his callash with four or five of them hanging about it some in the callash some behind and one Riding on the horse. He had lost a good deal of his Command over the Canadian Nations by selling them goods, a very extraordinary practice for a man of his consequence and a Chevalier de St. Louis, but it is so common in this country that the first franch people in the country do it. At his funeral he was attended with uncommon ceremony having expressed a desire to be buiried with Millitary honors. He had a Capt.'s Guard or Rather fifty men for they had no Capt in town there for Lt. Houghton to the Command as Capt. [In the absence of a Captain, Lt. Houghton and fifty men did the honors?]

but what was more strange the Colours were permited to make part of the form. A vast Concourse of french pople attended and many English but contrary to the expectations of every Body very few Indians. The funeral was conducted by Mr. St. George Dufrè and Coll. [John] Campbell, Gentlemen who had married two of his daughters and by the infuence of the latter more than his own he had procured these last honors. I am told I displeased the English Clergy men by walking in a Roman Catholic Procession arm in arm with one of that Religion.

Luc de Chapet de La Corne St. Luc (1712–84) was former director of Indians affairs in Quebec under the French and a participant in King George's War and the Seven Years War. In the Revolution Burgoyne gave him command of a band of Indians, many of whom deserted when they were restrained from plundering. Anburey, *With Burgoyne from Quebec,* pp. 151, 157, 165n.; Graymont, *Iroquois,* pp. 81, 150–54. La Corne died October 3, 1784, six days after Enys' arrival at Montreal. Since Enys probably wrote the interpolation in later years, he could easily have fallen into error.

Major John Campbell obtained an appointment as superintendent of Indian affairs for the Province of Quebec, very likely because he had married one of De La Corne's daughters. The De La Corne genealogy is in Cyprien Tanguay, *Dictionnaire généalogique des familles canadiennes. . . ,* 7 vols. (Montreal, 1871–90), III: 286. See also Maximilien Bibaud, *Le Panthéon canadien* (Montreal, 1891), p. 141.

27. The assembly was a kind of dancing club or class that met regularly during the winter. Its members were the social leaders in the community. Ester Singleton, *Social New York under the Georges* (New York, 1902), p. 301.

28. Isaac Weld noted that in Canada winter was "the season of general amusement." By means of their carioles or sledges the Canadians traveled over the snow with almost incredible swiftness covering as much as eighty miles a day with the same horse. The cariole held two persons and a driver and was usually drawn by one or two horses. The shape of these vehicles varied. Some were open and some were covered, usually with furs. Many Canadians preferred the former type, for the chief pleasure of carioling consisted "in seeing and being seen," and the ladies always went out "in most superb dresses of furs." So smoothly did the carioles glide over the snow that it was necessary to have a number of bells attached to the harness or a person continually sounding a horn to guard against accidents. Weld, *Travels,* pp. 391–93.

29. Lancelot ("Capability") Brown (1715–83) was a noted British landscape architect.

30. The Indians to [?] do not as a Body punish Crimes of this kind but the nearest Relations in general retalliate on the Murders.

31. The Caughnawaga Indians had scarcely any penal laws. The chief punishment was

degrading. Even murder was not punishable by any formal law, but the friends of the murdered person were at liberty to kill the murderer if he did not make any atonement. James Smith, *An Account of the Remarkable Occurences in the Life and Travels of Colonel James Smith during his Captivity with the Indians* (Philadelphia, 1831), pp. 150–51.

32.   The water was so high in this River at present that we Rowed over the lower falls with ease so that if it was not for some Remarkable trees we should not have known where it was. This fall is about ten Miles from the Rivers Mouth. The second is three Miles higher.

33.   The "Yankee Settlement" was probably Plattsburgh, N.Y., located at the mouth of the Saranac River at Lake Champlain. The town was recognized in 1785, and at that time, according to J. H. French, *Gazetteer of the State of New York* (Syracuse, N.Y., 1860), pp. 233, 239, the only settlements (in what was to become Clinton County in 1788 and through which flows the Saranac River) were located on the shores of Lake Champlain. For a list of the original proprietors of Plattsburgh, which included Nathaniel and Zephaniah Platt, see W. H. Hurd, *History of Clinton and Franklin Counties, New York* (Philadelphia, 1880), pp. 148–50.

34.   Enys is presumably referring to either the Atlantic Salmon (*Salmo salar*) or its close relative, the Landlocked Salmon. Although it had disappeared by the middle of the nineteenth century because of the destruction of its breeding habitat, "early settlers of the valley of Lake Champlain, found the streams upon both sides filled with Salmon." Winslow C. Watson, "A General View and Agricultural Survey of the County of Essex in New York State," *Transactions of the New York State Agricultural Society* 12 (1852): 745–46. Sir William Johnson may or may not have fly fished in the Mohawk River watershed earlier in the eighteenth century. See Austin S. Hogan, "Fly Fishermen's Bicentennial, 1761–1961," *The Conservationist* (April–May 1961): 46–48, 45; Milton W. Hamilton, "More about Sir William Johnson," letter to the editor, *The Conservationist* (October–November, 1961): 42–43; and Austin S. Hogan, "An Introduction to the History of Fly Fishing in America," *The Museum of American Fly Fishing* (Manchester, Vt.: The Museum, 1973).

35.   It may seem strange to one unacquainted with the place why we did not take boats directly from the town of Montreal but the Rapid just above that place for the above distance being very strong the Kings Boats are in general kept at La Chene. When any Boats do go up this Rapid it is only ½ loaded and it is attended with a great deal of Labour. In order to obviate this difficulty the french had began a Canal from La Chene the Remains of which are still to be seen near the ferry at that place which was to communicate with a small

River called the little Lake which falls into the St. Lawrence just at the Market Gate of Montreal. This was an excellent plan and it is much to be Lamented it was not executed as it would have facilliated all kinds of Transport the Roads being at All times extreemly Bad and in a wett season some times impassable. But the English tho they have made great improvements higher up the River have neglected this.

The earliest canal in Canada was constructed at Lachine at the beginning of the eighteenth century to overcome the turbulent falls at Lake Saint-Louis. Lock canals were built at the Coteau du Lac and the Cascades between 1779 and 1783. As the improvement would benefit commerce, General Haldimand called a meeting of Montreal merchants in February 1781 to see if they would share in the cost of maintenance; they agreed to pay ten shillings for each bateau. Robert Hunter, *Quebec to Carolina in 1785–1786 . . .*, edited by Louis B. Wright and Marion Tinling (San Marino: Huntington Library, 1943), p. 326; Burt, *Quebec,* pp. 287–88.

36. This was the house of the Sulpicians or Grey Nuns. Some insane persons were cared for here. Hadfield, *Diary,* pp. 50, 50n.; Kalm, *Travels,* II: 412. The old Manor House, purchased from the Roboutel de la Noue family, was rebuilt in 1774 following a destructive fire. The house that may be seen today, although substantially rebuilt and renovated several times, stands on the very same site. Information provided by Miss G. D. Beauvais, Public Archives of Canada.

37. Thomas Coram, philanthropist, initiated the Foundling Hospital in London, which opened in 1741.

38. These two Locks as well as others that I shall have reason to Mention hereafter were made during the late disturbances to facilliate the Transport of Provisions to the upper Posts. Before they were made it was with great difficulty a boat could pass and is I believe one of the worst places of the Whole River. The Cascades which you first come to are only a strong Rapid full of Rocks and extreemly dangerous to go down without a good Pilot. This place was very fatal to General Jeffrey Amherst. The Trou is of a different Nature and is formed by a very large Rock at a small distance from the shore from whence there is a Ledge that strikes the current away to the center of the River so the only passage down this place is between this Rock and the shore. This is also shallow except close to the Rock where the fall is I suppose about 7 or 8 feet high, down which the Boats go into a sort of hole or trou from whence it takes its Name. As this place was also fatal to General Amherst it may not be improper to give such an account as I got from our pilot who said he was one of those who come down with that Army. This man said he was one of fifteen Pilots that were

taken at fort Live [Lévis] and was therefore obliged to pilot the Boats down but this Number was very inadequate to the task. They were however seperated in the different divisions and passed the Long Sault very well (by the bye I have been told a good many boats were lost at that place) but this man made no mention of any being lost until they came to the Buisson, when by some accident some of the boats took a wrong Chanell and were lost. Wither this is the place where the Cannon were lost or at the Trou I could not hear for certain. Some say one some another. The Trou is the one they lost most men at, for this Reason at that place you are obliged to turn a sharp point so that the Boat before you, is out of Danger before you come to it, and being once down the shoot at the trou instead of keeping the mid Channel you are obliged to Row into the north shore tho you can perceve no better Channel there than in the Middle. By this means the boats which had no Pilots on bord were deceved and keeping too far out got on the Rocks in the Cascades and great numbers lost.

On September 4, 1760, Lord Jeffery Amherst lost "84 men, 20 batteaus of Regts, 17 of Artillery, 17 whaleboats, one row Galley, a quantity of Artillery stores and some guns," despite the fact that every corps had a Pilot and several had two. The water in the river was unusually high at the time. *The Journal of Jeffery Amherst*, edited by J. Clarence Webster (Toronto: Ryerson, 1931), p. 244.

Fort Lévis was located on one of the Galops in the St. Lawrence, near Ogdensburg and Prescott. It was beseiged and taken by the British in August 1760. Hadfield, *Diary*, pp. 68, 68n; David W. Smyth, *A Gazetteer of the Province of Upper Canada* (New York, 1813), p. 37.

39. See page 277, note 20 and Hunter, *Quebec to Carolina*, pp. 61–62.

40. This was probably Adam Empey's public house at the Cedars. Hunter, *Quebec to Carolina*, pp. 61, 326.

41. This place is in the Map called Coteau de St. Francois instead of Coteau du Lac, the Common Name.

42. A "terrible" rapid which receives its name from the violence of the current. Hunter, *Quebec to Carolina*, p. 62. The Pointe is a prominent headland. Hadfield, *Diary*, pp. 53–54.

43. Robert Hunter, who also visited this region in 1785, wrote: "At the Coteau du Lac, I think the rapids are still stronger, if possible, than any I have seen yet. They have three canals or locks here to avoid them, and you must produce a pass for each boat to one McPherson, a sergeant here who has the care of the canals." *Quebec to Carolina*, pp. 62–63.

44.   Other visitors complained of the "cursed" mosquitoes whose bites were enough to make one "grow mad." Ibid., p. 62.

45.   In this place one McAlpin, an officer of Royalists executed such crueltys by whiping some, half hanging others and it is said binding some with cords and puting them out in that state Naked to be stung by the Muskeetoes, that however dangerous, some of the Prisoners was tempted to make there excape but being taken the[y] told the General the Reasons for endeavoring to get away was the above crueltys. This young man was tried for the above and Broke by a court Martial in 1782.

The island, surrounded by rapids, was made use of to secure prisoners, particularly those taken at Cedars by Captain Forster. Despite the "inconceivably great" current here some men managed to escape. Hadfield, *Dairy,* pp. 54–55. Much controversy developed over British treatment of prisoners taken at the Cedars. American charges of cruelty were aired in the Continental Congress on July 10, 1776 (*Journals,* V: 533–37). The British convincingly refuted these charges in *An Authentic Narrative of Facts Relating to the Exchange of Prisoners taken at the Cedars* (London, 1777).

An account of McAlpin's court-martial has not been found, but two letters in P.R.O. B 2864, War Office, Head Quarters Records (microfilm in Public Archives of Canada) indicate that a McAlpin was dismissed from the service in 1782. Both letters were written by John Johnson to Major Sernoult. The first one (Jan. 2, 1783) read: "It will be necessary that the Vacancy, Occasioned by Ensign McAlpin's Dismission from the Service be filled up first." The second one (May 29, 1783) read: "Mr. Anderson would succeed to Mr. McAlpin's Vacancy of near a year standing."

46.   Now Lancaster, Ontario. Hunter wrote of the inhabitants at this place: "A great many officers of the Eighty-fourth are settled down the River aux Raisins here, who live on their half pay and upon what they are allowed from government. They have each so much land allotted them, which they cultivate with great care." *Quebec to Carolina,* pp. 66–67. Hadfield noted that the lands settled by the Royal Yorkers, 8th Reg., were very good. *Dairy,* pp. 56, 56n. A grouping system was followed in the settlement of land according to which men of the same regiment and of the same nationality and religion were kept with their own kind. For example, Number I Royal Township was planted by Roman Catholic Highlanders of Johnson's first battalion. The Scottish Presbyterians were established in Number 2. The German Colonists, the German Lutherans, and the Anglicans in Numbers 3, 4, and 5, respectively. In the distribution of land, fifty acres were alloted to a single civilian, one hundred to the head of a family, and fifty additional acres for each member of the recipient's family. Reduced privates received one hundred acres, ex-captains seven hundred, etc., according to rank. To Frederick Haldimand goes the credit for the successful settlement of Upper Canada. Burt, *Quebec,* pp. 370–76.

47. The St. Regis Reservation, established in 1755, lies on the south shore of the St. Lawrence, near Cornwall, Ontario. The St. Regis Indians belonged to the Mohawk nation. Hadfield, *Dairy*, p. 57n. The geographical location of the Reservation is 45°00′ 74°35′.

48. Cataraqui is today's Kingston, Ontario.

49. Pointe Maligne "or Sr. Willm, Johnsons Point" is shown in "A map of the inhabited part of Canada" from the large survey by Claude Joseph Sauthier, Engraved by Wm. Faden, 1777. Smyth, *Gazetteer*, pp. 40–41: "Grande Pointe Maligne, on the St. Lawrence River, is opposite the Grand Island of S. Regis. Petite Pointe Maligne is on the North shore of the river, not far above the lower end of Grand Island St. Regis."

50. Johnstown is today's Cornwall, Ont. Like Enys, Robert Hunter was not impressed with the town: "We arrived in the parish of Johnstown and pitched our tents in a place as bad as any pigsty among hogs, cows, and horses, just to please the Canadians who complained they could not get wood anywhere else for their fires." *Quebec to Carolina*, p. 69.

51. Jeremiah French (?–1805), a Loyalist, served during the Revolution as lieutenant in the King's Royal Regiment of New York. French received land grants near Cornwall in Upper Canada. He married Elizabeth Stewart. Hadfield *Dairy*, pp. 54, 59, 59n.

52. In coming up these two Rapids I had taken a Pole to do what I could which had taken up my attention so much as not to feel during the time the depredation carried on against me by the sand flies, but I had no sooner got out of the boat than some one remarked my face was covered with small blisters which in about an hour became very painfull. This fly is not near so big as the Musketoe but the bite is much worse and of a different Nature. The Bite of the former is exactly like the sting of an nettle in England, Whilst that of the sand fly raises a small blister like a burn from whence the french call them Brulae. This blister is very troublesome and in general makes the skin of the part near it Peel off.

53. These strong rapids, which elicited vivid comment from all early visitors to this area, have been flowed out by the great hydroelectric Carillon dam near Cornwall, Ont.

54. The man who lives at the head of the fall told us of a Brigade of Boats which had come up that Spring one of which had Emborded as the Canadians call going Round with the Current. The Conductor whose name was La Pense [Pensée] ordered some of his hands into one of the Boats which was at the Head of the Sault and going on board himself went out into the middle of the

Rapid threw Relief into the boat that was in distress and brought both Boats in at the Bottom of the Sault but this was Reconed a very daring Act.

A Boat of our Regt was lost in this manner in June 1786 but the men and most of the goods were saved. Having Run uppon an Island at the foot of the Sault, had the current once taken them outside of that Island it is said to be impossible to save them as the[y] must go into what is called the Chanell Scartie[?].

Some of the Royalists have ventured down this Long Sault by the way boats go up in canoes. I have not heard of any Boat going down this way as a passage yet, and the Reason which they Assign is not the danger of the Long Sault but that of the Milles Rockes and Moulinette which are so very Rapid Rocky and Shallow that it would be almost impossible to go down them. But this is not the way which the Canadians go or even ever have attempted to go.

They leave this Channel at the head of Isle aux Chats [Cat Island] and proceed down close to the south shore. There is but little if any danger in going down this way if they mind to keep the south shore but there is a Chanel strikes off among the Islands which leads into the Channel Scartie. Having once passed this Chanell you cannot go wrong. There is at this place what they call the nine Mile Reach where current is remarkably strong. Some people say they have gone it in twenty minutes but I believe we were an hour. At the foot of this is the only fall you can perceive of the Long Sault going down this way. It is just at a point and if the Garde keeps as ours did close to the South Shore it seems as if the current would drive you on the point but you get into an Eddy time enough to avoid it if your guide knows his buissiness, but [i]f I had not a good Guide I should prefer the Middle of the River as I am told there is water enough all across. At the foot of this fall there is a spot of very Rough water where almost all Boats take in some water but some of the Pilots take in less than others. It is very seldom you hear of a Boat being lost in this Chanel. A little below this shoot you come into the main River at the foot of Rapid aux Cheverale. Since writing the above I have spoken to La Pense therin mentiond who says the Boat which he went after had passed the Long sault altogeather and going down the Chanel scartie had got on some Rocks at the Bottom of that Chanel where the current is not very strong that he had followed her down the Channel Scartie and taking her from the Rocks had brought her up by the common Rout. He says also that the Channell Scartie is not so dangerous as many seem to think and that a light Boat if well managed may go down it with a tollerable degree of Safty. He could not tell exactly how high the fall is, thinks it from Eight to ten feet. Having passed this there is nothing of any consequence.

In going down the Long Sault by the common Rout the Canadians I am told sometimes tie two boats togeather and lett them drive with the current.

"All this time the poor Canadians were stripped naked in the water, pulling the boats against the rapid rapids of Mille Rockers." Hunter, *Quebec to Carolina*, p. 71.

". . . a rapid which is known as Mille Rockes . . . nothing can equal the exertions which the men made here. The very appearance of the difficulties would deter an athletic European from attempting it, but the Canadians are brought up from infancy in this employ." Hadfield, *Diary*, p. 59.

55.   Point Iroquois on the St. Lawrence is now incorporated in the village of Iroquois, Ontario. Hadfield wrote that the "remarkable points" after leaving Rapid Plot were "Pointe aux Iroquois, Presqu'Ile Pointe, Pointe au Cardinal, Pointe au Galots and Pointe de L'Ivrogne." *Dairy*, pp. 64, 64n.

56.   New Oswegatchee is one of the Richest and most flourishing of the New Settlements, consists of Eight Townships. Indeed it was perfectly surprizing to see the Progress they had made in so short a time. They had not only got good houses built but large Farmes Cleard and sowed with Grain of all kinds, all sort of Vegetables and Indian corn in the greatest abundance. The Canadians who were in our boats seemed to fear these people tho at 120 Miles distance would be in a short time able to under sell them in the Montreal Markets which I realy think will be the case. We were the first who brought up the account of a Vote having passed in parliment for allowing Rations to the Royalists for a longer time than they expected. They all expressed great joy at it tho they acknowledged that government had before done so much for them as they could well expect and that most of them were in as good a way and many in a much better than when the War first Broke out, and to this Rule I believe there are very few exceptions altho it must be allowed there are some. Altho to draw a Comparrison beween this settlement and that on Lake Champlain may appear vanity in an Englishman and an officer yet I cannot help saying a few words on that subject. They are both settled by the troops who have been emp[l?]oyed during the war, which Lands are given them in Reward for past services and Losses. On the part of England you here find a flourishing settlement well supplied with Provisions for more than three years and not only that which gives them full time to work at their Land and houses but a division of farming tools made among them, nor was even the means of providing fish for there subsistence forgotten, two Netts being given to each township for that purpose, with many other advantages, Cloathing, shoemarkers tools &c. &c. which I do not know and if I did would

be too tideous to mention. On the other hand you find poor wretches who came to these places with out Provisions to live uppon which obliges them to seek for food in the woods and Lakes that takes up a great deal of there time, and to purchase tools or cloathing they are obliged to work for there more Oppolent Neighbours some few of which have brought money with them. By this means the Poor people are in a most distressed state by being obliged to Neglect their own farms but I must here acknowledge that they undergo these hardships with Spirit, and labor with such unremitting perseverance that they make great Progress and it will in time no doubt Prove a flourishing settlement.

Near Oswegathee or Fort La Gullatte [Galette] is the Black River which at some times of the Year is so full of fish that I am told you cannot throw a spear into it without striking a Fish. This they say is but for a few days.

In 1784 the Oswegatchie settlement consisted of 223 men, 101 women, 262 children, and 11 servants. Livestock was scarce. In June 1784, Haldimand ordered that these Loyalists be "victualyed" at two thirds allowance until 1 May 1785, and at half that much for the subsequent year. Tools and seed were also provided to the Loyalists. Ernest A. Cruikshank, *The Settlement of the United Empire Loyalists on the Upper St. Lawrence and Bay of Quinte in 1784* (Toronto: Ontario Historical Society, 1966), pp. 123, 140–41, 169. The Loyalists who settled in Upper Canada were different from those who went to the maritime provinces. Many of the former belong to the artisan class and had been accustomed to living away from large towns. Few of them had possessed large properties. Burt, *Quebec,* pp. 360–61.

Fort La Galette was on the North shore of the St. Lawrence, opposite Ogdensburg N.Y. A redoubt had been constructed about 1728. Hadfield, *Diary,* p. 72n.

57.   Amherst's design in 1760 was to invade Canada simultaneously from east, west, and south and to form a junction at Montreal. Amherst was to lead the main army, consisting of eight weak battalions of British numbering fewer than 6,000 men, 4,500 provincials, and 700 Indians, from Oswego down the St. Lawrence. By August 15, this force had reached Oswegatchie, or La Galette, on the site of present Ogdensburg. On August 26 Amherst invested Fort Lévis, which had a garrison of 300 men. After a cannonade of three days the fort surrendered. Repair of the fort and of his boats detained Amherst for three days; on the 31st the expedition began the hazardous and, as it turned out, costly descent of the rapids. Fortescue, *History,* II: 401–405.

58.   Carleton Island is on the American side near Cape Vincent, N.Y. Construction on Fort Haldimand, an oblong square, flanked on each side by four bastions, with barracks to accommodate as many as 2,000 men, was begun in 1778 and completed three years later. The island became the strongest British port west of Montreal. Here ships were built and supplies for the upper ports were transferred from bateaux to vessels. The

island was also a refuge for Loyalists and a rendezvous for the Iroquois who attacked the New York frontier. Hadfield, *Diary,* pp. 73, 73n.

59. The *Seneca* was a brig of 130 tons with 18 guns, built for navigation on Lake Ontario. It belonged to the Crown. Ernest A. Cruikshank, *Ten Years of the Colony of Niagara, 1780–1790* (Welland, Ont., 1908), p. 23; Hadfield, *Diary,* p. 73.

60. Either John or Jonathan Jones. Cruikshank, *Loyalists,* p. 90n.

61. Charlevoix wrote: "Five or six leagues from la Galette, is an island called Tonihata, the soil of which appears tolerably fertile, and which is about half a league long." P. De Charlevoix, *Journal of a Voyage to North-America,* 2 vols. (London, 1761), I: 280. This is present-day Grenadier Island, one of the Thousand Islands.

62. Enys was seeing the Thousand Islands. The editor has been unable to find "Rocks at Plumbton." There are several examples of the place name "Plumpton," however. Hackfall is a romantic valley, 5½ miles northeast of Ripon, North Riding of Yorkshire. Ledford (Lydford) is a parish and Village, 7 miles north northeast of Tavistock, Devonshire.

63. It is asstonishing how these trees can find Nourishment as they appear to grow from the Solid Rock. Many of the Cracks in which they grow can hardly be seen yet certain it is that Trees of a considerable size grow in this manner quite from the top of the Rocks down to the Waters Edge.

64. In coming up if the wind is not fair the best way is to go between Isle au Coulais [Couchois?] and the Main. This passage at first appears like a Bay terminating in a swamp but is the shortest way and covered from they [the?] wind. The West and South west winds are said to prevail here in general about ⅞ of the year.

  Cataraqui stands in the spot where the old french Fort Frontenack [Frontenac] formerly stood and is of the same size & form. In the French time i[t] was kept in good Repair and was regular square with a strong stone wall round it. The Bastions at each Angle from the ruins appear to have be[en] thicker than the rest and had Loop Holes for Cannon, with two good Bomb Proof Magazeens. The Plain round it is Cleard of wood for a great distance, and has in many places the traces of old Lines and encampments of which the French Nation are so fond they leave marks wherever they go. The fort as it stands at present does not seem to be intended for any defence. The Barracks are Cheifly built on the old walls of the Fort, and form a Square Closed at each Angle with Pickets. There is no Well in the Barrack Yard or any means of supplying it with water but by the Lake. This is called and is intended to be the Capital of the New settlements above the Milles Isles, in consequence of which there is a very large town laid out, into Square Building Lots, many of which have small houses erected thereon, but it does not yet appear much like a town. The only Public Building yet compleated is a school house the most part of which was done by the King, but Lots are Laid out for a Market house and Church. A clergyman of the English Church resides here, and has Charge of the Schooll. Not far from hence is the Bay de Quinty [Quinte]. One of the Best of the New Settlements consists of six townships well settled. The Number of Souls in the Settlements dependent on Cataraqui are about two thousand. Not far from hence is a very fine Grist and Saw Mill most beautifully situated. They were built by the King for the use of the Settlement. They pay by what I can find the tenth board for cutting at the saw Mill but the Grist Mill grinds free at present but how long it is to continue so to do I do not know. In the farthest part of the Bay de Quinty is a small Settlement of the Mohawk Indians with a Cheif called Capt. John. He is exteemed one the best Speakers in the Nation but is much adicted to Liquor. The remaining part of the Mohawks are at the head of the Lake at a place called the grand River with Capt. Brent [Joseph Brant] and most of the other Cheifs. These people do not like the other Indians live on hunting. They have their Land divided among them and Recive all the implements of husbandry which they till the same as the Royalists and have at each place a Mill, Church, and Schoolhouse erected by Government for them, besides the presents they Receive as Indians. Cataraqui is about 200 Miles from Montreal and 160 from Niagara.

Fort Frontenac guarded the outlet of Lake Ontario into the St. Lawrence. Defended by a French garrison of a little over one hundred men, it surrendered to Col. John Bradstreet, 27 August 1758. Fortescue, *History*, II: 338, 344.

A town plan for Upper Canada is in *United Empire Loyalists*, edited by Leslie F. S. Upton (Toronto: Copp Clark, 1967), pp. 126–27; Burt, *Quebec*, pp. 270–75. The fertility of the soil about the Bay of Quinte was generally recognized. Smyth, *Gazetteer*, pp. 54–55.

"The Saw Mill is a very good one, but an expensive Job, and [has] taken much longer time building than what Mr. Brass of the Rangers told me was necessary." Major Ross to Genl. Haldimand, 14 June 1784, Cruikshank, *Loyalist Settlements*, p. 125.

Capt. John [Johan] was a chief of the Lower Mahawks. Joseph Brant (Thayendanegea) was the most famous (or infamous, according to the Americans) Indian of this period. Cruikshank, *Loyalist Settlements*, pp. 32–128 passim; William L. Stone, *Life of Joseph Brant* (New York, 1838); Graymont, *Iroquois*, passim.

65.   The *Limniade,* or *Limnade,* 220 tons, 16 guns, was the largest vessel sailing on Lake Ontario. It belonged to the Crown. Cruikshank, *Ten Years of Colony of Niagara,* p. 23; Hunter, *Quebec to Carolina,* pp. 83, 95, 330.

66.   The eighth township was later called Elizabethtown. Burt, *Quebec,* p. 372.

67.   Genl. Henry Hope to the Command whilst I was in town and was with many others just going to embark on board of a s[l]oup on his way to Quebec when the Darkness came on on the 16th.

On Sunday the 16th of October 1785 at Montreal in Canada the day had been extreemly Dark and lowering all day as well as for some days before, but of a Sudden at ½ past two oClock P.M. it became as Dark as it ever was in this World. I am sure I never saw a Night so dark. It continued so nearly about a Quarter of an hour in which time we had some thunder with Lightening & Rain but no means Violent. It then Cleared off so as to be tollerably light and again came on as dark as before which again Cleared off and was succeeded by a third Darkness but not so great as the former during which time some people say they smelt sulphur others that the Air made them Sick. It was so dark the whole eveng we kept the Candles burning nor was I out after the storm till near 8 oClock at which time it was as fine Moon light as I ever saw.

An Account of What is Called Dark Sunday
1785

Although this does not form any part of the history of the 29th I think it of so singular a Nature as to be worth Noting. The Account here given is what I saw myself in Montreal and took notes of it on the following day.

The weather during the 14th & 15th of October 1785 had been remarkbly Dark & Sultry, But on Sunday the 16th much more so than before so that the Poultry went to Roost and the Cattle went under there Sheds for Shelter so early as nine or ten in the Morning. About ½ past two it began to grow dark and by 3 was darker than the darkest Night I ever beheld in my life, in short utter darkness. This continued for rather more than a Quarter of an hour when we had some Thunder lightening & rain but by no means what could be called Violent. It then became something lighter but very soon the darkness returned as bad as ever. This again cleared up a little but was succeeded by a third darkness which however was not quite so bad as the two former but lasted longer. During the time some people said they could smell Sulphur, Others that the Air made them sick but I cannot say I felt any thing of the kind myself. From between 5 & 6 it began to grow gradualy lighter and about 8 oClock I went out into the Streets and found it as fine star light Night as ever I beheld in my life and the Streets full of people of all kinds & Ranks congratulating each other on the escape they had experienced from an expected Earthquake.

On reading Coxe's Travels into Russia I could not help being very much struck with the similarity of his situacon (Volume 1 Page 377) and ours on the 3d of October mentioned on the other side of this Page.

He says he was so much interupted by Hoggs during the night that he determined to resign to his unwelcome Guests that litter which he could no longer enjoy himself. He accordingly raised himself from his straw and sitting down comtemplated by the light of a slip of Deal the scene arownd him. His companions he says Lord Herbert & Coll. Floyd were streched upon the same parcel of straw from which he had just emerged. A little beyond them their servants occupied a separate heap. At a small distance Three Russians with long beards and coarse sackcloth shirts & Trowsers lay extendd upon their Backs on the bare floor. On the opposite side of the Room Three Women in there Clothes slumbered on a long bench while the Top of the Stove offered a bench for a Woman dressed like the others and four sprawling Children almost Naked.

The manner in which they build thear houses are also very much in the same method as like what he says of the Russians. Their houses are generaly square formed of whole Trees piled one upon the other, secured at the corners where the extreemities meet. The interstices betwen the piles are filled with Moss. Within the Timbers are smoothed with an Axe, but without left with the Bark in there Rude state. They usualy construct their whole house with the assistance of a hatchet alone, and cut the planks of the floor with the same Instrument, and mostly finish the shell of the house before they begin to cut the Windows and doors. It is likewise the Custom in all the New Settlements to make use of slips of Deal or Rather Splinters from the Root of the Pitch pine in place of Candles which I have often seen.

The Quebec Gazette (October 27, 1785) reported that on the sixteenth "the air was darkened by a thick fog which dissipated about 10 o'clock. The atmosphere was of a luminous fiery color. About two o'clock in the afternoon, it became dark by degrees, in such a manner, that about half an hour after two, people could not see one another in the houses. This lasted twenty minutes, and was followed by lightning, thunder and rain which gradually diminished the darkness; it was however very difficult to read without candle light at three o'clock. This period was of short duration, for darkness came on again at 7 minutes past three, and it grew by degree as dark as before insomuch that no night was ever more obscure than it was at this time. The black clouds dispersed about 14 minutes past three, but lightning, thunder, and heavy rain continued till about half after five."

Quebec experienced uncommon darkness during the day on October 9, 15, and 16; the last was the most phenomenal. The ministers of the English and Presbyterian churches had to resort to candles during service and people were obliged to dine by candlelight. Both in Quebec and Montreal the rainwater was almost black. Ibid., October 20, 1785.

William Coxe wrote: "The cottages are built in the same manner as those of Lithuania, . . . they are of square shape; formed of whole trees piled upon one another, and secured at the four corners with mortises and tenons. The interstices between these piles are filled with moss. Within, the timbers are smoothed with an axe, so as to form the appearance of wainscot; but without are left with the bark in their rude state. The roofs are in the penthouse form and generally composed of the bark of trees or shingles, which are sometimes covered with mould or turf. The peasants usually construct the whole house solely with the assistance of the hatchet and cut the planks of the floor with the instrument, in many parts being unacquainted with the use of the saw: they finish the shell of the house and the roof, before they begin to cut the windows or doors. . . . At Tabluka, . . . a party of hogs, at four in the morning, roused me in grunting close to my ear. Not much pleased either with the earliness of the visit, or the salutation of my visitors, I called out to my servant, 'Joseph, drive these gentry out of the room, and shut the door.' 'There is no door that will shut,' replied Joseph with great composure; 'we have tried every expedient to fasten it without success; the hogs have more than once been excluded, but have as often returned.' This conversation effectually rousing me, I determined to resign to my unwelcome guests that litter which I could no longer enjoy, and contemplated, by the light of a slip of deal, the surrounding scene. My two companions were stretched upon the same parcel of straw from which I had just emerged; a little beyond our servants occupied a separate heap; at a small distance three Russians, with long beards, and coarse sackcloth shirts and trousers, lay extended upon their backs on the bare floor; on the opposite side of the room three women in their clothes slumbered on a long bench; while the top of the stove afforded a couch to a woman dressed like the others, and four sprawling children almost naked." William Coxe, *Travels in Poland and Russia* (New York: Arno, 1970), pp. 269–71. The Editor was unable to locate a copy of the edition used by Enys.

68.   The Queen's birthday was celebrated on January 18. Hughes, *Journal,* p. 138.

69.   Carleton Island or as it is Called in most Maps Isle a la Bech is about 27 Miles from Catarqui if you go round by water the whole way, but if you cross the carrying place on Grande [Wolfe] Isle, it is only 11. This place was built in the year 1778 or 79 in order to facilitate transport of Provisions &c.

&c. to the Upper Posts, which until that time was carried on from Oswegatchee and often suffered very much from the Vessles being detained in the Narrows by foul Winds. It is well situated for the purpose being an Island just at the very entrance of the Lake. The Fort stands uppon a very high Precipice which forms one side of it, with very little Rampart but a line of sloping Pickets. The other part of the works is in a semi cercular form, and has three Bastions towards the Land, but the heavyest Batterys are on the Precipice over the Water. It has a very good Magazeen and has a Well the water of which is not fit to use. The whole works are now gone very much to decay for at the Peace this place coming within the American Line every one thought they did Right to destroy it as much as possible. It is here also the Vessels are built and kept. What is calld Navy Point is a low Point under the fort in the form of a Rams Horns which makes a Bay on each side of the Istmus in one of which is the Dock with all its stores Artifices, Barracks &c. in the other one the shiping Rownd [?] which is all the Publick stores of every other kind with houses for the Navy employed thereon. On the other side of the fort is the Merchants Point where all the Merchants Suttlers live and have their Private stores for Lodging of Merchant goods. Thus are the Army, Navy, Dock men, and Merchants, kept entirely sepperate a thing I never saw so compleatly done in any other place in the Province. For the Number of shipping seamen &c. &c. See the Annexed Retons [returns]. The fort will contain about 400 men.

Having in the Former Page mentioned the Transport it may not be impropper to say what it is. I have already given an account of the Communication betwixt Montreal & this place therefore have only here to observe that all stores provisions and every thing wanted for the upper Posts is forwarded up by this Rout. The Batteaux come in what they call Brigades of No Determind number from 4 to 16 or 18, always in equal numbers because when they come to any strong current the Crew of two Boats unite and take up one boat which being place above the current they return and bring up the other. In the like manner Do all the others. These Boats generaly Bring up 24 Barrells of Pork of 300 lb. but when they bring flower or any Lighter specicies they sometimes bring more. They are manned with four men each Boat, and another who is conductor has charge of the whole. They receive their Loading at La Chene and are obliged to deliver it as Per Invoice at the Island, where if any thing is lost that they cannot account for in a sattisfactory manner their Wages are stoped to pay for it. Their pay is Different at different seasons and different men. The Conductor thos [has?] Sixteen Dollars for the Voyage which is I believe the same all the year through as I do not remember to have heard his pay is augmented in the Spring and fall as that of the men is. From the first of the Spring to June they have at the Rate of ten Dollars per Man to those who are in the head and stern of each Boat who are supposed to be the best hands and the two Center men at that time 8 Dollars. From then to September they [the?] end men have only Eight and the Center men Six Dollars, after which they again receive the same pay as in Spring. The days for this Change are fixed but I forgot them. They have also the Perquisite of taking down passengers or goods in thear Return Boats provided the King has nothing to send down but if any thing is going down on government account the Commanding Officer orders as many Boats to be set apart as may be wanted who receive nothing extraordinary for their trouble as their agreement is to bring down goods for the person who engages, "them". This agreement is the same with the Merchant Boats. The great thing is taking down the Packs of peltry in the fall of which there annualy come down several thousand, and when the Merchants have not boats enough to take them down which is never the case they then have the Kings boats whom they pay at the Rate of half a Dollar for each Pack. Each boat will carry from 36 to 40. The Number of Packs which went down the Year I was in this place was not so many as usual being only about 3000 each of which is Valued at 10£.

Annexed is the number of Boats that went Round the Lake the above year and the number of Barrell Bulk transported upwards in the ships during my residence, with other explanatory Returns. The whole goes over these Lakes in the Kings Ships who thereby becomes carrier for the Merchants who pay [?] Per Barrel. The Naval storekeeper keeps the Rotations and puts down every Boat Load as it arrives which is forwarded in its turn when ever there is Room on board the ships for if the King has work for the Ships the whole year merchandize cannot go on as it only is put on board when the King has no more goods or Provision on the Island. Thus during the war I am told merchant goods has lain a long whiles. Boats that go Round the Lake seldom carry more than 18 Barrel Round in their Boats, therefore if they bring up the usual quantity, 25, they generally leave the seven to be sent in the Rotation. The Rotation for Boats is kept by the Commanding Officer but the storekeeper examens all as well those which go Round as those which go on boats to see in the first place they do not carry other things than are specified in their pass, in the Second to see also they do not put more Barrell Bulk on bord than what they are Rated to pay for. During my stay here I was orderd to Muster the ships crews as soon as they came into port to see they had their Complemen realy on Board and to make returns of the same to head Qarters.

Carleton Island, formerly Deer Island, is in the St. Lawrence on the south side of Wolfe Island, which is opposite Kingston.

For a description of the fort somewhat similar to that of Enys, see Hughes, *Journal,* p. 150. Hughes had supper at Carleton Island with Enys on August 1, 1786.

On November 28, 1791, Patrick Campbell visited the island: "I went on shore on Carleton island where the British had a garrison last War; the barracks, dry ditch, and ramparts are still remaining, but in a decayed state. A sergeant and twelve men are kept here to preserve the barracks from being burnt by the Indians, and the Americans from taking possession of it, and the dismounted guns thereon. The cause assigned for our forsaking this port is said to be because it is doubtful whether these islands be within the British or American lines." *Travels,* p. 144. After the War of 1812 the island was recognized as belonging to the United States.

Geography favored Canada in the fur trade, which, however, suffered from two annoying restrictions. One was the prohibition of private vessels on the Great Lakes; the second was the regulation that passes or licenses were necessary for every man and all goods going up from Montreal. In 1788 the first restriction was entirely abolished; the second one was terminated in 1791. The execution of the Jay Treaty in 1796 gave no shock to this commerce because, as it was expected, Montreal would probably continue to draw a considerable portion of the furs gathered on the American side of the line. Moreover the commercial advantages derived from the fur trade were offset by the cost of keeping the posts and maintaining their garrisons and of providing shiploads of Indian presents. Burt, *Quebec,* pp. 346–49.

As was stated earlier, in 1777 the Spanish dollar was given a rating of 5s.

The "Annexed" list or lists of "shipping seamen" and "number of Boats that went Round the Lake" have not been found.

70.   On the Evening of the 17th I was so much exhausted with Packing up, writing & together with the heat that on some very trivial occasion I burst into a fit of Laughter that lead Tanling who was present to conceive I was in Hystericks and I had enough to do to make them desest from throwing water in my face for altho I could tell all that passed I could not for my life speak a word.

71.   Salmon Creek runs into Lake Ontario. Salmon and Salmon trout were in great abundance here. Michael Smith, *Geographical View of the Province of Upper Canada* . . . (New York, 1813), pp. 28–29.

72.   Robert Hunter, who visited Fort Ontario "(alias Oswego)" shortly before Enys' arrival there reported that Capt. Forbes was "a very genteel man." The fort, Hunter continued, "is not so large, but stronger and more regular than that at Carlton Island. It consists

of five bastions and a strong drawbridge. That facing the river Onandago—which derives its source from Lake Oneida about fifty miles from Oswego—has ten pieces of cannon." *Quebec to Carolina,* p. 88. Old Fort Ontario was across from Oswego. Graymont, *Iroquois,* p. 64.

73.   When they were employd in Erecting this fort the French made an attack on the works and were defeated, during which a small redoubt near the extremity of the point with one Gun did very great excution by taking them in flank whilst in a Ravine coverd from the fire of the fort. This same Redoubt was in the course of the attack assailed three times by a solid Collum and repulsed it as often.

In 1722 the British established Oswego as a trading post to offset the French at Niagara. In 1727 a stone redoubt was constructed. On August 9, 1756, Montcalm appeared before the fort and after three days' cannonade forced it to surrender. After burning Oswego, Montcalm retired to Ticonderoga.

During the Revolution, Haldimand, for whom the problem of the West was "a veritable nightmare," built more vessels on the lakes, founded an important depot at Carleton Island, reoccupied Oswego in 1781, and dug the first Canadian canals. Burt, *Quebec,* pp. 286–87; Hadfield, *Diary,* pp. 82–83, 82n; Fortescue, *History,* II: 291, 302–304; Lossing, *Field-Book,* I: 216–19.

74.   The Fort will contain if all the Barracks were in good Repair about 800 Men which would be a good number for its defence and with which it ought to make a good stand.

During the nineteenth century the bar was dredged and Oswego became an important lake port.

75.   Having in the course of the Spring been informed that there was a Beaver Damm not far from hence I determined on going to see it. It was, however, a long while before I could get an opportunity to do it. At lenth on the 19th of May about Eight in the Morng I left the fort in Company with Mr. Price (the Interpreter), two soldiers of the garrison and two Onondaga Indians. We went in a Boat about three Miles North East of the place, passing on our way the place still called the french Landing from being the place where the french landed when they attacked this place at the time it was first building. There is however nothing more remarkable in it but a small remains of an Entrenchment on a high grownd and an old Cannon near the water side. Having proceeded to the distance above mentioned we all Landed and hauled our Boat out of the water and left it dry on the Beach then taking to wood we set off nearly a South Course for about five or Six Miles when we came to a small swamp where we perceived several trees cut by the Beaver.

I beleive the largest I saw was cut more than ten Inches in diameter tho the Interpreter & Indians sayd they have seen them cut more than twice that thickness. We passed Round this swamp on one side of which was the Damm we were in search of. The place Dammed up was about twenty or thirty yards long and in some parts the water was four feet Deep. The Bank was not made of large trees felled as many say they are but cheifly of the smaller size from the thickness of my Arm downwards so mixed with Clay as to make a solid, walk three or four feet Wide hard enough to bear a horse of any Wheight. There were besides this many other places where the water was stopped in the like manner. We had no sooner Arrived than the Indians set to work & cut down the Damm to lett the water out of the swamp, which kept us waiting an hour or an hour and half, during which time the Black flies and Musketoes troubled us very much. At lenth the Indians told us the Damm was low enough and that we could get to the house, and directed us the way we shouls go without being wet. Mr. Price and myself accordingly set off and keeping along the edge of the swamp and sometimes passing over places where the water had been Dammed up as above we soon Reached an old Beaver house which had been broke up in the Spring. Here I in Vain looked for all those Accomodations I have Read of and the Suite of appartments which they are said to build. There were however two or I beleive had been three appartments that were formed under the Root of an old tree which had a good communication with the water. Over the apperture of one of these Rooms we could perceive all the sticks to have been hauled by the Beaver. This they told me was their Dining Room, as these Animals make it a Rule never to eat in the same place they sleep in. Passing this we crossed over by means of an old Damm to a small Island in the center of the Swamp which we also Crossed. We had no sooner got to the other side than we saw the Beaver House. Here we were again joined by the Indians who had taken another way. This House appeard to me to be quite of another kind from the one before mentiond. It stood by itself, was of a excelent form of about twelve or fourteen feet diameter. It was made of sticks, Leaves & Mudd, was about Ten feet high so that it may be said to have been in the shape of an Hemisphere very much Like those built by the Musk Rats only of a more solid nature. The first thing they did on our meeting at this place was to find out the places where the house had communication with the water, at the opening of which the Indians stood with their Beaver Spears and desired Mr. Price and I would jump in the House which we did & threw sticks into it wherever we could. The Indian very soon told us there were young ones in it, one of which soon made its appearance and retired again into the house. Having waited for a short time in hopes of the old ones coming out they conjectured they were not at home, and calling for the Dog made a hole in the top of the house and sent him in. He soon killed a Musk Rat and brought it out. This I at first feared was what the Indian had taken for a Young Beaver, but on sending the Dog in a second time he Returned with a Young Bever in his Mouth which he had likewise killed. This so disturbed the Rest that they ran out of the house as fast as they could. They were four in number and were taken with great ease as they could not Run fast. The Indians took each one, Mr. Price a third and a soldier and myself between us the fourth. I confess I did not at first like to touch them being fearfull they would bite but the Indians said they would not, that they were the most harmless things in Nature which we soon found to be very true and began playing with them as with a young Puppy. They were compleatly formed Beaver in every Respect tho not larger than a large Guinea Pigg to which I thought they have some resemblance.

The house was now open in two places but we could not see much of it. It must have however several appartments from the Dog who could not turn round in them being obliged to back out of them before he could proceed to [?] but wither this house was two story high or no I cannot say. Being now thoroughly convinced the old ones were not within the Indians began to hunt about the swamp for them. It was not long before one make its appearance near the place where the Damm was broken and was fired at by a Soldier who was left at that place. He however did not kill him. It was not very long before he again made his appearance and one of the Indians made a strake at her with his Spear and She again escaped. It was now a good while before we saw her again and they began to think they should see no more of her when the Youngest of the Indians saw and threw his Spear into her. The other Ran instantly to his assistance and they very soon killed her. They had no sooner got this then [they] began to think of going home as they said they were certain from the little work which had been done to the Damm there was no more there, tho there were many places we could see New earth brought and placed just above the edge of the water. Before they left the place the[y] made a sort of Grating with pretty strong sticks where they had broken the Damm in order to facilitate the repair of it to any Bever that might fix in this place in future. This done we sett off on our way home again, Crossing in our way many tracks of Deer, Bear and otter which would have certainly escaped my Eye had they not pointed out to me. On our Return they brought us out exactly at our boat which we launched and Arrived at the fort again about two the same day with all our Game where I order the Young Beaver to be taken care of intending if possible to Rear them.

Next day May the 20th was a very wet day and one of the Indians took his Gun and after being out between a half or three quarter of an hour returned with about two Dozen of Snipes and Sand Larks. I could not conceive how he could get so many in so short a time, till he told me they flew in large flocks, which was the first time I ever knew snipes to do so—nor are snipes more common here in general than in other places.

The teats of the Beaver were but four which were on her Breast not like other Animals on the belly. All the trees we saw cut by these Animals were cut in such a manner as to fall Clear and not to lodge on any other one near it. Among other storys I was told even the old Beaver were so harmless, that the Messasaga Indians take hold of them by their Teeth that Project, and drag them out of their holes, without danger of being Bitten, but will no[t] Vouch for the Veracity of it. Certainly the young ones are very innocent and would make very pritty Petts could they be Reard but this is very difficult to do.

76.	1786	BATTEAUX PASSED OSWEGO	
	Octr		
	2	Mr Kingsby[?] to Niagara.	
	13th	Mr John Service[?] with Coll Harvey[?] Mr Clark[?] Mr Van Camp	each a Batteau to Cataraqui & the Island
	22	Capt. Myers & some Women & Children	to Cataraqui
	23d	Mr Tollier[?] of Datray[?] & Mr Disger[?] and a Negro	To Niagara
	Octr	Mr Bachelor Spring[?]	
	10th	Mr Seaver[?] this[?] fall	
		James Cruiklands[?]	
	[?]	John Van Altber[?]	to the States
		Abraham de Grave	
		Lancaster[?] Lightall[?]	
		John Haver[?]	
	Novr	John McEwen	to return in
	6	Peter Ferguson	Spring perhaps
		Robert McKinley	not together
	Returned May 10th 1787		
		Clark[?] returned to the States but I have lost the date of his passing	

[1787]   EXPRESSES IN WINTER——
Jany
18   Lieut Thacher[?] 34th Regt ⎫
          La Pensè——————   ⎬ from Canada
                                 ⎭
21   Left this [place?] on ther way to Niagara
Feby
5   Corpl Proctor[?] left this for Cataraqui
6   Winny[?] arrived from Niagara
7   Left this[?] on his way to Montreal
21   Proctor returned.
23   Hale of the 29th [25th] Regt went to Cataraqui
March
3   Hale returned to this place
4   [?] George came from Niagara
5   Set[?] of[f] again for Niagara
12[?]   Winny[?] return'd from Montreal
16   Left this [day] in a Canoe for Niagara

                    ARRIVALS IN SUMMER 1787
April
17   Mr Chisholm from Albany
23d   Ramsay with a Boat to Niagara
27   Mr MacLean left this [day] for Cataraqui
——   ⎰ Mr Barney[?] Wemp[?] and a man[?] of Tarleton's Corps
——   ⎱ with [?] a boat from Albany to Cataraqui with their familiys.
29   Some Cayuga Indians who gave me an account of the
          return of the Big Tree from Albany.
May
[?]
3   Mr Todd with 3 Boats from Canada arr
4   left this with two of the above Number
5   Mr Farrand[?] and Mr Robertson[?] left this in the
          other one for Canada
6   Corpl Proctor[?] returned from Cataraqui
——   Mr & Mrs[?] Roy MacKinsey[?] & Graham[?]
          Arrived with each a Boat from Canada.
8   They left this on their way to Niagara
9   A Boat from Canada belonging to Mr Graham which he had
          left [?] Chamberlin[?]
          Conductor, left this the Same day

10	a Boat from the States owner Mr Michen[?]

John McEwen
Peter Ferguson   } went in to the States
Robert McKinley   } on the 6th of Novr last
Adam Brown
Wm Gass [Goss?]   } who have no pass but are
and two women   } said to have been loyal

11	Three Boats Mr Hummeten[?] Niagara
	part[?] the same day
12	Three Boats Mr & Mrs Frobisher[?] & Co[?] to the
	grand portage passed the same day
12	A Boat from Niagara to the States went on directly[?]
	Mr Lampman[?] who left his boat at this post & who[?]
	took the one of [Street or Short?] per order
13	Mr Valentine went off to Cataraqui
14	Major Donalston[?] and eleven other in one boat by the States
—	Mr Campland[?] with a boat to Niagara.
—	Mr Chishom with a boat to the States.
21st	Mr Donaldson[?] with a boat from the
22d	States left this the 22d.
22d	Lapensè arrived with four boats from Canada went of[f] next day
23d	Mr McLean arrived in the Boat that took Mr Valentine.
	A Number of Cheifs from Canada went by in two Canoes
	to the Can[?]
25	Two Boats from the States with Mr Kart[?] and others to Cataraqui
28th	They left this Mr Levy[?] & on board sent[?] a Boat
	for Mr Connor in which Mr McLean went[?] Pasenger
29	a Boat from Canada in which Mr Connor Arrived.
30th	The Boat left this for Niagara
June	
3d	Mr Long came to the fort having left the Boat at Salmon Creek
6	the Boat went for Mr Connor Return'd and brought Mr Valentine.
11	A Royalist named Winny came in on foot. He went with
	Chisholm & returned with an american Trader to the [?]
21st	A boat from the States to Niagara
	Mr Johnston Paas from [& Parted?]
	another to Cataraqui Mr Phas[?] Chisholm[?]
	a Boat[?] from [?] to Do Mr Smith
22	A Boat from Niagara to the States
	Mr Stevens & others

—   a Boat from Cataraqui to Falls[?]
        the Road[Recd?] Mr Stewart
—   two Boats from the States for Cataraqui
        ————Laught[?]
        Jacob Smith

26   Four Boats from the States for Cataraqui,
                         Burges[?] Huyck
                         Willett Copey[Cossey?]
                         John Robin
                         Nicholas [?]

The April 29 reference to "Big Tree" probably pertains to the Cayuga Chief "Great Tree"; see Graymont, *Iroquois,* pp. 180, 216.

NIAGARA FALLS AND A ROYAL VISIT, 1787

1. "Commodore" David Betton was senior naval officer on Lake Ontario and acting commodore 1786–94. Hunter, *Quebec to Carolina,* p. 330.

2. The False Duck Islands are located in Lake Ontario close to Long Point and are a part of Prince Edward County. These two islands are also known individually as Timber Island and Swetman Island. The main Duck Island is located approximately in the middle of Lake Ontario east of the False Duck Islands and close to the international boundary line.

3. Fort Niagara is at the mouth of the Niagara river on the United States side. Its history goes back to 1678, when La Salle built storehouses there and surrounded them with a palisade. Burnt in 1680, the fort was abandoned in 1687. Charlevoix mentions a blockhouse there in 1721, strengthened in 1726 by adding four bastions. It was rebuilt in 1749 as part of the French project of a chain of forts from Canada to Louisiana. In 1759 Sir William Johnson besieged and captured Fort Niagara. By the terms of the Treaty of Paris of 1783 the fort fell within the American side but was not surrendered until 1796. *The Makers of Canada Series,* XII, *The Oxford Encyclopedia of Canadian History,* edited by Lawrence J. Burpee (Toronto: Oxford University Press, 1926), p. 209. Patrick Campbell reported that it was "a pretty strong stuccade fort with regular bastions, pallisades, pickets, and dry ditch." *Travels in the Years 1791 and 1792,* p. 147. For a detailed account of Fort Niagara see Janet Carnochan, "Fort Niagara," *Niagara Historical Society* 23 (n.d.): 1–15.

4. Fort Schlosser at the Lake Erie end of the Lewiston portage was built under the direction of Col. John Joseph Schlosser in 1760. Haldimand's familiarity with European fortresses was probably responsible for the location of the fort at this point. Robert W. Howard, *Thundergate: The Forts of Niagara* (Englewood Cliffs, N.J.: Prentice-Hall, 1968), p. 104. Thomas Hughes, who visited the fort in August 1786, reported that it was "a miserable place, no defence but a few pickets." Hughes, *Journal,* p. 152.

5. John Butler earned a reputation for cruelty toward the American enemy during the Revolution. Whether he merited the opprobrium is subject to dispute. Carnochan, *Fort Niagara,* p. 9. He commanded a corps of Loyalist Rangers, which attacked the New York and Pennsylvania frontiers. Graymont, *Iroquois,* pp. 167–74; *Oxford Encyclopedia of Canadian History,* edited by Burpee, p. 70; Sabine, *Loyalists,* I: 278–79.

6. The report that the Americans built a fort in 1787 at what is now Franklin, Pennsylvania, was correct. The fort was called Fort Franklin. Bruce Grant, *American Forts Yesterday and Today* (New York: Dutton, 1965), p. 83.

7.   At the lower end of the Niagara portage. A report of that period stated: "From Niagara to the landing place below the Falls is about seven miles and a quarter. There is a tolerably good road but merchandise, stores, etc., are carried up the river in batteaux or in vessels . . . ; beyond this place the current becomes too strong to proceed any further by water without great difficulty; boats, indeed, but not vessels, can go about a half mile higher. . . . From the wharf at the landing goods are drawn up the side of the bank about fifty feet high upon ways, on an easy slope, by a capstan fixed at the top. From this place there is a waggon road of seven miles to Fort Schlosser, which is one mile and a half above the falls, where the goods are again put into boats and carried up (eighteen miles) to Fort Erie." Cruikshank, *Ten Years of Niagara*, p. 27.

8.   Commerce was carried over the Niagara portage precisely as it had been since the capture of Fort Niagara by the British in 1759. The goods were brought to Lewiston in ships and hoisted to the top of the mountain by cradles, first devised by Colonel John Montresor. Montresor studied the portage, particularly the edge of the mountain that he might place to the best advantage a rope hoist with cradles above and below, for the raising of provisions, ordnance, and other supplies. Louis L. Babcock, *The War of 1812 on the Niagara Frontier, Buffalo Historical Society Publications* 29 (1927): 18; Frank H. Severance, "The Achievements of Captain John Montresor on the Niagara, and the First Construction of Fort Erie," *Publications of The Buffalo Historical Society*, edited by Severance (Buffalo, 1902), V: 11. For a brief description and a view of Montresor's inclined tramway, see Theodora Vinal, *Niagara Portage* (Buffalo: Foster and Stewart, 1949), pp. 20–21.

   Philip Stedman, Sr., had the contract with the British Government for carrying goods over the Niagara portage. Stedman was paid handsomely for this privilege—a thousand guineas, one report stated. Another one stated that Stedman paid the Government £1,500 sterling annually for the privilege. His returns were reported to be £3,000 and £1,000 per annum. He kept sixty horses and as many oxen and three hundred tons of hay. The enterprising Stedman also kept a small public house. Hunter, *Quebec to Carolina*, pp. 97–98, 332; Hadfield, *Diary*, pp. 92–93.

9.   Pierre Francois Xavier Charlevoix, *Histoire et description generale de la Nouvelle France*, . . . (Paris, 1744). The first English translation of this work was in 1761. Charlevoix had visited Niagara Falls in May 1721.

10.   Enys was probably referring to the Devil's Hole Massacre which occurred during the Indian uprising led by Pontiac. Only three forts resisted the concerted Indian attacks— Detroit, Pitt, and Niagara. The assault on the last was in part caused by the British eliminating the traditional role of the Indians at the Niagara portage. For years this place had been a source of income to the Indians, two hundred of whom were employed in carrying furs from the west. The English, however, proposed making a road for wagons and thus conveying goods by teamsters with oxen and horses, a less expensive

operation than the former. The hostility of the Senecas necessitated placing a guard at the foot and at the head of the portage. On 14 September 1763 a wagon train which had come from Lewiston with supplies for Detroit set out with an escort of twenty-five men accompanied by John Stedman. Suddenly this contingent was attacked by five hundred Senecas. The survivors who were not killed by fire were slaughtered with tomahawk and scalping knife. Terrified by the ensuing din some of the teams went over the cliff and men flung themselves over it to escape Indian torture. Only two persons survived the massacre—John Stedman, who had charge of the portage, and a drummer boy. On hearing the firing, some troops from the fort went to the rescue, only to suffer the same fate as the victims of the first ambush; only eight men escaped. By the time the entire garrison of the fort reached the scene of the massacre, the Senecas had disappeared. Carnochan, *Fort Niagara*, pp. 7–8; Francis Parkman, *The Conspiracy of Pontiac*, 2 vols. (Boston, 1913), II: 84–87.

11.   Of Miss Stedman Hunter wrote: "She is a charming, lively girl and is going soon to Detroit." *Quebec to Carolina*, p. 103.

12.   Grand Island.

13.   Fort Erie, on the Canadian side opposite present Buffalo. It had a barrack for troops and a blockhouse. Soldiers were quartered here for the purpose of transporting the public stores. Smyth, *Gazetteer*, p. 23.

14.   John Burch came to America in 1772 and went into the business of lacquering in Albany, N.Y. A Loyalist, he escaped to Niagara during the Revolution and took up land there. By 1783 he had cleared twenty acres. In 1786 he erected the first commercial sawmill in Upper Canada on Chippawa Creek. Hadfield, *Diary*, p. 100n; Hunter, *Quebec to Carolina*, pp. 103–104, 333; Cruikshank, *Ten Years of Niagara*, p. 42. Burch's Mills were two miles above the falls. *Mrs. Simcoe's Diary*, edited by Mary Quale Innis (Toronto, 1965), p. 96.

15.   Francis Ellsworth, a Loyalist and one of Butler's Rangers, received a land grant bordering the Horseshoe Falls, Niagara. Table Rock was on his land. By 1783 he had cleared five acres. Hunter declared that Ellsworth's house was situated "on the most delightful spot in the world" and that everyone who came to see the falls had to call at their house. *Quebec to Carolina*, pp. 104, 333–34; Hadfield, *Diary*, p. 101n.

16.   Andrew Ellicot, the first American surveyor to measure the Falls, estimated the perpendicular pitch to be 150 feet, to which he added 58 feet for the descent in the upper rapids and 65 feet for the lower rapids for a total of 273 feet. Frank H. Severance, *Studies of the Niagara Frontier* (Buffalo, 1911), pp. 176–78.

17.   Mrs. Elizabeth Simcoe wrote on September 24, 1795: "We stopped near Painter's

House to look at the Ft. Schlosser fall. . . . [Later] I rested myself at Painter's House where they prepared besides Tea those Cakes baked in a few minutes on an Iron before the fire which the people of the States make so well, eggs and sweetmeats and bacon or salt fish they usually offer with Tea." *Diary*, pp. 162–63.

Today Painter's Point is located along the River Road in Niagara Falls, Ontario, about a half mile from the Falls. It was so named because of its vantage point for painting or sketching the Falls from the Canadian side. It is also known as Bender's Point from the Bender family who settled here in 1782 and acquired this point in their land grant.

18.   It is surprising that Enys did not hear of the feat of Joseph Hadfield and Robert Hunter, both of whom had gone under the Falls on July 13, 1785. Of this deed Hadfield wrote: "We arrived at a small detached fall of water that is separated from the great fall about 20 to 25 yards broad. It was necessary to pass through this on our hands and feet. My flannel jacket protected my skin a little, for I can only compare this sheet of water for a large hail, and descending 120 feet the power and weight was excessive distressing. We had then to encounter another, which being effected, we advanced to the foot or base of the Great Cataract falling from a height of 180 feet. The effect on my skin was like to that I would suppose would be occasioned by a hail storm. However, onward I pushed until I arrived at the second small fall, but which was much greater and more severe than the other I had encountered, for the pressure and weight had nearly overcome my powers of resistance. Having passed it, I soon came to the base of this tremendous cataract. It is necessary here to explain that the force and impetus with which the water is hurled from the summit, gives it an oblique or rather describes an inclined plane, leaving a considerable aperture between the rock and the water [Cave of the Winds]. I had heard of this body of water being so great as by its density to become opaque. I was determined to prove it. I entered boldly and might advance 15 to 20 feet or a little more. I did remain long enough to ascertain it, for I found the heat to be so intense my breathing became difficult, and in a violent perspiration I sought the opening and was very happy to emerge freely again. I must here remark that not withstanding I had the full power of the sun's rays acting on the body of water all was dark, as if I had been entombed in a cavern." Hadfield, *Diary*, pp. 104–105.

19.   Generally a sulfur smell is not perceivable today, but ocasionally some people can detect such an odor.

Harrogate was a fashionable watering place of England, in the West Riding of Yorkshire.

20.   The spray evaporates, or, if the droplets are too heavy, they fall via gravity.

21.   Very few Ladies attempt to visit these falls by [but] I am told the name of a Lady (Lady Susan O Brion) "I think" is still to be seen not [?] by herself on the bark of a Tree near the Table Rock. Wither she went to the Bottom or no

I never heard nor what kind of Dress she wore upon the occasion. Certain I am that [a dress] normaly worn by Ladies is not at all calculated for the purpose it would not render it utterly impossible for them to pass in that habit.

The courageous lady mentioned by Enys was probably Lady Susan Sarah Louisa (1744–1827), eldest daughter of Stephen Fox Strangways, first Earl of Ilchester. In 1764 she eloped with William O'Brien, actor and dramatist, who went to Quebec in 1769. Plate 3 in Charles P. De Volpi, *The Niagara Peninsula* (Montreal: Dev-Sco, 1966), has this inscription: "From a Drawing taken on the Spot by Lt. Pierie of the R1. Artillery 1768. . . . To the Right Honble. Lady Susan O'Brien, this view of the CATARACT of Niagara, with the country adjacent, is most humbly Inscrib'd by her Ladyship's most obedt. & Obliged h'ble. Servt. Will'm Pierie."

On July 30, 1792, Mrs. Elizabeth Simcoe made her first descent at the Falls, going as far as Table Rock. On August 24, 1795, she made another, more daring descent: "We stopped near Painter's House to look at the Ft. Schlosser fall & then descended the hill which I found much easier than had been represented, & very little more difficult than the usual way to the Table Rock although it carried us so many feet below it. I rested half way & sketched the Rock & Ladder above me. The view from the Margin of the water is infinitely finer than from Table Rock. We were near a mile distant from it." *Diary,* pp. 76–77, 162. Unfortunately, Mrs. Simcoe did not describe her dress on these occasions.

22. Probably Enys was referring to Robert Hamilton, "a gentleman of the first rank and property in this neighbourhood, and now one of the governor's council." He came to Canada during the Revolution and settled near Queenston on the Niagara River. He was engaged in mercantile business along with Richard Cartwright. Campbell, *Travels,* p. 151; Hunter, *Quebec to Carolina,* pp. 95, 97–98, 332. Mrs. Elizabeth Simcoe, a frequent companion of Mrs. Hamilton, thus described the Hamilton home: "Mr. Hamilton has a very good Stone House the back Rooms overlooking on the River. A gallery the length of the House is a delightful covered walk both below and above in all weather." *Diary,* p. 76.

23. Table Rock fell June 26, 1850. According to Mr. Francis J. Petrie of Niagara Falls (July 16, 1975), "It was a large table-like ledge of rock, hence its name, that was over 60 feet long, extending some 30 feet out over the Niagara River gorge at the Canadian end of Horseshoe Falls. A large piece of it remained until the 1890s but this then gradually receded. The last of this rocky ledge was blown off deliberately in two explosions —July 1st and July 4th, 1935—by the Niagara Parks Commission as it was considered unsafe. . . . There is no longer any trace of Table Rock remaining."

24. Wind conditions could affect the flow of water downstream to Burch's Mills, but not on a regular schedule as that of ocean tides.

25. On May 29, 1787, Major Matthews wrote to Brant to the effect that the British planned to continue giving presents to the Indians and protecting the post against American encroachments. If, however, the Indians thought it more to their interests that the Americans should have possession of the posts and be established in Indian country, they ought to say so, in order that the English might no longer be put to the "vast and unnecessary expense and inconvenience" of keeping the posts, the chief object of which was to protect the Indian Allies. Stone, *Brant,* pp. 270–74.

26. Sayenqueraghta (Kayenquatah), a Seneca war chief, was the most influential leader in the Six Nations. Graymont, *Iroquois,* pp. 33, 159–60, and passim.

27. This stone, fort-like building, the original part of Fort Niagara, still stands. The Large House or the Castle, as some call it, was constructed in 1726 by the French. The 1726 plans show three doors on front, none to the rear. Mrs. Simcoe wrote: "There is a large Stone House built by the French in the Fort at Niagara & from thence it is said to take its name as Niagara in the Indian Language signifies great House." *Diary,* pp. 94–95.

28. "The Bottom" was the civilian area to the west of Fort Niagara's walls. It is still there, in effect; the U.S. Coast Guard uses it today. The civilians at Niagara engaged in trade up the Lakes.

29. John Butler was handsomely rewarded for his services in the Revolution. In 1796 he enjoyed a salary of £500 sterling per annum and a pension as a military officer of an additional £200. He also received a large grant of land. His Rangers, however, were not so generously treated. For one thing, they complained of not having received an equal proportion of clothing and of farming utensils with other Loyalist settlers. They were also jealous of the tenure in which they held their lands. Some of Butler's Rangers went back to the United States in disgust. In 1783 Haldimand received instruction to confer 1,000 acres on field officers; 700 to captains; 500 to subaltern, staff, or warrant officers; 200 to non-commissioned officers; 100 to privates, and the same quantity to every head of a family; 50 to every single Loyalist; and 50 to every individual in a family. In 1787 Lord Dorchester was instructed to confer 200 additional acres on those settlers who had improved their land. Sabine, *Loyalists,* I: 278–80; Hadfield, *Diary,* pp. 62–63; Cruikshank, *Ten Years of Niagara,* pp. 22–33, passim; Burt, *Quebec,* p. 397; Hunter, *Quebec to Carolina,* p. 75, 329.

30. The frontier movement in this area was indeed from South to North. At the close of the Revolution a number of individuals from Vermont, New York, and Pennsylvania came to Canada to prospect for and obtain land. Many of them asserted that for various reasons they had been unable to fight for the British cause, or, if they had fought on the American side, they had done so against their will. Even Major André's executioner, one Strickland, was able to procure land until he was recognized and whipped out of

the settlement and sent back to the United States. In Strickland's behalf, though, he was a Tory and a reluctant executioner. Burt, *Quebec,* pp. 362, 426, 468; Hunter, *Quebec to Carolina,* pp. 75, 329. According to Enys' record, "Batteaux passed Oswego," October 2, 1786, to June 26, 1787, it would seem that as many people went to the United States as came from there; see p. 311, note 76.

31.   Navy Hall, a group of four wooden buildings which had been used as winter quarters for the sailors on the lake and to hold stores, was built during the Revolution. After the War the buildings at Navy Hall were in "exceeding bad repair" and the wharf was in ruins. Of the Ranger's barracks one pile was virtually "dismantled." Cruikshank, *Ten Years of Niagara,* p. 26; Janet Carnochan, *History of Niagara* (Toronto, 1914), pp. 10–11. When Colonel John Graves Simcoe was appointed lieutenant-governor of Upper Canada in 1791 and, with Mrs. Simcoe, arrived at Niagara July 26, 1792, he found Navy Hall not ready for their occupancy and settled in three marquees pitched on the hillside. Simcoe *Diary,* p. 7, and passim. Hadfield and Weld also noted the Indian graves. Hadfield, *Diary,* p. 101; Weld, *Travels,* II: 149.

32.   Hadfield recounted that John Burch showed him a musket ball that he had extracted near the center of a large tree. By counting the circles in the trunk he estimated the age of the tree to be at least 120 years. *Diary,* p. 101.

33.   This was apparently a combination of blind man's buff and tag.

34.   Mrs. Simcoe refers to Mineral Springs in the vicinity of Niagara Falls. One was said to cure lameness, blindness, and every disorder. *Diary,* p. 167.

35.   This Lady was Mrs. McCormack, daughter to Arnoldy of Montreal.

36.   Peter Arnoldi kept an inn at Montreal. Hunter, *Quebec to Carolina,* pp. 39, 43–44.

These Narrows I had not before seen as I had always gone up and down under the No[r]th Shore as many or most Boats do which go to Cataraqui but I rather think this is the best way to go down even from thence for although it may be rather further the distance seems more than ballenced by the current being stronger down in this than the north Chanell but I should certainly prefer the North side to go up to Cataraqui.

There are several "Narrows" in Ontario.

37.   Also spelled *Messesagnes.* At a Council of Chiefs and Warriors at Albany in August 1746, the leading spokesman of the Six Nations informed the English commissioners that they had taken in the Messesagnes as a seventh nation. Samuel G. Drake, *The Aboriginal Races of North America* (New York, 1880), pp. 13, 500n.

38. The *Leander* had 52 guns. All of these vessels are listed in Colledge, *Ships*. The *Thisbe* was the newest vessel, built in 1783.

39. The *Quebec Gazette* (August 2, 9, 16 Supplement, 23, 30; September 13, 20, 27; October 11) devoted much space to the Prince's visit. The press account is quite similar to that of Enys. The former adds that on this "memorable and happy" occasion all prisoners except murderers were freed.

40.   Mrs. Alsop is the celebrated Belle Farmer of Mrs. Broke in her *Emly Montague.*
"Belle Farmer" should be "A. Fermor." The motto should have read: *Regiis gloria Nauticis,* Glory to the Royal Navy.

41. The *Quebec Gazette* (August 23) states that the ladies had the honor of being introduced "at a Drawing-room" to the Prince.

42. Prince William Henry, later William IV, was born August 21, 1765.

43.   I could not but admire the manner in which he answered the addresses presented to him. In that of the French Clergy they were profuse in their compliments of their happyness under his Solders [?] Mild beneficent govenment. To which he cooly replied that he was glad to find they were so happy and had no doubt but so long as they behaved themselves as good subjects that those blessings which they so much esteemed would be continued to them. The French Merchants were as profuse of their compliments as their clergy had been before and amongst the rest congratulated England on her future hopes in such an Prince who promised to be the Bulwark of the Nation by his early attention to his profession in the Navy. He told them he was extreemly obliged to them for all their compliments and hoped one day to prove himself worthy of them by doing the very utmost in his power to crush the Enimys of his country whoever they might be.

The newspaper accounts include the addresses.

44. Here, in an interpolation, Enys includes tediously detailed instructions for a military review and a sham battle to be executed before Prince William Henry and Lord Dorchester. This part of the journal has been omitted as it contains little of historical value. The *Quebec Gazette* (August 30) briefly reported that the Royal Artillery in the garrison and the 29th, 31st, and 34th Regiments were reviewed by the Prince and Lord Dorchester.

45. "The Chateau," wrote Weld, "is a plain building of common stone, situated in an open place, the houses round which, form three sides of an oblong square. It consists of two parts. The old and the new are separated from each other by a spacious court. The

former stands just on the verge of an inaccessible part of the rock; behind it, on the outside, there is a long gallery, from whence, if a pebble were let drop, it would fall at least sixty feet perpendicularly. This old part is chiefly taken up with the public offices, and all the apartments in it are small and ill contrived; but in the new part, which stands in front of the other, facing the square, they are spacious, and tolerably well finished, but none of them can be called elegant." *Travels*, I: 351. See also Kalm, *Travels*, II: 427.

46. Kalm wrote that the Indians of Lorette had made the French "their patterns" in several things beside their houses. These consisted of two rooms—bedroom and kitchen. In the former, beds were placed near the wall; in the latter, there was a small oven of stone, covered on top with an iron plate. The Jesuits had converted the Indians to Roman Catholicism. The village contained a "fine little church" with a steeple and a bell. Kalm *Travels*, II: 462–63.

47. Of this fall Weld wrote that it "is not half the height of that of the Montmorenci, but then it is no less than two hundred and fifty feet in breadth. The scenery round this cataract is much superior in every respect to that in the neighbourhood of Montmorenci. . . . As for the fall itself, its grandeur varies with the seasons. When the river is full, a body of water comes rushing over the rocks of the precipice that astonishes the beholder; but in dry weather, and indeed during the greater part of the summer, . . . the quantity of water is but trifling." *Travels*, I: 359–60.

48. Fraser was a member of the firm of Fraser and Shaw. In addition to a large wharf, he owned a warehouse at Quebec. Hadfield, *Diary*, p. 125.

49. For a more detailed yet similar description of an Eskimo kayak, see Kalm, *Travels*, II: 500–501. Kalm wrote that the Eskimos were "false and treacherous" and would not permit strangers among them. Shipwrecked Europeans, he added, might as well drown as fall into the hands of the Eskimos. See also Edwin Tappan Adney and Howard I. Chapelle, *The Bark Canoes and Skin Boats of North America* (Washington, D.C.: Smithsonian Institution, 1964), pp. 190–91, 205–207. The remains of an Indian canoe, brought from America by Enys, is in a stone shed at the Enys estate, Enys-Penryn, Cornwall. According to Miss Elizabeth Enys: "There is no documentation [regarding the Canadian birch-bark canoe] but I have always understood that he acquired it in Canada, & brought it back from there down the mighty Hudson River, presumably man-handled by porterage across Ticonderoga, & thence home by sailing ship. It might well have been packed with some stupendously big Buffalo horns which we used to have, but which were stolen some years ago, & other things, which he thought of interest & worth transporting."

50. Parkman, *Conspiracy of Pontiac*, II: 139–40; Weld, *Travels*, p. 346.

51. Thomas Hughes, as was shown above, pages 289–90, note 22, agreed with Enys.

52. A veiling was indeed a major tourist attraction, in fact and in fiction. Hadfield, *Diary,* pp. 156–59; [Brooke], *Emily Montague,* I: 27–34. For richness of detail Enys' account is by far the best. Hadfield confessed that he never went into a convent without feeling some distress that women under thirty should lead a celibate life.

53. The Grand Vicar in Quebec was Msgr. Jean-Olivier Briand, after he retired as bishop of Quebec in 1784; the Grand Vicar in London was Father Thomas Hussey, 1784–88. The Coadjutor was Msgr. Jean-François Hubert. The Bishop was Msgr. Louis-Philippe Mariauchau d'Esgly (or D'Esglis), first Canadian-born bishop of Quebec, who died in 1788. The Editor is endebted to M. Armand Goqué, Archivist, Les Archives de L'Archidiocèse de Quebec, for this information.

54. Kalm wrote that he had been told "that none of the nuns went into a convent till she had attained an age in which she had small hopes of ever getting a husband." *Travels,* II: 445–46. Hadfield remarks that there were novices of only seventeen or eighteen years of age and that some of the nuns were "very handsome" women. *Diary,* p. 158. Of the Ursulines, Mrs. Simcoe wrote: "Their dress is black with a white hood & some of them looked very pretty in it." *Diary,* p. 43.

55. David Garrick, *Lethe. A dramatic Satire* . . . (London, 1767); Isaac Bickerstaffe, *The Padlock: A comic opera* . . . (London, 1768). Both pieces had been performed at the Theatre-Royal in Drury Lane.

56. The nuns who served the sick at the Hotel Dieu were of the Augustinian order. Kalm, *Travels,* II: 428.

57. Muirson, a staunch Loyalist, was attainted by the state of New York and his extensive estate in Suffolk County was sold. Harry B. Yoshpe, *The Disposition of Loyalist Estates in the Southern District of the State of New York* (New York: Columbia University Press, 1939), pp. 18n, 48, 201; Sabine, *Loyalists,* II: 111.

58. There follow eight pages of manuscript which contain repetitive material—what appear to be the notes used by Enys in describing Chaudière Falls, the two veilings, the concluding festivities for Prince William Henry, and the reprieve of the sailor about to be hanged. These notes did state, however, that after the performance of *Lethe* and *The Padlock* there was performed "a scene or two of a Pantomine for the amusement of the Prince, the whole of which concluded with the song of Rule Brittania in which was introduced a transparent Drawing on Sattin of the Prince suported by Brittania."

59. *Quebec Gazette,* October 11, 1787.

VISIT TO THE UNITED STATES, 1787–1788

1. Miss de Lisle was probably the daughter of Dr. David Chabrand de Lisle, Military chaplain for Montreal. Hunter, *Quebec to Carolina,* p. 324. Miss Livingston was either Margaret Livingston (b. 3 June 1768), daughter of Peter Robert and Margaret Livingston, or Maria Livingston (b. 1767), daughter of Walter Livingston and Cornelia Schuyler. *The Livingston Family in America and Its Scottish Origins,* compiled by Florence Van Rensselaer, arranged by William Laimbeer (New York: Colonial Dames New York Genealogical and Biographical Society, 1940), pp. 91–92. There were quite a few families by the name of "Fortier" in 1787.

2. Pearl was a prominent citizen of Burlington, Vermont. *The Vermont Historical Gazetteer,* edited by Abby Maria Hemenway, 3 vols. (Burlington, Vt., 1868), I: 496–97, 516. Jack Rowe was the son of Jacob Rowe of Quebec. *Letters and Diary of John Rowe,* edited by Anne Rowe Cunningham (New York: New York Times, 1969), p. 13.

3.
Boundary of the Province of Quebec
Latitude 45° . .0. .0. . North
Variation   8° . .0. .0. . West

fixed by Order of the honorable Hector Theophilus Cramathy Esqr. Commander in Chief of the Province of Quebec and the Earl of Dunmorre governor of the Province of New York 15 Augt 1771

John Collins Esqr.
A. Benzzell Esqr.

Altho we had not yet left the British post yet we were in the Province or rather now the State of new York the Boundarys of which are as follows

Miles
Length   290   40 and 45° North Latitude
Between
Breadth   70   74 and 76 West Longitude

It has the Ocean for its Southern Boundary at New York from whence it extends to the Northern end of Lake Champlain is Bounded by Canada on the North by Connecticut Massachusets & Vermont on the East and by New Jersey & Pennsylvania on the West. It extends about 30 Miles to the East and 40 to the Westward of the Hudsons River.

The Island of New York as well as the River was discovered by a Englishman Named Hudson in the year 1608 and after being alternately several times Possessed by the English & Dutch until the 1674 when it was given to the English by treaty to whom it belonged untill the late revolution in its government.

The winter of 1771 saw progress in running the limits of the provinces of Quebec and New York at the 45th parallel. The Vallentine-Collins line extending eastward from Lake Champlain to the Connecticut River was completed in 1772. The westward line, from Lake Champlain to the St. Lawrence, was run in 1773–74 under the direction of Collins and Claude Joseph Sauthier. Lawrence S. Mayo, "The Forty-fifth Parallel: A Detail of the Unguarded Boundary," *The Geographical Review* 13 (April 1923): 255–65. Adolphus Benzell or Benzel, a civil engineer, was of Swedish origin. As Inspector of the King's Unappropriated Lands and Woods, Benzell was a dedicated guardian of the royal timber. See Benzell to the King, P.R.O., CO5:114; to Governor Wentworth, P.R.O., Adm. 3820; to Earl of Dunmore, P.R.O., CO5:72. Cramahé was the governor of Quebec. New York was taken by the English in 1664. It came again into Dutch hands in 1673, but was restored by treaty to the English the following year.

4. This was probably the schooner, *Maria,* of six guns, in service on the Canadian lakes. Colledge, *Ships,* p. 345.

5. Benedict Arnold burned his ship, the galley *Congress,* and four other gondolas in a bay on the east side of Lake Champlain some ten miles above Crown Point according to his own account. This is exactly the location of Button Mould Bay which is sometimes called by the British "Destruction Bay." This could also be Ferries's Bay, or Ferries's Bay could be part of Button Mould Bay. The Editor is indebted to Gordon Bowen-Hassell, of the Naval Historical Center, for the above information.

6. During Burgoyne's Campaign, Col. Brown surprised an outpost between Ticonderoga and Lake George, and took possession of Mount Defiance. He also destroyed a number of vessels, seized a large quantity of stores, released one hundred American prisoners, and captured about three hundred British soldiers. Benson J. Lossing, *The Empire State* (New York, 1887), p. 275.

    The "Mills" were most likely those of John Stoughton, the original patentee of Ticonderoga, just downstream from the outlet of Lake George, or else the mills at the lower falls in today's village of Ticonderoga.

    The landing place at the foot of Lake George was often called "The Landing Place." "South Landing" was probably at the southern end of the lake at today's Lake George Village.

7. "This pump sounds like something someone made. On large boats, such as sloops, the pumps were hollowed out logs with a shaft running down with a disk. Attached to this was a long handle at a right angle and it would pump the water up on deck and the water would run over the side. I am sure that all sorts of pumps were in use at that time but for small boats I don't think so." Letter of James A. Knowles, Smithsonian Institution, July 11, 1974.

8. This is one of several methods still in use for locating hives.

9. In late summer 1755, William Johnson encamped at the head of Lake George. Learning from scouts that there was advancing a force of fifteen hundred men, composed of French regulars, Canadian Militia, and Indians, he dispatched Col. Ephraim Williams with a large body of provincials and Mohawks to meet them. The detachment fell into an ambuscade and suffered severe losses. The survivors fell back to Johnson's camp, pursued by the elated victors under Baron Dieskau. Here the French met with a most stubborn resistance and were driven back in disorder, and the wounded Dieskau was taken prisoner. Although Johnson did not follow up this success, he was rewarded by a vote of five thousand pounds from the British Parliament and by a baronetcy from the King. Lossing, *Empire State,* pp. 165–66; Fortescue, *History,* II: 289–90.

10. Fort Amherst, a little north of Glens Falls, was a stockade erected in 1759 according to plans drawn by Col. John Montresor. The rear was protected by an impassable swamp. The remains of the fortification were visible as late as 1830. Louis F. Hyde, *History of Glens Falls, New York, and Its Settlement* (Glens Falls: Privately printed, 1936), pp. 33–34, 34n.

11. Wing's Tavern was seven miles from Fort Edward. Hill, *Fort Edward,* pp. 247, 299. Abraham Wing was the founder of Glens Falls. Hyde, *Glens Falls,* pp. 95, 134–35.

12. Chastellux thus described the falls: "Here the river is confined and interrupted in its course by different rocks, through the midst of which it glides and falls precipitously, as it forms several cascades . . . here the Hudson frets and fumes, it foams and forms whirlpools, and flies like a serpent making its escape, still continuing its threats by horrible hissings." Marquis De Chastellux, *Travels in North America* . . . , translated and edited by Howard C. Rice, Jr., 2 vols (Chapel Hill, N.C.: University of North Carolina Press, 1963), I: 216.

13. There were sawmills in operation at this locality as early as 1763. The second sawmill, as primitive as the first one, was probably erected in Queensbury in 1764. John Glen (1735–1828) was a trader. In 1755 he bought a tract of land, which later became known as Glens Falls. After the Revolution, Glen, a member of the Albany County Militia, rebuilt the mills, destroyed during the conflict. Hyde, *Glens Falls,* pp. 114–16, 125, 174. *The Quebec Gazette,* September 23, 1784, reported the marriage of Miss Southouse, daughter of Judge Southouse, to Jacob Glen of Schenectady, an officer of Johnson's 2nd. battalion of Royal Rangers. The same issue of the *Gazette* announced the arrival of the *Speedy,* Captain Auvergne.

14. Fort Edward, built by Phineas Lyman of Connecticut, was originally called Fort Lyman. Sir William Johnson renamed it Fort Edward, for Edward Augustus, Duke of York and Albany. The fort was razed in 1775. Hill, *Fort Edward,* passim.

15. Much has been written about Jane McCrea, who was en route to meet her Tory lover, David Jones, serving in Burgoyne's army, when she was killed by Indians. This tragic event proved to be a boon to American propaganda efforts to mould public opinion and increase enlistments. Hill, *Fort Edward*, pp. 272–75, 351–65, 373; Chastellux, *Travels*, edited by Rice, pp. 214–15, 351–65.

16. During Burgoyne's advance, Duer's house at Fort Miller served as British headquarters. Apparently Enys' informers were correct in stating that Duer was "seldom" at home. On 11 April 1780, Duer authorized Abraham Wing "to permit such families as he shall think proper . . . to inhabit my new house at Fort Miller and to make such regulations for the preservation of the Building and keeping order in the house as he shall think proper." Hill, *Fort Edward*, pp. 307, 340.

17. Several sawblades mounted side by side in a single vertically reciprocating frame cut several boards at each pass of the carriage holding the log.

18. This was perhaps the house of Mrs. Sara McNeil, the friend of Jane McCrea.

19. Schuyler also kept a store at Saratoga. Don R. Gerlach, *Philip Schuyler and the American Revolution* (Lincoln, Neb.: University of Nebraska Press, 1964), pp. 53–58. This, the third house built by Schuyler at Saratoga, is still standing. The first one was burned by the French in 1745, the second by the British in 1777. Francesco dal Verme, *Seeing America and Its Great Men*, edited by Elizabeth Cometti, (Charlottesville, Va.: University Press of Virginia, 1969), pp. 15, 107.

20. General Fraser died of wounds received at the Battle of Bemis Heights. For details of Fraser's burial and sketches of his grave and of the house occupied by Burgoyne, see Lossing, *Field-Book*, I: 64–66.

21. Accounts of Burgoyne's Campaign are in Piers Mackesy, *The War for America 1775–1783* (Cambridge, Mass.: Harvard University Press, 1965), pp. 130–44; Ward, *Revolution*, II: 504–542; Fortescue, *History*, III: 233–42; Lossing, *Field-Book*, I: 43–81.

22.   Not far above the half Moon [Halfmoon] are the Kahoz [Cohoes] falls which are the whole breadth of the Mohawk River but only 30 feet high. They were out of our way and would have given but little pleasure to one so lately from Chaudre [Chaudière] Montmorency & Niagara.

The Lansings, northerly neighbors and relatives of the Vanderheydens, laid out their land in building lots shortly before the Revolution and established the village of Lansingburgh. The name Troy was adopted at a public meeting in Ashley's Tavern on January 5, 1789. Writers' Program, Work Projects Administration, *New York: A Guide to the Empire State* (New York: Oxford University Press, 1940), p. 344.

23.   At this tavern, wrote Count Dal Verme in 1783, "they served us tobacco, pipe, brands, and candles, and everyone . . . spent more than two hours alternately parching his throat with smoke and moistening it with wine." *Seeing America*, p. 12.

24.   Some [of] these old Houses are said to be built with bricks brought from Holland when they first came to form the settlement and from their gothic appearance it may be true for ought I can tell.

The earliest settlers of Albany were of Dutch descent.

25.   This was Fort Frederick, on the site of the present state capital.

26.   The elegant home of Philip Schuyler, originally called "The Pastures," is still standing. Harold D. Eberlein, *Manors and Historic Homes of the Hudson Valley* (Philadelphia: Lippincott, 1924), pp. 222–36; Anna K. Cunningham, *Schuyler Mansion* (Albany: N.Y. State Education Dept., 1955). The Rensselaer and Yates homes are no longer standing.

27.   I have since learnt they have a few Artillery men in many places just to take care of the Stores and a Regt in the Western Country under the Command of General [George Rogers] Clark.

Clark had just been deprived of his command. Temple Bodley, *George Rogers Clark* (Cambridge: Houghton Mifflin, 1926, pp. 318–24. Enys' description of West Point, a military depot at this time, is correct.

28.   The Sloop of War which took Major Andre up and brought Arnold down the River was called the *Vulture*.

The account Enys heard was essentially correct. In the no-man's land near Tarrytown, plagued by the depredations of "cow-boys" (mostly Tory refugees) and "Skinners" (those supporting the Revolution), one could expect to meet either friend or foe. The three men who took Arnold were John Paulding, Issaac Van Wart, and David Williams. Labeled as "volunteer militiamen" by Congress, they were operating under a recent New York act which permitted them to claim as prize any property they might find on a captured enemy. André made the fatal mistake of taking these men to be Loyalists instead of adherents of the Revolutionary cause. Had he shown Arnold's pass, which he had in his possession, he probably would have been permitted to proceed. Carl Van Doren, *Secret History of the American Revolution* (New York: Viking, 1968), pp. 339–41; Lossing *Field-Book*, I: 753–54.

Included in the Enys manuscripts is a copy of John André's "The Cow-Chace," a satirical poem which poked fun at General Anthony Wayne's expedition against a blockhouse near the village of Bull's Ferry for the purpose of reducing the post and driving the cattle on Bergen Neck within the American lines. The Americans failed to take the blockhouse, but succeeded in obtaining some livestock. André's verse was published in Rivington's *Royal Gazette,* the last, or third, canto appearing on the day André was taken at Tarrytown. Enys' heading of the poem is "The Cow Chace Elizabeth town August 1st 1780." Lossing, *Field-Book,* II: 622n., 684–86.

29.   The Van Cortlandt mansion built by Frederick Van Cortlandt in 1748, now transformed into a museum, is near the entrance of Broadway and 242 Street. The gray stone structure, a fine example of Georgian Colonial architecture, was occupied by Washington for a short time after the Revolution.

30.   During the Revolution the extensive property of Frederick Phillipse, a Loyalist, was confiscated. Phillipse applied to the British government for compensation and was awarded £62,075 sterling. In 1809 the property was estimated at six or seven hundred thousand pounds. Sabine, *Loyalists,* II: 185–88. The leasing arrangement described by Enys was a common one.

31.   The northern end of the Harlem River in today's New York City. For a view of Manhattan Island and Kingsbridge in 1782, see I. N. Phelps Stokes, *The Iconography of Manhattan Island, 1498–1909,* 6 vols. (New York: Dodd, 1915–28), I: plate 50.

32.   For a brief description of these fortifications, dominated by Fort Washington, renamed Fort Knyphausen by the British, see Lossing, *Field-Book,* II: 610n; John A. Kouwenhoven, *The Columbia Historical Portrait of New York* (New York: Doubleday, 1953), pp. 71–72; Wilbur C. Abbott, *New York in the Revolution* (Port Washington, N.Y.: Friedmann, 1962), pp. 202–204.

33.   Verdine Elsworth's Lodging house was located at 19 Maiden Lane. It opened in January 1784. Stokes, *Iconography,* VI: 387, 612; Maiden Lane *Independent Gazette,* January 8, 1784.

34.   In 1771 the population of New York City was 21,863. At the end of the Revolution it was probably less than that number. The census of 1786 showed a population of 23,614. Sidney I. Pomerantz, *New York: An American City, 1783–1803* (New York: Columbia University Press, 1938), p. 21; Stokes, *Iconography,* I: 331; V: 1207. The fires of September 21–23, 1776, and of August 3, 1778, caused heavy property losses and much distress among the poor. The first and more destructive of the two fires consumed virtually all of the buildings between Broadway and the Hudson River as far as St. Paul's Church, which was saved. Trinity Church and the Lutheran Church were burned. The second conflagration destroyed more than sixty dwellings and many stores near the waterfront. Stokes, *Iconography,* I: 324, 333–34; George W. Edwards, *New York as an Eighteenth Century Municipality, 1731–1776* (New York, 1917), pp. 128–41.

35.   St. Paul's Chapel (1764) was the first authentic Georgian Church in New York. It

was inspired by St. Martin's-in-the-Fields in London. The light, spacious interior is handsomely decorated with a barrel vault carried on slender columns, and a gallery on each side. On the Broadway side of the church is a monument to Montgomery, executed by Jean Jacques Caffieri, a French sculptor, on order of the Continental Congress. Montgomery's grave is beneath the monument. Federal Writers' Program, New York City, *New York City Guide* (New York: 1939), pp. 98–99; Chastellux, *Travels,* edited by Rice, II: 657–58. The Charity School was supported by Trinity Parish.

36.   New York is said now to contain between 3500 and 4000 houses most of which are larger and better than before the fires.

        The Harbour of New York so very large comodous and safe may be easyly defended and is but very seldom obstructed by the Ice, altho in 1780 it was frosen so hard that they carried large Cannon, Stores and Provisions under an Escort of Dragoons to Staten Island. Ships may be at the Warfs on either side of the town.

        In the City Hall are the portrats of the French King and Queen that are said to be very well done.

The winter of 1780 was excessively cold in all parts of the country.

    The full-length portraits of Louis XVI and Marie Antoinette, executed by Wurtmuller and presented to the United States by the French King and Queen, continued to hang in the Senate Chamber when the Capital was moved to Washington. When the British fired the building in the War of 1812, the portrait of Marie Antoinette was entirely consumed and that of Louis partially injured. The latter was removed into a lumber room in the General Post Office and afterwards disappeared rather mysteriously. Stokes, *Iconography,* V: 1197.

37.   Stokes, *Iconography,* I: plate 46, map by Claude Joseph Sauthier. Half of the land on which the fort was located is now Bennett Park, Fort Washington Avenue, and 143d Street. *New York City Guide,* p. 301.

38.   There were some breastworks at M'Gowan's Pass, between 105 and 108 Streets and Fifth and Sixth Avenues, now known as Mount St. Vincent. Lossing, *Field-Book,* II: 610n.

39.   Before I leave New York it may not be Amiss to relate a Story which was told me for a certain fact. The proposal was said to have been made by one of the people called Quakers But rejected with Scorn by the General who then Commanded the American Army before New York. It was as follows.

        In the early part of the American War, when his Majesties Ship Asia was at Anchor before the town of New York, Various Plans were proposed for her destruction. Among the Rest was the following: That a Boat loaded with Gunpowder should be sent as if attempting to cross the River, but so managed as to fall into the hands of the English, Under a full perswasion that they would put it on board of that ship. In one of the Barrells was to be placed a piece of Mecanism so contrived as to go for a day or two, at the end of which time it was to press upon a Spring which was to fire a Gun Lock contained in the Powder by which means it was to explode and blow up any Magazeen in which it might have been placed.

For an account of the attempted submarine attack against a large British warship (*Eagle* or *Asia*) in September 1776, see *Naval Documents of Revolution*, VI: 736–37, and Appendix B, 1499–1511. The "Diary of Samuel Richards" (p. 736) states: "The admirals ship—the *Eagle* of 64 guns appearing in full sight, . . . Capt. [David Bushnell]—of the sappers & miners—having prepared his submarine engine—it was sent one night with a magazine of powder attached to it." The "Journal of the *Asia*" (p. 736) states: "at ½ past 10 sent 4 Boats to the Assistce of the Advanced Guard p. Signal." The guard boats could have been alarmed by a strange object in the water: Bushnell's submarine, the *Turtle,* operated by Sergeant Ezra Lee. In a letter to Jefferson, 26 September 1785, Washington wrote that Bushnell was a "man of great Mechanical powers," who had come to him highly recommended. Bushnell, Washington continued, "had a machine which was so contrived as to carry a man under water at any depth he chose, and for a considerable time & distance, with an apparatus charged with powder which he could fasten to a ships bottom or side & give fire to in any given time (sufft. for him to retire) by means whereof a ship could be blown up, or sunk" Bushnell's own detailed description of his invention prepared for Thomas Jefferson and Ezra Stiles is in *Naval Documents of Revolution*, pp. 1501–1507. Bushnell attributed the failure of the attempt made near Governor's Island to the fact that Lee, in trying to fix the woodscrew in the ship's bottom, struck a bar of iron. Had Lee moved a few inches, he would have found wood to which he could have attached the screw. See also Frederick Wagner, *Submarine Fighter of the American Revolution: The Story of David Bushnell* (New York: Dodd Mead, 1963).

40.   There was an Indian tradition that at one time it had been possible to cross Hell Gate by stepping from one exposed rock to another. Reginald P. Bolton, *Indian Paths in the Great Metropolis* (New York: Museum of the American Indian, 1922), pp. 184–85.

"Hog's Back" is a shoal in the ship's channel of East River as one is going toward Flushing Bay. "The Pot" was a rock directly in the ship channel of the East River. "The Gridiron" and "the Frying pan" certainly sound like shoals, as they are typical names for shoals and are in the same area between Long Island and Barran Island in the Hell Gate Passage. The *Huzzar,* twenty-eight guns, sunk September 1779, was a victim of the Pot.

41.   The Narragansett pacer, a breed of American saddle horse, is now extinct.

42.   During the Revolution, Newport's population was greatly reduced, and property valued

at $624,000 specie was destroyed. Lossing, *Field-Book,* II: 656–57. Not until 1900 did Rhode Island have one capital. Prior to 1854 there had been five capitals—Providence, Newport, East Greenwich, Bristol, and South Kingstown. The General Assembly traveled around from one to another. In 1854 the number was cut to two—Newport and Providence. In 1900 by constitutional amendment it was reduced to one—Providence. *Providence Journal–Bulletin Almanac* (1973), p. 199.

43.   These islands in Narragansett Bay are named Prudence (by far the largest), Patience, and Hope. In using the term "Proprietors," Enys meant "settlers." Rhode Island was never a proprietary colony.

44.   "A very excellent house" according to Robert Hunter, *Quebec to Carolina,* p. 117.

45.   There were five church buildings in Providence in 1787. The "Anabaptist church" mentioned by Enys must refer to the First Baptist Church erected in 1775 and still standing. The Episcopal church, first known as King's Church, was built in 1722 and torn down in 1810. There were two Congregational Churches in 1787, the original congregation having split in 1743. The Congregational Meeting House of the First Congregational Society was built in 1723. In 1795 it was taken over by the town as a Town House and used as such until 1870. The splinter group from the original congregation built the New Light Meeting House in 1746 which it occupied until 1807. The fifth church in Providence in 1787 was the Quaker Meeting House built in 1725 and used until 1844.

There were two public school houses in Providence in 1787; both were built in 1767. One was called Whipple Hall, the other was known as Brick School House. An almshouse and workhouse, standing in 1787, was built in 1753.

Rhode Island College was established in Warren in 1764. It was moved to Providence in 1770 when the College Edifice was built. That building now called University Hall is still standing. Rhode Island College became Brown University in 1804. Information kindly provided by Nancy F. Chudacoff, Reference Librarian, The Rhode Island Historical Society.

46.   The first Boston Directory (1789) states that Mrs. Mary Loring had a boarding house on Hanover Street.

47.   The first pier for this bridge was laid 14 June 1785; it was opened to traffic in a little more than a year. The bridge was considered a major engineering feat and its completion was celebrated by a public procession, salutes, and fireworks. The bridge was 1,503 feet long, 42 feet wide, and cost $50,000. The contractor was Lemuel Cox of Medford. Samuel A. Drake, *Old Landmarks and Historic Personages of Boston* (Detroit: Singing Tree, 1970), p. 24. The Editor is indebted to Harriet R. Cabot for some information on Boston.

48.   The Harbour of Boston is esteemed as good as any on the continent. It is in the form of a Large Bason in which stand a good many Islands. Several Points also Project into it forming Peninsula's on one of which stands the town of Boston. This harbour is perfectly safe in any Wind and is well fortified against an Enemy by a Castle called Castle William on an Island a little below the town. It is at Present Garrisoned by a Company of Artillery who serve at once the purpose of keeping up the Works, firing Signals & Salutes and taking care of Prisoners this being a place where they confine convicts to hard Labour for any stated time which they may be convicted for. Their employment is making Nails by which I am told they more than maintain themselves. I cannot help thinking this employment better than any I have seen addopted in England where Culprits of this kind are kept to heaving of Ballast or Beating of hemp. There when they leave these places they have learnt no trade by which they can maintain themselves and finding themselves once more thrown upon the Publick and branded with infamy no one wishes to employ them. They are obliged to have recourse to their former malpractices and in place of being by any means mended they come from thence more compleat Rogues than they went in. On the contrary this System it appears to me that having acquired a Profitable trade during their confinement as well as a habit of industry, on their coming out they would be able to employ themselves to the benefit of the society to which they were formerly the Pest.

Prisoners were kept at Castle William, also known as Fort Independence.

49.   The Malden Bridge of 1787 took six months to build. It replaced the "Penny Ferry" which was built by the Malden Bridge Corporation over the Mystic River from Charlestown to Malden.

50.   The fire at the time of the Battle of Bunker Hill destroyed most of Charlestown; 380 houses were lost as well as public buildings. There were 2,000 homeless.

51.   The rope walks were on Pearl Street and at the bottom of the Common, now Charles Street. The markets were at Faneuil Hall.
        Mrs. Molesworth was the former Suzanna [Susan?] Sheafe, who eloped at the age of fifteen with Captain Ponsonby Molesworth, nephew of Lord Ponsonby. She and her husband went to England in 1776. Esther Forbes, *Paul Revere & the World He Lived In* (Boston: 1942), p. 146; Sabine, *Loyalists*, II: 280–94; Zobel, *Boston Massacre*, pp. 100, 141.

52.   The locality referred to near the Ohio River is probably "big bone lick" which Frank Witmore of the U.S. National Museum is investigating. The Museum of Comparative Zoology, Harvard University, contains a number of the older specimens which were the property of Harvard at the time of Louis Agassiz' arrival in Cambridge during the first

half of the nineteenth century. Very likely the specimen cited in the Enys journal is still in the Harvard Collection. The editor is indebted to Professor Farish A. Jenkins, Jr., for the above information.

53. "The Honorable Judge Belcher of Halifax, Nova Scotia, purchased a pair of globes for Harvard in 1765. The terrestrial globe is no longer in exhibitable condition, but this celestial sphere, twice restored, has survived two centuries of use remarkably well." A picture of the celestial globe is given in *Early Science at Harvard: Innovators and their Instruments,* December 18, 1969, through February 1, 1970 (Cambridge, Massachusetts: Fogg Art Museum, Harvard University, 1969), pp. 36–37.

54. Breck (1747–1809) was a prominent merchant and a member of the Massachusetts House of Representatives. *Recollections of Samuel Breck with Passages from His Note-Books, 1771–1862,* edited by H. E. Scuddler (Philadelphia, 1877), pp. 17–29.

55. No Beaton is listed in the Cambridge Vital Records or in Lucius R. Paige, *History of Cambridge, Massachusetts 1630–1877* (New York, 1877). No reference to Lieut. Beaton or Beton can be found in the Ministry of Defence Library, London.

56. Estimates as to the length of the Long Wharf vary. Harriet R. Cabot of the Bostonian Society informed the Editor that it was 1,800 feet long. For a description of the wharf see Drake, *Landmarks,* pp. 114–15.

57. There was a hospital for sick and "infectious" patients on Rainsford Island. This dealt largely with smallpox. There were inoculating hospitals at Castle William and Point Shirley in 1764 and a military hospital near the present Massachusetts General Hospital in 1783.
    The Manufactory House was established in 1748 and there were the Bridewell Almshouse and Workhouse.
    Boston had five publick schools for boys between 1760–66. There were two grammar schools and three writing schools. The Boston Latin School was then (1787) and is now flourishing.

58. The Arsenal at Springfield was a United States arsenal. Francisco de Miranda, who visited the arsenal at Springfield in 1784, wrote: "Two wooden warehouses contain seventy-five hundred muskets of French make, some ancient weapons of the same type as was used when the war began, about ninety bronze artillery pieces . . . , two thirteen-inch mortars, four or six twelve-inch cannons, some howitzers and miscellaneous artillery, and carriages, etc. The powder is kept in a brick warehouse." Francisco de Miranda, *The New Democracy in America: Travels of Francisco de Miranda in the United States, 1783–84,* translated by Judson P. Wood, edited by John S. Ezell (Norman, Okla.: University of Oklahoma Press, 1963), pp. 113–14; Mason A Green, *Springfield, 1636–1886: History of a Town and City* (Springfield, Mass., 1888), passim.

The arsenal at Springfield was one of three established by the United States Congress. The other two "Magazines" were located at West Point and Carlisle. *Journals of the Continental Congress,* XXV: 738. When the American army went into winter quarters at Morristown in 1777, Henry Knox was sent to Massachusetts, where he started a government arsenal at Springfield.

59. An uprising (1786–87) took place in western Massachusetts under the leadership of Daniel Shays in protest of the state's conservative fiscal policies that benefited the merchant class at the expense of the farmers. When the county courts became more rigid in the collection of private debts as well as taxes, imprisonment for debts increased and sales of personal property and farms to satisfy creditors and tax collectors mounted. Petitions for relief were presented to the legislature, but they were refused.

Denied paper money and tax payments in kind, the debtors prevented the courts from sitting and the sheriffs from selling their property. In September 1786, a group led by Shays broke up a session of the Massachusetts State Supreme Court at Springfield. To enforce the law the legislature raised troops and Gen. Benjamin Lincoln was placed in command. In January 1787 Shays led a band of "rebels" against the arsenal at Springfield, but they were repelled by forces under Maj. Gen. William Shepherd. By early spring the rebellion was broken. Some of the rebels were captured, tried, and given the death sentence, but were later pardoned. A farmers' victory at the polls in the spring elections produced laws affording them the relief which had formerly been denied.

60. I was told of a singular advertisement which was in a Hartford paper last fall of a Mariage which Actualy took place at that place which Ran thus. Last Sunday was Married at the Church in this place Mr. Daniel Dolittle, to Miss Sarah Lovit, bothe of this parish.

The Connecticut River as well as all those to the North East of it abound in very fine Salmon whch they cure and send to the Southern Markets as there are none taken to the Southward not even in the Hudsons River which is so very Near.

There was a grammar school in Hartford in 1787, but no college.

There were great quantities of salmon and shad in the Connecticut River during the seventeenth and most of the eighteenth centuries. In 1795 a dam was erected at South Hadley which prevented the salmon from swimming to their breeding areas. Information provided by Michael G. Fitch, Connecticut Historical Society.

61. Chastellux made a similar comment about American inns: "I determined therefore to go straight to the tavern, where I was still unlucky enough not to find Mr. Phillips the landlord; so that I was received, to say the least, with indifference, which often happens in the inns in America, when they are not in much frequented situations. Travelers are there considered as bringing more trouble than money. The reason for this is

that the innkeepers are all of them well-to-do farmers who do not stand in need of this slight profit: most of those who follow this profession are even compelled to it by the laws of the country, which have wisely provided that on any road there shall be a 'public house,' as these taverns are commonly and appropriately called, every six miles." *Travels,* edited by Rice, I: 81–82.

62. For an account of the destruction of New Haven and Fairfield, see Lossing, *Field-Book,* I: 422–28.

63. This name was given to the Peninsula extending into the Sound at Greenwich from the fact that many horses used to be pastured there. Ibid., I: 411–12.

64. In September 1788 a controversy arose between Virginia and the Board of Treasury respecting the double settlement of Dr. George Draper's accounts with the United States and the state of Virginia for the same services in the army. Edmund C. Burnett. *Letters of Members of the Continental Congress,* 8 vols. (Washington: Carnegie Institution, 1921–36), VIII: 801n.
    Constable may have been a member of the firm of Constable, Rucker & Co., which purchased North Carolina tobacco. Ibid., pp. 558, 584n.
    William Seaton of New York is reputed to have attested the will of Major John André drawn up at Staten Island, June 7, 1777. Sabine, *Loyalists,* II: 273.

65. The best-known work of McComb (1763–1835) included the Brick Church, 1767, the North Dutch Church, 1769, and the New York Hospital, the cornerstone of which was laid in 1773.

66. Lossing (*Field-Book,* II: 422n.) wrote that a feeling of security made the American garrison careless and when the sudden British attack came, they were unprepared to repel it. A more probable account of the British capture of Paulus Hook, now Jersey City, is as follows: After the American retreat from Long Island and New York in late summer 1776, much of the artillery and stores and many wounded were taken to the New Jersey shore for transportation to Newark. A number of the wounded, "Invalids," as Enys called them, however, had to be left at the Hook. After several days of British cannonading the Americans withdrew and the British held Paulus Hook for the remainder of the War. *History of Hudson County and of the Old Village of Bergen* (The Trust Company of New Jersey, Jersey City, n.d.), pp. 33–34. Still another version states that after the reverses suffered by the Americans in New York, it was recognized that the fortifications at Paulus Hook would have to be abandoned. General Mercer removed all guns, stores and troops with the exception of a small guard under orders to leave upon the first appearance of the enemy. On September 23, 1776, the British ships cannonaded the fort. When they took it, they found but a few guns unfit for use. Mercer and his troops retired to Bergen. Harriet P. Eaton, *Jersey City and Its Historic Sites* (Jersey City, 1899), pp. 50–51.

67.

It was not until I arrived at Philadelphia that I found out there was a Manufactory in Hackingsack [Hackensack] for making Wompum for the Indians although I frequently enquired in New York where it was made without being able to procure the least information.

On the Banks of this River there was formerly a Copper Mine which was wrought with advantage to its proprietor until it became necessary to Erect a Steam Engine the Expence of which togeather with the late war coming on at the same time occasioned it to be dropped.

On the Pessiaeck [Passaic] River about 30 Miles from New York is a fall which is by some esteemed curious but for the reasons already given for not going to those on the Mohawk River, as well as the badness of the Roads and quantity of Ice and Snow I did not visit them. It is said to be from 70 to 80 feet high and from what I can learn is in appearance like that of the hudsons River near fort Edward but not near so large.

Wampum, beads made from shells and used as money by the Indians, was manufactured at Pascack, New Jersey, by John W. Campbell and his descendants, from 1775 until 1889. The black and more expensive wampum was made from the thick and blue part of sea clam shells; the white was made from conch shells, brought from West Indian ports as ballast to New York and sold to the Campbell firm. To procure the hard shell clams necessitated a trip by rowboat from New Milford on the Hackensack river to Rockaway, Long Island, via Newark Bay. When the clams arrived, they were placed under trees and the neighbors were invited to take all the flesh they wanted, but to leave the shells. After the opening of the Washington Market in New York City, the Campbells contracted for all the empty clam shells. Farmers who made wampum at home could get cash for their product at the Pascack trading post or from the Campbells. Some of these farmers "worked out the blanks," as the unfinished work was called, and the Campbells did the polishing at their mint. As the American frontier receded westward, the Campbells sold their product to professional fur traders, among them, it is said, John Jacob Astor. Wampum money began to decline about 1830, but the "moons," circular bits of white shell chopped out of conch shell and polished wafer thin, and the "pipes," long pieces of shell ranging in length from one to six inches, and other ornaments continued in demand long after that. Frances A. Westervelt, "The Final Century of Wampum Industry in Bergen County, New Jersey," New Jersey Historical Society Proceedings 10 (1925): 283–90; John T. Cunningham, "The Campbells Shell Game," The New Jersey Sampler (Upper Montclair, N.J.: n.d.), pp. 124–27.

The copper mine mentioned by Enys probably belonged to Arent Schuyler, whose mine was located "near the confluence of the Passaic and Hackensack rivers about eight miles west of New York City." In 1753 the first steam engine in America was used there to pump water from the mine. Benjamin Franklin visited the operation, and in his Papers, III: 465, mention is made of it. Fires apparently brought the operation to a halt. Information obtained through the courtesy of E. Richard McKinstry, Reference Librarian, New Jersey Historical Society.

Passaic or Totowa Falls, described as 72 feet high and 350 feet wide, was one of foreigners' chief points of interest at this time. Michel-Guillaume St. Jean de Crèvecoeur, *Journey into Northern Pennsylvania and the State of New York*, translated by Clarissa S. Bostelmann (Ann Arbor, Mich.: University of Michigan Press, 1964), p. 601.

68. It is quite likely that at the time of Enys' visit the barracks were occupied by a number of poor families. Constructed in 1758, the barracks were used by British troops from 1767 to 1771. In July 1765, the Rev. "Leo'd" Cutting was living in the barracks, for which he paid £20 yearly rent. In 1775 they were occupied by Continentals or state militia. In 1783 John Sheridan was holding school there in "a very comfortable room." After the Revolution the barracks were used as city hall, court house, and jail. They were consumed by fire in 1796. William Benedict, *New Brunswick in History* (New Brunswick, N.J.: Privately printed, 1925), p. 111. Letter of Leo'd Cutting, July 11, 1768, Special Collections Dept., Library, Rutgers University; *The Political Intelligencer and New Jersey Advertiser*, November 11, 1783; *The Brunswick Gazette*, May 10, 1791; *Guardian or New Brunswick Advertiser*, October 18, 1796.

69. The battle of Princeton was fought on 3 January 1777.

70. Enys would have been pleased with the following authoritative statement regarding the vandalism committed at Princeton: "For five months after the battle American troops in Nassau Hall did more damage than the British; they wrecked the organ and orrery, stole the books, and smashed things generally. For an ensuing year the dismantled place was used for a military hospital." The college had ninety students in 1786. Charles G. Osgood, *Lights in Nassau Hall* (Princeton, N.J.: Princeton University Press, 1951), p. 10.

71.   The repasts provided for us at the Different houses where the Stage stopped were Rather singular. Our Breakfast was as you very often find in this country, Composed of Beaf Steaks sasuges and Tea Coffee &c. Our principal dish at dinner was a Cold Baked Pig which no one could touch and our Supper consisted of nothing but a smoking hot Goose.

72. The Indian Queen Tavern was situated on Third Street, between Market Street and Chestnut Street, and was not far from the center of the City. It was maintained "in an elegant style" consisting of "a large pile of buildings, with many spacious halls and numerous small appartments appropriated for lodging rooms." "New York and Philadelphia in 1787: Extracts from the Journals of Manasseh Cutler," *Pennsylvania Magazine of History and Biography* 12 (1) (1888): 103.

73.   On his return to America in 1785, Benjamin Franklin was chosen president of the Pennsylvania Executive Council.

74.   David Franks, father of the Philadelphia belle, Rebecca, was a Tory sympathizer. He lived at the corner of Lodge and Second Streets opposite the old State Roof House, once the home of William Penn. Franks's will, proved 22 July 1794, states that he was "formerly of Philadelphia in North America, but now of Isleworth, County Middlesex." Frederick D. Stone, "Philadelphia Society One Hundred years Ago," *Pennsylvania Magazine of History and Biography* 3 (4) (1879): 367; 29 (3) (1905): 315.

    The concert, advertised in the *Pennsylvania Packet, and Daily Advertiser* (January 3, 1788), was held at the City Tavern. The "Plan" of the concert was as follows:

Act I

Overture first	Stamitz
Song	
Concerto flute	Brown

Act II

Trio, Piano Forte, Flute and Violoncello	Schroeter
Song	Gretre [Grétry]
Concerto	Corelli

Act III

Overture	Abel
Solo Violoncello	Schetky
Symphony	Bache [probably J. C. Bach]

75.   Stewart was said to have been "the handsomest man in the American Army." *Pennsylvania Magazine of History and Biography* 47 (3) (1923): 275n. He was born in Londonderry, Ireland, in 1756. On April 11, 1781, he married Deborah, daughter of Blair McClenachan, a wealthy Philadelphia merchant who amassed a fortune during the Revolution by privateering, supplying the American troops, and writing marine insurance. Hunter, *Quebec to Carolina*, p. 357. A succinct account of the Battle of Germantown is in Ward, *Revolution*, 1: 362–71.

76.   This French bank was authorized by Turgot on 24 March 1776. It enjoyed so much prosperity that it was independent of the state. At first a simple discount and deposit bank, it began in 1777 to issue notes in very modest proportions, but later more extensively. In 1783 it had a circulation of about forty million and its notes were preferred to specie. That same year, however, it underwent a grave crisis when Controller General d'Ormesson forced it to make an advance of twenty-four million to the Treasury. It weathered this crisis but it was not successful under Calonne. After him it sought to preserve itself from governmental interventions which compromised it. In

1788 Brienne imposed on it the value of its notes, although it had no need for this measure. It continued to pay in specie, and its credit, once again sound, was nearly the sole resource of the government for survival during the extremely difficult period that preceded and immediately followed the meeting of the Estates General. Necker valued it very highly and wanted to rely on it at the time of the Constituent Assembly to put the public finances back on their feet. Marcel Marion, *Dictionnaire des institutions de la France aux XVIIᵉ et XVIIIᵉ siècles* (Paris: Picard, 1969), p. 67.

77.   Howard married Peggy Oswald Chew. His Baltimore home, "Belvidere," was the scene of much entertainment.

78.   Colo. Howard was thus far on his way to New York as one of the Members of Congress for the State of Maryland.

I had hitherto intended to leave Philadelphia on the 9th but the day before the time of my departure came I received an invitation from Mrs. Bingham for a Ball on the 14th which was said would be one of the most splendid things of the kind the continent could produce which induced me to postpone my departure for a week.

79.   Bond, like Chew, had been a British sympathizer during the Revolution. By profession he was a physician, educated largely in Europe. He was one of the founders of the University of Pennsylvania and a professor in that institution. After the Revolution he was appointed Consul-General from Great Britain for the Middle and Southern States. Sarah Cadbury, "Extracts from the Diary of Ann Warder," *Pennsylvania Magazine of History and Biography* 18 (1) (1894): 63; Sabine, *Loyalists,* I: 235–36.

80.   Abigail Adams was as enthusiastic as Enys about the Philadelphia belles: "The room became full before I left it, and the circle very brilliant. How could it be otherwise, when the dazzling Mrs. Bingham and her beautiful sisters [the Misses Willing] were there; the Misses Allen, and Misses [Harriet and Maria] Chew; in short, a constellation of beauty." Quoted in William S. Baker, "Washington after the Revolution," *Pennsylvania Magazine of History and Biography* 20 (1) (1896): 76.

81.   Benjamin Franklin had five brothers who lived to maturity, but none of these men had sons or grandsons that were living in 1788. Probably Enys was referring to William Temple Franklin, who was the illegitimate son of Benjamin Franklin's illegitimate son, William Franklin, the Tory governor of New Jersey. William Temple Franklin was in Philadelphia in 1788.

The Marquis, if his title was indeed that of Marquis, probably belonged to the Breton branch of the Chappedelaine family. On 9 January 1791, he wrote from Savannah to President Washington, soliciting Washington's favor in the establishment of a colony on Sapelo Island by "three heads of noble Breton families" who were with the Marquis.

Washington Papers (L.C.), Vol. 248, ff. 110–111; *Dictionnaire Des Familles Français Anciennes ou Nobables a la fin du XIXe siècle* (Evreux, 1910), pp. 381–83.

82.   Enys' description of the Chew home differs somewhat from that of George Grieve, translator of Chastellux, *Travels:* "In 1782 I visited and passed a very agreeable day at this celebrated stone-house, so bravely, and judiciously defended by Colonel Musgrove, and saw many marks of cannon and musket shot in the walls, doors, and window shutters, besides two or three mutilated statues which stood in front of it. It is a plain gentlemen's country-house, with four windows in front, and two stories high, calculated for a small family, and *stands single, and detached from every other building.*" "Cliveden," as this house is called, is still standing and still owned by the Chew family, who bought it back in 1797. Chastellux, *Travels,* edited by Rice, I: 304.

   Musgrave's action was commemorated by a silver medal, which was at one time worn as a regimental (40th Foot). Chew's house is represented on the medal and is in the background of one of the engraved portraits of Musgrave in the British Museum Prints.

83.   Miss Markoe was probably the daughter of Abraham Markoe by his third wife, Elizabeth Baynton. The Markoe Mansion at 9th and Chestnut Streets was one of the finest in the city, being the first house to use marble lintels over the windows.

84.   Joseph Hadfield, returned to the United States in 1787, at which time he visited the homes "of the leading characters of the country." *Diary,* p. 7.

85.   Among other Jeu D'Esperits during the American War was a little Poem called the Battle of the Keggs which is to be found in a small Volume of Select Poems Printed at this place which is said to have been produced by the following story.

            Soon after the British Troops took possession of Philadelphia, a Small Kegg was seen floating down the River, when two Boys went off in a Canoe to see what it was, when to their great surprise the Canoe no sooner touched it, than it exploded, killed one of the Boys and had nearly destroyed them both for their curiosity. It was then found to have contained a quantity of Gunpowder, and the Lock of a Gun so fixed as to communicate with some Springs which passed to the outside of the Keg, which being loaded at the bottom was kept floating in an upright position, so that the ends of these Springs projecting from the upper edge of the Keg, might strike against any thing it met with in its way down the Stream, such as the sides of Ships, Boats, Wharfs, &c. when so delicate were the Springs of the Gun Lock that the slightest touch let it off, which giving fire to the Powder contained in the Keg, caused it to explode & blow up any thing with which it had come in contact with. The success of this was no sooner known in the American Camp "whch was above the town" than some Waggs thought they might have some Amusement by sending down a number of empty Keggs which being done soon after daylight one Morning, On their being seen from the Batteries were supposed to be of the same nature with that which had killed the Boy & therefore fired upon to prevent their getting among the Transports below the Town, to the great Amusement of the Americans who called it the Battle of the Keggs to cellebrate which a Mr. [Francis] Hopkinson wrote the above named poem.

An undated broadside entitled "The Battle of the Kegs" is in L. C. Portfolio 163 no. 3. See also Francis Hopkinson, *The Battle of the Kegs* (Philadelphia, 1866).

The ingenious David Bushnell claimed responsibility for the incident that inspired "The Battle of the Kegs." "I fixed several Keggs under water, charged with powder, to explode upon touching anything, as they floated along with the tide," Bushnell wrote. "I set them afloat in the Delaware, above the English shipping in Philadelphia, in December 1777." Unfortunately, the kegs were set adrift too far from the enemy vessels to do them damage. One of the kegs, however, blew up a boat, with several persons in it, and "thus gave the British that alarm, which brought on the battle of the Keggs." *Naval Documents of the American Revolution,* VI, 1507.

86. The observant Abigail Adams wrote to her sister that she had not seen a lady in England who could "bear a comparison with Mrs. Bingham, Mrs. Platt, and a Miss Hamilton, who is a Philadelphia young lady." Margaret L. Brown, "Mr. and Mrs. William Bingham," *Pennsylvania Magazine of History and Biography* 41 (July 1937): 293.

87. The large room of the Duke of Queensberry probably concerns Queensberry House, Cholmondeley Walk, at Richmond, Surrey. George, 3rd Earl of Cholmondeley, built the first house in 1708 on some of the foundations of the old Richmond Palace. The house was sold in 1780 to the 4th Duke of Queensberry, notorious in the early decades of the nineteenth century as "Old 2," a decrepit roué. The house was pulled down in 1829. The Editor is indebted to E. J. Huddy, Department of Printed Books, British Museum, for this information.

The very elegant Bingham Mansion, located on the northwest corner of Third and Spruce Streets, was surrounded by spacious gardens protected by a high wall. Brown, "Bingham," pp. 286–324.

88. John Penn (1760–1834) was the son of Thomas and Lady Juliana Penn. He attended Eton 1773–76. On the death of his father in 1775, he became hereditary Governor of Pennsylvania. He was admitted to Clare Hall, Cambridge, 17 December 1776. He received the M.A. degree in 1779 and Ll.D. in 1811. He spent the years 1782–89 in America. He died unmarried at Stone Park 21 June 1834. The Editor is indebted to H. A. Tarrant, the Old Etonian Association, for this information. See also Howard M. Jenkins, "The Family of William Penn," *Pennsylvania Magazine of History and Biography* 21 (4) (1897): 423–34.

89.   The description of Market Street is correct, but the Market house is no longer standing.

90.   The church was the German Reformed (Dutch Calvinist) church that stood on Race Street, east of Fourth. It was built in 1772 and is now being restored.

91.   In 1788 the university was known as the "University of the State of Pennsylvania." Episcopal Academy was founded in 1785.

92.   The State House (now called Independence Hall) and Pennsylvania hospital are still standing. The Poor House and Prison are not. For a description of the prison, see François Alexandre F. duc de la Rochefoucauld-Liancourt, *Voyage dans les Estats-Unis d'Amerique, fait en 1795, 1796 et 1797*, 8 vols. (Paris, 1799), VI: 244–66.

93.   The Quaker influence was largely responsible for legislative action against theatrical entertainment, but until 1773 there had been a theatre at Southwark. The Continental Association of 1774 and an Act of the Pennsylvania legislature in 1779 effectively terminated this form of amusement by professionals. There continued to be amateur theatricals, however, and with the coming of peace in 1783 even the professionals returned to Philadelphia, although they were obliged to disguise their presentation as moral dialogues or historical lectures. *Richard III*, for example, was advertised as "a serious Historical Lecture in five parts—on the Fate of Tyranny." Each season the disguises became thinner until the Act of 1779 was repealed ten years later. Whitfield J. Bell, Jr., "Social History of Pennsylvania, 1760–1790," *Pennsylvania Magazine of History and Biography* 42 (July 1938): 281–308.

ON TO VIRGINIA AND HOME, 1788

1.   The "Lower Ferry" became known as Gray's Ferry; a street and bridge now cross the river at the site of the old ferry. The place of amusement Enys doubtless referred to was Gray's Gardens close by the Ferry. Gray's Gardens was a popular resort on summer days for all classes of Philadelphians. The gardens stood on the eastern bank of the river, at the foot of Gray's Ferry Road, just far enough from the city proper to be a delightful walk or drive. The river banks were laid out with pleasant walks and ornamental shrubbery. Enys probably referred to Gray's Gardens as the "Green Room" because nearby was Israel Pemberton's country seat known as "Evergreen." This estate was right on Gray's Ferry Road so Enys must have passed it on his trip from what was then Philadelphia to the Ferry. Joseph Jackson, *Encyclopedia of Philadelphia* (Harrisburg, 1932), III: 650; Henry G. Ashmead, *Newspaper Cuttings* (clipping file in the Historical So-

ciety of Pennsylvania), V: 17–19; Thompson Westcott, *Historic Mansions and Buildings of Philadelphia* (Philadelphia, 1877), pp. 502–505.

2.   For a succinct account of the Battle of Brandywine, see Ward, *Revolution,* I: 341–54.

3.   One great reason I am told for these Mills getting so great a Name was their being among the first that made use of the French Burr Stones which are preferred to all others in this part of the world, and some even go so far as to aledge it is impossible to make fine flower with any other kind.

Of these Mills Robert Hunter wrote: "The river Brandytown [*sic*] is famous for turning fifteen mills, which are the first in America and perhaps the world. They were never known to cease working, summer or winter. The sloops come close up alongside of them and take in the flour. . . . These mills belong to eleven people and bring them in an immense income. Four of them are in the possession of one person." *Quebec to Carolina,* p. 176.

4.   Dover was actually the capital of Delaware.

5.   Howe had disembarked unopposed at the head of the Elk on August 25, 1777. "The mystery of Howe's movements is very easily explained," wrote Fortescue (*History,* III: 214). "He had made up his mind originally to land in the Delaware, so as to be nearer to New York and to Burgoyne, but gave up the attempt on the remonstrances of the naval officers, and sailed on to the Chesapeake. Whether the naval officers may have exaggerated the risks of disembarkation in the Delaware I cannot pretend to decide; but the fact remains that the voyage to the Chesapeake was disastrous, since contrary winds prolonged a passage of three hundred and fifty miles over no fewer than twenty-four days." Piers Mackesy states that Howe's army which landed at the Head of Elk on 25 August had been embarked for forty-seven days. *The War for America,* p. 126.

6.   We had not gone above two Miles before we came to a small new place Called Abington [Abingdon] which appeared to be agreeably situated on a Hill but the most conspicuous thing in it is a New Building to the left of the Road which is designed as a Colledge whch is a very handsome Brick Building.

Not far from Abington is a pretty high hill from whence there is a very extensive Noble View of the Ajacent Country terminated by the Chesapeak [Chesapeake] Bay but it is unfortunately not well cultivated.

Enys was referring to Cokesbury College, built on a high knoll overlooking Bush River and Chesapeake Bay. The building was of brick, 108 feet in length, 40 feet in width, and three stories high. On each side of the large hall were two classrooms. The premises were enclosed by a fence, and a pool six feet square was provided for bathing. The curriculum, which stressed the classics, was based on that of the Kingswood, John Wesley's famous school in England. On December 4, 1795, the College was destroyed by fire. C. Milton Wright, *Our Harford Heritage* (Havre de Grace, Md.: Privately printed, 1967), 236–39.

7. In 1777, Ebenezer Hazard noted that a "good" tavern was kept on the Baltimore road by a man who bore the unusual name of "Godsgrace," one of a series of proprietors. In November 1784, Clement Skerrett advertised the reopening of the tavern in the *Maryland Journal*. "Ebenezer Hazard's Travels through Maryland in 1777," edited by Fred Shelley, *Maryland Historical Magazine* 46 (1) (March 1951): 47.

8. This Mr. Daniel Grant is a Native of Scotland and must be a man of very large propperty. The whole House which is extreemly large with stabling for near 50 horses are his own propperty. He has a very large family all of whom receive the Best Education the country can give them & I am told his eldest son died on his way to Europe wither he was going to make the Tour. He has two Daughters grown the Eldest of which was married a few days before I arrived to a Mr. Hacket. She is not very tall but I realy think is as pleasing a little person as any in town. She is also accomplished in Music, Singing, Dancing &c. and although they live in one end of the house you never see her or her sister unless you are expressly invited to see them. Mr. Grant keeps a very elegant Carriage and horses chiefly for the use of his daughters as he and Mrs. Grant are as Plain people as I ever saw particularly the latter who is continually bustling about the house and seems so much at home in the Line of her Business that I do not think she could be happy in any other.

"Mr. Hacket" was a merchant. He married Miss Jenny Grant on January 1, 1788. At the end of the eighteenth century there was a merchant firm called Hacket and Grant in Baltimore. Information provided by Richard J. Cox, Curator of Manuscripts, Maryland Historical Society.

In December 1782 Daniel Grant moved from the Indian Queen Tavern on the corner of Hanover and Baltimore Streets to his fine new house in Light Lane, between Market Street and Ellicott's Wharf, called Fountain Inn. J. Thomas Scharf, *The Chronicles of Baltimore* (Baltimore, 1874), p. 206.

9. There were several furnaces in the vicinity of Baltimore. The Kingsbury Furnace and the Lancashire Furnace were the properties of the Principio Company. William Hammond was the manager of the Hocksley Forge on the Patapsco. G. D. Williams, "Mines and Minerals," in *Maryland: Its Resources, Industries and Institutions* (Baltimore, 1893), pp. 102–104; Earl C. May, *Principio to Wheeling* (New York: Harper, 1945), pp. 45–46. See Bayley Ellen Marks, "Notes on the Maryland Historical Society Manuscript Collections: Iron Manufacturing in Maryland—A Look at Surviving Records," *Mary-*

land Historical Magazine 44 (Fall 1969): 297–99; J. Louis Kuethe, "A List of Maryland Mills, Taverns, Forges, and Furnaces of 1795," ibid. 31 (June 1936): 155–69.

10.   William Seton [Seaton?] had married Anna Maria Curson, the daughter of Richard Curson (1763–1808), who was a Baltimore merchant.

11.   "The two Miss Smiths" were probably the daughters of William or John Smith, or of General Samuel Smith. Robert Purviance, *A Narrative of Events Which Occurred in Baltimore Town During the Revolutionary War* (Baltimore, 1849), pp. 30–31, 103–104.

   "Miss Ireland" could have been one of the daughters of Edward Ireland (1736–1816), a native of Barbados and a merchant in Baltimore for many years. His eldest daughter, Anna, died June 30, 1788, in her nineteenth year. Elizabeth Ireland married Zebulon Hollingsworth on April 22, 1790. Mary Ireland died January 9, 1792, also in her nineteenth year.

12.   By the Bye these Reels are not altogeather the Highland Reels tho I do not know how to describe the difference. They are I find much used in the back parts of Virginia.

   For a description of pioneer dancing, see Joseph Doddridge, *Notes on the Settlement and Indian Wars of the Western Parts of Virginia and Pennsylvania* (Pittsburgh, 1912), pp. 121–25.

13.   A New Yorker called the locale of the dances "the most elegant dancing Assembly Room in the U.S. It is a 2 story brick building very long and has a very elegant appearance in Front." "A New Yorker in Maryland: 1793 and 1821," *Maryland Historical Magazine* 47 (2) (June 1952): 139. See also, Scharf, *Baltimore*, p. 283. Subscriptions to the Assembly dances were for gentlemen over twenty-one and for ladies over eighteen. Six managers distributed the places in the quadrilles by lot. A card of April 18, 1788, read: "The Juvenile Amicable Society requests the pleasure of Miss Cox's company at a ball to be held at the Old Fountain Inn at six P.M." Marie Letitia Stockett, *Baltimore: A Not Too Serious History* (Baltimore: Norman Remington, 1928), pp. 100–101.

14.   George and Andrew Buchanan were also prominent in Baltimore. Scharf, *Baltimore*, passim; Purviance, *Baltimore*, pp. 30–31.

15.   The observations of the astute West Indian exile, Moreau De Saint-Méry, are quite similar to those of Enys. Baltimore had two thousand houses, mostly constructed of brick. The streets were broad, paved, and straight. The courthouse was two stories high with a wooden balcony and pediment facing Calvert Street. "But what gives Baltimore an air that is pleasing as it is unique," Saint-Méry continued, "is a hill, owned by Colonel Howard, that dominates the town on the north. The main residence and its de-

pendancies occupy the forward part, while a park embellishes the rear." "Baltimore as seen by Moreau De Saint-Mery in 1794," edited and translated by Fillmore Norfleet, *Maryland Historical Magazine* 35 (3) (September 1940): pp. 225–28.

16.   The Methodist Church, the First Light Street Church, was destroyed by fire in 1796. Scharf, *Baltimore,* p. 78; Writers' Program, W.P.A., *Maryland* (New York: Oxford University Press, 1940), pp. 230–31.

Baltimore had a high tax rate to meet expenses for public improvements, among which were the grading, leveling, and paving of streets. In 1784 provisions were adopted for lighting the streets at night with oil lamps and for policing them. Scharf, *Baltimore,* p. 500. In the latter part of the century it became the practice to dispose of lots by leases for long terms, mostly ninety-nine years renewable forever. The rents stipulated after the Revolution were so high that the lessees or tenants frequently abandoned the lots, and the town lost some valuable citizens who fled from prosecution. The census of 1790 assigned to Baltimore a population of 13,503, including blacks. Clayton C. Hall, *Baltimore, Its History and Its People,* 2 vols. (New York, 1912), I: 18–45; Thomas W. Griffith, *Sketches of the Early History of Maryland* (Baltimore, 1821), pp. 112–32. In 1782 Baltimore contained eight houses of worship—Episcopal, Presbyterian, Lutheran, Dutch Calvinist, Catholic, Baptist, Quaker, and Methodist. In mentioning the "State house," Enys was probably referring to the building known as Old Congress Hall.

17.   Howard was elected Governor of Maryland in October, 1788. His home, Belvidere, is no longer standing.

18.   The earliest fortifications in Whetstone Point were constructed during the Revolutionary War, when the Provincial Convention of Maryland directed the Council of Safety to provide for the defenses of Baltimore. In 1781, Fort Whetstone consisted of a battery, magazine, military hospital, and barracks. The channel obstructions included the sinking of small vessels and the installation of a boom and iron chain between the two points. Felix Louis Massenback designed the gun batteries and James Alcock the "star fort." The enclosed fortification could be described as an earthen embankment conforming to a five-pointed star. Fort McHenry replaced the earlier structure. Harold I. Lessem and George C. Mackenzie, *Fort McHenry* (Washington: National Park Service, 1950); Lee H. Nelson, *An Architectural Study of Fort McHenry* (Philadelphia: Historic American Buildings Survey, 1961), pp. 3–12. Writers' Program, *Maryland,* p. 254.

19.   In 1782 a line of stages was established between Philadelphia and Baltimore, which was later extended to Alexandria. Hall, *Baltimore,* I: 41.

20.   The custom of Sleeping two or sometimes more in one Bed is by no means uncommon in this part of the world. Indeed the Marquis de Chastelleuse [Chastellux] or his translator Mr Graves says that it is not uncommon after you have

been in bed some time to have a person come and get into bed to you. However I never mett with or herd of any such thing except from the above Book.

It was George Grieve, the English translator of Marquis de Chastellux, *Travels in North America,* who wrote about sleeping accommodations at American inns. Grieve's sojourn in America lasted only one year, 1781–82. Enys was doubtless referring to the following statement of Grieve: "Throughout America, in private houses, as well as in the inns, the several people are crowded together in the same room; and in the latter it very commonly happens, that after you have been some time in bed, a stranger of any condition (for there is little distinction), comes into the room, pulls off his clothes, and places himself, without ceremony, between your sheets." Chastellux, *Travels,* edited by Rice, II: 603.

21.   I was told at Alexandria that farenhights Thermomether was so low as ten Degrees, others say so low as seven or Eight within doors altho this place is in Latitude 39.

  When at Mount Vernon Colonel Humphries told me the Mercury of their Thermometer which is upon the above scale placed in an exposed Situation was in the Ball for some hours of the above day.

22.   This Warehouse is the place where a good deal of the Maryland or Kites foot Tobacco is Lodged for sale, which is much more valuable than any other. It is of a Bright Yellow colour and of a Superior flavour to any other very little of which is grown in Virginia. The place most famous for it is near the Elk Ridge [Elkridge] about Eight Miles from Baltimore.

  There is one very singular circumstance rellative to the Tobacco Trade that deserves notice which is that it answers the purpose of ready Cash by the following means. A planter Brings down as many Hogshead of Tobacco as he can make which is inspected and lodged in the Warehouse whre it remains, the Inspector giving a Recept or Note that so many Hogsheads of Tobacco of such a Quality are lodged in such a Warehouse. This Note the Planter can pass to any Merchant he pleases and it may pass thro several Hands like a Bank note before it gets into the hands of one of the Shippers who purchase them up, and going to the Warehouses, on Producing the notes receive the Quantity of Tobacco threin mentioned, at a Port ready to be shipped whenever he pleases to demand it. In this country in Speaking of any mans estate they do not say he is worth £800 a year but that he makes 80 Hogsheads of Tobacco.

The tobacco business in Georgetown had its start with the "inspection house" or "the rolling house," as a tobacco warehouse was often called, built by George Gordon near the mouth of Rock Creek between the years 1734 and 1748. The original structure must have been of logs; it was succeeded by two large brick buildings. The tobacco business flourished and ultimately assumed such proportions that three large warehouses were required to accommodate it. The planters adopted the method of "rolling" the tobacco, that is, putting it in large hogsheads, averaging 1,000 pounds, rigged with an axle and tongue and drawn by horses or men over roads ("rolling roads") to the nearest warehouse.

The Maryland Kite-foot tobacco was a bright tobacco, highly prized.

A guinea was a British gold coin worth 21 shillings in 1788. The hogshead averaged 1,000 pounds in weight. According to Tooke's *History of Prices* (as cited by Mulhall below), which quoted tobacco at 33 shillings per hundred weight in 1788, the price of tobacco in Georgetown must have been depressed. "Old Georgetown," *Records of the Columbia Historical Society* (Washington, 1908), II: 151–54; Joseph C. Robert, *The Story of Tobacco in America* (Chapel Hill, N.C.: University of North Carolina Press, 1967), p. 55; Michael G. Mulhall, *The Dictionary of Statistics* (London, 1899), p. 471.

23.   Prior to 1792 the "Bunch of Grapes" was in the old Herbert house on the northeast corner of Fairfax and Cameron Streets. Mary G. Powell, *The History of Old Alexandria, Virginia* . . . (Richmond: William Byrd, 1928), p. 129.

24.   Sketches of Fitzgerald and Hunter are in Hunter, *Quebec to Carolina*, pp. 361, 363–64. Fitzgerald, a merchant of Alexandria, had served as aide to Washington during the Revolution. He was a director, with Washington and others, of the Potomac Navigation Co. William Hunter, also a merchant, carried on a thriving business with London and Liverpool. He was mayor of Alexandria in 1788–90.

25.   Washington's birthday was 11 February 1732, according to the Julian calendar. By change to the Gregorian calendar there was a loss of eleven days, hence February 22 for Washington's birthday.

26.   Not far above George town are the great falls of the Potomack which have hitherto impeded the intercourse by water with the back country but they have now A Navigable Canal in great forwardness so much so that they expect to begin to reap the benefits of it in the course of a few Months by which they will be able to take Boats up to the very head of this amazing River from whence it is only twelve miles to one of the heads of the Manogahala [Monongahela] River which empties itself into the Ohio at Fort Pit [Pitt] or Pitsburgh [Pittsburgh]. This is the Rout by which I conceive the Americans will carry on the Indian Trade, for as by the above rout they have a communication with the Ohio, so by going down that River untill they come to the Muskingham [Muskingum] 172 Miles below fort Pit and going up the latter its sources lead them to within a mile or two of a River which falls into Lake Erie not far from Sandusky. A very large Settlement is now making at the Mouth of the Mus-

kingham [Muskingum] by a party of people from New England at the head of which is the old Genearl [Rufus Putnam] Putman. They left Boston in December last with every thing necessary to begin with. Hutchens [Thomas Hutchins] in Speaking of the Siato [Scioto] River which is 390 Miles below Fort Pit says the Stream is gentle and passable for Large Boats or Barges a Considerable distance and for small Boats for near 200 Miles to a Portage of only four Miles into the Sandusky. His Map however does not make the Branches of this River extend so far so that I am rather lead to think it a false Print and that he means the Great Meamis [Miami] which runs that way. This seems to me an Eligible rout from Kentucke [Kentucky] to the Western Lakes.

Enys was referring to the Chesapeake and Ohio Canal, at this time under the direction of the Potomac Navigation Company. Archer B. Hulbert, *The Great American Canals,* 2 vols. (Cleveland, 1904), I: 33–168.

The Cheat River, a branch of the Monongahela, divides at Parsons, Tucker County (West Virginia), into the Blackwater and Dry Fork Rivers. The head of the Potomac River is slightly west of the Tucker County line. The distance between these streams is approximately five or six miles as the crow flies.

During Washington's visit to Western Virginia in 1784, he talked with local people about the distance between the heads of the Potomac and Monongahela. *The Diaries of George Washington 1748–1799,* edited by John C. Fitzpatrick, 4 vols. (New York: Mt. Vernon Ladies Ass'n. of the Union, 1925), pp. 279–305.

The *Ohio River Handbook and Picture Album,* edited by Benjamin and Eleanor King (Cincinnati, 1950), D 37, does state that Marietta is 172 Miles below Pittsburgh. At the time that Enys was visiting Alexandria, Rufus Putnam was, indeed, laboriously pushing his way westward. *Memoirs of Rufus Putnam* (Boston, 1903), pp. 103–105.

A facsimile of Hutchins' map is in *A Topographical Description of Virginia, Pennsylvania, Maryland, and North Carolina,* edited by Frederick C. Hicks (Cleveland, 1904). Hutchins' map, as Enys suggests, bears very little resemblance to reality.

27. This Society may have been the Society of St. Andrew founded by William Hunter, Jr., who emigrated from Galston, Scotland. Hunter, *Quebec to Carolina,* pp. 363–64.

28. Here is also the first attempt at a Turnpike road I have seen in this country. The Gates are standing at each end of the town but I did not perceive them take any Toll nor indeed does their Efforts yet merret any whatever. They may hereafter.

By an Act of October 1785, Commissioners were directed to "set up and erect . . . one or more gates or turnpikes across the roads . . . leading into the town of Alexandria, from Snigger's and Vestal's gaps, within five miles of said town, and the tolls and duties following shall be paid and received." By an act of December 2, 1787, "All coaches [etc.] . . . passing up or down the country to, from, or through the town of Alexandria, . . . shall pass and repass toll free." Hening, *Statutes*, XII: 75–80, 522–27.

29.   General Nelson had several sons who, at the time, were young men: William (b. 1763), Thomas, Jr. (b. 1764), Philip (b. 1766), Francis (b. 1767), and Hugh (b. 1768). Richard C. M. Page, *Genealogy of the Page Family in Virginia* (New York, 1883), pp. 171–72.

30.   This defect in the soil is a great misfortune no doubt but it could not have happened to any one who was so able to remedy it, as its owner from his knowledge in husbandry is able to take every advantage which may offer as well as the amazing quantity of Manure which he makes every year from his large stock of Cattle, so that I am convinced that any person who visits this place twenty Years hence will find it in a high state of cultivation.

Enys was, for the second time, referring to Lancelot "Capability" Brown, the well-known British landscape architect.

31.   Mrs. Stuart, née Eleanor Calvert, was the wife of Dr. David Stuart. Her first husband had been John Parke Custis. Charles Moore, *The Family Life of George Washington* (Boston: Houghton Mifflin, 1926), pp. 91–103.

32.   At the top if the house instead of a Weather *Cock* is placed a Dove with an Olive branch in its mouth.
    He also pointed out a point below his house which he said was only connected to the main land by a Narrow Istmus, that the Neighbourhood abounding in Deer, the Proprietor used to drive them on to the Point where by guarding the Istmus he kept them in a sort of natural Park.

Charles G. Wall, Resident Director, The Mount Vernon Ladies' Association of the Union, has provided the following information: "While George Washington was in Philadelphia presiding over the Constitutional Convention during the summer of 1787 he found time to procure a weather vane for his Mount Vernon Mansion. It features the Dove of Peace returning to the ark. The original installation, which has also functioned as a lightning rod through the years, is still in position, the wooden finial which supports it being the only replacement.
    "There was a park, an enclosure, for deer on the slope between the Mansion and the river in George Washington's time. It existed for some years but the enclosure did not hold the deer, they became a nuisance in the formal planted areas and the enclosing palisade was eliminated."

33.   Warburton Manor was the seat of one branch of the Digges family. George Digges of Warburton was the "neighbour Digges" of Washington's letters. His son was Thomas

Atwood Digges. Information provided by Elizabeth M. Daniels, Maryland Historical Society, December 4, 1974. See also, Robert H. Elias, [pseudo. of Thomas Atwood Digges], *Adventures of Alonso,* edited by Thomas J. McMahon, United States Catholic Historical Society, Monograph Series, XVIII (New York, 1943).

34.   This was probably a true white-tailed deer, either an albino or a melanistic color phase.

35.   Washington had a longstanding interest in mules derived from his awareness that mules had a longer life span and better work performance than horses. After the Revolution, the renowned farmer of Mount Vernon set about obtaining a jack or two "of the first race in Spain" to cross with mares for the breeding of mules. The desired acquisition was not easy, since the rulers of Spain had for many years forbidden the exportation of blooded stock. Washington's initial efforts were disappointing, but in 1785 through the good offices of José Moñino, *conde de* Floridablanca, Washington obtained one of the coveted animals, which he named "Royal Gift," as indeed it was, being the personal gift of Charles III of Spain. Washington was delighted with the nearly fifteen-hands-high animal, "very bony and stout made, of a dark color, with light belly and legs." On learning of Washington's desire for an ass, Lafayette had also set about procuring one for him, and finally secured one from Malta. This addition to the Mount Vernon stables, named "Knight of Malta," was " 'youthful, clean-limbed, and active.' " To make the stable truly international, there arrived from Surinam a Jennet ordered by Washington. In covering season, Washington advertised his asses in papers as far away as Philadelphia. For a sprightly account of Washington's success in the breeding of mules, see John H. Powell, "General Washington and the Jack Ass," in *General Washington and the Jack Ass and Other American Characters* (South Brunswick, N.Y.: Yoseloff, 1969), pp. 176–90.
    Magnolio was Washington's Arab stallion.
    A much more scholarly and detailed account of Washington as a mule breeder is found in "Royal Gift—The Story of a Present from the King of Spain to George Washington," an unpublished manuscript written by Julian P. Boyd. While Washington cannot have the honor of being the first American or Virginian to experiment with the breeding of mules, "he does have the honor of seeing an opportunity, and of seizing it vigorously." Moreover, Washington made "a great and lasting contribution to American agriculture simply because he was America's first citizen and because he fixed his eye upon the mule's potentialities." Here the jack is described as being nearly sixteen hands high, with a large head and clumsy limbs; he was grey in color and lethargic in movement. Washington paid the cost of bringing the ass and his groom from Spain to Mount Vernon. Initially Royal Gift's breeding capacity was disappointing and caused no little embarrassment to its illustrious owner until it was found that a jennet rather than a mare might produce the necessary "excitement" in the stubborn jack. Oddly enough, it was New England, rather than the South, that soon led in the exportation of mules, most of

them going to the French West Indies. In 1789, the United States exported 8,628 horses and 237 mules. By the end of Washington's administration only 4,283 horses were exported and 1,718 mules.

Inserted in the Enys journal is a clipping of January 19, 1895, touching on the value of mules with particular reference to Royal Gift. The clipping includes a February 23, 1786, advertisement offering a "Jack Ass of the first race in the kingdom of Spain" for covering mares and jennies at Mount Vernon.

36. Doubtless a member of the firm of Porter and Ingraham of Alexandria. *Diaries of Washington,* edited by Fitzpatrick, III: 162n. The guest list, including "Captn. Enys" and "Mr. Ingraham" is carried on pp. 304–305.

37. The Stuarts lived at Cedar Grove, built by Richard Stuart. Paul Wilstach, *Tidewater Virginia* (Indianapolis: Bobbs-Merrill, 1929), p. 299; ———, *Potomac Landings* (Indianapolis: Bobbs-Merrill, 1932), p. 345.

38. In his later years all that Washington remembered regarding the origin of his family was that in his youth he had been told that the family had come from one of the northern counties of England. "He was not sure whether it was Lancashire or Yorkshire or a region still farther North." Douglas S. Freeman, *George Washington,* 7 vols. (New York: Scribner's, 1948–57), I: 527 ff. In the thirteenth century the "Wessington" family resided near the border of Lancashire and Westmorland. John, the emigrant, was born at Sulgrave Manor, the family seat in Northhamptonshire.

39. The mansion is ninety-six feet long. Information provided by John A. Castellani, Librarian, Mount Vernon Ladies' Association of the Union, August 22, 1974.

40. In speaking of this perfect whole of which General Washington furnishes the idea I have not excluded the exterior form. His Stature is Noble & lofty, he is well made, and exactly proportioned, His Physiognomy mild and agreeable, but such as to render it impossible to speak particularly of any of his features, so that in Qu[i]ting him you have only the recollection of a fine face. He has neither a grave nor a familiar Air. His Brow is sometimes marked with thought, but never with inquietude. In inspiring respect, he Inspires conficence, and his smile is always the smile of benevolence. Chastellux Travels, Voll. 1 P. 138.

Enys was quoting from the first English translation of Chastellux, *Travels in North America in the Years 1780, 1781, 1782,* translated by George Grieve, and issued January 1787 in London by G. G. J. and J. Robinson, Pater-Noster Row, pp. 138–39.

41. Frances Bassett was the niece of Mrs. Washington. Moore, *Family Life of Washington,* p. 215.

42.   The Marquis instead of continuing his Journey with me returned to Mount Vernon where he staid two days.

Chappedelaine did not return to Mount Vernon until the 14th. There he spent that night and returned to Alexandria on the 15th. *Diaries of Washington*, edited by Fitzpatrick, III: 304–305.

43.   About a Mile & ½ above Fredricksburgh we crossed the River at a small place called Falmouth whch is by some called the head of the Navigation of the River. For my part I cannot think it Navigable higher than Fredericksburgh as from thence to falmouth they can only go in Flats or Skows as they call them to the Northward.

44.   Watson was a leading merchant of Alexandria. Hunter, *Quebec to Carolina*, p. 361.

45.   A Thomas O'Connor, 1770–1885, who would appear to have been too young to be the man Enys met, was editor for a time of a weekly entitled *The War*. The War of which O'Connor wrote, however, was that of 1812. The editor is indebted to Milton C. Russell, Virginia State Library, for this information.

46.   Heth, a lieutenant with Morgan's Riflemen, was taken prisoner at Quebec December 31, 1775. John H. Gwathmey, *Historical Register of Virginians in the Revolution* (Richmond: Dietz, 1938), pp. 373–74. "It would be unpardonable to omit mentioning the humanity of General Carleton," wrote Anburey, "who has cloathed all those who were taken prisoners, they being almost in a state of nakedness; many of them he suffered to return to their homes upon their parole of not bearing arms again during the war. Those who are here to be exchanged are cloathed, and fare the same as our own soldiers." *Travels* I: 134.

47.   Near the Bridge over this River are several very large Poplar Trees which are said to be twenty three feet in circumference three feet above the grownd.

48.   Anderson's Tavern was damaged by fire on January 11, 1787. The fire began with the storehouse formerly occupied by John Hartshorn and spread to the Tavern. Between forty and fifty storehouses and dwelling houses were consumed, together with Byrd's warehouses and seventy hogsheads of tobacco. *Tyler's Quarterly* 8 (July 1926): 67.

49.   The jambs of the basement windows of the Capitol are at least five feet thick so it is very likely that the foundations are at least six feet thick.

The Masonic Hall, a white frame building, was erected in 1785 largely through the efforts of John Marshall. It has been occupied by the Masonic Order longer than any other building in America. Lafayette was feted here in 1824. Writers' Program, W.P.A.,

Virginia: A Guide to the Old Dominion, p. 294; Dept. of Interior, National Park Service, *National Register,* Virginia.

50.   Between 1786 and 1789 the amount of tobacco exported from Virginia, as stated in official returns was as follows:

From Oct. 1786 to Oct. 1787	60,041 hogsheads
From Oct. 1787 to Oct. 1788	58,545 hogsheads
From Oct. 1788 to Oct. 1789	58,673 hogsheads

The average price per pound in 1787 was 15d. The average price per pound in 1788 was 25s. per hundredweight. In 1789 the average price per pound was 15d. The hogshead averaged about 1,000 pounds. William Tatham, *Historical and Practical Essay on the Culture and Commerce of Tobacco* (London, 1800), pp. 196–97; Melvin Herndon, *Tobacco in Colonial Virginia: The Sovereign Remedy* (Williamsburg: Virginia 350th Anniversary Celebration Corp., 1957), p. 49; Joseph C. Robert, *The Tobacco Kingdom, Plantation, Market, and Factory in Virginia and North Carolina, 1800–1860* (Durham: Duke University Press, 1938), p. 236.

51.   The North African Arab states of Morocco, Algiers, Tunis, and Tripoli had for many years levied tribute on Mediterranean shipping, the European powers finding it simpler to pay them protection money than to subdue them.

      American independence terminated the favorable as well as the unfavorable effects of English mercantilist regulations.

52.   Jefferson estimated that in 1782 there were 296,852 free inhabitants in Virginia and 270,762 slaves. The census of 1790 gave 442,117 whites and 305,493 blacks. Enys' statement is therefore not entirely correct. Thomas Jefferson, *Notes on the State of Virginia,* edited by William Peden (Chapel Hill, N.C.: Institute of Early American History & Culture at Williamsburg, Virginia), pp. 86–87; Dept. of Commerce and Labor, Bureau of Census, *Heads of Families* (Washington, 1908), p. 9.

53.   In Coxes Travels in Russia I met with the following account of the Cossacs (Page 356 Voll 3) which bears so strong a resemblance to what I have seen among the American Indians I could not help copying of it.

            The whole Character is very much the same but he particularly says That by examining a Tract which has been lately traversed by the enemy in the most tumultuary manner the[y] can discover with tolerable exactness the number of horses which have passed over it and how many of them were led. Some of them by appling their Ears to the ground can distinguish the Buz of men or the Clattering of horses feet at a very considerable distance. He also says they are the best troops to pursue a flying Enemy, extreemly Vigilant on out posts and form the best patroles.

Enys' interpolation appears out of place here.

54.   Petersburgh is one of the Largest Markets for Tobacco in the State and is by some said to export one third of that Article or equal to 20,000 Hogsheads annualy. If it is remarkable for any thing also it is for being the residence of Mrs. Bowling [Bolling] a person of very large fortune decended from the celebrated Indian Princess named Pocahunta [Pocahontas] Daughter to Powhatan formerly King of this country. She was much atached and of great service to the first English Setlers and was afterward married to an Englishman named Rolle [John Rolfe] and taken to England with him.

Early land and water routes in the Roanoke Valley led to Petersburg. The observant Italian traveler, Count Luigi Castiglioni, reported in 1786 that a great quantity of tobacco was brought to Petersburg, even from North Carolina, and was exported to Europe as James River Tobacco. James G. Scott and Edward A. Wyatt, *Petersburg's Story, A History* (Petersburg: Titmus Optical Co., 1960), pp. 40–41.

Robert, son of John and Mary Bolling, of Tower Street, London, the first of the name who settled in Virginia, was born December 26, 1646. He arrived in Virginia October 2, 1660. In 1675 he married Jane, daughter of Thomas Rolfe and granddaughter of Pocahontas. Philip Slaughter, *A History of Bristol Parish, Va.* (Richmond, Va., 1879), pp. 140–47.

55.   Besides the great advantage to be drawn from a water conveyance to the now Capital of the State, from its most distant parts it appears from all the Maps that the heads of the Fluvana [Fluvanna] or James River runs thro the Mountains up to the Foot of the Allagany's on the opposite side of which are the heads of the great Kanavaw [Kanawha] River which falls into the Ohio near the northern boundary of Kentucky.

The General Assembly of Virginia passed acts for clearing and improving the navigation of the James River in 1765, 1772, and 1773. The canal was eventually extended to Buchanan in Botetourt County. Hening, *Statues,* VIII: 148–50, 564–70; IX: 341–42; Kathleen Bruce, *Virginia Iron Manufacture in the Slave Era* (New York: Century Co., 1930), pp. 61–62, 88, 92–93.

56.   Enys was probably referring to the Deep Run pits owned by the family of Samuel Du Val. Jefferson wrote that the coal found near Richmond was of excellent quality. Bruce, *Iron Manufacture,* pp. 87–93; *Notes,* edited by Peden, pp. 28–29.

57.   Alexander is mentioned in William G. Sumner, *The Financier and the Finances of the American Revolution,* 2 vols. (New York: Kelley, 1968), II: 169–74.

58.   Cornwallis arrived at Petersburg May 20, 1781. It was late June when he withdrew, not retreated, toward the coast, arriving at Portsmouth in late July. Fraser's ordinary, or inn, has not been located.

59.   Bird's was open during the Revolution. *Virginia Magazine of History and Biography,* 79 (October 1971): 403, 407; *Calendar of Virginia State Papers,* II: 156, 627.

60.   The main street, called the Duke of Gloucester Street, was 99 feet wide and seven-eighths of a mile long from the college to the east end of town where the capitol building was located. Jane Carson, *Travelers in Tidewater Virginia, 1700–1800* (Williamsburg: Colonial Williamsburg, 1965), p. 20.

    In his "Tour of Scotland" (1783), Enys gave the following description of the Duke of Hamilton's "palace": "we Reached the Village of Hamilton, famous for nothing but the house or as they call it the pallace of Duke H——n. . . . It is a very large rather than Elegant building. The principal front being spoild, by the Wings being a Vast deal too heavey for the Body of the House, the Suite of Rooms are large and Elegant, and contain a great many good Pictures by capital hands."

61.   The students were complaining about the food served to them by the college. Information provided by Mrs. Dortha H. Skelton, Reference Librarian, The College of William and Mary in Virginia, August 16, 1974.

62.   The "handsome church" was the Bruton Parish Church, still standing.

63.   The two creeks are Queen's Creek and College Creek (once called Archer's Hope).

64.   See William H. Gaines, Jr., "Thomas Nelson, Jr.—Governor-at-Arms," *Virginia Cavalcade* 1 (2) (Autumn 1951): 40–43, and Randolph W. Church and W. Edwin Hemphill "View at Little York in Virginia," ibid., pp. 44–47. The latter article contains sketches by Benjamin Henry Latrobe which throw light on Enys' text. See also Freeman, *Washington,* V: 363: " 'Mr. Secretary,' as he [Nelson] was called by his friends, had retired from public life in 1775 and had lived at Yorktown. Now, at 65, he still was observant and was able to give the camp the first reliable news that had come from Yorktown after the siege began: The bombardment, he said, already had done much damage and had forced many of the British to take shelter under the cliff, where Cornwallis had established himself in a grotto."

65.   "Between the marsh above Moore's Mill, which was on Wormeley's Pond, and the steep ravine of Yorktown Creek the open plain was not much more than half a mile wide and was known in part as Pigeon Quarter." Freeman, *Washington,* V: 348–49. See map, p. 348. See, also, Fortescue, *History,* III: 400–402. After recounting Cornwallis' mistakes prior to the defeat at Yorktown, Fortescue adds: "Even so, all might have been well had he held fast to his outer line of defense, in which he could almost

certainly have prolonged the siege for another week; whereas he knew that by abandoning them, he rendered his inner line untenable."

The upper marsh is formed by Yorktown Creek, the lower, or downstream marsh by Wormeley Creek. Pidgen or Pigeon Hill is that ridge formed between the headwaters of the two previously mentioned creeks. It was here that Cornwallis had his primary outer defenses.

66. Point of Rocks is the shore immediately upstream from Redoubt Ten of the British outer works. It is identified on 1965 U.S.G.S. Maps, Series AMS 5758111, NW, Series V834, Poguoson West Triangle, Va. Information provided by James N. Hackett, Chief Park Historian, National Park Service, Yorktown, Virginia.

67. The Franco-American commissioners negotiating the surrender of Cornwallis were Viscount de Noailles and John Laurens. The British commissioners were Lieut.-Col. Thomas Dundas and Major Alexander Ross. The meeting place was the Moore House. Freeman, *Washington,* V: 382, 382n.

68. "General" Thomas Nelson, signer of the Declaration of Independence and Governor of Virginia, was actually the nephew of Secretary Nelson. William Nelson was the father of Governor Nelson. Emory G. Evans, "The Rise and Decline of the Virginia Aristocracy in the Eighteenth Century: The Nelsons," in *The Old Dominion,* edited by Darret B. Rutman (Charlottesville, Va.: University Press of Virginia, 1964), pp. 62–78.

69. Mann Page married Elizabeth Nelson on June 5, 1788; therefore he was not yet the son-in-law of Governor Nelson. *Genealogy of the Page Family,* pp. 74–75. Page was not a member of the Virginia Federal Convention of 1788. Hugh Blair Grigsby, *The History of the Virginia Federal Convention of 1788* (New York: Da Capo, 1969).

70. Hampton is a very small place inhabited chiefly by Pilots.

71. After the destruction of Norfolk early in 1776, Fort Nelson, named for General Thomas Nelson, was erected on Windmill Point. Writers' Program, W.P.A., *Virginia: A Guide to the Old Dominion* (New York: Oxford University Press, 1940), p. 254. The fort was burned by the British in 1779.

72. Enys' informers minimized the damage sustained by Norfolk as a result of British fire on January 1, 1776. For seven hours, shot from sixty guns descended on the seaport and landing parties set fire to wooden structures along the wharves. Even the Whig defenders took part in the destruction, setting fire to Tory homes. The fires raged for almost three days, consuming most of the town. What was left was subsequently laid waste by order of the Virginia Convention in order to deprive Dunmore of quarters in Norfolk. The severity of both friend and foe reduced Norfolk from a bustling seaport to a charred ruin with losses estimated at more than 300,000 pounds sterling. Elizabeth

Cometti, "Depredations in Virginia during the Revolution," in *Old Dominion,* edited by Rutman, pp. 137–38.

73.   See *The Lower Norfolk County Virginia Antiquary* I: 35–36n.

74.   Robertson probably belonged to the firm of Silbert, Robertson, & Munro. See *Calendar of Virginia State Papers,* VI: 633; VII: 504. For Pollard, see "The Norfolk Academy," *Lower Norfolk County Antiquary* I: 27. References to Dr. Taylor are in *Calendar Va. S. Papers* IV, VI, VII. A notice of Dr. John Ramsay's marriage is in *Lower Norfolk County Antiquary* III: 127.

75.   What will render Norfolk always a disagreeable place is the disputes which subsist among themselves so much that those of one [part of the] town will not asociate with them of the other, to which you may add the old idea of Whig and Tory which subsists here as strong as ever. They had no public Amusements of any kind so that I do not know what kind of Women they have. Those who came within my observation were very indifferent.

INDEX

Abby: xxvi; provisions for, 267
Abercromby, General Ralph, xxviii, xxix
Aberdeen, 66
Abingdon, 345
Adams, Abigail, 341, 343
Adirondack Museum, xl–xli, 280
Agassiz, Louis, 335
Albany: description of, 185–86; early settlers, houses, 329
Alder, Lieutenant William, 28, 32
Alexander, William, 256, 357
Alexandria, Norfolk route, 252–67
Algerians. *See* Algerines
Algerines, 255, 356
Allen, Ethan, xx, xxii
Allen, Miss, 218, 222
Allen, Misses, 341
Allsop, George, 289
Alsop, Mr., 84, 155
Alsop, Mrs., 95, 290
Amherst, General Jeffery: 280, 293, 294; strategy in 1760, 299
Anburey, Thomas, 276

Anderson's Tavern, 253, 256, 355
André, Major John: will, 101, 190; capture, 191–92, 329–30; "Cow-Chace," 329–30
Anticosti Island: 59, 77; Thomas Wright Survey, 275
Arbuthnot, Lieutenant Robert, 30
Ariadne, 154
Arnold, General Benedict, xx, xxii, 20, 176, 275, 326
Arnoldi, Peter, 321
Ash Island, 51
Ashley's Tavern, 328
Asia, 331–32
Assembly, dancing club, 291
Astor, John Jacob, 338
Atkin, Lieutenant Maurice, xxiv, 61, 64–65, 68
Aubrey, Captain Thomas, 13
Augustinian Nuns, 324
D'Auvergne, Captain Philip: xxv, 22, 72–73, 77–78, 80–81, 283; predictions on voyage to Quebec, 74

Baillie-Balruthrie House, 66
Baker, Captain John, 119
Balls: for Prince William Henry, 156; assembly ball at Alexandria, 244–45
Ballston Spa, 48, 281
Baltimore: ground rent Methodist meeting house, State House, churches, 235; fortifications, Baltimore Assembly, 238; description of, 347–48
Baltimore-Alexandria route, 238–45
Banff, 64
Banter, 60, 282
Barnsfair, Captain, 174
Barra Castle, 66
Barra Island, 63
Barracks, New Brunswick, 339
Barron, 172
Basin Harbor, 176
Basset, Captain James, xxii
Basset, Captain Thomas, 3
Bassett, Frances, 252, 354
Bateaux sinking, 280
Bath, xxxv, 68–69, 72
"Battle of the Kegs," 342–43
Bay of Seven Isles, 79
Beaton, Mr., 204–205, 335
Beaton, Mrs., 205
Beauport, 286
Beckwith, Colonel George, 156
Bedel, Colonel Timothy, 277
Bee hives, locating, 177
Belcher, Judge, 335
Beloeil, 53
Bennet, Lieutenant Thomas, 7
Bennist, Captain, 105
Benzell, Adolphus, 326
"Belvidere," 341, 348
Beron, Mons., 151
Betton, "Commodore" David, 117, 315
Bibby, Captain, 194, 209

Bic Island, 79
Big Tree, 313
Bingham, Mrs. Anne Willing, 217–218, 341, 343
Bingham, William: xxxviii; source of wealth, 217; ball, 221–22; mansion, 222, 343
Bird Rocks Islands, 77
Bird's Ordinary, 257, 358
Black River, 299
Blackshiels, 67
Bladensburg, 241
Blockhouses, 279
Blodget, Asa, 278
Bloody Pond, 178
Boatmen, Canadian, 298
Bobbenson, Captain, 61
Bolling, Robert, 357
Bolling, Mrs., 357
Bolton, Captain, 266
Bond, Phineas, 218, 341
Bond, Miss, 218
Booker, Lieutenant Thomas, 48
Borough Tavern, 266
Botetourt, Lord, statue of, 258
Boston: Massacre, xx, 272
Boston: rope walks, 204, 334; Beacon hill, 201, 205; markets, 204; inhabitants, 205; houses, 205; public buildings, 205–206; Faneuil Hall, 205; Long Wharf, 205–206, 334–335; Workhouses, 206, 335; public school, 206; bridges, 201–202, 333; hospitals, 335; harbor, 334
"Bottom," 320
Boundaries: Province of Quebec, U.S.–Canada, Vallentine-Collins Line, 325–26; between English and American settlements, 173
Bouquet River, 50

Bowdoin, James, 202
Bowling Green, 253
Boyd, Julian P., xiii–xv, 353
Boyd, Robert, 265
Boyd, Captain William, 58, 60, 63
Bradford, Colonel Gamaliel, 204–205
Bradstreet, John, 185
Brandywine: flour mills, 229; battle, 345
Brant, Joseph, xxxviii, 120–21, 143–44, 147, 277, 301, 320
Breck, Samuel, 205, 335
Breed's Hill, xx, 203
Brehm, Captain Diedrick, 54–58, 282
Breynton, Lieutenant John, 128–29, 131
British Queen, 276
Brooke, Frances, 289
Brooke, Mrs., 160
Brooke, the Reverend John, 289
Brooke, Thompson, 106
Brown, Mrs., flutist, 217
Brown, Colonel John, 23, 176, 278, 326
Brown, Lancelot, 89, 252, 291
Brunstone, Mr., 73
Bruton Parish Church, 358
Brymner, Douglas, xl
Buchanan, Andrew, 347
Buchanan, George, 347
Buchanan, William, 235
Bugs, 95
Buisson, 294
Bunch of Grapes Tavern, 244, 350
Bunker Hill, 203
Burch, John, 131, 143, 317, 321
Burgoyne, General John, xxiii, 14, 23
Bush. *See* Harford
Bushnell, David, Submarine, 331–32, 343
Butler, John, 93, 121, 315, 320
Butler's Rangers, 146, 320

Butterfield, Major Isaac, 377
Button Mould Bay, 326

Caffieri, Jean Jacques, 331
Caisse d'Escompte, 340
Caithness, 64
Calash (caleche), 287
Caledonian Hotel, 67
Campbell, Major Archibald, xxv, xxvii, 8, 10, 49, 89, 91, 116, 150
Campbell, Colin, 24
Campbell, Captain George: 124–25; grave, 125
Campbell, Major John, 291, 338
Canada, invasion of, xxii
Canadians, description of, 7
Canadian League, 289
Canadian Squaw, 151
Canal, James River, 255
Canals, 292–93
Canete, 61
Canoe, 326
Cape Diamond, 286
Capitol (Richmond): foundations of, 355, 254; Capitol (Williamsburg), 258
Carillon dam, 296
Cariole, 89, 291
Carleton, 33, 277
Carleton, Major Christopher, 8, 10, 23–24, 26–28, 32, 34–36, 40, 68
Carleton, Guy: xxii, 6, 14, 155–57, 165, 168, 253, 271, 276, 322; humane treatment of prisoners, 355
Carleton, Thomas, 253

Carleton Island: xvi, xxv, 101, 106, 116, 150, 299; description of fort, 305, 307; communication, 305; transportation costs, 305–306; volume of cargo, 306; rotation, 306; fur trade, 307
Carrington, Colonel Edward, 209, 264
Carron Iron Works, 290
Castiglioni, Count Luigi, 357
Castle. *See* Large House
Castle Craire, 59, 282
Castle Town [Castleton?], 40
Castle William, Convict labor, 334
Cat Island, 297
Cataraqui, xxv, xxvi, 103, 105–106, 221, 300
Cathcart, Lord William, xxvi, xxvii, xxviii
Caughnawaga Indians, 23; burial, 89, 291–92
Cedar Grove, 354
Cedars: 153, 275; prisoners taken at, 295
Chambers, Commodore, 278
Chambers, Commodore William, 36
Channel Scartie, 297
Chapel Segget, 66
Chapman, Mr., 209
Chappedelaine, Marquis, 218, 238–40, 245, 253, 267, 341, 355
Charlesbourg, 286
Charlestown, destruction by fire, 203, 334
Charlevoix, Pierre François Xavier, 124, 274
Chastellux, François Jean, Marquis de, xxxix, 252, 274, 327
Chateau, 322–23
Châteauguay Convent, 92
Chatham Barracks, 3
Chaudière falls, description of, 157, 160–61, 323
Chazy River, 90

Cheat River, 351
Chesapeake and Ohio Canal, 350–51
Cheviot Hills, 67
Chew, Benjamin, 217, 341
Chew, Harriet, 218, 341
Chew, Juliana, 222
Chew, Maria, 218, 341
Chew, Peggy Oswald, 341
Chew, Sophia, 222
"Children's" dance, 218
Chipman, Captain John, 49
Chippawa Creek, 131, 143
Cholmondeley, 343
Chowder, 76
Church dignitaries, 324
City Tavern, Albany, 183, 340
Clark, General George Rogers, 329
Claus, Daniel, 279
Claverack, 188
Clinton, Governor George, 196
Clinton, General Henry, 50
"Cliveden," description of, 342
Close, Farman, 115
Coadjuter, 166
Coal, 256, 357
Cochrane, Alexander F., 174
Cod, 76
Coffee house, Albany, 183–85
Coffin, Captain Isaac, 154
Cohoes Falls, 32, 328
Clow, Mr., 239–40, 252
Cokesbury College, 345–46
Concert, Philadelphia, 215, 340
Congress, 326
Constable, Mr., 209, 337
Convent, Three Rivers, 86
Cooke, Captain, 65
Cooling Water, 150
Coon, Mr., 215
Coote, Major General Eyre, xxxi

Copper Mine, 338–39
Coram, Thomas, 293
Cornwall, Ontario. *See* Johnstown
Cornwall County Council, 272
Cornwallis, Lord Charles, xxiv, xxx, 53, 257, 358
Cortland Manor, 192
Cossacks, passage of horses, 356–57
Coteau de St. Francois. *See* Coteau du Lac
Coteau du Lac, 294
Cottages, Lithuanian, 304
"Countess of Schlosser," 120
Coupar, Angus, 66
Coxe, William, 304
Cradle, Niagara Portage, 122, 316
Craig, Mrs., 222
Cramahé, Hector, xxii, 326
Cranberries, 80
Crook, Lieutenant Joseph, 27
Croton-on-Hudson, 191
Crown Point, 48
Cruger, Henry, 188
Cumberland Bay, 51
Curson, Mr., 232
Curson, Anna Maria, 347
Cutler, Benjamin Clark, 204–205
Cutting, Rev. "Leo'd," 339

Dal Verme, Count Francesco, 329
Dancing: xxxviii, 106; dance clubs in Baltimore, 234–35
"Dark Sunday," xxv, xxxix, 105–106, 302–304
Davis, Colonel Thomas, 154

Dawes, Thomas [?] William, 200, 202
Deblois, Gilbert, 282
Deblois, John, 282
Deblois, Stephen, 282
"Defence during Napoleonic Wars," xxxiii
De La Bouverie, Marquis, 222
DeLancey Square, 196
De Lisle, Dr. David Chabrand, 172, 325
De Lisle, Miss, 172, 325
Devil's Hole Massacre, 124–25, 316–17
Dieskau, Baron Ludwig August, 327
Digges, George, 352–53
Digges, Thomas Atwood, 352–53
Digges, William, 246
Distilling salt water, 5
Dixon [Dickson?], Major Hugh, xxvii, 27, 32, 89, 150
Donald, William, 255
Donaldson, Captain Thomas, 91
Dorchester, Lord. *See* Guy Carleton
Douglas, Captain Charles, 4, 11, 17, 275–76
Douglas, Captain Robert, 276
Douglas, Ensign, 121, 128
Douglass, Mr., 121, 138, 140–41
Doune, 65
Dow, Charles M., xl
Draper, Dr. George, 209, 337
Dress regulations, xxix–xxx
Duck Islands, 117, 315
Dudevant, Arnaud-Germain, 61
Duer, Colonel William, 179, 328
Duff House, 65
Dufré, St. George, 291
Duke of York, xxxii
Dundas, Colonel Alexander, 157
Dundonald, Lord, 174
Dunmore, Murray, John, 4th Earl of Dunmore, 265–66, 326

Dutchess County, 190
Dyce, 66

Eagle, 331–32
Elegood, Colonel, 266
Elk Head of, Howe's debarkation, 345
Elkton, 230
Ellicot, Andrew, 317
Ellsworth, Francis, 132, 317
Elsworth's lodging house, 193, 208, 330
Emily Montague, 84, 160, 322
Empey's (Adam) Public House, 294
Enys, Reverend C. R. Saltren, xl
Enys, Charles, xl
Enys, Dorothy: xxxv; death of, 69
Enys, Elizabeth, xxxix, 323
Enys, Francis (Frank): xviii, xxiv–xxv, 222, 283; letters to, xxxix
Enys, Francis Gilbert, xl
Enys, John: death, xxxv; death of uncle, 68; depositories of manuscripts, xxxix–xli; education, xviii–xx; family background, xviii; "History of 29th . . . ," 272; likenesses, xxxv; memoranda, xxxix; performs marriage, 112–13; profile of, xxiv; promotion to major, xxvii; promotion to lieutenant-colonel, xxix; removal to Bath, xxxv, retirement, xxxiii–xxxv
Enys, John Davies, xl
Enys Library, 271–72
Enys, Mary, xxxv
Enys, Sarah L.: xxxix; discovery of John Enys' journals, 272–73
Episcopal Academy, 344
Esquimaux canoe, description of, 158

Esquimaux. *See* Labrador Indians
Eton College Register, 272
Evelyn, General William, xxiv, 3, 72, 275
Everard, Major H., *History of Thos. Farrington Regiment,* xli, 272
Exeter, 72
Eyre, Henry, 69

Faggot bond, 128
Fairfield, 337
Falmouth, 72, 355
False Duck Islands, 315
Faneuil Hall, 334
Fares: New York–Providence; Providence-Boston, 200
Farquhar, Lieutenant William, 28, 32, 42, 44
Federal Constitution, adoption of, 246
"A. Fermor," 322
Ferrero, 26
Ferries's Bay, 176
Fife, 65
Fireworks, 156–57, 165
Fish, Colonel Nicholas, 196
Fish, abundance of, 112
Fishing: xxxviii, in Atlantic, 75; fly fishing, 90–92; fishing spears, 104–105; for eels, 151; for salmon, 90, 104–105; night fishing, 152; for herring, in Lake Champlain, 292
Fishkill, 190
Fitzgerald, Colonel John, 245
Fitzgerald, John, 350
Flat Rock, 128
Forbes, Captain David, 45, 109, 307
Forfar, 66

Forglen, 66
Forster, Captain George, 93, 277, 295
Fort Amherst, 178, 327
Fort Ann, 44, 151, 279
Fort Edward, 44, 179, 327
Fort Erie, 131, 317
Fort Franklin, 315
Fort Frederick, 329
Fort Frontenac, 300–301
Fort Gage, 280
Fort George, 44–45, 48, 151, 280
Fort George, England, 282
Fort Haldimand, 299
Fort Independence. *See* Castle William
Fort Knyphausen, 330
Fort La Gallet, 299
Fort Le Boeuf, 121
Fort Lévis, 101, 294
Fort McHenry, 348
Fort Miller, 328
Fort Nelson, 265, 359
Fort Niagara, 131, 144–46, 315
Fort Ontario, xxvi, 108, 112, 307–308
Fort Oswegatchee, 101
Fort Oswego, 109
Fort Pitt, 350
Fort Rascal, 110
Fort Schlosser, 120, 122, 125, 315
Fort Washington, 196, 330
Fort Whetstone Point, 348
Fort William Augustus, 101
Fort William Henry, 46, 280
Fortier, Miss, 172, 325
Fountain Inn, 232
Franklin, Mr., 218
Franklin, Benjamin, 215, 275, 338–41
Franklin, William Temple, 341
Franks, David, 215, 340
Franks, Rebecca, 340
Fraser, 323

Fraser, Captain Alexander, 23, 48, 109
Fraser, Captain Hugh, 37
Fraser, John, 157–58
Fraser, General Simon, 328
Frasers Tavern, 257
Fredericksburg, 252
French, Jeremiah, 98, 296
Frontier movement, 320
Fruit, 146
Frying Pan, 332
Furnaces, Maryland, 346
Fyvie Castle, 66

Gages Heights, 45
Gallop, 100
Game, abundance of, 112
Games, 148
Gardening, 106
Gardens, 96
Gairnstown, 65
General Elliot, 165
General Green, 197
Georgetown, 241
Germain, Sergeant, 118
German Reformed Church, 344
Germantown: battle of, 340; visit to, 219, 221
Giant Steps, 56
Glamis, 66
Glen, Jacob, 327
Glen, John, 327
Glenn, Mr., 179
Glens Falls, 45, 178
Globes, 204, 335
Goat Island, 136
Godfrey, Captain, 199–200

Gordon, General Benjamin, 18, 273, 277
Gordon, George, 349
Grand Batture, 93
Grand Vicar, 161
Grand voyer, 287
Grant, Daniel, 232, 346
Grant, Miss Jenny, 346
Grant, Mrs., 346
Gray's Ferry. See Gray's Gardens
Gray's Gardens, 344
Great Tree. See Big Tree
Green Island (Verte Isle), 59, 81
Green Room. See Gray's Gardens
Grenadier Companies, 53, 281
Grenadier Island, 108
Grey Nuns, 293
Grey Sisters, Montreal, 92
Gridiron, 332
Grieve, George, 349
Griffeth, Mr., 197, 200, 238
Guinea, value of, 350

Haarlem Heights, 196
Hackfall, 300
Hadfield, Joseph, 22, 281, 295, 318, 342
Haldimand, General Frederick: xxiv, 53, 109, 293, 320; achievements of, 308; familiarity with European fortresses, 315; house of, 54, 58, 82, 281–82, 295
Half Moon Point, 183
Halfmoon, 328
Hamilton, Duke of, palace, 358
Hamilton, Miss, 222
Hamilton, Mrs., 343
Hamilton, Robert: 128, 131, 141, 143, 319; Hamilton home, 319
Hamilton, Thomas, 125

Hampton, route to, 264
Hancock, John, 202
Harford, 231
Harmar, Miss Arabella. See "A. Fermor"
Harpooner, 59, 282
Harrison, Lieutenant Hercules [?], 26
Harrogate, 139, 318
Hartford, 336
Harvard College, 204–205
Haughton, Richard, 278
Haughton, Lieutenant William, xxv, 23, 29, 37, 73, 82, 278
Hay, Captain Adam, 155
Hay, Mrs. A. Hawkes, 193
Hay, Colonel Udny, 178
Hayley, Mrs. Mary, 202
Hazards of winter travel, 239–42
Hazen, General Moses, 174
Heights of Abraham, 12
Helder Campaign, xxxi–xxxii, 274
Hell Gate, 198, 332
Heth, Colonel William, 253, 355
Highlands, 190
Highways, care of in winter, 287
Hill, Lieutenant Thomas, 3
Hives, locating, 327
Hog's Back, 332
Holland, Major, 54, 282
Hollingworth, Jesse, 235
Hollingsworth, Zebulon, 347
Hope, General Henry, 153, 157, 255, 302
Hopkinson, Francis, 343
Howard, John Eager, 217, 235, 341, 348
Howe, Lord George Augustus, 48, 280
Hoy Head, 64
Hoyt, Winthrop, 32
Hughes, Lieutenant Thomas, xxv, 73, 82, 283

Humbert, General Jean, xxx
Humphrey, Mr., 126–27, 132, 138
Humphreys, Colonel David, 246
Humphreys, Mr., 128, 130
Hunter, Major-General Peter, xxx
Hunter, Robert, 294–95, 315, 318
Hunter, William, 244–45, 350
Hutchins, Thomas, map, 351
Huzzar, 198
Hyde, Captain Jedediah, 175

Icebergs, xxxvii
Indians: 16; council, 143, 148; kindness, 31; ladders, 137; mounds, xxxvii; punishment for crimes, 291; raiders, 35–36; regatta, 152; St. Regis, 37, 96; squaws, 119–20
Indian Queen Tavern, 215, 339
Inflexible, xxiii, 20, 277
Ingraham, Mr., 251
Innkeepers, rude treatment by, 207
Inns, American, 336–37
Intelligence, Quebec, 9–10
Inverkeithing, 66
Ireland, Edward, 347
Ireland, Elizabeth, 347
Ireland, Miss, 234, 347
Irish insurrection, xxx
Iron Ore, 232
Irvine, Colonel William, 14, 276
Isis, xxii, 4, 8, 278
Isle aux Noix, 24, 51
Isle La Motte, 36
Isle Royale, 101
Isle Tonianta, 102

Jackson, William, 222
Jacques, Ensign William, 54
James River Canal, 357
Jamestown, 258
Jane, 165
Jeffery, Mrs., 202
Johns, Mr., 24
Jersey Island, xxvii–xxviii
Jersey, 20, 278
Johan, Captain, 301
Johnson, Sir John: 16, 23, 37, 48, 96, 277, 295; corps, 50
Johnson, Lieutenant William, 37
Johnson, Sir William, 96–97, 280, 292, 327
Johnson's Point. *See* Point Maligne
Johnstown, 97, 152, 296
Jones, Mr., 32–33
Jones, Captain, 102
Jones, John or Jonathan, 300
Jordan, Mr., 239–41, 243

Kayak, 323
Kayenquatah. *See* Sayenqueraghta
Kelso, 67
Kemble, Captain William, 155
Kennon, Mr., 209
"Kent House," 282
Kentucky, 351
Kinderhook, 188
King's boats, 292
King's ships, 108
Kingsbridge, 192, 330
Kingston. *See* Cataraqui
Kinross, 66
Knox, General Henry, 336

Labrador Indians, 78, 284
Lachine, 53, 91
La Corne St. Luc, Luc de Chapet de, 290–91
Lake Erie, 143
Lake George, 37, 279–80
Lake, General Gerard, xxx
Lake Ontario: navigation, 110; traffic, 113
Lake St. Francis, 95, 150
Landing, 122
"Landing Place," 326
Lansing family, 328
Lansingburg, 183
Laprairie, 171
La Pensée, 153, 296, 312
Large House, description of, 144–46, 320
Lauder, 67
Laurencekirk, 66
Leander, 154, 322
Ledford, 300
Lee, Sergeant Ezra, 332
Lee, Henry "Light Horse Harry," 244
Lee, 22, 50, 278, 281
Limniade, 103, 116, 118, 149, 302
Linzee, Captain Robert, 6, 9–10, 275
Lion's Den, 124, 141
Literacy, New England, 206
Liverpool-London, 270
Livingston, Maria, 172, 325
Locks, 92, 293
Log, Hampton-Liverpool, 268–69
London road, Morpeth to London, 67–68
Long Sault, 98, 152, 294, 297–98
Lorette Indians, 157, 287, 323
Lorring, Mrs., Boarding House, 200
Loyal Convert, 277
Loyalists, 26
Lyman, Phineas, 327
Lyon, Colonel James, 245

McAlpin, 295
McCauley, Alexander, 258
McClenachan, Blair, 217, 219, 340
McComb, John, builder, 209
McCormack, Mrs., 321
McCrea, Jane, 179, 328
McDonald, Miss, 82, 87
McDonald, Captain John, 82
McFarlane, Lieutenant Robert, 47
Mackenzie, 276
McGowan's Pass, 196, 331
McIntoch, Donald, 32
Mackenzie, Captain Thomas, 10
McKinzie. See Mackenzie
Maclean, Lieutenant Allen, 115, 276
McNeal, Mr., 179, 328
Magnolio, 353
Mail, 81
Maîtres de poste, regulations, 289
Mall, Boston, 202
Manor House, Roboutel de la Noue family, 293
Maria, 20, 27, 36, 49, 174, 277, 326
Marietta, 351
Marine mammals, 284
Market Street, Philadelphia, 344
Markoe, Abraham, 342
Markoe, Elizabeth Baynton, 342
Markoe, Miss, 221–22, 342
Marshall, John, 355
Martin, xxii, 3
Martin, Luther, xxxviii, 234
Martin, Mrs., 234
Masapagas. See Missisaugas
Mascouche le Page, 53
Maskinenge. See Muskellunge
Masonic Hall, 355
Matthews, Major, 320
Maurage, Major Philip, 171
Maxwell, General William, 196

Meade, George, 215, 221
Mercer, General Hugh, 337
Merritt, Ichabod, 280
Messassagnes, 152
Messesagnes, 321
Miami, 351
Michilimackinac, 112
Middlebury, 28, 278
Middlebury River, 278
Military review, 322
Mill Bay, 49–50
Mille Rockes, 298
Mills: grist and saw, 131, 301, 326;
    Brandywine, 345
Minchin, Captain Paul, 154
Mineral springs, 321
Mingan Islands, 78
Missisaugas, 103–104
Missisquoi Bay, 173
Mohawk, 149
Mohawk Indians, 36
Molesworth, Captain Ponsonby, 334
Molesworth, Mrs. Suzanna Sheafe, 334
Monkton, destruction of, 32–33
Monongahela River, 350
Monsell, Major William, 100, 108, 116
Montcalm, Louis Joseph Marquis de
    Montcalm, 280, 308
Montgomery, General Richard, xxii, 275,
    331
Montmorenci Falls, 54–58, 82, 136,
    157, 282, 323
Montreal: xxvi; social life, 88–89
Montresor, Colonel John, 280, 316, 327
Mosquitoes, 94, 296
Motto, 322
Mount Defiance, 326
Mount Independence, 49, 53, 279, 281
Muirson, George, 168–69, 171, 176,
    178, 186, 324

Munro, Captain John, 34–35, 37, 48,
    279
Musgrave, Colonel Thomas, 217, 342
Musicale, 63
Muskellunge, 290
Muskingum, 350–51

Narragansett Bay, islands, 333
Narragansett pacer, 199, 332
Nassau Hall, vandalism, 339
Naval craft, construction of, 16
Navy Hall, 147, 321
Navy Point, 305
Negroes: population, 255; quarters, 255
Nelson, Elizabeth, 359
Nelson, General Thomas: sons, 352; 245,
    264, 359
Nelson, Secretary Thomas, house, 261
Nelson, Thomas, Jr., 358
Nesbit, Lieutenant Colonel William, 13
Newark, 211
New Brunswick, 212
New Haven, burning of, 208, 337
New Mackar, 66
Newport, population, 199, 332–33
New Year Eve Celebration, 214
New York State, raid against, xvii–
    xxiii, 35–52
New York, military parade, 197
New York City: population, houses, port,
    churches, Columbia College, charity
    school, monument to Montgomery,
    balls, 193–94; fortifications, 194–96;
    population, fires, houses, harbor, 330–
    31

Niagara Falls: xvii, xxvi, xxxvii; boat over, 132; description of, 134–40; geological, 141–43; Horseshoe, 126
Niagara Portage, principal waggoner, 129–30, 316
Niger, 81
Norfolk: destruction by fire; town disputes, 265–66, 359–60
Northern lights, 50
Northumberland, Duke of, 67, 72
Nunnery, 290
Nuns, their ages, 324

O'Brien, Lady Susan Sarah Louisa, 318–19
O'Connor, Thomas, 355
Old Meldrum, 66
Oliver, Lieutenant George, 149
Orleans Island, 82
Oswegatchie, xxv, 101, 106
Oswego, xxv, 308

Page, Mann, 264, 359
Painter's House, 317–19
Painters Point, 136, 140
Pardon to midshipman, 165–66
Parker, Colonel Josiah, 267
Parks Farm, 40
Paterson, Allan, 282
Paterson, Charles, 61, 282
Patroon, 185

Paulus Hook: fortifications, 211; Paulus-Philadelphia route, 209–15, 337
Payne's hòstelry, 176
Pearson, Captain, 81
Pegasus, xxvi, 154
Pettyagar. *See* Pirogue
Pirogue, 209
Passaic Falls, 338–39
Pearl, Colonel Stephen, 173–74, 325
Pearson, Robert, 284
Peekskill: travel accommodations; military activity of landlord, 190
Pendennis Castle, 73, 283
Penn, John, 222, 343
Penrose, Miss, 69, 72
Penrose, Sarah, 283
Penrose, Reverend Thomas, 283
Pennsylvania, University of, 344
Pentland Firth, 64
Perth, 66
Petersburg, tobacco exportation, 357
Philadelphia: description of, 224–26; diversions, 226, 277–78
Philadelphia-Baltimore route, 227, 232
Phillipse, Frederick, 330
Pictet, Captain Marcus, 172–73
Pidgeon, Mr., 140–41
Pierie, William, 319
Pigeon Hill, 261, 358–59
Pilotage, 94
Pittsburgh. *See* Fort Pitt
Plains of Abraham, 159
Platt, Mrs., 343
Plattsburgh, 292
Plays: *Lethe, Padlock,* 164
Pocahontas, 357
Pointe au Cardinal, 99
Point aux Iroquois, 99, 298
Point Maligne, 96–97, 296
Point of Rock, 261, 359

Pointe aux Pins, 102
Pointe de Barrè, 100, 102
Pointe aux Trembles, 84, 169
Points in St. Lawrence River, 298
Pollard, Mr., 105
Pollard, Benjamin, 266
Pollard, Edward, 149–50
Ponsonby Molesworth, Captain, 204
Ponsonby, Suzanna Sheafe, 204
Poplar trees, 355
Porpoises, 78
Porter, Captain William, 116–17
Porter and Ingraham, 354
Portraits: Louis XVI, Marie Antoinette, 331
Portsmouth, description of, 266
Post Road, Quebec-Montreal, 288
Pot, 198, 332
Potan, Mathew, 173
Potomac Falls, 350
Potomac River, head of, 351
Potts, Major William, 104
Poughkeepsie, 190
Powell, Brigadier Henry Watson, 36
Pratt, Sheila, xxxix
Presque Isle, 99
Preston, Thomas, xx
Princeton, battle of: College, vandalism committed at, 212, 339
Princeton University Library, xl
Prison Island, 153
Prisoners, American, 94
Prize money, xxviii
Property losses, 52
Providence, 200
Provisions, 103
Pump, 176–77
Punch Bowl, 110
Putnam, Rufus, 351

Quebec: 58; description of, 284; origin of name, 285–86; Castle of St. Louis, 285; churches, 285; convents, 286; fortifications, 286–87
Queen's birthday, 106
Quinte, Bay of, 150, 301

Ramsay, Dr. John, 110, 266
Randolph, Governor Edmund, 253, 255
Rapid aux Cheverale, 297
Rapids, Mille Roche, Moulinette, 98
Rates of Transportation, 288–89
Rattlesnakes, 132
Reels, 347
Regimental reorganization, 53
Rensselaer, Miss, 186
Rensselaer, Stephen, 185
Resource, 154
Returns of 1780 raid, 52
Review, 26th Regiment, 165
Rhode Island, capitals, 333
Rice's Tavern, 200
Richmond: description of, 253–54; fire, 355
Richmond, Green, 68
Rimside Moor, 67
Rivière des Raisins, 96, 295
Roads, conditions of, 289
Robertson, Daniel, 86
Robertson, Gilbert, 266
Roche, Lieutenant James, 45
Rock Creek, 242
Rodney, Admiral George Brydges, Battle of Saints Passage, 59, 282
Roe. See Rowe

Rogers, Mr., 173–74
Rogers, Major Robert, 280
Roger's Road, 47
Roger's Rock, 48
Rolfe, Jane, 357
Rolfe, John, 357
Roll, Colonel Johann Gottlieb, 214
Roman Catholic liturgy, Philadelphia, 221
Rona Island, 63
Rose, Lieutenant, 20
Rosekrans, Major James, 50
Ross, Captain Andrew, 28, 33–34
Ross, Major John, 109, 217
Rowe, Jack, 173, 176
Royal Savage, 20, 277
Russell, Thomas, 204–205

Sabbath Day Point, 177
Saguenay River, 80, 284
St. Andrew, Society of, 351
St. Antoine, 53
St. Charles, 53
St. Clair, Captain David, 24, 69
St. Denis, 53
St. George, Colonel Richard, 171
Saint-Henry-de-Mascouche, 53
St. Kilda, 63
St. Lawrence, rapids, 153
St. Leger, Colonel Barry, 53
Saint-Méry, Moreau de, 347
St. Patrick's Lane, 125
St. Paul's Chapel, 330–31
St. Regis Indians, 296
St. Regis reservation, 296
Salisbury, 68

Salmon, Connecticut River, 336
Salmon Creek, 108, 307
Salt water, distillation of, 5
Sandflies, 99
Sandusky, 351
Saranac River, 90, 292
Saratoga: block house, 179–80
Sault du Buisson, 93
Sault du Trou, 92
Sauthier, Claude Joseph, 296
Sawmills, 43, 125, 178–79, 317, 327–28
Sawyer, Admiral Herbert, xxvi, 154, 156–57
Sayenqueraghta, 144, 320
Scalping, 45–46
Schuyler, Arent, 338
Schuyler, General Philip, 328–29
Schuyler's Island, 281
Scotch Bonnet, 49
Seals, 6, 78
Sears, David, 202
Seaton, William, 209, 337
Selwyn, Dr. Alfred, xl
Seneca, 102, 116–18, 300
Sept Îles, 59
Sernoult, Major, 295
Seton, Miss, 234
Seton, Mr., 227, 230, 232
Seton, William, 347
Settlements: above Thousand Islands, 301; Americans in Canada, 147, 175; contrasts in 298–99; crops, 298; land-grouping system, 295; Loyalists, 99; Mohawk Indians, 301; Oswegatchie, 299; royalists, 102, 119; Scottish Catholics, 96; town plans, 301
Seven Isles, 79
Severance, Frank H., xl
Shays, Daniel, 207

Shays's Rebellion, 336
Sheafe, Mary, 204
Sheafe, Roger Hale, 204
Shepherd, Major General William, 336
Sheridan, John, 339
Sherwood, Captain Adiel, 280
Sherwood, Captain Justus, 49, 281
Sillery, 84, 159–60, 289–90
Simcoe, Mrs. Elizabeth, 317–19, 321
Simcoe, Colonel John Graves, 321
Skenesboro, 50, 176
Skenesborough, 281
Skerett Tavern, 232
Slavery, xxxviii
Sleeping arrangements, 240–41, 348–49
Smith, Dr. Abiel, 203
Smith, Misses, 234, 347
Snakes, 138
Somnambulist, 256
Sorel, 15
South Landing, 176, 326
South Traverse, 81
Southampton, xxviii–xxix
Southans, Mr., 105
Southouse, Miss, 179, 327
Spanish dollar, value, 307
Speedy: xxiii, xxv, 72; accommodations, 283
Springfield Arsenal, 206–207, 335–36
Springs, 149
Sprouts, 183
Stagecoach: Boston-New York, 206; Philadelphia-Alexandria, 348
State House (Independence Hall), 344
Stedman, Miss, 317
Stedman, John, 317
Stedman, Philip, Sr., 316
Stedman, Philip, 129–30, 131, 146, 148–49
Sterling, Lord William Alexander, 53

Stewart, Elizabeth, 296
Stewart, 173–75, 217
Stewart, Mrs. Deborah, 340
Stewart, General Walter, 340
Stonehaven, 66
Stoughton, John, 326
Strathmore, 66
Stromness, 64
Stuart, Eleanor, 246, 252, 352
Sue, Miss, 222
Sullivan, Brigadier John, 276
Sulpicians. See Grey Nuns
Surprize, xxii, 3, 275
Surveyor general of highways. See Grand Voyer
Swinglebar, trouble with, 231

Table Rock, 134, 138, 317, 319
Tavern fare, 339
Taverns, 183, 346
Taylor, Dr. James, 266, 360
Teeth, prehistoric, 204, 334–35
Temperature, 349
Temple, Lady, 202
Temple, Sir John, 200
Terrebonne, 53
Theatrical performances, 324, 344
Thisbe, 154
Thompson, General William, xxii, 14, 276
Thomas, General John, 276
Thorp, Mrs., 68
Thousand Islands, 102–103, 300
Three Mile Point, 49
Three Rivers, 86
Thunderer, xxiii, 277

Ticonderoga, 23, 37, 48
Tidd, Captain, 73
Tingling, Lt. William, 136
Tobacco, 243, 255, 270, 349–50, 356
Tonianta Island, 151, 300
Tonihata. *See* Tonianta
Tory, Escape to Canada, 109–10
Townshend, Thomas, 68
Transparencies, 155
Treeing, 25–26
Trou, 293
Truro, 72–73
Trusty, xxxii
Tryon, General William, 72
Tuileries, 156
Tumuli, 147
Turnpikes, 107
Turriff, 66
Turtle, 332
Tweed, 67
Twenty-ninth Regiment: Boston Massacre, xx; departure for America, xx–xxii; dress regulations, xxvi–xxvii; departure from Canada, 165

Ursulines, 324
Ushant, 73

Valcour Island: xvii, xxiii, 18–20, 36, 51, 273, 278
Van Cortlandt, Frederick, 330
Van Seciek, Mr., 188

Vehicles, 82
Veiling: xxxvii, 324; at General Hospital, 161–64; Hotel Dieu, 166–68
Vergennes, 31
Vermont, raid in, xvii, xxiii, 28–35, 49, 178
Venango, 121
Virginia, population, 356
Voyage to England (1782), 58–68
Voyers, 84
Vulture, 329
Vyvyan, Lady, 73, 283

Wampum, manufacture of, 338
Warburton Manor, 352–53
Washington, General George: xviii, 20, 252, 278; ancestry, 251–52; birthday, 350; character, 251–52; conversation with John Enys, 244, 246; deer park, 352; description of, 354; Mount Vernon, 245–46, 249, 251–52; mules, 249, 353–54; visit to Western Virginia, 351
Washington, Major George Augustine, 251–52
Washington, Mrs. Martha Dandridge Custis, 246, 251–52
Water pump, 326
Waterbury, General David, 20
Waterford. *See* Half Moon Point
Watson, Captain Jonas, 119
Watson, Josiah, 252, 355
Wayne, General Anthony, 329
Weedon, General George, 253
Weld, Isaac, 281
West Point, description of post, 190

Whitcomb, Lieutenant Benjamin, 18, 277
White, Captain, 60
White, Henry, 282
White Porpoises, 80
Whores Eggs, 76
Wild cattle, 121
Wilkes, John, 202
William IV. *See* William Henry
William Henry: xvii, xxvi, 153, 162, 322; birthday, 156; entry in Quebec, 154–55
William and Mary College: 257; student fare, 358
Williams, Colonel Ephraim, 327
Williams, Major Griffith, 276
Williamsburg, appearance, 257–58, 358
Williamson, Miss, 234
Wilmington, Delaware, 229
Wing, Abraham, 280, 327–28

Wings House, 44, 178
Wings Tavern, 327
Wooster, Major General David, 276
Worcestershire, xxix
Wolfe's Cove, 159
Wolfe's Landing, 159
Wrath, Cape, 63
Wright, Thomas. *See* Anticosti Island

Yale College, 208
Yankees, spirit of resignation, 29–30
Yankee settlement, 90
Yates, Abraham, 185
Yorktown: 53, 257–64; battlefield, 261, 264; British surrender, 264; negotiation of surrender, 359; siege, 358

THE AMERICAN JOURNALS OF Lᵗ JOHN ENYS

was composed in 11-point Fairfield and leaded two points
with display type in handset Egmont Light by
Joe Mann Associates, Inc.;
printed on Warren's 1854–55 lb.,
Smyth-sewn and bound over boards in Holliston Roxite,
by Vail-Ballou Press, Inc.;
and published by

SYRACUSE UNIVERSITY PRESS
SYRACUSE, NEW YORK